GEOFFREY ELBORN

Edith Sitwell: A Biography

SHELDON PRESS
LONDON

950997   181

First published in Great Britain in 1981 by
Sheldon Press, SPCK, Marylebone Road, London NW1 4DU

Thanks are due to the following for permission to reproduce photographs:
Cromack of Scarborough; Cecil Beaton photographs, courtesy of Sotheby's
Belgravia; Victor Hey of Scarborough; Lisa Larsen, *Life* Magazine © 1948 Time
Inc.; Fox Photos; and Erich Auerbach.
Thanks are due to the following for permission to quote from published and
unpublished material:
Mrs. Valerie Eliot (for T. S. Eliot); Geoffrey Grigson; Mrs. Alison Waley (for
Arthur Waley); Auberon Waugh (for Evelyn Waugh); Pamela Hansford Johnson
(for herself and C. P. Snow); Frank Magro (for Osbert Sitwell); David Horner; The
University of Texas (for Sir George Sitwell and Denton Welch); Robert Robinson;
The Britten Estate (excerpts from the letters of Benjamin Britten are © The
Britten Estate, and are not to be reproduced without written permission); Laurence
Pollinger Ltd and the Estate of the late Mrs. Freida Lawrence Ravagli (for D. H.
Lawrence and Freida Lawrence); the Trustees for the Copyrights of the late Dylan
Thomas © 1981; W. B. Yeats (from *Letters*); Weidenfeld & Nicolson publishers of
Diaries of Evelyn Waugh edited by Michael Davie; the Literary Estate of Virginia
Woolf, and The Hogarth Press for extracts from Volumes II and III of *The Diary of
Virginia Woolf* edited by Anne Olivier Bell; and William Heinemann publishers of
Lytton Strachey by Michael Holroyd.
The author and publishers also thank Mr. Francis Sitwell, Edith Sitwell's literary
executor, and David Higham Associates Limited for permission to quote from the
writings of Edith Sitwell.

Printed in Great Britain by
Ebenezer Baylis & Son Ltd,
The Trinity Press, Worcester, and London

ISBN 0 85969 323 6

For my parents
and my sister Gillian
with love

Contents

Introduction

EDITH SITWELL was one of the most colourful and contro-
versial women of the twentieth century, so it is not surprising
that she is mainly remembered as a personality, rather than as
the serious poet she was. Many of her most fervent admirers, who
saw her frequent television appearances, recall with affection her
clothes, rings, and hats, but have never read a line of anything
she wrote. The personal trappings loved by the general public
did not particularly amuse the academic critics, who found it
hard to accept that a woman they believed led a campaign of
vulgar self-advertisement could also be a poet of outstanding
ability. Paradoxically, Edith Sitwell disliked personal publicity
and seldom mentioned her private life in public; any publicity
was for the benefit of her own work, for her brothers, or for any
particular creative artist who she believed had special talents. Always lacking the ability for self-analysis, she was unable to realize that by some of her methods she was actually hindering
rather than furthering the serious appreciation of her own poetry.

No matter what the cause was, whether a campaign for James Purdy, an attack against the frivolity of the upper classes in the 1930s, or simply remarks about "bad" poetry, Edith Sitwell was always guided by her own sense of justice, no matter how idiosyncratic it might appear to others, and no matter what the consequences might be. Thus it was perfectly compatible for Edith to support her friends with great loyalty and kindness with one breath, and with the next to be vitriolic about someone who had dared to criticize a favourite writer.

Of the public to whom Edith Sitwell was almost *over*familiar, many could never have guessed that she led an "extremely unhappy" private life. Her unhappy love affair with the Russian artist Pavel Tchelitchew brought her great joy and more sorrow, and to a large extent the course it ran explains why Edith was never able to accept the fame with which she was crowned during the years of World War II, and why she became sadly embittered in the last years of her life.

It has been difficult to document in any detail her relationship with Tchelitchew, because the letters they wrote each other during World War II have been sealed from access by mutual consent until the year 2000. Edith Sitwell was always reluctant to discuss her innermost secrets, even with her family, and particularly private griefs were rarely detailed in letters but would be discussed face to face when Edith and correspondent next met.

In her autobiography, *Taken Care Of*, Edith Sitwell wrote: "During the writing of certain chapters of this book, I realised that the public would believe anything—so long as it is not founded on truth." This was especially true of the details Edith Sitwell used to circulate about her early life. There is no doubt that she had a difficult time with her parents, but her brother Sacheverell does not agree that the accounts she gave to friends and those she published were exactly true. In old age, Edith came to believe the reality of the legends she created, but because there is so little written evidence of those early years to contradict her, her own autobiographical statements about this period are all we have to go on, although they have to be regarded with extreme caution.

I first became interested in Edith Sitwell when, as a schoolboy, I discovered one of the poet's own recordings of her verse. The dust on the sleeve, and the price reduced to bring it within the

capacity of my pocket-money, led me to buy it. At once I was fascinated by the strangely individual poems, and curious about
the rather haunted-looking poet whose photograph, by Baron,
formed the record cover. Almost at the same time, I had been
reading the poetry of Sacheverell Sitwell, whose work is even
more unjustly neglected than his sister's, and I began a friendship
that has been an inspiration in many ways. It is at the suggestion
of Sir Sacheverell that this book came to be written, and I can
never fully express my gratitude to him and his wife, Lady Sitwell, for innumerable kindnesses over many years, and more recently while this book was written. Much of it was prepared in
their home, Weston Hall, and there I had access to the letters
written to Sir Sacheverell and Lady Sitwell by Dame Edith and
Sir Osbert.

All the opinions are of course my own, as are, indeed, any errors, and I am grateful to Sir Sacheverell for his comments and
his tactful reticence about certain sections I suspect he may have
disagreed with.

I am also indebted to Dame Edith's nephew Francis Sitwell,
who, as her literary executor, has granted me permission to quote
passages from Dame Edith's letters and papers, of which he holds
the copyright. His help and patience have been invaluable. I
must also thank Frank Magro, Sir Osbert's literary executor, for
permission to quote letters to Sir Sacheverell Sitwell. I greatly
benefited from assistance given to me by Elizabeth Salter, whose
book *The Last Years of a Rebel* provided a starting point for this
book, and also from her making available certain papers in her
possession.

John Pearson, whose own book *Façades* was published in 1978
(titled *The Sitwells: A Family's Biography* in the United States),
has helped me in many ways, not least by his unfailing sense of
humour, which has encouraged a greater sense of detachment
than I might otherwise have had.

Many others either lent me letters, granted me interviews, or
assisted by correspondence, and to them I am indebted: H.M.
Queen Elizabeth the Queen Mother; the late Dowager Lady
Aberconway; Sir Harold Acton; Lorna Andrade; the late W. H.
Auden; the late Sir Cecil Beaton; Jessie Bradley; Virginia Carr;
Lord Clark; Peter Dickie; C. H. Ford; Michael Goodwin;
Geoffrey Gorer; Graham Greene; the late C. M. Grieve (Hugh

MacDiarmid); Geoffrey Grigson; Sir Alec Guinness; Allanah
Harper; David Horner; Craig Kennedy; the late Viva King; Lin-
coln Kirstein; the late F. R. Leavis; John Lehmann; David Lut-
yens; Jordan Massee; Arthur Miller; Henry Moore; the late Ray-
mond Mortimer; Barbara Nopper; Derek Parker; Sir Peter Pears;
Myfanwy and John Piper; James Purdy; Kathleen Raine; the late
Sydney Goodsir Smith; Lady Snow; Stephen Spender; Michael
Stapleton; Gertrude and Bernard Stevenson; Ronald Stevenson;
Gore Vidal; Sir William Walton; Ian Watson; and Malcolm Wil-
liamson.

For unpublished letters and papers I must thank in particular
the staff of the Humanities Research Center at the University of
Texas, at Austin, whose unfailing courtesy, help, and kindness
made my search of their vast Sitwell collection a pleasure. Letters
from Edith Sitwell to Choura Tchelitchew Zaoussailoff were
translated from the French by Michael Goodwin.

Other institutions who made their papers available were the
British Library, the Beinecke Rare Book and Manuscript Library,
Scarborough Public Library, Sussex University, Yale University,
and the Berg Collection of the New York Public Library.

I am also grateful to my friends from the College of Ripon and
York St. John, who have endured incessant Sitwell conversation,
and especially John Crampsie, who travelled to the United States
with me to assist with my researches, and without whose help the
task of reading many hundreds of letters would have been labo-
rious.

Lastly, I am grateful to Jane Roslington, Mary McKerrow, and
Genine Graham for typing the manuscript, and to my editors,
Darley Anderson, Julie Davis, and Derek Hudson, for their con-
structive criticism.

Edith Sitwell:
A Biography

ONE

A Member of a Family

I was unpopular with my parents from the moment of my birth, and throughout my childhood and youth. I was in disgrace for being a female. . . .

Taken Care Of

"CANNES," Augustus Hare wrote in 1890, "has turned into a fashionable place, chiefly dependent upon society for its recommendations." Amongst those it attracted was Queen Victoria herself, who, during one of her last visits there, in 1891, was driving quietly past the La Bocca woods when she met a girl with a plump face surrounded by golden hair, clutching the hand of her nurse, Miss Davis. "*Her* carriage is coming," the nurse said severely. As they curtsied, the Widow of Windsor held up her hand and the royal party drove on.[1]

The "fashionable place, chiefly dependent upon society," was favoured by Sir George and Lady Ida Sitwell, Edith's parents, as suitable to a member of Parliament and his wife. Sir George Sitwell was the Conservative member for Scarborough, and it was at his constituency house, Wood End, in the northern resort's fashionable Crescent, that "Miss Edith" was born.

But the affluence and social standing that brought the young girl South did not derive from a background of calm aristocratic family life. Her mother, Lady Ida, was the daughter of the Earl and Countess of Londesborough, owners of most of Scarborough. There was an impressive array of ancestors: the Duke of Beaufort, Lady Ida's grandfather; Lady Conyngham, favourite of George IV; and Joseph Denison, who had built the family fortune in London as a banker. Lady Ida's marriage to Sir George Sitwell in 1886 seemed an unusual combination and was to be a sadly tragic partnership. Lady Ida, a great beauty, had appealed to Sir George for her looks rather than her intellect, and although not unintelligent, she had enjoyed all the prosperity of being a member of the landed aristocracy, a privilege that put aside the need to give her an education. She had only a remote idea of the value of money, and even less of the facts of life. She married George Sitwell having met him only twice, over luncheon, and after a few days the surprises of marriage proved too much for her; the frightened young girl of eighteen, unprepared for life outside the family home, ran back to her mother. (Edith later wrote that Lady Ida's mother sent her back.)

Edith's father, Sir George, was of necessity more self-reliant, having been orphaned at the age of two on the death of his father. There had followed a rapid depletion of the family fortune, and his mother, Louisa, was forced to live cheaply in Scarborough, leaving Renishaw Hall, the family's Derbyshire mansion, shut up for the greater part of the year. His mother, the daughter of a Colonel Hely-Hutchinson, was religious to the point of mania, helped by having Bishop Heber and Archbishop Tait amongst her relations, and this dominated the family life. The suffocating atmosphere alienated Sir George; he was a lonely child and remained an atheist all his life. His scepticism remained unmoved in the face of an incident that took place when he was nineteen, at a meeting of the National Association of Spiritualists. George found himself "capturing a spirit," apparently seizing a girl in her underwear through streaks of ectoplasm.

The loneliness that his daughter, Edith, was to inherit was relieved by an absorption in history, and he had a distinguished career at Eton and Oxford. But his childhood, smothered by religious relations, had already marked his character with a strong sense of independence. Renishaw was to be his ivory tower where he was able to exercise complete control and expend some of his rather eccentric energy. In a pamphlet he wrote on his family seat, he described the house:

Renishaw Park contained at the beginning of the present century [the nineteenth] about 450 acres, but it is now somewhat smaller, a corner having been cut off by the Midland Railway. The ground lies well for picturesque effect, and the present owner has added much to the beauty of the scene by the formation of a lake at the foot of the hill, upon which the house stands. This fine sheet of water, extends over twenty acres, and is more than a mile in circumference. The greatest length is 670 yards. The cost including the trees and planting, was not less than £4,000 and of this sum, a very large proportion was paid to labourers from Scarborough. The house of Renishaw is of considerable size, the north front being exactly 300 feet long. The body of the house . . . is believed to have been re-built shortly before . . . 1627. . . .[2]

But the relief was only temporary. The religious fervour from which Renishaw was an escape was not confined only to obsessive family prayer at Wood End. Lady Sitwell ran a Scarborough home for fallen women, supervised by Sister Edith Woods, whom Edith remembered as "a bursting woman like an advertisement for tomatoes in a railway station."[3] The "unfortunates" ran a laundry, but its integrity was ruined when it was discovered that every girl in the house was pregnant, because of the inclusion of a young man. He had been mistaken for a girl and had refused the compulsory bath that new arrivals enjoyed.

Sir George would never escape the influence of his austere upbringing, but with his work at Renishaw, rebuilding and altering the gardens, he believed he was helping to conserve the family fortune that had been restored by his mother. He remembered with horror the hordes of parasitic relations who ate and drank their way through the Sitwell money during the long hot summers of his youth at Renishaw. At least he was being constructive, for it was "such a mistake to have friends."[4]

So it was from backgrounds of such varying fortunes that the Sitwell and Londesborough crests were united in November 1886 at St. George's, Hanover Square, London. After their honeymoon, Sir George and Lady Ida were welcomed into Scarborough with a procession lit by six hundred torches. The pageantry, as ever, pleased Sir George; their carriage was pulled by the lifeboat crew, and as they drove through Scarborough, crowds gazed curiously to see his new bride.

The following September, Lord Londesborough opened the

1887 Scarborough Cricket Festival, of which he was president, and enjoyed the few days consorting with the visiting "actresses" who came to "entertain" at the spa. Unfortunately, Lady Londesborough discovered her husband's unfaithfulness and a blazing row ensued in Lady Ida's bedroom. Lady Londesborough was placated by a gift of emeralds, but the furious row was to speed the birth of the child Lady Ida was expecting. Lady Ida was taken to luncheon at the Cricket Festival two days later, on September 7, but was rushed back to Wood End, where between one and two o'clock Edith Louisa Sitwell was born.

Edith was a shock to her parents, for she was not the boy they had been counting on, and they remained heirless. For her part, Edith repaid this disappointment with a distinct lack of duty. From the beginning she lacked any real affection from her parents, and as the family travelled from one house to the next—Renishaw, Wood End, and London—she had little opportunity to feel a sense of belonging or being at home amongst the confusion of nurses and distant relations. Inevitably, while her father was concerned only with his remote pastimes, and her mother spent long mornings in bed to relieve her intense boredom, Edith was left to wander amongst servants, whom she learnt to love.

The child had an insatiable curiosity and managed to dispel feelings of loneliness by her ability to read, acquired at the age of three. Before that, she always listened, enraptured, to the endless fairy stories her nurse at Scarborough would repeat to her. This vivid imagination provided her with the childhood friends she lacked, and Renishaw or Londesborough Park easily became to her the setting for the mysterious characters of the nurse's stories. Not a gregarious child, Edith was impossibly shy—a state that was not helped by her being stared at for her ugliness—and had inherited her mother's bad temper, which she displayed often. With unsociability came a gift for amusing herself.

Of course, she lacked no material comfort, and to please her her father bought her a pug dog, whom she called Dido, but this did little to assuage her irritability. Edith guarded her jealously. Once when she was walking with her in the private garden by Wood End, some boys tried to entice the dog to come to them behind the locked gates. Edith was furious and screamed, "How dare they! How dare those commoners even look at my Dido!"

When her brother Osbert was born, in 1892, Edith's status was lower still, for he was now the future baronet and Lady Ida's favourite child. Edith was enraged at his appearance and could not understand why the lobster-faced boy was receiving so much attention. She would yell into the cot, "You little beast, you horrible little beast," and when her nurse's back was turned, she would lose no time in pinching him spitefully.

By the time Edith was four, Lady Ida was slowly drifting apart from her husband, finding consolation only in her social life. She was impatient and impulsive, with an extravagance she had to keep hidden from her husband. Hats would be concealed in the house; another time it was boiled sweets, especially humbugs, and the staff at Wood End were invited to help themselves as they passed the jar in which they were kept.

As Lady Ida lost touch with her husband, she also became more distanced from Edith. Osbert held most of her affection, and "Miss E" was made well aware of her mother's feelings towards her. At Renishaw there was only the comfort of her pets and birds; an early companion was a bullfinch that she called Bullfy, but the bird was also "taken up" by her nurse. Edith felt it was hers, like Dido, and not to be shared, as it was amongst her few friends. Edith found a pin and gave it to the bird, which took it in its beak and laid it at the bottom of the cage. The nurse told her that if she continued, the bird would die, and when Edith asked what dying meant, she was told that it meant going away and never coming back. That, Edith decided, was the answer to her problem—that the bird should go away and not come back, thus ensuring that the nurse could not enjoy a share in its friendship. But Edith was caught putting more pins into the cage, and when she was now told that dying also meant being in pain she burst into tears. Recalling this bird many years later, she wrote:

Perhaps if I had a great wisdom, I should see everything that has ever happened to me comes from the same misunderstanding, in darkness in the mind . . . since there is no cruelty which does not come from either fear or miscomprehension.[5]

Peaky, a peacock, followed Bullfy in her affection, and yet another permanent black mark was placed against her father, "when, with his usual tactlessness, he got Peaky a wife."[6] Edith's next pastime arrived on her fifth birthday, when she was given a copy of Hans Christian Andersen's *Fairy Tales*. She was fas-

cinated by the horrific and cruel stories, but frightened herself
again and again by repeated readings of them, daubing the line
drawings with purple crayon.

Like one of these fairy tales in reverse, the fat child was now
growing thin, with deep-set eyes, and it was unlikely that she was
going to have her mother's beauty. The section of "The Ugly
Duckling" in Edith's copy was torn; her fervent imagination must
have rebelled against a story that so cruelly reversed her own
conception of her situation.

These isolated incidents indicate how important to her was this
imaginative world where she could retreat for safety. Although
her undoubted misery was to become legendary to her friends in
later life, as much a necessary part of her as her jewels and fondness for quoting her ancestry, and just as suspect from a spectator's point of view, it was at Renishaw that she endured the
greatest loneliness.

But of course her misery was not uninterrupted. However
much Edith came to dislike her mother, as a child she made Lady
Ida repeat endless tales of her own childhood and her parents.
Edith would have been reluctant to admit it later, but she nevertheless believed that her mother's story-telling "has always been
one of the great pleasures of my life. . . ."[7]

Another great comfort to the children in this unhappy family
was Henry Moat, Sir George's servant and later his butler, who
came from a long line of whalers from Whitby. Osbert wrote of
Henry Moat that his whole outlook was ". . . that of a sailor, and
his talk was spiced with nautical phrases, some of them hard for a
landsman to understand. . . . Occasionally, there would be a
rumpus and he would leave for months—or even years—until, in
fact, he came back again. My father, in the end, was always
pleased to see him, however tiresome he might have been. . . ."[8]

Henry Moat was infallibly kind to the three children and
would often warn Edith when Lady Ida was in a bad temper and
was looking for her daughter. "You'd better run, Miss Edith," he
would say. "Her Ladyship is in one of her states."[9]

In *Taken Care Of*, her autobiography, published posthumously
in 1965, there are details of her early unhappiness at Scarborough, but elsewhere, when Edith was less bitter, she declared
that her recollection of Londesborough Park, the seat of her maternal grandparents, the Earl and Countess of Londesborough,

was "one of the loveliest memories of this time in my life."[10] The
Earl was often considered in the London society in which he
moved to be a "swell," but despite his enthusiasms for the traditional Victorian aristocratic pursuits, he found time to be fond of
and to amuse Edith. Apart from founding the Scarborough
Cricket Festival at which Edith was nearly born, he also started
an annual Tennis Carnival. His generosity with money enabled
lifeboats to be maintained, and his ability to mix well with the
local traders and fishermen ensured his popularity in the town.
Edith herself was to hate sport (except reviewer baiting), but her
grandfather was absolved from any blame because of his indul-
gence towards her, and was to her a "singularly delightful grandfather . . . for he made us seem important and . . . turned everything into an adventure. . . ."[11] His speciality, which Edith
enjoyed more than anything, was jaunts in a light carriage driven
by four horses, when he would race over fields and bump across
ditches, his expert horsemanship making the outings great adventures.

Her grandmother was more formidable, with white hair and
beautiful hands, kept covered by long black gloves to preserve
their whiteness. Her main occupation was knitting pink shawls.
She had been an opera-lover in her youth but was too old to travel
to the theatres by the time Edith was seven, so Edith's aunts Lady
Lily and Lady Mildred Londesborough would play piano duet
arrangements of Rossini and Bellini. The results were not always
musical, and Edith found it difficult at times not to laugh.

Londesborough Park provided a variety of interests for the
young Edith. A large retinue of cooks, gardeners, and footmen
was kept, and the hierarchy of different liveries fascinated her.
There was a "pleasure ground," where she would often wander.
The great cedar and magnolia trees bordered a stream, where a
half-witted old woman had a cottage. Edith often enjoyed tea
there, while her hostess sewed patchwork. Outside the cottage,
the Scottish gardener, Macpherson, tended the lawns. He was to
be the inspiration for a character in *Scotch Rhapsody*, a poem
from her collection *Façade*, published in 1922, and also for the
gardener in her long poem *The Sleeping Beauty*, published in
1924.

From Belvoir House in The Crescent, Scarborough, where her
younger brother, Sacheverell, was born in 1897, Edith was taken

to the beach by her maternal aunts Lily and Sibyl. In the summer there were always Punch and Judy shows, which Edith adored, although the faces of the puppets frightened her. Her aunts left her in charge of a boy who sold donkey rides, and when she was later taken to see his house in a poor slum area of Scarborough, she wanted to share Sir George with the boy, as he had no father (Sir George must have been in favour at that time). Although the plan came to nothing, for years Edith was haunted by the memory of the drunks lurching across the shabby street, carrying half-empty bottles. For the first time she was touched by a glimpse of misery working its way on somebody other than herself. The memories of her own childhood, and the misery she saw endured by others, were carefully absorbed and later transformed into her own poetic world.

Edith agreed that she was an "exasperating child," and recalled an example of how difficult she could be:

. . . a train between Scarborough and London had to be stopped, and I taken out and restored to Scarborough, for I fainted with rage because another train had passed us with a shriek, and I could not endure that any train should go faster than ours. After this lèse majesté on the part of the second train I was ill for some time.[12]

Edith's awkward behaviour as a child was emphasized by the contrasting example of her two brothers. Osbert was an attractive baby, and he behaved well. Sacheverell had a quiet and more retiring nature than either his brother or his sister and revealed none of the snobbery Osbert showed even when a very young child. Sacheverell once commissioned a rug from a poor black man whom he used to see often in Scarborough, to give the man some work, and like Edith he was haunted by the poverty of the miners' children they saw in Eckington, near Renishaw. When Osbert and Sacheverell (or Sachie, as his family called him) grew old enough to be companionable, Edith's private world still flourished in their company. She took pleasure in sharing her discoveries with them, and it was Sachie who was the more responsive; he listened to Edith repeating the family stories she had heard from her mother. Edith felt some closeness towards her brothers, but this affection did not bring her any nearer to her parents, and she tended to use her brothers as allies in the continuing battle.

Edith was fourteen when she went with her parents to Naples. She had been to Italy often, but this visit was particularly memorable for her. The family arrived in the middle of a plague, and when a bell rang they had "to keep back with the crowd, as a victim was carried along the street." Edith was made to hold her breath by Lady Ida until the plague carrier had gone. It was the New Year of 1902, and Edith looked on the crowds of fishwives selling wriggling eels for the holiday feasts and felt that

if a century had lost itself and I had woken up one morning to find myself in 1802, I doubt if I should have found adaptation difficult . . . the people we met discussed blood and brigands as casually as if they were fireworks on Guy Fawkes Day. . . . I was not kept away from life like the modern child, I was just as aware of plague and violence as I was of the small sweet oranges or the lizards on the sunny walls.[13]

During a visit to Vesuvius, Edith was scolded by her father for poking her toe in the lava puddles. She was determined to climb to the top to prove to her father that she could manage, even if the way was hot and steep. Sir George conceded and gave her a helping hand, pulling her up behind him. In their enthusiasm to climb together, neither realized that they had mislaid Lady Ida. She had chosen an easier route, meeting other people, and despite her protest was forced into a chair and carried halfway up by a group of men whom she encountered on the way. Her angry shouts eventually reached Edith and Sir George, and they realized that Lady Ida's porters would not move her further until paid. Sir George was on his guard and refused to pay them until they returned her safely to the station, and the family slid down to the bottom in ten minutes. The ascent, Edith lamented, had taken two and a half hours.

Edith's recollections of this Italian holiday display none of the malice she felt for her parents in later life; there was only the feeling of a happy holiday with her parents, whom she found the courage to tease during a visit to the zoo, even if it was only a temporary break from their role as scapegoats for all Edith's troubles.

The Italian visits were to provide Sir George with his greatest chance to play the feudal lord. In 1908 his car broke down in a Tuscan valley, and when he looked up to find where he was, he spotted the Castello di Montegufoni. He was impressed and told

Osbert that it had an "air of fallen splendour," and he bought the property. In no time he was full of plans to grow his own fruit and produce his own wine and champagne, adding by way of recommendation that "the drains can't be wrong as there aren't any." Sir George's preoccupation with gardens and "improvements" compensated for the isolation he felt from Lady Ida. It also helped his wife, as she was now able to entertain in the splendour of the castle.

Edith had just celebrated her twenty-first birthday in misery, having been taken to the Doncaster Races, where she sat with her back turned in protest. The race-meeting was not intended as an insult by her father, however much it seemed so to Edith. Sir George had discovered in Renishaw Hall a silver ticket that granted the Sitwells free entry to the Doncaster Races in perpetuity. He at once saw this as a way to celebrate Edith's birthday, but forgot to ask his daughter if she approved, having been as usual carried off into a world of his own by his enthusiasm. Lavish food that took several days to prepare was available for the huge invited party, and in the chilly September evening several bands serenaded Edith. The original purpose of the celebration, to introduce Edith to Sir George's friends, misfired because Edith was too shy to meet them.

It seems paradoxical that a young woman so shy and withdrawn should be absolutely determined to behave as *she* felt *she* wanted. The resulting consequences were not always happy, but at least Edith gained satisfaction from standing her own ground. Her most constant image of herself as a young woman was that of a shy bird. Recalling later how she felt at this time, in 1908, Edith said she ". . . had the remote elegance and distinction of a very tall bird . . . had not the look of one who has many acquaintances . . . was plain and knew it."[14] Her mother ignored her as much as possible, but for the time being the days of running away from home, which she had tried as a child of five, were over.

She had by now the companionship of a governess, Helen Rootham, who had arrived in 1903. She was ten years older than Edith and was to exert some considerable influence on the young lady's development. Miss Rootham was interested in poetry and introduced Edith to Verlaine, Rimbaud, and Mallarmé. The French writers were a shock to Edith, whose adolescent passion

had previously been aroused only by Swinburne. She never tired
of recounting how she escaped at the age of fifteen, accompanied
by a maid, to the Isle of Wight, equipped with a jug of honey to
pour over Swinburne's grave, where she also left flowers. But in
the meantime the two poetic young ladies were confined in the
family mansion, to them a prison.

The uneasy atmosphere existing at Renishaw was also noticed
by guests. Edith's cousin Constance Talbot became a frequent
visitor there, and she recorded her impressions in a diary. Constance, who was one year older than Edith, observed the Sitwells
from a position outside the immediate family, providing a rare
source of something like an impartial view of the family, and
Edith struck Constance as "very literary and artistic of course
. . . plays the piano all day . . . very well too. . . ."[15]

While they were staying in the same house, Constance went
to a church service, where the canon attacked Swinburne in his
sermon. This she duly reported back to Edith, who was furious,
and as a result Constance had to listen to an enforced reading of
Swinburne. Edith's mannerisms infuriated Constance, especially
since Edith liked to imagine that *she* was the only one who was
interested in writing, while Constance had herself been writing
secretly. Their rivalry meant they would never become close,
even when Constance married into the Sitwell family,* but Edith
realized there was some good sense in the lectures that her cousin
gave her on her arrogance.

Renishaw seemed to Constance "like an Italian palace with its
tapestries and cushions, inlaid cabinets and stamped velvets and
gold chairs from Venice." Visual impressions apart, Constance
felt that it had an atmosphere of *John Inglesant*.† She wrote in
her diary of summer 1906:

there seemed only a thin veil between the supernatural and it, and the
ghosts which were said to walk the house; one expected to meet one
in the quiet "great drawing room" with its musty smell "as though
someone dead was always there", as Edith said.

Lady Ida arrived, dressed in tweeds with a handkerchief knotted round her neck, and Constance liked her at once, as she was

* Constance Talbot married Colonel William Sitwell of Barmoor Castle, North-
umberland, in August 1912.

† A philosophical and mystical novel, set in seventeenth-century England and
Italy, by Joseph Henry Shorthouse, and published in 1881.

"tall and handsome with a lisping voice." Sir George, too, made a favourable impression on the young girl, despite what Constance judged to be his seventeenth-century appearance and his "punctilious little bows and stiff speeches."

The Lawrencian aspect of the countryside that was to form a background for *Lady Chatterley's Lover* struck her: "an Inferno . . . those furnaces always going and lighting up the smoke from the high chimneys with a red glow." The family took Constance to see a rose-garden at Chesterfield, and Edith was quiet, apparently something fairly usual when she was with her mother. At Renishaw there had been little distraction from the tension that arose from unhappy family relations, except in ensuring that they were all occupied in finding their own amusements to pass the summer days. While Edith played Brahms's intermezzi, Constance sketched the gardens. Later they all went for a walk in the garden, and the four children climbed onto a roof. Henry Moat and the footman could not be persuaded to go with them; they were obliged to be in attendance on Sir George, who ate his luncheon at a different time from the others.

In the evening, though, Sir George dined with the rest of the family and guests, and after the family had grumbled about the food, Edith entertained them with music in the ballroom. She was undoubtedly pleasing Sir George with her drawing-room accomplishment, one of the few things she did that seemed proper for a young lady of seventeen. Sir George did not particularly care for music, but he arranged for Frederick Dawson to ride over to Renishaw to give Edith piano lessons. Dawson, who was born in Leeds, had studied under the great Chopin player Vladimir de Pachmann and was one of the finest pianists of his day. Later, against her will, Edith studied the cello with Rubio in London.

The uneasy atmosphere at Renishaw was only heightened by a visit to dinner with neighbours, where everyone was so pleasant and "nice after the Sitwell family." Sir George found the party "stupid" and it was this feeling of dissatisfaction that the Sitwell family found with everything outside their own circle that Constance felt was their hallmark. It arose out of boredom, and gradually Constance came to feel that she was at Renishaw only as an amusement for the family. This may well have been true—the tutor called "Gibs" felt a romantic attachment for Constance, which she at eighteen found highly embarrassing. But no one seemed concerned, and even Edith was amused as the young man strolled around whistling the *Indian Love Lyrics*. Soon his attention, which continued to annoy Constance, became something of a rather ponderous joke to the family; although she wanted to leave, they persuaded her to stay on for another few days. A visit down a local coal-mine proved a diversion, but one which, recounted over dinner, bored Sir George. Instead, the family joked and winked over the one-sided love affair: "Lady Ida will talk of nothing else (*anything* for a topic). I asked if I might go into dinner with Sir George that night as a bulwark, but Gibs kept his eyes on me the whole time."

After dinner, Edith came and slept on her cousin's floor, for they were both afraid of the ghosts that were said to haunt the house, and in the morning Lady Ida repeatedly pleaded with Constance to stay on. This continued for another day until, driven to desperation, "I got quite rude in the end. I said 'I'll put it up in the hall; the *day* and the *hour*'. Sir George kept repeating 'we are all very depressed over your unnecessary departure—very sad, aren't we?'"

At last Constance escaped, feeling that she had been the victim of a plot, and that "it amused their empty days to watch the episode and get some fun out of it." The visit seemed a charade, but it was the kind of episode that would often be repeated in Renishaw, so desperate were the family for distractions that would relieve the tense and often nervous atmosphere.

Constance was the only girl Edith knew, and despite their differences her departure brought her to the verge of tears. She had been amused by the behaviour of the tutor, but Constance believed her when Edith told her that "the world was to her a hideous place, like a pot of vipers, each trying to sting each other."

Christmas was generally spent at Scarborough, in Belvoir House, and Constance joined the family there in 1908. While Lady Ida attended bridge parties, Constance, Edith, Osbert, and Sachie went for walks to watch the stormy waves. There they were terrified by the storm, which brought out "the terrible nervousness, apparently innate," in them that guests at Renishaw noticed.

When Constance went with Edith to a hunt ball, they were

both excited by a "young man in a pink coat who danced beautifully, and Edith and I talked of nothing else all the time." As at Renishaw, this house bore the marks of its inhabitants:

There was an odd mixture of extreme comfort, and the opposite in that house; there was the all pervading smell of gardenias and white lilacs and carnations; and always the big vase of tuberoses and soft sofas and wood fires and good coffee and cigarettes and the feeling that no one *need* do anything, and the more money they spent the better . . . it seemed to me they were living quite blindly and not seeing life clearly. . . .

Constance was always aware of a strange feeling that she was torn between longing to stay with the Sitwells and longing to get as far away from them as possible, but by the time she was in her early twenties, in 1911, she could accept them for what they were, as she wrote in her diary:

I can see Sir George walking about with his head in the air, and grey flannels and a green hat on: he looks very young for his age, and certainly a Patrician—his brow is never ruffled; he calls Sachie "darling" and Edith "pet"; he bows and says "Quite charming, Yes,". He is the Egoist intact. I can see Osbert coming out from the house now, tall, his fine face looking cross, and closely followed by the inimitable Sachie, who has his odd white felt hat on, and who carries a small walking stick. To watch those three walking along together, as I could from my window, Sir George explaining why the late Baroque furniture is better than the earlier ("less restless," he says) is more like a scene in a novel or a play. . . .

The observant Constance noticed that her servants liked Sachie because they "adored his voice." She felt that Osbert, on the other hand, had been spoilt and "took patience to be with." From the impressions Constance has left it is clear that it was only when Sir George and Lady Ida left that the young Sitwells could enjoy themselves, and the mood then changed to one of

the greatest fun! This lovely house and no old people at all! Laughed and talked all day, and listened to music. Edith talks of nothing but Yeats and Swinburne, and they all tell the most amusing stories—it is unlike anything else. Walked about with Edith down the dusky path and woodlands, talking and talked to . . . these have been days to remember.[16]

Edith was forming a literary taste that was to exert considerable influence on her own poetry, and her early "likes" in literature remained unchanged for much of her life. But time embellished the truth, and although she liked to claim she had memorized *The Rape of the Lock* as a girl of thirteen, she did not in fact read eighteenth-century literature until encouraged to do so by her brother Sacheverell when he was at Eton. Helen Rootham was now a decisive influence. She was encouraging Edith to read widely, and her sense of tact helped her to avoid rows and have her advice accepted. It was with her that Edith went to France and Germany to be "finished off," as she phrased it, in 1908, when she was twenty-one.

Her father still hoped that Edith might pursue a musical career, and in Berlin Edith continued her piano lessons, writing to Sachie about Josef Lhévinne, whom she had heard there. But when she returned she decided that the rigours of the concert platform were too much of a strain and abandoned any aspirations towards a musical career. She was uncertain *what* to do.

Looking back in later life, summing up these formative years, Edith was determined to give a bitter impression of her early life at Renishaw, but was always reluctant to give many substantial facts. The anxieties she endured included being made to kill bluebottles; incarceration in an orthopaedic device designed to strengthen and straighten her spine; her father's staring at her face in trains from behind *The Times* and then looking away again; and her mother's making her hide her face with a veil when out walking. These Edith would talk about in later life, but it is impossible to know how much was real and how much was imagined. Her "Bastille," as she called her orthopaedic device, was the best-known treatment, and the most expensive, for correcting curvature of the spine, but the *effect* it had on her appears to have been damaging and was to remain a lifelong nightmare. Although it was not a deliberate punishment, as she suggested, it did humiliate her in a way that impressed itself on her mind, leaving a mental wound that would not be erased.

Further descriptions of herself that she wrote in prose and poetry were more often of insubstantial, ethereal beings, like "a little cold air wandering and lost,"[17] or ghostlike figures than a "tall thin bird." Her writing gave her the chance to forget her cumbersome, awkward body and substitute instead the way she actually felt. "Changeling that I am,"[18] Edith wrote, she was never to forget that she was the unwanted, unloved child, born into the wrong world. In fact, Edith was already nearly six feet tall, with a slight stoop, and a prominent, "Plantagenet" nose that she detested. Her eyes were deep-set and her large eyelids resembled those of an owl.

Out of the confusion of memories, two clear aspects of Edith's character emerge: the shy, frightened child who found comfort in animals and birds; and the young woman who was becoming increasingly absorbed in a world of literature. The shy, frightened child was never far from Edith, even when older, but she was developing a protective defence of quick repartee. Some sort of self-reliance was vital, as her parents were absorbed in their separate worlds, Sir George in his gardens and family history and Lady Ida in her own society. They did nothing to help Edith through her confused adolescence and contributed more than anything to her constant sense of being persecuted. Lady Ida remained unfulfilled after the birth of her two sons, and she made Edith the scapegoat for her own personal misery in marriage. Whenever Edith met her mother there were scenes and displays of temper on both sides, and Edith probably gave as good as she got.

Worse than the bad temper was the start of the slow disintegration of Lady Ida, which was observed with concern by all the family except, apparently, Sir George.

Used to the extravagance of the Londesboroughs, Lady Ida was finding it difficult to live on the income Sir George had settled on her and could not prevent herself from living beyond it. In 1912 Osbert, aged twenty, left the family home to sign on for duty in the Eleventh Hussars at Aldershot. The situation at home worsened, with Lady Ida drinking heavily, and on Boxing Day Sachie, a fifteen-year-old schoolboy, wrote to his elder brother:

Mother is still very ill. I never knew how seriously ill she had been. She has had clots of blood, and congestion of the brain and very nearly became off her head.[19]

The "squandering" was obvious to her family, and although efforts were made to stop it, Sachie reported that

in fact things were worse than usual. . . . Father tells me Mother is liable not to £6,000 but to £11,000. It is quite impossible to see what will eventually happen. . . .[20]

Sachie was so worried that he called a family meeting at Renishaw, where Edith and Osbert discussed their mother's problems
with him, but impending disaster could not be averted. Osbert
had been taken into his mother's confidence and knew that in
1910 Lord Londesborough had offered to pay Lady Ida's debts.
Rather than lose face, Sir George had grudgingly paid them off
himself, but by a year later the new debts had rocketed to £2,000,
despite Lady Ida's promise that she would never overspend again.
She was terrified of her husband's knowing the true position and
turned in desperation to Osbert for advice.

Osbert shared his mother's extravagance, although on a smaller
scale, and felt some sympathy. Amongst his army colleagues he
found a friend who seemed to have the solution. According to
him the answer was a certain Julian Field, who seemed a cut
above the average money-lender. Field impressed Osbert, for he
had known Swinburne, knew half of literary France, moved
amongst the aristocracy with ease, and had published books. But
none of that was important to Lady Ida; all she was interested in
was the money. A confusing plan was put to her by which she
might borrow the £6,000 without difficulty. Cautious at the
start, Lady Ida protested that she needed only £2,000, but Field
told her that she might as well have £6,000. She agreed. With
life assurance to repay the loan, all seemed well, until the whole
deal resulted in Lady Ida's being given only £200 out of the
£6,000 she had signed away after the £2,000 debts were paid
off. Field told Lady Ida that there were expenses to be met and
that if she was dissatisfied she should tell Sir George. Field, of
course, was well aware that this was the last measure Lady Ida
would resort to. Becoming increasingly desperate, she was persuaded to borrow again. One method she tried was to find a
wealthy banker, and she also tried pleading with wealthy friends,
but this produced nothing. The friend who had introduced Field
to Lady Ida guaranteed one bill, and a young cricketer guaranteed another for £4,000.

Throughout the manoeuvring, Lady Ida in her innocence
never suspected that Field was using her, and that there was soon
to be a crash. Soon all her creditors were sending demands by
every post and Lady Ida was unable to meet any of them, for the
expected life assurance had not materialized. Pressure was building up against Osbert, for the officer who had introduced Field to

Lady Ida was being harassed to settle the bill he had backed. Should the money-lender tell his colonel about this business, his own career as a soldier would be ruined.

Osbert had no choice but to tell his father, who quickly settled the debts Osbert's friend had guaranteed, paying out £5,000 in all. However, £6,000 remained unsettled, and Sir George refused to pay it. He had found out that the whole transaction was illegal and decided that Field must be run to earth before he attempted to ruin another family. Field had a long history of fraud and blackmail, and Sir George knew that he had succeeded in black-mailing his relations, the Worsley family of Yorkshire, who had paid him off to avert a scandal. No matter what disgrace it brought to his own family, Sir George was determined that his principles must remain firm. Field, for his part, had never sus-pected that Sir George would bring the matter out into the open and that his own criminal career was near its end, but things were coming to a head.

The effect of all this on the children cannot be overestimated. Edith only saw her mother as wishing "to escape from the results of that which she had, out of sheer stupidity, done."[21] It was nat-ural that Lady Ida should wish that the appalling nightmare should pass, but to Edith this desire to run away from it all meant that her mother lost any credibility she ever had.

Until now Edith had been protected from her mother's rages by the servants, and especially by the gigantic Moat. But now that Edith had the knowledge of her mother's behaviour as an added weapon against her she used it, and announced that she was going to London to live. Edith had been writing poetry privately for several years, encouraged by Helen Rootham. Curiously, the idea for the first poem she wrote came to her while she was taking a bath. Helen Rootham noticed that Edith's poetry showed some promise and helped Edith with her technique. When in March 1913 the *Daily Mirror* published her poem *Drowned Suns* (for which she received two pounds), Edith was convinced, after the encouraging omen, that she must leave Reni-shaw to follow a literary life of her own in London.

> The swans more white than those forgotten fair
> Who ruled the kingdoms that of old-time were,
> Within the sunset water deeply gaze
> As though they sought some beautiful dim face,

> The youth of all the world; or pale lost gems,
> And crystal shimmering diadems,
> The moon for ever seeks in woodland streams
> To deck her cold faint beauty; thus in dreams,
> Belov'd, I seek lost suns within your eyes
> And find but wrecks of love's gold argosies.[22]

Lady Ida tried to persuade Edith to stay, as she found her enthusiasm to leave a cruel psychological blow. Ignoring frantic pleas, Edith left Renishaw in April 1913 and was driven to Sheffield, where she caught the London train with Helen. They had already found temporary lodgings, with Osbert's help, in St. Petersburgh Place, Bayswater.

Uncomfortably new in the city, they were faced with problems, not the least of which were financial. If it had not been for the money Helen had saved, it would have been impossible to have gone at all, and as Sir George lived in a mediaeval world "when a groat was worth something," Edith found money very hard to come by. Osbert had managed to bamboozle Sir George over his accounts, but Edith, then less cunning, was obliged to give him a lengthy account of her expenses at her lodgings:

You understand I was only able to be at Miss Russell's for nine months in the year . . . so the whole year would have worked out at one hundred and twenty pounds plus extra food which we had to get in, and of course, we had only one sitting-room with which we really cannot manage.[23]

With the help of some intervention from Lady Ida, Edith borrowed money from Sir George, which she intended to repay by selling a diamond necklace that had been left to her. Sir George came to London later in May, but it was not until early June that he promised curtains and carpets that he considered "just passable" from a family house, Balcombe Tower. Edith refused the shabby furnishings and moved to another address in Bayswater, 22 Pembridge Mansions, Moscow Road. Although it sounded rather grand, visitors were surprised to find that the flat was at the top of a dark stair and resembled one room of a workman's house. But it was a beginning, and furnishing it gave Edith great pleasure, using red and gold hangings that Osbert brought to her. Although Edith had often declared that she "hated the country," she regarded herself as a "country poet," and she was pleased with the view over Kensington Gardens, which reminded her of the trees at Renishaw.

Money was scarce, and when the First World War broke out Edith took a job in the War Supplies Depot. She hated the work, but stuck with it for the duration of the war, and by the time peace came she was established at last in a place large enough to accommodate her expanding ambition and self-regard.

TWO

London Calling

Having in many ways a feline nature, it amuses her to sharpen her wits upon the wooden heads of her adversaries as much as it amuses a cat to sharpen his claws upon the leg of a table.

"That English Eccentric Edith Sitwell," *Sunday Referee*

WITH THE BEGINNING of the war came a false dawn for the Sitwells when, in November 1914, a one-day hearing found Field guilty of misappropriating money borrowed in Lady Ida's name. But the matter did not end there; the shadow of some outstanding debts loomed large.

Sir George was responding by becoming more cautious about money and more idiosyncratic in his behaviour, turning to his younger son for company. "Father and I are always lunching at Rowntrees," Sachie wrote to Osbert; "the rolls are so charming—it is really quite a nice little luncheon."[1]

But Sir George could not escape the reality of his wife's debts. One money-lender had died and his estate was pressing for settlement. Sir George refused to pay, insisting that Field must bear the responsibility of his cheating. But the matter was not as simple as that. The estate announced that it would prosecute not only Lady Ida, but Field too, for conspiring to defraud the money-lender whose services Field had used.

Field, now desperate, tried to blackmail Sir George by making him aware of the contents of a letter Lady Ida had written him; and when Sir George again refused to co-operate, the letter was sent to the prosecution.

Lady Ida came to trial in March 1915, before Mr. Justice Darling, and the trial dragged on for several days. She was cross-examined for seven hours, during which time the prosecution, ignoring Field, managed to transform her from a lady of leisure into a wicked, grasping woman who did not care what she did to get money.

Osbert, who was with his regiment at the front, had been forced to return from France in case he was called as a witness to testify to his slight involvement. The prosecution made much of his part in the affair, but he did not go into the witness box. If he had testified, he would have incriminated his mother even further, and so he gallantly remained silent.

Lady Ida was found guilty and sentenced to three months in Holloway Prison, while Field received three years for his part in the affair. In a passage most of which she excised from her published autobiography, Edith wrote:

I was living in London when the first law-case began (there were three before the final débâcle). This was during one of the most appalling battles of the war. The morning after . . . I went to see her [Lady Ida] she was lying in bed, buffing her nails, always with her, a sign of ill temper and disordered nerves.

She said to me, "Why are you wearing black?"

I was dressed in a hideous dark blue coat and skirt. I said to her, "What would you say if I had come to tell you that Osbert had been killed?"

She shrank away from me, then said "I suppose you would like to hit me" . . . I will not say what I replied. . . .[2]

It was possibly the involvement of Osbert in his mother's case, and the accusations he was having to endure, rather than the "childhood cruelty" she suffered herself that finally turned Edith against Lady Ida. And because Sir George could possibly have saved the family from the scandal by "stumping up" he was to become another *bête noire,* the hated "Ginger," a nickname fittingly enough born in contempt. It arose from an incident that took place during the First World War. Not long after he had grown a red beard, Sir George gave a London taxi driver a tip of twopence. The driver was so furious with this miserly gift that he

said to Sir George, "After the war, Ginger, the streets will be running with the blood of people like you." Sir George replied
calmly, "Perhaps they will be. . . ."

The scandal had acted as a catalyst on the Sitwell children,
prompting a closeness seldom felt before. As Sachie wrote:

[it] . . . was to tie the three of us together, two brothers and a sister,
in our determination to live, and leave a mark of some sort or kind
. . . and was to precipitate us into action . . . into taking pen in
hand. . . .[3]

Edith, who was moved to tears over donkeys beaten on the
Scarborough sands, found it impossible to consider her parents'
feelings with sympathy. All the bitter memories of home were re-
vived, and within the dreary walls of Pembridge Mansions she
wrote *The Drunkard* and *The Mother*. They were added to some
of her poems that had been published in the *Daily Mirror*, and,
desperate to put herself in print and to try to redeem the name of
Sitwell, she paid Blackwell's of Oxford five guineas to have them
published as a small volume. Edith's *The Mother*, published in
1915, was not a particularly striking first book and did not sell
many copies. But it contained some remarkably individual lines
that showed the genesis of an original poetic talent. In *The
Drunkard*, a poem in her first collection, the opening lines:

> This black tower drinks the blinding light,
> Strange windows livid white . . .

give an indication of what was to become a preoccupation with
light and shade, whether in literal terms of colour or to represent
life and death. The couplet:

> Once more wild shriek on shriek would tear
> The dumb and shuddering air. . . .[4]

takes this vivid use of sensory impressions further by merging
sound with feeling. The young girl's imaginative buttressing of
the physical world had become a poetic strength in adulthood.

Unpromising and to a large extent unnoticed as *The Mother*
was, it contains a theme that was to be developed and praised in
Edith's later work: whether death of the body brings with it the
spiritual death of the soul. Often in her early work Edith wrote of
some act of treachery, where the problem of reconciling infamy
and death is examined within the context of a firm belief in

"good." In the title poem, *The Mother*, the spirit or soul of a
mother murdered by her son cannot rest, because of the thought,
torturing to her, that she was murdered *despite* the love she had
given him. The woman is not cast in the role of an accuser; neither does she blame her son for her own death. Instead he suffers
in purgatory:

> "His body is a blackened rag
> Upon the tree—a monstrous flag"
> Thus one worm to the other saith,
> Those slow mean servitors of Death.

The mother concludes the poem:

> "He did no sin. But cold blind earth
> The body was that gave him birth.
> All mine, all mine the sin; the love
> I bore him was not deep enough."[5]

Edith's determination to dedicate her life to poetry meant
more than just writing her own. In 1912 Edward Marsh had published the first of an intended annual series of collections of Georgian verse called *Georgian Poetry*. It ran until 1922 and included
the kind of work Edith disliked intensely. She felt that it dealt
only with the ramblings of English village cricket matches and
country-loving beer drinkers. This was a less than fair assessment,
but in any case she wanted to oppose the bulk of pastoral sentimentality that the Georgians produced.

Through her brother Osbert, Edith met Nancy Cunard and Iris
Tree, and it seems that together they formed the idea for opposition to Marsh with a rival anthology, called *Wheels*, although it
is not entirely certain whose idea the periodical originally was:
the title may have come before or after Nancy Cunard's poem of
that name, which was included in the first number, published in
1916. Edith's name as editor does not officially appear until 1921,
but she was deeply involved from the beginning.

Although *Wheels* was launched to oppose Marsh's anthologies,
it was not to be an entirely effective riposte. The contributors
(who included Edith's brothers and Helen Rootham, who translated Rimbaud) were, with the exception of Aldous Huxley, less
well known than many of the Georgians whom Edith attacked.
T. S. Eliot, although he had praised Sachie's work in 1918, considered by 1921:

The poets who consider themselves most opposed to Georgianism, and who know a little French, are mostly such as could imagine the Last Judgment as a lavish display of Bengal lights, Roman candles, Catherine wheels and inflammable fire balloons, *vous, hypocrite lecteur*.[6]

Other reviewers found Edith "brilliantly accomplished," but towards those who did not, or those who dared to criticize *Wheels*, such as Miss Jones of *Common Cause*, Edith was merciless. It was then that she began her habit of rapping short-sighted reviewers on the knuckles, and in an open letter to Miss Jones at the back of the 1919 *Wheels*, she wrote:

Dear Miss Jones (if you will pardon the expression)
Though the above is unsigned, I detect in it the traces, less of the cloven hoof than of a certain wooden head. I can quite understand your taking a rooted dislike to skilled technique in poetry, but may I suggest that the loss of subtlety is not always (as is the case with my poems) the result of polish. . . . I like you personally, Miss Jones, so I prefer to draw a veil over the rest of this painful scene, which the magic of your touch has converted from a *Fête Galante* into a family party at Lyons' Popular. Frankly, darling, what a stinker! Don't ever do it again, *please*, Miss Jones! Poetasters indeed!
Believe me, in spite of this little rift in the lute,
Yours faithfully,
The Editor of *Wheels*[7]

Edith had more opportunities of capitalizing on this emergent notoriety by meeting artists and writers at her brothers' house in Chelsea. It was a more "bohemian" area than Bayswater, and Osbert was able to entice a larger selection of people to dine in Swan Walk than Edith could ever afford to invite to her house.

Many of his friends would come on later to see Edith, amongst them Roger Fry, whom she persuaded to paint her. The last portrait was completed in 1918. As in all the accounts she left of her sittings with various artists, her sittings with Fry seem to have been almost farcical. For one portrait she wore a lily-green evening dress and, together with Fry—his long, grey hair covered by a large black sombrero—provided great amusement for the children who saw them walking in Fitzroy Square. Towards Edith, Fry was warm and friendly, and she quietly savoured the more eccentric aspects of his character. (During one sitting the coal merchant arrived and delivered his goods on the bed, at Fry's request.) In his paintings Fry sympathetically softened the bone structure of her face to emphasize the rather dreamy look of a poet.

The most interesting portrait, said to be the best likeness of her, was painted in 1915, by the Chilean artist Alvaro de Guevara. It is likely that Fry introduced Edith to "Chile," as he was known, and it has been suggested, though with little evidence, that they were in love with each other. What is true is that they began a close friendship after admiring each other's writings, for Chile also wrote poetry, and for some time they were often seen in each other's company. Guevara's biographer, Diana Holman-Hunt, noted that "it was obvious to everyone that Chile worshipped Edith, their visits to the ballet and concerts, her tea parties and poetry readings, her love, her wit and sympathy all provided solace."[8]

But he was, in fact, actually in love only with Nancy Cunard, although he felt a close spiritual affinity for Edith. He went with her to see the première of Sachie's ballet, *The Triumph of Neptune*, and the gossip journalists commented on this widely. Several years later, when Allanah Harper, editor of the Paris magazine *Échanges*, asked Edith about Chile, she said she would indeed have married him had she not been told that he had venereal disease.

This remark was typical of the evasive answers Edith would give when quizzed about her private life. Later, when asked by a correspondent about the Guevara portrait, she replied, "Yes, Señor Guevara did paint a portrait of me, but then so have many artists."

These artists were not the only ones Edith met through Osbert. In May 1917 he had a telephone call from Robert Ross, the writer and one-time friend of Oscar Wilde, asking him to go to meet a young poet whom their friend Siegfried Sassoon had discovered, and who Ross thought might interest Osbert. Osbert found in Ross's rooms "a young officer about my age, he was three months younger than myself—of sturdy medium build and wearing khaki uniform." It was Wilfred Owen, and the two men found they shared a common hatred of the war. Then in June, C. K. Scott-Moncrieff, the translator of Proust (who was to become a deadly enemy of Osbert), showed the Sitwells Owen's *The Deranged* (published as *Mental Cases*), and they were so impressed they wrote at once to Owen in Scarborough, saying they would like more poems to publish in the 1918 edition of *Wheels*.

Owen was anxious to see some of the Sitwells' work before committing himself and went to buy a copy of the 1917 *Wheels* in Scarborough. This proved more difficult than he had thought, as he was in territory fiercely hostile to the Sitwells. One bookshop had refused to stock copies, but he was so persistent that the assistant "loudly declared she knew all along I was Osbert himself." In the letter describing this to Osbert, Owen continued, "This caused a consternation throughout the crowded shop, but I got the last laugh, 'No madam, the book is by a friend of mine, Miss Sitwell.'"[9]

In fact, much to her great distress, Edith never met Owen, and various problems of changing publishers prevented the poems being published in the 1918 *Wheels*. In November, a week before the Armistice, Owen was killed, and it was not until March 1919 that Osbert received a selection of poems from Owen's mother, Susan, sent from Oswestry. Edith wrote to acknowledge them and told Susan Owen that she wanted to publish selections in *Wheels*. She had decided on *The Show, À Terre, Strange Meeting, The Sentry, Disabled, The Dead-Beat,* and *The Chances,* which she felt "should overwhelm anybody who cares really for poetry."[10] Edith was not exaggerating her feelings about the poems because she was writing to Owen's mother; she was genuinely moved and excited about them, and the letters are full of reverential phrases such as "I should feel it such a privilege to see you," and "copying out these poems of his for *Wheels*. They get home so hard that one finds oneself crying. . . . It has been sometimes impossible to go on."[11]

Susan Owen, aware of Edith's feelings, sent her a photograph of Wilfred. By this time Edith had made careful copies of the poems and sent in the proofs to Mrs. Owen; she thought, "They look magnificent in print."[12] Edith had been helped by Sachie to arrange and decipher the poems, many of the manuscripts of which were bespattered with mud, with parts missing. Finding the task difficult, she invited Siegfried Sassoon to come over to discuss the possible readings of the poems, but on arrival he announced that, as he had been a close friend of the poet, it would have been Owen's wish that Sassoon should prepare the poems for publication. By then Edith had worked very hard on the poems for some time, interrupting everything else, and felt bitter that they should be taken out of her hands. Sassoon's behaviour rankled with her, but she knew better than to make any difficulties; at least she was having the pleasure of printing them in *Wheels,* and her foresight did not pass unnoticed. Many years later, when Sassoon's fondness for the Sitwells had worn thin (mainly due to rows with Osbert) he wrote: "As far as I can remember, the selection was made entirely while I was in America. . . . But Edith Sitwell should be given full credit for being the first person to realize that Wilfred Owen's genius was more than highly promising talent."

If the reviews of *Wheels* had been discouraging, Edith found an unlikely champion in the shape of the novelist Arnold Bennett, who was not afraid to say that he admired her work and that of her brothers. She was pleased when he wrote:

The Sitwells can all write. . . . Further they all afflict the public—I mean the poetic public—which is a grand thing to do! They exult in a scrap. Battle is in the curve of their nostrils. . . .[13]

Such remarks only encouraged Edith, for she was now totally loyal to the cause of her own idea of poetry. Gradually she felt more able to take a breath, conquer her naturally shy personality, and bare her teeth if she felt a fight was necessary for her to demonstrate her loyalty to her poetic convictions. Of course, it brought her troubles, and many years later, when thinking over her battles, she noted about herself:

And to learn humility is my hardest trial. My friends try hard to teach me this. For instance, when I told Mr. Arnold Bennett "I have just met Middleton Murry and have come to the conclusion that I infinitely prefer God", Mr. Bennett reflected for a moment and replied "Spiritual pride is an awful thing". Then he gave a short laugh, "Remember this Edith, God sees you and Middleton Murry in just the same way. He sees no difference between us". At the time I did not care for that reflection. But the deepest lesson I have to learn is how not to love people in the wrong way, and how not to hate them in the wrong way, and this is very difficult.[14]

Edith would have done well to have remembered Bennett's advice, especially in her dealings with his French wife, Marguerite. Marguerite Bennett had no particular talent apart from reciting poetry in French, but Edith thought she had discovered a valuable ally. With Helen Rootham, they founded the Anglo-French Poetry Society to promote the cause of poets such as Verlaine and Baudelaire, and after hectic arrangements the first meeting was held in Bennett's house in June 1920. Sixty seats had been hired from Harrods, and with the help of Bennett's valet a recital room was arranged. Marguerite Bennett wore a rather pretentious dress of white brocade satin with silver and gold, and Egyptian veils embroidered with silver, but was assured it was perfectly suited to the occasion. Not to be outdone, Edith wore a glittering dress of gold and silver, which Marguerite told her was "magnificent." The poems Marguerite read were by Ronsard, Baudelaire, and Verlaine, and on the whole the meeting was a success, despite her reading through a bad cold. Edith herself considered the recital a major triumph, as influential critics such as St. John Ervine turned up. With such an audience, the Anglo-French Poetry Society seemed a useful platform for the Sitwells' poems, because Edith managed to slip in some of her own and Sachie's work.

For some months the Society ran smoothly, with Marguerite taking Edith's advice to read all the poems in a "somnambulistic voice." They lacked permanent headquarters and moved around various London drawing-rooms giving lectures and recitals. Edith was asked to give a lecture at Lady Baring's "Lend-a-Hand Guild" on "Modern English Poetry and Its Effect on Modern French Poetry," and taking the name of the Guild literally, asked those present to give their names if they were interested in becoming members of the Anglo-French Poetry Society. For some time Edith remained friendly with Marguerite and even became quite close to her, inviting her to stay at Renishaw, where she felt obliged to warn her about the family ghosts. However, Marguerite Bennett had an added interest in the Anglo-French Poetry Society, for it was at one of its readings, in Bedford College, that she met Pierre Legros, who eventually wrecked her marriage to Bennett. It is probable that Bennett encouraged Marguerite to go to Scotland, where she gave readings in Glasgow and Edinburgh, simply to get her away from Legros. If Edith was aware of this, there was no indication of it in a letter to Marguerite, which expresses hope that the readings would go off well.

Not everyone was as enthusiastic as St. John Ervine. Lytton
Strachey, who was a guest on one occasion, noted:

Last night, the Sitwell dinner was dreadfully dull, and they took me
off afterwards to an incredibly fearful function in Arnold Bennett's establishment. *He* was not there, but *she* was—oh my eye, what a
woman! It was apparently some sort of poetry society. There was an
address (very poor) on Rimbaud etc., by an imbecile frog [Helen
Rootham]. Then Edith Sitwell appeared, her nose longer than an
ant-eater's, and read some of her absurd stuff; then Eliot—very sad,
and seedy, it made one weep. Finally, Mrs. Arnold Bennett recited,
with waving arms and chanting voice, Baudelaire and Verlaine until
everybody was ready to vomit. As a study in half-witted horror the
whole thing was most interesting. The rooms were particularly disgusting and the company very miscellaneous.[15]

Marguerite Bennett had a stronger personality than had been
reckoned with by Edith. Close proximity to another woman
nearly always grated on Edith's nerves, and the first sign of trouble between them came in January 1922 when a certain Mme
Gabrain, whom Marguerite had chosen to read, criticized Helen's
choice of Rimbaud's poems. Edith wrote in a great fury that
Helen was well known in the literary world and that Mme Gabrain "still had to make a name for herself." Whatever Marguerite wrote in reply provoked a furious riposte from Edith:

I don't know why you thought you dared write such a letter about
Helen to me. Your spiteful impertinence merely throws a most un-
pleasant light upon yourself. Conceit, about any form of art, is really
the last thing that Helen can be accused of. As for Art, I do not choose
to discuss Helen's art with you.

Yours, EDITH SITWELL[16]

By now Edith had convinced herself that if she was to be successful, she must be absolutely ruthless in her campaign to persuade others of her own gifts. Nothing would be allowed to stand
in her way, and if her methods annoyed many, they were also
proving effective on others, for she received a steady flow of letters from young would-be writers. Edith enjoyed the role of poetic counsellor, and when a certain Brian Howard sent his poems
to her she replied:

I get a very great many manuscripts sent to me, and I invariably return them with a short note of regret, but in your case it is different.

You quite obviously have a very real gift and I hope to publish some works of yours in *Wheels*, perhaps this year, perhaps next, it depends on you.[17]

Howard found the advice Edith gave him encouraging, and after making some changes he wrote again in a few days with the revised poems. Edith was not entirely satisfied and told him to put some of his work aside for two months and then look at it again. To his delight she hoped that he might come and spend the afternoon with her. "We will work at your poems together before tea, and after tea we will talk about books, pictures and music."[18] He gave a striking impression, his outward manner being like Oscar Wilde's. Edith was convinced that Howard was a writer of talent, and there is no doubt that although her faith in him now seems to have been exaggerated, at the time he had at least some promise.

The publicity that *Wheels* had been given had not been all useful, and by 1921 her publishers were refusing to handle the next edition. It was taken over by a new publisher, and some of the earlier contributors had to be left out. Howard, because of the promise he showed, was represented with one poem, *Les Barouches;* he had written under the name of Charles Orange. The reviewer of the *Athenaeum* noted that "he jazzes with the macabre, the ghosts of lovers drowned in the lake change hats in the old barouches." Of some of the other contributors, "Mr. Aldous Huxley is at his liveliest, grimaces, and concludes with an arsenical benediction; Mr. Sacheverell Sitwell indulges now a sombre, now a quaint fancy; Miss Edith Sitwell's very special fruit (pomegranates) falls into her mouth in rhymes." The reviewer considered *Wheels* "a queer game but it has its points even though we have nothing more to say of it at the end than Holy Cockatrices and Boot-buttons."

Edith, to use one of her own phrases, believed that "bad publicity was better than no publicity at all."[19] The advertisements quoting favourable and unfavourable reviews at the back of *Wheels* were only part of a publicity campaign that was not always confined to the printed page.

Edith had grown more experienced in public debate since the days of the Anglo-French Poetry Society and was willing to travel to any part of the country where she was invited to lecture. *Where* did not matter: the important point was that her name was becoming known. Indeed, she was often invited because it was the very aggressiveness of her views on poetry that attracted large audiences. In 1923 a hospital committee that invited several guest speakers to a weekly debate invited Edith to discuss "the comparative value in old poetry and the new" with the poet Alfred Noyes as her opponent. They arranged to meet in the London School of Economics. Alfred Noyes was fairly representative of the Georgianism that Edith disliked, and, aware of this, he felt that he might "suddenly be attacked by a furious flock of strangely coloured birds, frantically trying to peck my nose." The debate was chaired by Sir Edmund Gosse, the poet, critic, and translator of Ibsen, who asked Noyes not to be too hard on Edith, for he was informed she was on the point of fainting, owing to nerves.

The debate began uneasily when Edith asked if her supporters might sit on the platform with her. Noyes agreed, but took advantage of the opportunity by telling the audience that he wished he could bring his along as well, naming Shakespeare, Dante, and others. This had the desired effect. Edith sat alone with Noyes and Gosse, having lost the first round.

Noyes and Edith were oddly matched in battle: Edith in a purple robe and laurel wreath, and Noyes in his rather American-cut suit, wearing horn-rimmed spectacles. Edith sat and read from a manuscript, ending:

We are always being called mad. If we are mad—we and our brothers in America who are walking hand in hand with us in the vanguard of progress—at least we are mad in company with most of our great predecessors. . . . Schumann . . . Coleridge and Wordsworth were all mad in turn. We shall be proud to join them in the Asylum to which they were consigned.[20]

Noyes, for his part, kept his promise to Gosse that he would not attack the "new poetry," but instead declared with Sainte-Beuve that "true poetry is a contemporary of all ages." When the debate ended, Gosse turned to Edith, whom he led away on his arm, and remarked, "Come along, Edith, I have no doubt that in his day Shakespeare was thought mad."[21]

The following day the press reported that Miss Sitwell, the champion of modernity, spoke without notes, whereas the old-fashioned Alfred Noyes delivered his text from a ponderous manuscript. It was, of course, the other way round, but the report started a furious controversy in the press about the debate. Rudyard Kipling joined in, declaring a letter from one of Edith's supporters to be "one of the most impertinent" he had ever read, more welcome notoriety for Edith.

Shortly afterwards Edith was the guest speaker at the Woman Writers' Club and repeated the London School of Economics lecture, but this time with disastrous results. Her attacker now was a woman of about sixty, who told Edith that the so-called new poets thought too much of themselves and that their poetry dealt not with human beings but "puppets, things of paint and sawdust" that had no life. She also objected to the artificial manner in which Edith described scenery in her poetry, saying that it resembled toy trees and "such that came out of Noah's Ark." The charges went on, and the last straw for Edith was when her accuser told her that what she and her followers produced was of "curiosity, vulgarity and primitive childishness" and "that most of what they had done might have been written by raw cave-men if they could write." By now Edith was shaking with fury and said, "I shall not reply to that speaker, I never answer rude and insolent remarks." This apparently upset the chairwoman, a Miss Woods, who told Edith that she was certain that Edith's accuser had not meant any discourtesy, and that it was the custom of those in the Club to speak frankly. In reply, Edith told Miss Woods:

I agree that no writer is entitled to attack another merely because they write in a different style and on different principles.[22]

St. John Adcock of *The Bookman* then rapped Edith and told her he frankly thought all the quarrelling she was involved in was nonsense, and in any case surely some of the critics had been kind to Edith. "Some," Edith said, laughing, for she was feeling less angry, "but I don't quarrel, and only when someone hits me on the head, so I slap their faces."

The debate ended in laughter, with Edith joining in, when Adcock remarked, "That is misleading, for it looks like quarrelling to me!"

By 1920 Edith had published two more volumes of poems: *Clowns' Houses* appeared in 1918, and *The Wooden Pegasus* in 1920. The poems in both books were much more original than

Edith's earlier work and showed a strong development of her poetic personality. This was not just chance; she was beginning to enjoy her independence and, free from the restrictions of Renishaw, where she was in a constant state of nerves, had at last been able to write to a strict daily timetable. Edith had realized that the only way to produce poetry was not to wait for inspiration but to sit and write. Even when she was a famous poet, Edith still practised her technique daily like a pianist working at her exercises, a habit she began at the outset of her poetry career.

Helen's introduction to Edith of Verlaine and Rimbaud was proving a useful influence on Edith's own work, though mainly as a catalyst, rather than as an example to imitate. Her gift of apparently endless word-spinning was by now highly accomplished, as in her *King of China's Daughter*, which was published in 1920:

> The King of China's daughter,
> She never would love me
> Though I hung my cap and bells upon
> Her nutmeg tree.
> For oranges and lemons,
> The stars in bright blue air
> (I stole them long ago, my dear),
> Were dangling there.
> The Moon did give me silver pence,
> The Sun did give me gold,
> And both together softly blew
> And made my porridge cold;
> But the King of China's daughter
> Pretended not to see
> When I hung my cap and bells upon
> Her nutmeg tree.[23]

Although Edith was interested in the work of Verlaine and Rimbaud, the poetic method she developed was almost entirely original. She remarked, however, in an essay published in 1925 that Rimbaud's "power of concentrating visual things into a spiritual essence" and the fact that he was "one of the most powerful influences on the rhythms, the peculiar expressiveness and the visual sense of our time" had been of great value to her early work, and his influence was still apparent.[24]

Edith felt that if poetry was to make an impact on the reader, it must present "natural objects" in a new way. Most people had become too used to looking at natural objects in only one way, and consequently through familiarity they had become rather boring. Edith's idea was to make use of all the senses equally: "When the speech of one sense is insufficient to convey his [the poet's] entire meaning, he uses the language of another." The poet knows, Edith suggested, "that every sight, touch, sound, smell of the world we live in has its meaning; it is the poet's duty to interpret these messages."[25] Using one sense to describe sensations normally associated with another, although relatively neglected in poetry until utilized by Edith, was not altogether new. Francis Thompson, the nineteenth-century poet, and Symbolists such as Baudelaire used the technique frequently, but Edith's adoption of it was still innovatory in her era.

One such poem whereby Edith demonstrated her method was *Aubade:*

> Jane, Jane,
> Tall as a crane,
> The morning light creaks down again;
>
> Comb your cockscomb-ragged hair,
> Jane, Jane, come down the stair.
>
> Each dull blunt wooden stalactite
> Of rain creaks, hardened by the light,
>
> Sounding like an overtone
> From some lonely world unknown.
>
> But the creaking empty light
> Will never harden into sight,
>
> Will never penetrate your brain
> With overtones like the blunt rain.
>
> The light would show (if it could harden)
> Eternities of kitchen garden,
>
> Cockscomb flowers that none will pluck,
> And wooden flowers that 'gin to cluck.
>
> In the kitchen you must light
> Flames as staring, red and white,
>
> As carrots or as turnips, shining
> Where the cold dawn light lies whining.

Cockscomb hair on the cold wind
Hangs limp, turns the milk's weak mind. . . .

Jane, Jane,
Tall as a crane,
The morning light creaks down again![26]

The first surprising image is "creaks," describing light experienced as an auditory image. Edith explained in an essay written in 1925 that she used it because "in a very early dawn, after rain, the light has a curious uncertain quality, as though it does not run quite smoothly. . . ."[27]

Other images may at first glance appear unusual, but in the context they are all exact, and apt. "Cockscomb-ragged" not only describes the hair, but also reminds us of the rustic setting of the poem. "Rain" is not just any rain; its weight, texture, and intensity are all explained with great economy in the phrase "dull blunt wooden stalactite." The poem even ends with a touch of humour, with the pun "turns the milk's weak mind."

It is true that the poems are not easily analysed, and this was one reason why Edith's work was so disliked by some of her early critics. But the impact of these startling new uses of words is chiefly emotional rather than intellectual. With repeated readings, however, the meanings become clear in a logical sense, too, and show that Edith *was* achieving, with her own method, a fresh conception of natural objects.

THREE

Façade

This modern world is but a thin match board flooring spread over a shallow hell. . . .

Essay in *Bucolic Comedies*

APART from the language of poetry, Edith was interested in the rhythms of words when placed in various orders. She was fascinated by the transcendental études of Liszt, in which the composer had written music to cover every pianistic complexity possible, demanding a dazzling technique in performance. The idea of writing similarly technically difficult poems did not materialize until Edith wrote her *Hornpipe*, which contains all the accents and rhythms of the sailors' dance. But after that others were to follow, where not only rhythms of dances such as the *Waltz*, *Polka*, and *Fox Trot* are used, but also there is a remarkably skilful playing with language, where the vowel sounds actually telescope into each other. These lines from "*I do like to be beside the Seaside*" resemble the quickening trill in the G-sharp minor étude of Liszt:

> Thetis wrote a treatise noting wheat is silver
> like the sea; the lovely cheat is sweet as
> foam; Erotis notices that she

Will
Steal
The
Wheat-king's luggage, like Babel . . .[1]

This group of poems was a maturing of her early penchant for simple word-play. They were to be arranged under the title of *Façade*. The remainder of the poems following *Hornpipe* were all actually written in close collaboration with a composer, a young friend of Sachie's from Oxford. His name was William Walton.

In 1918 Sachie left the Grenadier Guards, where he had been since he left Eton in 1916, to go to Balliol College, Oxford. He met William Walton, then at Christ Church under Dr. Strong, who was Dean there. Walton was in the cathedral's choir school and had impressed Strong, who managed to alter the rules for entry so that Walton could become an undergraduate at Christ Church at sixteen. For some reason he did not pass his exams for the Mus.Bac. and B.A., which would have qualified him as a schoolmaster, and now his future seemed uncertain. Fortunately Sachie, who hated Oxford and hardly ever attended a lecture, deliberately got himself sent down and, convinced he had discovered a young genius, took Walton back to London, where they lived in Osbert's house at Swan Walk.

Walton learned of Edith's technical exercises when, as he recalled, "Sachie suggested that it would be a good idea if they were read to music, and as I happened to be the only composer around, they asked me to do it." There was also the threat, in fact, that they would ask Constant Lambert if Walton did not agree. Walton was not particularly fond of poetry to start with, and initially was "not very keen on the idea," but in 1921 he began work, and would either go round to Moscow Road, where Edith lived, or invite her round to Carlyle Square, where the Sitwell brothers and Walton had moved, when she would bring with her a new poem to work on.

Walton scored the work for flute, clarinet, saxophone, trumpet, cello, and percussion, an unusual combination of instruments chosen mainly because they were cheap. Although a private performance was arranged for January 24, 1922, Walton was scoring almost up to the last moment, getting assistance from Constant Lambert, whom he had now met. Lambert helped him to copy orchestral parts and even wrote a little of *Four in the Morning*.

The problem of how the speaker was to be heard above the music was overcome when Sachie remembered an instrument like a megaphone, called a Sengerphone, named after its inventor, Mr. Senger. Senger was an opera expert and had used his invention in Wagner's *Parsifal*. Sachie traced him, now an old man, to Hampstead, and he and Walton took a bus to see him there. Senger was fascinated by *Façade* and trained Edith in recitation at the rehearsals. She was shy at the beginning and her diction was unclear, and Senger became so exasperated at one rehearsal that he rushed up to her and, seizing her throat, told her, "You are using your voice the wrong way."

The music itself puzzled the small orchestra, who also slightly resented having to be conducted by such a young composer. Gradually, however, they came to like it, although the clarinetist remarked, "Excuse me, Mr. Walton, has a clarinet player ever done you an injury?"[2]

The first private performance was held in Osbert's house at No. 2 Carlyle Square, in a room so small that the sound was overwhelming to the large audience who had been packed in, although they were consoled afterwards with some hot rum punch. The programme announced that the poems of *Façade* were to be published in book form by the Favil Press, and they duly appeared in 1922, with a coloured frontispiece selected by Gino Severini which in fact Edith intensely disliked. (Severini, an Italian Futurist, was a friend of Sacheverell's.) The contents had now changed, and were to be altered yet again in 1923 by the first public performance. (In 1977 Walton resurrected several of the rejected pieces and they were performed in London. They went through further changes, as Walton reworked them for publication in 1979, when they were named *Façade 2*.)

The Aeolian Hall was booked for the second performance of *Façade*, on June 12, 1923, when it was to be unveiled to the public gaze. Amongst the audience who arrived there were Nancy Cunard, the writer Harold Acton, Virginia Woolf, the painter Augustus John, and the novelist Ada Leverson (who had been nicknamed "the Sphinx" by Oscar Wilde).

The backcloth was painted by Frank Dobson, famous for his sculpted bust of Osbert, and consisted of two masks, the first of which, in the centre, was half pink and half white and large enough to accommodate the Sengerphone through which Edith chanted her poems. Osbert announced each poem through the small second mask and explained to the audience that the Sengerphones were placed behind the backcloth to stop the reader's personality intruding into the poems. Acton noted that the audience tittered and made inopportune remarks.

Virginia Woolf did not understand what *Façade* was all about, as she admitted in her diary:

. . . the London season of course in full swing. So I judged yesterday in the Aeolian Hall, listening, in a dazed way, to Edith Sitwell vociferating through the megaphone. There was Lady [Sybil] Colefax in her hat with the green ribbons. . . . I should be describing Edith Sitwell's poems, but I kept saying to myself "I dont really understand . . . I dont really admire". The only view, presentable view that I framed, was to the effect that she was monotonous. She has one tune only on her merry go round. And she makes her verse keep step accurately to the Hornpipe. This seems to be wrong; but I'm all sandy with writing criticism, & must be off to my book again. . . .[3]

When the performance was over, Edith suffered all the harassment of a public figure. She had to be hurried behind the curtain as she was being pursued by someone she regarded as a sex maniac; eventually he discovered Edith, despite a kick from Sachie, who told him to get out. But after the maniac had departed there was still trouble in the form of an old woman who tried to hit Edith with an umbrella. At last she escaped to a party Osbert gave in Carlyle Square.

Edith felt exhausted by the performance and at the party lay back watching a game of charades where Lytton Strachey, Clive Bell, Eugene Goossens, and the critic St. John Hutchison acted the death of a Teutonic princess attended by a doctor and royal servants. Ada Leverson was present, and she thought *Façade* wonderful, as she told Acton. He introduced her to, amongst others, Evelyn Waugh. The conversation, Acton noted in his memoirs, "became a game of consequences complicated by the sphinx's deafness and air of mystery."[4]

The next day reviews appeared, and except for the *Daily Mail* they were all hostile. A critic noted that if Max Beerbohm wanted to do a really funny drawing of the Sitwells, instead of the stupid one of them on view at the Leicester Galleries, he should have gone to the "ridiculous recital" at the Aeolian Hall.

Another concluded, quite firmly, "Surely it is time this sort of thing was stopped."[5] The rumpus was not unfounded, nor entirely due to the misconception of the work. In truth, the orchestra was inadequately rehearsed and Edith had suffered badly from nerves and was not always audible, despite Mr. Senger's efforts.

Although the reviews were mainly hostile, Edith found a friend in Gerald Cumberland, a writer and journalist, who wrote in the July number of *Vogue:*

Miss Sitwell half spoke, half shouted her poems in strict monotone, emphasising the metre rather than the rhythm. Her voice, beautiful in tone, full, resonant and clear, could without effort, be heard above the din of the music. To this hour I am by no means certain what some of the poems mean, but if I do not understand their beauty, I divine it, and for that reason am all the more attracted, drawn, seduced.[6]

Edith was pleased and wrote to Cumberland to tell him how grateful she was. She said that she in fact owed his poetry a great debt of gratitude because it had "opened my eyes when I was first trying to write, to every new possibility. . . . You can understand," she concluded, "why, having learnt so much from a poem of yours, I am particularly delighted to know that you liked *Façade*."[7]

Although Edith appeared publicly quite confident about her work, she was privately quite nervous about its reception. It is perhaps surprising to find that as a result of this condemnation she was willing to take advice from John Freeman, who, as a noted Georgian poet, lived in the opposite camp, but she did so, perhaps reacting to the reviews with personal open-mindedness. She readily admitted to him that she had a distrust of his work because he was in the company of people like J. C. Squire, whose products she despised. Edith had, of course, certain prejudices towards some poets, but she honestly tried to understand their poetry:

Sometimes when I see a poet's work, I dislike it. This happened with many poets for whose work I now feel a great respect, but in the long run I am always won over by his qualities of music and sincerity.[8]

At that time, Edith was working on her poem *The Sleeping Beauty*. It was to be one of her best pieces of writing, for out of her difficult childhood she managed to draw from happy experi-

ences and recollections and transmute them into an imaginative
adaptation of the fairy story. Some of Edith's childhood memories, such as seeing pierrots and other figures of the commedia
dell'arte on the sand at Scarborough, had been reinforced and
taken on a new meaning when she saw them—or their Russian
counterparts—often featured in the Ballets Russes, then the sensation of the intellectual world, and especially in *Petrouchka*. In
1920 Edith had published a prose account of the stories of some
of the fables used by the Ballets Russes. In her preface she spoke
of how her generation of writers and artists had all been
influenced by the Ballets, for its movements "and the bright
shrilling of colour which is part of their speech, are an interpretation not of a mood alone, but of life itself. . . ."[9]

Referring directly to *Petrouchka*, Edith, commenting on the
scene where the Magician gropes for his puppet in the booth, felt
that the drum taps of Stravinsky's music were

nothing but the anguished beat of the clown's heart as he makes his
endless battle against materialism . . . we know we are watching our
own tragedy. Do we not all know that little room with the ancestral
portrait of God? Have we not all battered our heads through the
flimsy paper-walls, only to find blackness? . . . and with Claudius we
cry out for "light, lights, more lights" . . .[10]

This theme, originating in her prose, was to be concentrated in
some stanzas in *The Sleeping Beauty*:

> Like harsh and crackling rags of laughter seems
> The music, bright flung as an angel's hair—
> Yet awful as the ultimate despair
> Of angels and of devils. . . . Something dreams
> Within the sound that shrieks both high and low
> Like some ventriloquist's bright-painted show
> On green grass, shrill as anger, dulled as hate:
> It shrieks to the dulled soul, "Too late, too late!"
> Sometimes it jangles thin as the sharp wires
> Whereon the poor half-human puppets move;
> Sometimes it flares in foliage like hell's fires,
> Or whispers insincerities for love.[11]

and

> And there are terrible and quick drum-taps
> That seem the anguished beat of our own heart

Making an endless battle without hope
Against materialism and the world.
And sometimes terrible lumbering Darkness comes
Breaking the trivial matchboard floors that hide
From us the Dead we dare not look upon:
O childish eyes, O cold and murdered face—
Dead innocence and youth that were our own![12]

Edith's work now contained a message that was more directly stressed than it had been previously; the theme of the struggle for spiritual reality against the overwhelming forces of materialism. The opening passage of *The Sleeping Beauty* presents an allegory, where sleep is dark, to be gradually replaced by awakening into light:

When we come to that dark house,
Never sound of wave shall rouse
The bird that sings within the blood
Of those who sleep in that deep wood.[13]

It is a lost Eden, where, amongst other ideas, Edith explores the theme of a childhood innocence which, it seems, will never be destroyed:

Life was so still, so clear, that to wake
Under a kingfisher's limpid lake
In the lovely afternoon of a dream
Would not remote or stranger seem.[14]

But the childhood innocence is destroyed, and gradually a Vanity Fair appears. Edith may have been thinking of her life at Renishaw and Scarborough and combined her recollections with her impressions of *Petrouchka* to form a symbolic landscape where several themes are drawn together:

For Night and Day, and Hell and Heaven, seem
Only a clown's booth seen in some bad dream,
Wherefrom we watch the movements of our life
Growing and ripening like summer fruits
And dwindling into dust, a mirage lie:

Hell is no vastness, it has naught to keep
But little rotting souls and a small sleep.

It has the same bright-coloured clarity we knew
In nursery afternoons so long ago . . .[15]

The Sleeping Beauty was Edith's most ambitious poem up to
that time and is the one poem of considerable length where there
is a development of a theme without extraneous decoration,
which at times flawed some of her work. The traditional fairy
story served as a guide only, and in fact Edith changed the ending, for the Princess goes on sleeping in her world, undisturbed.

Before the poem was published, Edith sent it to John Freeman
for advice. So absorbed was she in Freeman's own work that she
accidentally incorporated into *The Sleeping Beauty* a line of his:
"then sleep came colder from the roses, blooming in desolation"
(which she slightly changed to ". . . colder than the rose . . .").
Freeman did not mind the alteration of this line, but for other
reasons accused her of flippancy, and Edith agreed: "I see your
point about avoiding flippancy and think there is a great deal to
be said for this point of view. In writing poetry using judgment is
the most delicate thing in the world."[16]

Edith was at the same time determined to improve Freeman's
taste and pressed him to read T. S. Eliot's *The Waste Land*,
which she had just read herself. "There are some wonderful lines
in it," she told Freeman, but much to Edith's disappointment he
did not agree: he had been unable to find any form in it. Edith
wrote to him that he must meet Robert Graves because

apart from the pleasure of meeting him, he can argue, and I can't, and
I do so want you to be converted to liking poems which you find at
the moment antipathetic. Robert is obviously the person to do this for
he has enthusiasm and I think, but I am not sure, at one time was un-
converted himself.[17]

Edith was asked to spend a few days with Graves and his wife,
Nancy, who lived at Boar's Hill, near Oxford. Graves met Edith
at the railway station and told her that he was unable to carry
her luggage because he had hurt an arm playing Rugby football.
As they struggled along together, things got worse when Graves
remarked, "It's nice to see a fine, strapping woman who can carry
her suitcases!"[18] Edith was not pleased, especially since they contained books and manuscripts and a heavy eighteenth-century
brocade cloak. Graves went on ahead, pushing his bicycle, and as
they approached the house, he cleared his throat and said to
Edith, after some hesitation, "Look here, Edith: you leave Nancy
alone and she'll leave you alone, see? She'll be all right if you are

all right. But don't try anything on with her, because she won't stand it. D'you understand?"

Edith agreed meekly, wondering just *what* Graves's wife would be like. As they walked up the path of the Graveses' home the suspense made her feel extremely nervous. Once inside, she was surprised to find Nancy Nicholson (as she preferred to be known) quiet and domesticated, and before long they were happily chatting together as they hemmed handkerchiefs. Later it transpired that Nancy had earlier received a warning from Robert in exactly the same words about Edith.

Nancy was an ardent feminist, and although Edith believed strongly in the acceptance and recognition of women in society, she felt that Nancy's views were too extreme. Nancy believed that their children should be allowed to behave in whatever manner they wanted, and her opinion prevailed, even though Robert and Edith found the combined noise of the three young Graveses intolerable. Although Robert shared many of his wife's views and was completely domesticated, the moment she departed for a country walk he grabbed the children and rushed them off to bed. Nevertheless, aware of what his wife would have said had she been there, he felt obliged to half-apologize to Edith, remarking, "I don't think we need worry Nancy with things like that."[19]

Edith discussed modern poetry with Robert and heard all his latest theories on Shakespeare, on whom he had cast a Freudian eye. At the same time, Edith was disconcerted to find him like a "high wind" as he "cooked sausages with one hand, and played with the children with the other." She felt that he did too much, although he "could not write enough poetry to please me."[20]

Edith was, however, fascinated by Graves's relationship with Nancy, and her observations of the life of a poet with a feminist gave her an indication of what she would have expected had she herself married. Nancy told her that no woman, however tiresome, should be quelled in any way and also that, in her eyes, all husbands were in the wrong—except Robert, of course. Nancy related to Edith the case of a man who was a poet who had left his wife and baby to go on writing. Such selfishness, Nancy decided. Women, she insisted, must be considered above anything else, they must be given way to. What did a man's art matter if his hand could rock the cradle?

Edith disagreed strongly, for she passionately believed that art came *above* domestic and married life and could not understand Nancy's defence of "the tiresome women she championed."[21]

However, she regarded the Graveses as sincere friends, and when the Sitwells were dismissed in Robert Graves's *Good-bye to All That*, in 1929, was bitterly hurt. Earlier, Edith had been upset rather than annoyed when the Graveses went to Cairo without saying goodbye, but she never knew the real extent to which she had apparently given offence. She had once declined to stay with the Graveses when she heard the children had tapeworms, for she always had a horror of illness, and for consolation told herself that the Graveses were offended at her refusal.

Her friendship with these two famous literary figures was just one of several she was making around then. Graves had met Virginia Woolf at this time, who with her husband, Leonard, was publishing a long poem of his, but they did not know each other well. When Edith was invited to tea with Virginia, she was interrogated about Graves and his wife, and her description of his energy "like a high wind" amused Virginia.

Edith was not a constant visitor to the Bloomsbury teas, for although she liked Virginia personally, and was fascinated by her appearance, she cared very little about her work. She had told Virginia that she was one of the few living writers whose work meant anything to her, but later in life dismissed her as a "beautiful little knitter."[22] To Edith

everything about her from the beautiful and delicate head with its large and delightful blue eyes, her birdlike delicacy of movement, her long and lovely hands, add to the feeling of charm. . . . Conversation with her reveals not only the beauties of her own mind, but unexpected richness in our own. She hovers like a benevolent hawk . . . she pounces, she brings up the smallest treasure from the depth of one's mind and holds it till it glitters in the light.[23]

On the occasion when Edith was asked to amuse Virginia about Graves, E. M. Forster and Victoria Sackville-West were also present. With Forster Edith felt uneasy, for unlike her he seemed incapable of making a hasty judgement, and was too silent for Edith to feel at ease:

Everything he says is so exact and tidy that I feel conversationally not so much my usual feeling of being a bird that has been out in a tornado of wind, as like a dockside policeman who has taken the wrong turning in every sense. I do not feel too big for my boots, but I feel my boots are too big for me.[24]

Forster asked Edith if she thought the impulse towards creating the arts had any foundation in the sexual urge. Edith decided that it had, but did not dare to say so after Virginia and Forster had said they thought not.

Because Vita Sackville-West, whose work Edith did not admire, was there, Edith was embarrassed when Virginia asked her what she thought of the Rugby football school of poetry, as she loosely included Vita in that group. Edith bravely told Virginia that, compared to herself, the novelist had led a sheltered life and could therefore hardly realize "how alarming it is to be pursued by flocks of enraged sheep . . . trying to knock down and trample one underfoot, and to eat one's brains."[25]

It is likely that the recollections Edith had of the Bloomsberries were in fact formed from a party Virginia Woolf gave in early June 1925. Virginia's diary entry for the fifth includes the same guests Edith mentions, and notes that Edith

was like a Roman Empress, so definite clear cut, magisterial & yet with something of the humour of a fishwife—a little too commanding about her own poetry & ready to dictate—tremulously pleased by Morgan's [E. M. Forster's] compliments (& he never praised Vita, who sat hurt, modest, silent, like a snubbed schoolboy).[26]

Evidently Edith's remarks about the "Rugby football school of poetry" had made a certain impact.

More revealing is a diary entry Virginia Woolf made a few weeks earlier, when she and Edith dined at Carlyle Square:

. . . Edith is an old maid. I had never conceived this. I thought she was severe, implacable & tremendous; rigid in her own conception. Not a bit of it. She is, I guess, a little fussy, very kind, beautifully mannered. . . . She is elderly too, almost my age, & timid, & admiring & easy & poor, & I liked her more than admired or was frightened of her. Nevertheless, I do admire her work, & thats what I say of hardly anyone: she has an ear, & not a carpet broom; a satiric vein; & some beauty in her. How one exaggerates public figures! How one makes up a person immune from one's own pleasures & failings! But Edith is humble: has lived in a park alone till 27, & so described nothing but sights & sounds; then came to London, & is trying to get a little emotion into her poetry—all of which I suspected, & think promising. Then how eager she was to write for the Press

[Hogarth Press, founded by Leonard and Virginia], which had always been her great ambition, she said. Nothing could be more conciliatory & less of an eagle than she; odd looking too, with her humorous old maids smile, her half shut eyes, her lank hair, her delicate hands, wearing a large ring, & fine feet, & her brocade dress, blue & silver. Nothing of the protester or pamph[l]eteer or pioneer seemed in her—rather the well born Victorian spinster. So I must read her afresh.[27]

Virginia appears to have been more impressed with Edith's work than Edith was with Virginia's, for Edith sent the novelist a copy of *Rustic Elegies* as soon as it was published in 1927. Virginia seems to have found a fascination with Edith, for when she invited Edith for tea in March 1927, she found a different way to describe her guest. Edith was

transparent like some white bone one picks up on a moor, with sea water stones on her long frail hands which slide into yours much narrower than one expects like a folded fan. She has pale gemlike eyes; & is dressed, on a windy March day, in three decker skirts of red spotted cotton. . . . All is very tapering & pointed, the nose running on like a mole. She said I was a great writer, which pleased me. So sensitive to everything in people & books she said. She got talking about her mother, blaspheming in the nursery, hysterical, terrible; setting Edith to kill bluebottles. "But nobody can take a liberty with her" said Edith, who prides herself on Angevin blood. She is a curious product, likable to me: sensitive, etiolated, affectionate, lonely, having to thread her way (there is something ghostlike & angular about her) home to Bayswater to help cook dinner. . . .[28]

Apart from her own published writings, there are almost no records of anyone's having troubled to note any of Edith's own intentions regarding her poetry. Virginia concluded her entry with a revealing remark Edith made about her poetry:

She said she would like to attach great bags & balloons of psychology, people having dinner, &c, to her poems, but she has no knowledge of human nature, only these sudden intense poems. . . .[29]

The two women were poles apart in thought, yet they shared something of the same attitude towards other writers, for Virginia had written that "every writer was a potential enemy," something Edith spent her whole life demonstrating. If Edith was jealous of Virginia's success, she did not show it publicly, for she never pretended to take the Bloomsbury Group seriously enough to consider its members a challenge to her own reputation. It is more likely that she distrusted them because they were an aspect of "intellectual society." She felt insecure educationally, for although Virginia had not been to university either, she had read widely, and knew Greek and Latin, owing to the encouragement of her father. Edith once half-jokingly remarked that the Bloomsbury Group "at once perceived that I had no culture, and had no original thought."[30]

There was always a certain pretentiousness in the Bloomsbury Group's behaviour that Edith found unacceptable; she felt that to be appreciated by them it was essential to have "furniture made of tin, and ostrich feathers on the floor."[31] Clive Bell annoyed her the most, despite his friendship towards her brothers. She poked fun at his "Francophilism" and the way in which he spoke about the "latest and most moronic Parisian poets as if they were equal to Dryden and Tennyson."[32]

Bell's obsession with all things French provided her with an incident she relished, told to her by her friend Arthur Waley (who became famous for his translations of Chinese and Japanese literature). Waley lived near Bell in Gordon Square, and as he left early each morning on his bicycle he would pass Bell's house. There on the steps were French rolls, which Waley observed the local dogs decorating daily in an unhygienic manner. Waley felt he ought to warn Bell about the additional flavour his rolls acquired after they left the bakery, but he was afraid he would be forced to confront a parlourmaid, and eventually, having kept quiet for several weeks, said nothing at all.

On a serious level, too, it was the silent aspect of Arthur Waley that Edith appreciated. He was one of the few early admirers of her work, and although he said little, talking only to the point, she would be invited to "bring a book" and then to sit in his garden, and they would read silently together. Just as she was prey to lunatics, Waley was host to his own brand of bores who thought he would be interested in discussing *The Mikado* because he was an oriental scholar. Edith was always amused to hear his high voice relating the latest invasion by some old lady or boring student.

When he stayed at Renishaw, he was the perfect guest to counter Sir George. He was also the only living figure Edith was to include in her *English Eccentrics,* a study published in 1933. She suspected that Waley kept a conversation book which he wrote up every night, noting down the conversations he had had that day, and that it would turn up one day to embarrass his friends. His air of silent intellectual superiority inspired no little awe in her.

While Edith was seeing the Graveses at Oxford she hoped it would be possible to arrange a performance of *Façade* there, but the work was now the centre of a new controversy. During the first performance Noël Coward had pointedly walked out, and, probably out of sheer jealousy of the Sitwells, had begun a rather silly campaign against them. Amongst his first attacks on the Sitwells was a parody entitled *Chelsea Buns,* ostensibly by one Hernia Whittlebot, edited by Noël Coward with an introduction by "Gaspard Pustontin." His signed preface did not endear himself to Edith. Part of it read:

In France, Hernia Whittlebot has been hailed and extolled even more perhaps than in England. Within the obscure translucent gloom of the bois, members of the Whittlebot "cult" may be observed wandering like contented spirits temporarily released from their narrow confines of ungarlanded graves, and in their shining eyes the knowledge that at last they have found the source of life's inspiration.[33]

The joke was probably one of Coward's most high-spirited routs, carried out in the same sense of fun that Edith herself felt when she played pranks on those she regarded as the opposition. But the poetry was not even a good parody:

Theme for Oboe in E Flat

Zebubbah zebubbah,
Zooboom tweet tweet,
Pidwiddy pidwiddy
Pidantipatiddy.

Dark—round—
Suggestive beads of sound
Zebubbah zebubbah,
Tweet, tweet.[34]

After *Chelsea Buns* came the show *London Calling,* of which he was part-author, and with this it seemed to the Sitwells that war had been declared. In this revue, which opened at the Duke of York's Theatre in September 1923, Coward gave his impression of *Façade*, which was so artless that it ought to have been ignored by Edith. But her nerves were shaken by it so that she made herself ill by worry. Writing to Harold Acton shortly after *London Calling*, Edith regretfully had to ask him to cancel the plans for the performance of *Façade* at Oxford, as she feared Coward's supporters might cause trouble. It is unlikely that she ever regarded Coward as a serious threat, but she was upset all the same and her brothers demanded an apology from Coward, which she eventually received. She never carried on a public campaign against Coward as she did against Wyndham Lewis, which must have disappointed Coward, for he probably hoped for some free publicity. The matter ended for the time being in 1926, when Coward, forced to apologize by Osbert and Sacheverell, received a note from Edith which made the point crisply and conclusively: "Dear Mr. Coward, I accept your apology. Yours sincerely, Edith Sitwell."[35] They were not to meet socially until 1962, when Coward had forged his reputation without the help of Sitwell publicity.

The storm that blew up over *Façade* had brought Edith endless letters and paragraphs in the gossip columns, and she found it increasingly difficult to work. She always wrote in bed, sometimes waking at six so that she could work undisturbed, but there were constant interruptions. Her problems included the stream of unwelcome visitors who arrived in Moscow Road. One was a man who resembled a gorilla, who one evening tried to invite himself into Edith's flat with the insistent salesman's technique of one foot in the door. He wanted, he told Edith, to see his "pretty baby," but Edith quickly stamped on his foot and he "retired, howling."

Nor was that the end of her problems. Living in London was proving expensive after the rent of the flat was raised. Also, Helen had been a devoted friend to Edith, but she was already unwell and her illness had begun to affect her mind. Earlier, when Edith had given parties in Moscow Road, Helen had always kept in the background, but now she demanded almost complete attention from visitors. After one operation in 1924 she finally decided to go to Paris, where Evelyn Wiel, her divorced sister, had a flat, and to take Edith with her. At the beginning, however, Edith lived only temporarily in Paris in Evelyn's flat in

the Rue Saint-Dominique, and kept her own rooms on in Pembridge Mansions.

For Edith the prospect of Paris was exciting, as she had heard
of the new movement of writers, artists, and musicians there. Not
that all musicians were acceptable to Edith; at one of her earliest
parties after arriving there, given in 1925 for the frequenters of
the Shakespeare & Company Bookshop run by Sylvia Beach, she
found amongst the guests the musician George Antheil. Antheil
was working on his *Ballet mécanique*, which he wrote for a
player piano, since the work was impossible for any pianist to
perform. Edith was told by his admirers that "he plays so loudly,
so fast and his music is so difficult, that he has to be carried out
and slapped with wet towels like a boxer, and rubbed and given
smelling salts."[36] Edith did not find his conversation any more impressive than his music, feeling that to talk to him was like talking "to a shut oyster that has been irritated by a pearl."

Parties apart, Edith kept quiet. "I see very few people," she
wrote to Harold Acton. This gave her a chance to do some writing, something she had found increasingly difficult in London.
She had been preparing *Troy Park*, a volume of poems that had
already gone to the printers, and was now working on *Poor
Young People*, a joint publication with her two brothers.

The same theme of betrayal developed in *The Sleeping Beauty*
was given emphasis in Edith's new collection of poems, *Troy
Park*. When questioned in the 1950s about her early poetry in a
BBC radio programme called "Frankly Speaking," and asked by
an interviewer whether her unhappy childhood had contributed
to her development as a poet, Edith replied, "Oh, I think so. I
mean, I think it probably did a great deal."

To another BBC interviewer, in 1957, Edith spoke of her autobiographical poem *Colonel Fantock*, which was published in
Troy Park:

It had a good many backgrounds . . . it had the background of Renishaw and the background of Montegufoni which I had seen but—well
of course we lived there also, and also the background of my grandmother's family house, one in Wales which was called Troy House
which I'd never seen but the name had a great effect on me. . . .

"Colonel Fantock" was the name given by Edith to Sachie's
tutor, Major Brockwell, and in the poem the three Sitwell chil-

dren became "Dagobert" (Osbert), "Peregrine" (Sachie), and Edith as "I." In the last stanza there is a deep sense of betrayal when

> . . . one cruel day in deepest June,
> When pink flowers seemed a sweet Mozartian tune,
> And Colonel Fantock pondered o'er a book.
> A gay voice like a honeysuckle nook—
> So sweet—said, "It is Colonel Fantock's age
> Which makes him babble." . . . Blown by winter's rage,
> The poor old man then knew his creeping fate,
> The darkening shadow that would take his sight
> And hearing; and he thought of his saved pence
> Which scarce would rent a grave. . . . That youthful voice
> Was a dark bell which ever clanged "Too late"—
> A creeping shadow that would steal from him
> Even the little boys who would not spell—
> His only prisoners. . . . On that June day
> Cold Death had taken his first citadel.[37]

The themes that Edith was repeating and expanding in her work were perhaps an effort to salvage something worthwhile from her childhood, to make the unhappy life she endured at home with her parents an experience that had a more universal validity.

It is clear that she had suffered some personal terrible crisis, which was never fully explained but only hinted at in her poetry. At the end of her poem *Pandora's Box*, also in *Troy Park*, the crisis is mentioned and appears with a tremendous sense of intensity without ever being explained in strict biographical terms:

> I crept to that small room . . . there was a box
> (A flat thin sea that seemed a crystal box) . . .
> And all the mad Cassandra tongues of birds
> Cried, "Troy is burning,"—there, outside the window,
> Yet all that box held was a small thin letter.[38]

As John Piper, the artist, wrote in 1947:

Once, as a girl—perhaps a very little girl inside a garden, Edith Sitwell's senses must have had some sudden blow, enduring in its effect. Probably it still hammers. But her poetry gives the impression that she has at some time experienced one all revealing moment, which as she goes on writing, she gets nearer and nearer to recapturing. . . .[39]

It was also in 1925 that she formed her friendship with Gertrude Stein, who kept an important artistic salon at her home in the Rue de Fleurus. Edith had reviewed Stein's *Geography and Plays* in 1923, not entirely favourably, and as Miss Stein and her "other half," Alice B. Toklas, never forgot a bad review, the first meeting was not a great success. It took place in March 1925 and Edith found her

an impressive oldish woman, her figure looks that of a German hausfrau, or perhaps headmistress, but she has a superb face with a sensitive modelling and she seems full of rich, earthy, Schumannesque life. Yet in some ways she is very limited in her understanding, for instance about the war. Her attitude towards the war horrified me; she can't understand suffering, but she is very dictatorial, never listens to anything anybody else may say, she merely interrupts them in the middle of a sentence, and says, "It isn't so at all" or "It's certain it's not for that reason" and takes matters into her own hands.[40]

Nevertheless, Edith admitted she "couldn't help liking her," and told Miss Stein that she hoped she would come to England, to which she was soon returning herself.

There were other reasons for Edith's attention to be directed towards England. Sachie had met the daughter of a Canadian banker, Georgia Doble, and after a short interval they had become engaged to be married. The idea of Sachie's marrying was a shock to Edith, as she feared the precious family trio would fall apart, but after she met Georgia she changed her mind and decided she must welcome Georgia into the family. Miss Doble was invited by Edith, now back in England, to Weston Hall, a house in Northamptonshire that she and Sachie would eventually make their home, to stay with her and her brothers. She told Georgia, "Your nature is as lovely as your appearance and it would be beyond words if one didn't value you at your real worth. Trust me implicitly—you can, you know." She determined Georgia would be her "loving sister" and not the sister-in-law she had initially dreaded.

Sachie and Georgia had decided to be married in Paris, in 1925, and Edith wrote sadly to Sachie that she was "so miserable, but there is absolutely no possibility of my coming to your wedding. You know I would strain every nerve to do it if it were possible. But it is utterly out of the question."[41]

Edith's problems had come to a head when she had returned

from dinner on her birthday in September. There was an unpleas-
ant present in the form of a letter from her bankers, Coutts, telling her that she had exceeded the allowed limit on her overdraft
by sixty-eight pounds. They wanted her to send funds at once,
and after a couple of sleepless nights Edith had to give up most
of her dress allowance for six months to pay off the bank; the rest
of her overdraft had to be paid the following year. It was the
worst financial crisis Edith had so far endured; as she told Sachie,
"I can afford *no* railway journeys, no books, no new clothes, no
taxis."[42] There was thirty pounds expected from a book, but that
would have to go on the rent. Edith wondered vaguely if Sir
George would pay her fare over to Paris for the wedding if she
went on to stay at Montegufoni; but even if he did, she still had
no clothes. There would be "at least two new pairs of shoes and a
new dressing gown" required, Edith considered ruefully. She
added, however, "I am going to give you and Georgia a really
lovely gramophone as a wedding present when you return to
England. Don't worry about that my darling, because by that
time my financial situation will have cleared itself up and I shall
be able to go on as usual."[43]

Life at Pembridge Mansions continued to be a struggle, and
Edith considered returning to Renishaw. But poor as she was,
Pembridge Mansions gave her precious independence, and Edith
felt that as she had "let Helen in for this" she could not possibly
abandon her and leave her to it. "We are absolutely obliged to
economize," Edith told everybody, and she decided quite firmly
they would struggle through.

A Sitwell wedding was unthinkable without Edith, and when it
arrived, Sachie arranged for money to be given to her. But just
before the wedding she tripped and sprained her ankle in the
street while out shopping, and it seemed that it would prevent
her from going to Paris. But eventually she arrived there and
managed to limp to the hotel where Sachie and Georgia were
staying.

Much as she wanted to be with Sachie as his protector and
sister, she wisely realized that she must not "badger" him, and
kept to her room until the wedding. As soon as it was over she
left for Montegufoni with Osbert. Mrs. Keppel, the late King Edward VII's friend, arrived there with "a party of monsters with
everybody behaving as though she were Queen Alexandra."[44]

It was Mrs. Keppel who had been so shocked when she heard that Edith was leaving her parents to write poetry. "Do you mean to say, Edith," Mrs. Keppel had said, "that you do not prefer human love to poetry?" "Not as a profession," Edith had replied acidly.

But if Edith found Mrs. Keppel tiresome she was amused by a cutting that arrived about the wedding:

The witty and beautiful daughter of the Earl of Londesborough . . . from whom her children inherit their brains has been the sensation of London more than once. She is a most keen ornithologist and her collection of birds' eggs is one of the most famous in Europe. . . . Sir George Sitwell, besides being a soldier is author of that amusing brochure, *Who Killed Cock Robin?* [It was in fact by Osbert.][45]

The chance of bringing Gertrude Stein to England came in the spring of 1926, when she was invited to address the Literary Society of Cambridge. Curiously, she felt quite nervous about it and declined. Edith, who heard of this from Geoffrey Gorer, the anthropologist, wrote to Gertrude insisting that she should change her mind, and stating that Oxford wanted Gertrude to speak there as well. Eventually Gertrude agreed, and while her aged Ford car was being prepared for the journey by mechanics, she sat in it, writing her lecture, which she named "Composition as Explanation." The prospect of lecturing to the Oxford and Cambridge intelligentsia terrified Gertrude, and she asked for advice from friends on delivery. Eventually, despite conflicting advice from friends, she decided she *would* go and ordered a new hat and dress for the occasion. She arrived in London with Alice Toklas and was given a party by Edith, who was helped by Siegfried Sassoon to make things run smoothly.

Later, when they arrived in Cambridge, Osbert and Sachie spent some time trying to dispel Gertrude's stage fright. By the time they all arrived at Oxford, Gertrude had lost her nervousness and seemed delighted to find an audience so large that many had to stand at the back. Harold Acton, who was there, remembered the arrival of Gertrude, who looked like

a squat, Aztec figure in obsidian, growing more and more monumental as soon as she sat down. With her tall bodyguard of Sitwells and the gipsy acolyte [Toklas] she made a memorable entry. After the lecture, which she read in a flat voice, she concluded by reading a word portrait of Edith called, "Sitwell, Edith Sitwell".[46]

With such a strange visual combination of people, it is not difficult to see why Edith sat trying not to look embarrassed. Osbert stared at a chair, and Sachie, as Acton described him, looked as if he were swallowing a plum. Time, Acton recalled, seemed to stand still as the audience were treated to "Miss Sitwell have and heard, introduces have and had, Miss Edith Sitwell have and had."[47]

If the lecture had been embarrassing, Miss Stein was not undaunted in facing question time. The young Lord David Cecil (later a famous biographer and critic) and his friend Robbie Calburn, an undergraduate, alternated with questions until Calburn asked Gertrude Stein what she meant by saying that "everything being the same, everything's always different."

"Consider, you dear boys," she replied, "you jump up one after the other, that is the same thing, and surely you admit that the two of you are always different."

"Touché," Calburn replied.[48]

Miss Stein had scored.

The Sitwells tried to persuade Gertrude to stay longer, but she felt the excitement had been enough, and with her "gipsy" friend, Alice, she departed the following day for Paris.

A few months later, Edith gave a reading from *Troy Park* in London, and amongst the audience was Allanah Harper, who was so impressed by Edith's recital that she bought the new book and then wrote an article for *Le Flambeau,* an avant-garde magazine, on the three Sitwells. Edith was sent the review, was delighted, and invited Allanah Harper to come to one of her Saturday teas. Feeling nervous, she climbed up the bare stairs, and Edith answered the door, holding a brown kitchen teapot. "How splendid!" Edith said. "We meet at last." Allanah Harper had expected a Queen Anne tea-service with a Chinese design and realized that Edith was unaware of how shabby was the room that she sat in, lit by an unshaded lamp.

On this occasion T. S. Eliot had also arrived with his wife, Vivienne. Edith had already met him in 1917, and he was a frequent guest at Pembridge Mansions. Their arrival was announced by angry voices on the stairs, as the two of them argued

on the way up. To Allanah Harper's horror, Eliot tried to read a
magazine in which she had attacked him for obscurity in certain
lines of *The Waste Land*, and after a brief tussle she snatched the
magazine from his hands. But the conversation was not all poetry; Edith was sympathetic to Eliot, who was also plagued by
obsessively adoring lunatics. He recounted a story of a man who
would not leave until Eliot had a brainwave. In response, Eliot
said, "I must let the cat out of the bag" and, picking up an empty
shopping-bag, turned it upside down, calling, "But it's not a cat,
it's out." The man ran off, thinking that Eliot was wickedly keeping a cat trapped in a bag.[49]

Despite this uneasy initiation, Allanah often returned to Moscow Road and she and Edith became close friends. Edith asked
her to go to Oxford and Cambridge with her, where she was giving the same lecture at two of the women's colleges, Lady Margaret Hall and Newnham. The Principal of Newnham, Julia Strachey, was a sister of Lytton Strachey, and she invited them to
what turned out to be a very dull lunch. After it Edith gave the
lecture, which was chaired by Tom Driberg, the future MP, and
then had to endure being heckled by undergraduates. "Why do
you like Swinburne?" one asked. Edith told her that it was because he was "a pure poet whose verbal beauty was perhaps the
most wonderful in our language." The undergraduate complained
to Edith that Swinburne had no ideas, upon which Edith told the
student that she had better go back to Browning.

Later the sister of Roger Fry presided over dinner, and after a
long, embarrassing silence asked Edith if she believed in God.
Edith's answer was sharp, since she hated philosophical arguments, and was designed to stop the discussion: "I do not wish to
say." None of her immediate family had any religious beliefs, and
Edith, like her brothers, was never confirmed. Probably as a reaction to overindulgence on the part of their fanatically religious
paternal grandmother and aunts, the three Sitwell children were
at that time agnostic. To cover the result of confusion, another
person present quoted a line of E. M. Forster's—"Perhaps life is a
mystery and not a muddle." "Yes," Edith replied, "but don't destroy the mystery by pulling off the wings in order to dissect the
butterfly."[50]

Unknown to Edith, amongst the undergraduate audience
lurked one of her future enemies, Geoffrey Grigson, later a poet

and critic. He recalled her standing "like a crane upon the platform, ornithological or mechanical, in a long unusual dress of some stiff fabric, wearing a large emerald ring."[51] Edith's enemies then, Grigson explained in his memoirs, were the poets Binyon and Noyes, whom Edith compared to rolls of cheap linoleum, and he was not impressed.

FOUR

Years of Achievement

In the 1890's, "superior" people discovered that ugliness is beauty. But the modern intellectual is a bigger fool than that. He has discovered that everything is ugly,—including beauty. . . .

Letter to Allanah Harper

EDITH remained in England in the spring of 1926 because it had been decided to hold a second public performance of *Façade* in April at the Chenil Galleries in Chelsea. The work had had several years to settle, and this time an actor from the Old Vic called Neil Porter was engaged to speak most of the verses, with Edith taking a few of the slower pieces. The reception was now completely different from that of the first performance, with the audience trying to encore many of the pieces. Arnold Bennett, who remained a friend of Edith's because he was independent of Marguerite, was there and noted in his diary:

I drove to the Sitwell concert, *Façade*. Crowds of people, snobs, highbrows, lowbrows, critics and artists and decent folk. I enjoyed the show greatly, the verses are distinguished, the music (Walton) equally so, the scene by Frank Dobson was admirable.[1]

The most distinguished visitor to this performance was the Ballets Russes impresario Diaghilev, who was taken by Sachie, and commented to him afterwards that he heard "the shades of Elgar" in *Façade*. Diaghilev was not particularly fond of English music and later rejected music that Walton proposed for a ballet.

The most perceptive notice came from the music critic Ernest Newman, who was to cross swords with Sachie over his books on Liszt and Mozart. Osbert had warned the audience that the speaker might not be able to get all the words over, and Newman indeed felt that some of the poems were improved by "our not being able to catch the words. We got the essential things alright, such as

> "Or the sound of the onycha
> When the phoca has the pica
> In the palace of the Queen Chinee!"[2]

Newman was certainly right when he suggested that the poems should not be read as ordinary poems, but that they required "the sledge-hammer insistence" on certain words, and he concluded that

the music, the words, the megaphone and the piquant phrasing of the lines by the reciter were as much bone of each other's bone and flesh of each other's flesh as the words and the music are of each one in *Tristan* or *Pelléas*. At its best, *Façade* was the journalist's entertainment of the season.[3]

The reaction in the popular press was not so comforting, and in their gossip columns the daily papers frequently commented on Miss Sitwell's appearance and her behaviour. While Edith claimed that she found them tiresome, it was at least good publicity. The first performance of *Façade* had annoyed Noël Coward, but an even feebler pamphlet than his *Chelsea Buns* now came from the pen of C. K. Scott-Moncrieff, called *The Strange and Striking Adventures of Four Authors in Search of a Character*. The fourth "author" was William Walton, but despite its title there is nothing striking about the pamphlet, which is flat and satirically obscure. In *All at Sea* (1927) Osbert relates his encounters with Moncrieff, or "Mr. X," as he calls him, whom he describes as having "decided, if unoriginal natural gifts."[4] Moncrieff had, curiously, inscribed a copy of Sachie's first poems to their mutual friend Wilfred Owen. He became famous as a translator of Proust, but in his attack on the Sitwells, which he wrote in a week, his gifts deserted him. He began:

Once upon a time, there were four dear little children, whose names were Frogbert, Sacharissa, Zerubbabel and Lincurston, inhabiting a stately home in the country, entirely surrounded by every attention that natural affection could prompt or luxury afford. Now, Sacharissa and Frogbert and Zerubbabel had all been born in this house, but Lincurston was a co-option, principally on account of his talents which lay in the direction of music.[5]

Moncrieff continued his attack by commenting on Walton's music and the Sitwells' battle with J. C. Squire. Osbert, writing in 1927, said:

Probably the very folly and futility of it will tend one day to give it a certain interest as an example of what modern poets have had to endure at the hands of the jackals and boot-snatchers of the literary world.[6]

The success of the 1926 performance of *Façade* led to an invitation from the BBC for the Sitwells to broadcast parts of it in a programme called "The Wheels of Time." The broadcast was to be divided into three sections, past, present and future, with the comedians Robert, Sonnie, and Binnie Hale representing the present with jazz and ragtime, and the Sitwells the future with extracts from *Façade*, and the past represented by Victorian songs. Robert Hale met Osbert for lunch so that he could familiarize himself with their work. Hale had never heard of the Sitwells, and after hearing their poetry and finding during conversation that their "highbrow stuff" was beyond him, he decided to withdraw. As a consequence Osbert made some unfortunate and long-remembered public remarks about the theatre, in which he said that he considered the stage was in a "deplorable" condition and that "actors and actresses are so busy trying to be ladies and gentlemen and golfers that they have no time left to pay attention to their jobs."[7]

Replacements for the Hales were sought, but the manager of the Vaudeville Theatre, Mr. Archibald de Bear, wanted no one to take part in the broadcast, because of the "impertinent and insolent attack upon the entire theatrical profession made by Mr. Osbert Sitwell."[8] Eventually the programme was broadcast, without Mr. Hale.

Whether Edith enjoyed the battles her family were now involved in hardly seems to matter; because of the "boring" Noël Cowards and Archie de Bears she was becoming a symbol of an elitist movement that refused to accept the commonplace. For many it was "daring" to say one admired the Sitwells, and young, impressionable figures such as Cecil Beaton were instant converts to all that was becoming known as Sitwellism. Allanah Harper had introduced Edith to Beaton over lunch at his house, and Edith had agreed to a photography session afterwards. She enjoyed a fish soufflé, "despite the bones," and then went to a bedroom Beaton was using as a studio. He recorded in his diary that she had the appearance of "a tall, graceful scarecrow, with the white hands of a mediaeval saint," and this delighted him.

She posed instinctively, no matter how many positions I had already taken I felt loth to call a halt. . . . I must perpetuate the image in front of me, a young faun-like creature, sitting against my leaping fawn design, looking surprisingly Victorian in her crudely cut pre-Raphaelite dress with her matador's jet hat and necklace, her long mediaeval fingers covered with enormous rings.

The film had to stick, and when it was developed part of it was spoilt. Beaton, however, was not particularly worried. "I caught an approaching twinkle in her eyes as she left. It meant we were going to be friends."[9]

Edith was quick to see the publicity value of these bizarre but highly original photographs, and in 1927 she included one as the frontispiece to her volume of poems *Rustic Elegies,* with Beaton's address as an advertisement. Had Beaton's photographs been of anyone but herself they would have been of no interest to her. Visual images bored Edith, who hated being taken to art galleries and would gaze vacantly at the buildings Osbert and Sachie enthused about. But showing typical favouritism when visiting Bordeaux, she went to the trouble (for her) to describe what she saw, because she knew it would interest Beaton. In a letter to him she wrote that as well as finding "flocks of widows," she found Bordeaux

so hideous that it was beautiful. Very flat sands and sea, hotels full of villas made of children's tower bricks . . . booths on the seashore with miniature mermaids, lovely shell boxes and wheezing marine music, and shooting galleries as bright as stars.

The flowers were in "large round beds full of yellow calceolarias surrounded by meat-coloured and corpse-coloured begonias fringed with pale sea-green faded dining-roomish leaves."[10]

At this time Edith was trying her hand at acting in a skit on
"society." The idea of satirizing a London hostess had already
been attempted in 1926, with a play called *All at Sea,* written by
her brothers. Edith had taken part in it when it was performed
the previous Christmas of 1927, but the play had failed disas-
trously because it was not savage enough for effect. On this occasion Edith waited in the Curzon Hotel for her Aunt Grace and
her cousin Irene Carisbrooke. Before they arrived she was
obliged to converse with the son and daughter of the Parsee High
Priest of Bombay. "What do you think of the new Prayer Book,
Miss Sitwell?" they enquired, then, looking puzzled, continued,
"You are the famous actress, Miss Sidwell?" Edith was wondering how to avoid the awkwardness of explaining that Miss *Sid-
dons* was an eighteenth-century actress when her aunt arrived.
Almost at once the conversation switched to Emerald Cunard,
the society hostess whom Edith was intent on lampooning in her
poem *Gold Coast Customs.* She told them she was going "to wipe
the floor with that old woman, and throw the remains on the
dust-heap." Her aunt agreed. "After all," she said, "we don't
know who she is, and she is living openly with the pill-man" (Sir
Thomas Beecham).[11] Edith's attitude to Lady Cunard remained
unchanged despite the fact that she was well aware Sachie and
Georgia were close friends with the society hostess.

In the meantime, Sachie had been writing the book of his
ballet *The Triumph of Neptune,* for Diaghilev, which had music
by Gerald Berners (Lord Berners) and décor by Prince A. Sher-
vashidze, inspired by *Penny Plain and Twopence Coloured* from
Mr. Pollock and Mr. Hoxton. The ballet was presented in Paris in
1927 after opening in London in December 1926, and although
Edith declared ballet "bored the pants off me" she went to the
Paris première.

While watching the ballet she was aware that she was being
stared at by a "young thin man who looked as if he had seen a
ghost." A few days later they met at Gertrude Stein's house,
when the young man, whose name was Pavel Tchelitchew, at
once accused Edith of being Russian. On hearing her denial,
Tchelitchew insisted, explaining that Edith bore an uncanny re-
semblance to the original of Father Zossima, the saint in Dos-
toevski's *The Brothers Karamazov,* who had been his own father's
confessor. It would have been pleasant to write that the strange

meeting between Tchelitchew and Edith, which began a friendship lasting until his death in 1957, meant love at first sight, but in fact it is more likely that Pavlik, as he was called by friends, did not really care for Edith, despite his initial fascination with her. Apart from the fact that he was living with his friend, an American pianist called Allen Tanner, he sensed he would soon be ditched by another friend, Gertrude Stein. Besides these personal problems, his artistic life was grinding to a halt, and he was looking for a new patron.

Pavel Tchelitchew was born on September 21, 1898, a member of the established aristocracy. His family had been attached to the Imperial Court but had a liberal outlook that brought them trouble at the time of the Revolution. In 1918 the family fled from Moscow to Kiev, and from there Tchelitchew went alone to Turkey, where he joined the Russian Theatre. He painted its scenery, as Edith noted, "in return for being allowed to sleep on the stage, and sharing with the company the potatoes and bars of chocolate which were their only food."[12] In 1921 he moved to Berlin, where he met Allen Tanner. He found life there difficult, but he met Diaghilev, who took an interest in his work. Diaghilev told him frankly that he "must first break himself in two as one might break a faltering branch and cultivate in all perseverance the still vital half with the young green buds," and also that his drawing was weak and ideas "not first-rate";[13] Diaghilev always demanded perfection. He suggested to Tchelitchew that he would succeed only in Paris. Taking the impresario's advice, Tchelitchew went there in 1923, with his by now devoted Allen.

At first it seemed they would be no more successful in Paris than in Berlin, but Tchelitchew struggled on until a surprise visit from Gertrude Stein changed his fortunes. She and Alice Toklas arrived at his studio one day while he was out, and Allen Tanner, who was there, explained that Tchelitchew's paintings were locked in a room. Gertrude pressed him to bring up a wrench from her car. He did so, and eventually they forced the door open. For three quarters of an hour Gertrude and Alice looked at Tchelitchew's work, but they realized that Tanner was holding something back. He explained that they might wince when they saw it. "Show it!" they chorused, and Tanner embarrassedly produced a detailed drawing of a sailor, naked except for a pompon hat. "Quite a peep show," Miss Stein commented, "but it's very good."[14] Tchelitchew had found a patron in Gertrude Stein, and she removed the entire contents of the room, paying for them all. Miss Stein was well aware of Pavlik's temperamental nature. "If I present Pavlik to you," she remarked to Edith, "it's your responsibility because his character is not my affair":[15] words of warning that Edith never really understood.

Most of Edith and Pavlik's correspondence is locked up in Yale until the year 2000 by their mutual consent, and until then the full extent of their relationship will be impossible to determine. Edith was now forty, and it is unlikely that at that age she seriously considered marriage. She must have noticed the string of men that accompanied Pavlik and the devoted attention Allen Tanner, in particular, paid him. However, it could have been that in the early stages of their acquaintance she was not aware of his homosexuality, and that by the time she realized it much later, she was too emotionally involved with him to give him up.

At once Edith became a champion of his work, and early in 1927 she helped to arrange an exhibition at the Galerie Vignon in Paris. She knew him well enough by now to call him Pavlik and, enlisting the aid of Allanah Harper, she wrote:

Pavlik's vernissage is on Tuesday the 2nd, at the Galerie Vignon. And he has asked me to "receive" the people, as Choura is too shy. . . .

I do feel this exhibition is very important. . . . Please *do* make people come. . . .

Let us have a real campaign.[16]

Choura was Pavlik's sister, who had joined him in Paris and often shared a house with him until she married. Later she was to become a confidante of Edith's, who thought of her as a tragic but beautiful figure, something like Anna Karenina. When Edith visited the Tchelitchew household, Choura acted as a rather unnecessary chaperone. But one person she infuriated was Allen Tanner, since he felt she was avoiding her household duties because of her frequent illness, and he fiercely resented having to do them instead.

Pavlik was grateful for Edith's assistance with the exhibition, and in June 1927, writing in French and still addressing her rather formally, he wrote:

Dear Miss Sitwell,
Thank you very much for your letter. It did me so much good to

feel that someone like you is thinking of me at a time when I am feeling sad, tired and ill. . . . Dear friend! My paintings are not going well. I am producing horrible daubs! I feel more dissatisfied with them than ever. I am very, very tired. My *morale* is quite dead. My dealer had just informed me that he has sent all my works to London to show them in the Redfern Gallery, I don't even know when. . . . Do help me, dear friend, as I feel I am without energy, coping with my dealer, who is a fool. He keeps changing his mind, and it is nerve-wracking attempting to do business with him. He has just refused my two best works, and I do believe they are the best I've done for ages. He understands nothing. Jean Cocteau, my enemy, who is backing "the great French genius" M. [Christian] Bérard, has been slandering me to him. It is very, very difficult to work in Paris in a city which hates foreigners. Paris is a magnificent city, but the French worship money too much and are stupidly and idiotically patriotic. I suffer enormously. . . . I went again to see the woman who already has taken a month to make the frame for your portrait. She is a genius, but she has also a genius for slowness. She promised to show me the frame today as she has changed her mind three times in the course of making it, and I shall go and see her today and I mean to make her hurry up immediately. . . .

Those people you told me about in your letter never turned up. I saw Jeffey [*sic*] Gorer when he passed through—a charming fellow but with a tongue that never stops wagging. One day he nearly caused a row between me and Gertrude.

Dear friend, thank you for your kind interest. I am sure you will give me friendly help with the exhibition and the general arrangement of my pictures in London. It is my *absolute* wish that you allow your two portraits to be shown. . . .

Yours ever,
P. TCHELITCHEW[17]

The letter must have delighted Edith, and she rewarded it by an article entitled "Miss Sitwell presents a genius?" to coincide with his first London exhibition in 1928.

London has been introduced to a really great painter, Paul Tchelitchew, and when I say he is a really great painter, I mean what I say. . . . I can say with honesty that the day on which I began to realise these pictures was one of the most important days in my artistic life.[18]

In the meantime, Edith *was* excited by Pavlik, and it was a relief for her to meet new friends. She stayed during the summer of 1928 at Guermantes, where Pavlik had gone with Allen to live in a house lent by Stella Bowen, an Australian artist and the mistress of Ford Madox Ford.

At first life seemed idyllic. Choura, Allen, and Pavlik sat in the garden with Edith, and as Tanner recalled:

We gossiped with the peasants, walked with the cows, passed fields of beautifully fashioned Gothic haystacks, picked wild berries, gathered our own orchard fruit and nuts and bought fresh vegetables out of the ground from the peasants.[19]

But this calm scene could not last with four such difficult personalities. Edith sensed this but was used to eternal rows both at Renishaw and with Helen and her tiresome sister, so the strange atmosphere at Guermantes did not worry her for a while; it was a relief for her to get out of Paris for a time.

For most of 1928 Edith had been working on her long poem *Gold Coast Customs.* This subject interested her after she had been sitting for a drawing to Nina Hamnett, and she discovered that Nina knew a Mr. Joyce who was keeper to the Ethnographical Department of the British Museum. They met at the Museum one afternoon, and Edith was fascinated by the collection of African masks and other more gruesome relics there. Gradually ideas formed as she read books on the tribal habits of the Gold Coast. She worked hard for nearly a year on her poem, determined to get it right. There were many more personal reasons, however, for the dramatic change of style from the childhood world of *Troy Park* to the savagery of *Gold Coast Customs.* The various poems Edith wrote before the publication of *Gold Coast Customs,* in 1929, had been "more or less a preparation" for that poem.

By the late 1920s various social events had impressed themselves on Edith, and however much she was thought of as part of the frivolous upper- and middle-class set, this was not in fact so. The play *All at Sea* was only one example of Edith's attempting to show her disapproval of snobbish society.

The General Strike of 1926 had showed her the mass dissatisfaction of the working classes, and through her journalism Edith expressed her indignation at the attitudes of the rich towards the poor. One such essay was called "Freak Parties," written in 1929:

Last week, two homeless men died of starvation and exposure . . . having collapsed in the street. It seems strange to me, that those, to my mind, murdered spectres had Christian names like the rest of us. A short time ago, I read of the hunger marchers' famine-stricken walk to London, and then I remembered the Freak Parties given by foolish people who have no other claims to be thought original, and I cannot avoid the reflection, that vulgar and half-witted as such exhibitionists would be at any time, they are not only vulgar, but heartless now. . . . A new form of entertainment . . . is to dress up as people much poorer than themselves . . . and make fun of their simple and unfashionable pleasure. . . . It may be as well to point out that . . . a few generations ago many members of this "new society" might well have found themselves amongst the hunger marchers whose misery they do nothing to allay. . . .[20]

It was this theme that Edith was to develop in *Gold Coast Customs,* and in particular she attacked the famous London hostess Lady Cunard, who appears in the poem as "Lady Bamburgher." Edith had her sights trained on Lady Cunard for some time, as the embodiment of the rich society woman Edith so disliked. The satire is not immediately obvious, and it is necessary to refer to the notes Edith provided with the poem. It was also prefaced by an explanation of the African customs:

In Ashantee, a hundred years ago [1829], the death of any rich or important person was followed by several days of national ceremonies, during which the utmost license prevailed, and slaves and poor persons were killed that the bones of the deceased might be washed with human blood. These ceremonies were called Customs.[21]

The physical appearance of the poem shows that right from the first verse Edith is exploring new territory in her use of poetic form:

> One fántee wáve
> Is gráve and táll
> As bráve Ashántee's
> Thíck múd wáll.
> Múnza ráttles his bónes in the dúst,
> Lúrking in múrk becáuse he múst.[22]

Nearly every second syllable is stressed, as indicated, and this emphatic rhythm is deliberately reminiscent of a drum beat.

But the first verse immediately poses a problem, for the word "fantee" is not in common usage and has to be searched for in a dictionary, where it is defined as "Member or language of a Negro tribe inhabiting Ghana." The poem goes on to describe a scene of grotesque savagery in Africa. In the ninth stanza we come across a reference to Lady Bamburgher, and the connection between London and Africa is established. The removal of a note in later editions, because of social change since the days of the depression, is regrettable, for it points out more clearly this link, which the poem fails to indicate clearly:

Any traveller from Monbuttoo visiting first of all our new "Original Parties" and then walking down the Embankment, or in those streets of Revue Theatres, where our late heroes [from the First World War presumably] sell matches in the gutter, could not fail to be impressed by the superiority of our civilization over that of the Monbuttoos.[23]

In the midst of all the slum squalor, Lady Bamburgher gives her smart parties and is seen as being simultaneously the London hostess and the Amazon Queen:

> With a bone-black face
> Wears a mask with an ape-skin beard; she grinds
> Her male child's bones in a mortar, binds
> Him for food, and the people buy.

Lady Bamburgher has the empty face of the puppet that recurred often in Edith's earlier poems, but the face is that of a "Worm's mask," which is painted

> . . . White as a bone
> Where eyeholes rot wide
> And are painted for sight,
> And the little mouth red as a dead Plague-spot
> On that white mask painted to hide Death's rot.

Both the London hostess and the Amazon Queen are spiritually blind. The puppet figure, which was half human in the Vanity Fair section of *The Sleeping Beauty*, reappears in the form of a prostitute called Sally who is doomed to wander the streets without finding the rest that should be the reward of the dead:

> So now I'm a gay girl, a calico dummy,
> With nothing left alive but my feet
> That walk up and down in the Sailor's Street.

She has become a kind of zombie, pleading for hope:

> O Christ, that bone was dead, alone!
> Christ, Who will speak to such ragged Dead
> As me, I am dead, alone and bare.

There is no relief in *Gold Coast Customs*, not even for the sun, a traditional symbol of life, transformed instead into a symbol of death and decay:

> He hangs like a skull
> With a yellow dull
> Face made of clay . . .[24]

The actual effect of the poem is best felt from the cumulative reading of the verses from beginning to end. The poem, Edith Sitwell tells us, was

built on three tiers like the floors of a house. The bottom tier is the negro swamp, which is a phantom, spiritual state, and on it the other two tiers—the terrible slum of the beggars, and the terrible slum of the cannibal rich—are built. . . .[25]

But despite the force the poem has, it nevertheless fails, perhaps for reasons that Kenneth Clark gave:

As a work of art, *Gold Coast Customs* suffers from being too close to an appalling spiritual shock. It leaves us in the chaos of despair, and art is the opposite of chaos. . . . At the end there is a chink of hope, but it is vague, improbable and unsatisfying:
> Though Death has taken
> And pig-like shaken,
> Rooted, and tossed
> The rags of me.
> Yet the time will come
> To the heart's dark slum
> When the rich man's gold and the rich man's wheat
> Will grow in the street, that the starved may eat . . .[26]

The ending, which Clark considered to be "vague, improbable and unsatisfying," was changed in 1930, something he overlooked (his essay was written in 1942), and the following lines were added:

> And the sea of the rich will give up its dead—
> And the last blood and fire from my side will be shed.
> For the fires of God go marching on.[27]

But it must be admitted that the new lines are just as enigmatic as the old. *Gold Coast Customs*, with its savage satire, reminded W. B. Yeats of Swift, and he wrote:

When I read her *Gold Coast Customs* . . . I felt . . . that something absent from all literature for a generation was back again, and in a form rare in the literature of all generations, passion enobled by intensity, by endurance, by wisdom. We had it in one man once. He lies in St. Patrick's now under the greatest epitaph in history. . . .[28]

It is extravagant praise, and Yeats continued it in a broadcast he made on modern poetry in 1936:

Miss Edith Sitwell . . . seems to me an important poet, shaped . . . by the disillusionment that followed the Great War . . . she interjects a horror of death and decay. . . . Her language is the traditional language of literature, but twisted, torn, complicated, jerked here and there by strained resemblances, unnatural contacts, forced upon it by terror or by some violence beating in her blood, some primitive obsession that civilization can no longer endure.[29]

In *Gold Coast Customs* the imagery as well as the rhythm helps to convey the impression of a "nightmare horror of death and decay," and especially the references to animals, including rat, wolf, ape, monkey, worm, fly, weasel, louse, pig, dog, leopard, and rhinoceros. Added to this is a list of noises, none of them pleasant: bellowing, blaring, braying, cackling, giggling, groaning, howling, rattling, roaring, squealing, whimpering, and whining. All these generate the momentum of the poem, but they do not allow a breathing space and the total effect is suffocating, though it must be conceded that this was perhaps Edith's intention.

Predictably, *Gold Coast Customs* was greeted with a great deal of adverse comment when it was published, and Edith felt almost completely discouraged. "No-one understands my *Goldcoaster*," she complained. "One man came to me and remarked, 'I have read your ripping little African satire, Miss Sitwell, and thought it awfully jolly.' "[30]

Her poetry was not a paying product, and her early royalty sheets for *Gold Coast Customs* show fewer than 200 copies sold from 1929 to 1930. Though her reputation was growing, demands from Pavlik and Tanner meant she had very little money. The frequent trips across the Channel and back were costly, and in desperation—because she hated writing prose—Edith had agreed to write a book on Pope for Fabers.

Pavlik undoubtedly thought that Edith was rich, and her affection led her always to answer his requests with some small sum. By supporting Pavlik, however, she was also obliged to take on Allen Tanner. He was essential to the smooth running of the ménages at Guermantes and Paris, between which they divided their time. Pavlik used him to do the housework and other domestic chores and, thinking that only *his* art mattered, forgot that Allen, too, was an artist, and moreover one struggling desperately to further his career. Tanner received encouragement from Leopold Godowsky but was obliged to sacrifice his career because he was afraid of losing his lover. At times he was almost driven mad by Pavlik's eccentric nature and, desperate for an outlet, bombarded Edith with his grumbles. Pages of pencilled letters reached her weekly with a fresh list of domestic disasters and complaints: "Gertrude began a plot against me that Pavlik abused and exploited his sister with housework for me. (Edith, I am an expert houseman—I've taken complete care of Pavlik and my little ménage for six years.)"[31]

It was true that Stein and Toklas now disliked Pavlik, and they brewed endless plots for their own amusement, which wore Pavlik and Allen out. They both longed to escape to England, but as Tanner wrote to Edith, "I should love nothing better than to come to London, but I am so poor and England is so expensive. You cannot imagine how poor I am—poor in every way—poor in spirit I suppose even." He explained in a hysterical way how he was not allowed to play the piano because of Pavlik, and how terrible it was that "to have a gift like mine and not be active, and in a measure, successful, is a tragic, living death. It is all because my nerves are too weakened."

He repeated obsessedly in his letters to Edith in 1930 that he *must* have money, but at last a stroke of pure good luck came his way. He said he had found a book on a stall on the Left Bank of the Seine that was inscribed by Thomas Jefferson. He sent it to Edith, asking her to take it to Sotheby's with instructions to them to sell it *privately* at not less than £1,000. They replied in a letter which was a model of tact that it would be better to put it up to auction, as it would fetch more that way than by private sale. They also explained at great length that under no circumstances

could the book hope to fetch anything like £1,000. Tanner was
incensed and complained to Sotheby's that they did not know
their business. He wrote to Edith: "They are really weird, those
Sotheby's I had such a strange correspondence with them, and I
have a hunch they intend to buy up the book themselves, for
nothing, and then sell it at a profit afterwards." He had asked
Edith not to tell anyone about the book, even if slightly apologetic about his secrecy: "don't forget to keep it a secret, it's better that way." Edith ought to have been suspicious, but naïvely
she believed him.

The book was auctioned for an unknown amount, and after
Tanner received the money, he asked Edith to lie to Pavlik about
his sudden wealth, which she refused to do. It transpired that the
book had disappeared from a château in France and, worse still,
that the owner was a friend of Tanner's.

Tanner completely panicked. Edith was shattered by the revelation, and apart from the horror that Tanner might be a thief
there was the danger that the press might find out that Miss Sitwell had been handling stolen goods. In desperation she asked
Geoffrey Gorer and his brother Peter for advice. She had decided
that from now on she could communicate with Tanner only formally, and even then only when absolutely necessary in order to
continue relations with Pavlik. Geoffrey Gorer wrote in agreement:

I think on the whole you are quite right—it is on the whole the only
way of reaching a *modus vivendi,* and it is also the kindest for our
friend . . . and I should not read or answer any more of his glutinous
correspondence.[32]

Edith bravely sent a note to Tanner on those lines, aware that
she was running the risk of alienating Pavlik at the same time. In
a rage, Tanner sent her a bombshell, playing the part, as usual, of
the hurt martyr.

2, Rue Jacques-Mawas

My dear Edith,
All through this business of ours, I have repeatedly appealed to your
intelligence, your judiciousness *and* your loyalty, to keep all this a
strict secret *between us*—asking you not even to tell Helen. The fact
that you proceeded to carry out whatever arrangements I asked you to

carry out was a promise, or *at least* an acquiesence [*sic*]. The "lie" I am so furiously accused of unwittingly linking your name to, was simply meant to be an arrangement in an arrangement, between two friends and another—for safety and for good results—and was committed (if "committed" it was!) in the greatest innocence possible. You have no right to invite Peter Gorer to tea, even if he might be good or kind, and divulge, not only the most sacred and intimate account of our friendship (our "hurts" and feelings) and our disputes, but also bits of our secret. . . . I have explained *repeatedly* to you, *why* I wanted it kept secret—the thousand and one reasons *why*, and Peter may have the best intentions, but he has simply been "taken in" in spite of himself into a matter which should not concern him, and I am amazed that you have done this, which is even worse than the insulting letter you wrote to me.

However: *when I love*—I LOVE, and I am more than willing to forgive, most readily, the most serious errors between friends. I have forgiven you your letter, and ask you to forgive me my misdeed—as you consider it. But I am exceedingly exasperated that you cannot keep our secret and above all that you have taken Peter into our *most intimate situation*. I have long ago, before receiving your telegram even, told Pavlik and explained everything. He understands and is happy and desirous to keep our secret—is it going to be you, after all, who will fail to, in spite of everything???

With love (but "annoyedly")

ALLEN

Do not mistake the tone of this letter—words always seem harsher on paper.
I received a letter from Peter, just now, offering to come between us as peacemaker!

The first letter was evidently not harsh enough, for to it Tanner attached another sheet:

Later—

Dear Edith,
Upon second thoughts—with a more lucid brain—I regret having sent off oh! exceedingly—the answer I did send. As a matter of fact—I regret having answered *at all*. Such a letter which for sheer cruelty—beats anything I have yet witnessed. Nor shall I encumber you again with thanks, for having helped along this thing, as I now realize that it was *not* on my behalf that you did it. This is just a word in conclusion to what I believed to be a lasting and comforting friendship. Since *this* is the way you feel about me, and my relationship to Pavlik—and

probably always have—I shall simply give back the money to my
friend who will of course be very glad to have it, and you will have
the extreme pleasure in your old age of meditating upon the destruction of something that came through prayer, to relieve great distress,
for us all. And this, through selfishness about Pavlik (for that was not
a *lie* I asked you to tell—there are lies and lies—of various degrees and
sorts and some that are not even lies and are entirely justifiable) with
whom I have always more than shared *all*, always, and I really must
say that as far as our (his and mine) relationship goes and has gone—
Pavlik *does not need* that selfishness which is entirely misplaced—but
not only all that will you have the pleasure of meditating upon—but
also upon the final breaking of a spirit (mine) which was just upon
the point of mending itself—after 30 years of unhappiness and despair.
A nice day's work, Edith.
just remember . . .

ALLEN

Edith had also confided in Stella Bowen, who in a letter to
Edith wrote:

I'm afraid you must be sad and worried if not actually ill— . . . I
imagine the affair of the Lafayette [*sic*] book must have been just
hellish for you. I can see that it has very disagreeable aspects to put it
mildly, which you, being you, must take very much to heart.

Allen and Pavlik had gone to tea with Stella and, unaware that
she already knew of the whole affair, told her all about it. She
gathered that the owner of the book had accepted Allen's story of
finding it in Paris, but in her letter she told Edith:

Frankly Edith, I find it hard to believe that he bought it on the Quai.
I'm perfectly sure that neither Allen nor Pavlik would hesitate to fab-
ricate any story and tell it to me as it suited them. And the story of it
having been bought on the Quai was only revealed after the owner
had denounced the sale. The only trouble with me is that I find it
equally hard to believe that Allen is a plain, cold-blooded thief. . . .
Also one is obliged—constitutionally—to give anyone the benefit of any
possible doubt.

Doubts were placed in Edith's mind, and although she resolved
not to see Allen again, she had no choice but to accept him if she
wanted to keep Pavlik as a friend. At least Edith was consoled by
the knowledge that Pavlik had known nothing about the book
until Tanner told him, but as Stella Bowen commented in the

same letter, "So long as Pavlik continues to protect Allen, what can we do?"

Inevitably, when Pavlik arrived in London to see Edith, Tanner was there too. Helen Rootham complained to a friend about Pavlik:

I am really most awfully sorry for Edith, who expected to have a very different sort of time with that man [Pavlik] than the time she is getting. But he has made my life quite impossible . . . but she has not the slightest idea, poor darling, how she keeps on. I do not quite understand what it is that she *does* want from him, because he has been most grossly and impertinently frank as to what he is prepared to give. But now he is being actually bad-mannered and churlish. Osbert and Edith gave a party for him last night, at Osbert's house, to which hostesses like Lady Wimborne [wife of the first Viscount Wimborne] were invited, and the ill-mannered brute left before they arrived.

The King of Spain was dining with Lady Wimborne, and this man knew that she could only come on after the King left, but he would not stay, because he was not pleased with the attention he was getting. I would like to wring his neck, because both Edith and Osbert really took very great trouble about this party, and incidentally, spent a good deal of money.[33]

Understandably, Edith was also annoyed at Pavlik's behaviour, and to teach him a lesson she asked Helen, even though she was ill, to telephone Tanner to say that she was unable to see him and Pavlik as arranged. Unfortunately Pavlik himself answered and screamed down the telephone to Helen that he knew there was nothing wrong with Edith, only that she was angry with him. He insisted that Edith must see him, and when she agreed, a violent scene broke out.

"Edith, *ôtez vos pantalons* [take your trousers off]," he shouted. For a minute Edith did not understand, but once she did she was furious. "Yes," he continued, "take them off immediately, you can't wear them, they don't suit you. Kindly leave the man's clothes to me and stop trying to be Joan of Arc or you will be beaten, understand that for once and for all." He told Edith that he would give her three days in which to decide if she was going to behave, by which he meant that she must understand that he was going to do the ruling. "Two people," he told her, "couldn't rule." Edith was to "take it or leave it, otherwise it would be good-bye."[34]

Edith noticed that he was livid with rage and looked, as she often called him, "a Tartare." It would have been an ideal chance for Edith to escape, but by now she was deeply in love with him; only to Pavlik would she have given in to such threats, which she did. As a result she was forgiven. The rest of Pavlik's London visit was peaceful, but he had been gathering confidence to have a talk with Edith about his personal difficulties. He felt he was living two lives, one with Tanner and one with Edith, and felt compelled to tell her about it.

They had been to the ballet with the Gorers, and, having left early, Pavlik found an opportunity to talk. He blurted out details of his private life, but Edith had apparently heard about it before, and when he began, "I am in Hell—I mean my private life," she became upset and, tearing her arm away from his grasp, walked slowly towards the Gorers' waiting car. Pavlik shouted behind Edith, "Don't be angry," and on reaching the car he asked her if she was returning to Paris. To spite him she lied and announced that she was going to Italy with Osbert. But by the time they reached Edith's house, Pavlik was desperately submissive; he followed her in and said, "Do not be angry with me, you *must* know all—you *must* know all about me." As he left, he kissed Edith on the forehead, his eyes full of tears, and departed, almost breaking down, in the Gorers' car.[35]

The lie about the visit to Italy produced complications. Edith would not go back on her word, and Pavlik wrote repeatedly to her, asking if they could travel over together. Edith knew that he thought she was incapable of lying, and eventually she heard that Pavlik was pursuing someone from the Russian Ballet, having arranged to go to Italy with Diaghilev. She waited nervously to hear more, until she discovered that "the ballet dancer turns out to be a highly respectable male companion whom the poor Boyar [Pavlik] has known since he was a child. Really, what liars some people are!"[36]

Edith was now forced to see her lie through, but abandoned Osbert and decided instead to go to Venice with Sachie and Georgia and to meet Pavlik there. They arrived there safely, but Edith waited in vain. It turned out that Diaghilev had died suddenly, and Pavlik, who was superstitious, would not travel to Venice, where his compatriot had been buried.

Edith was slowly realizing the painful reality of her relationship with Pavlik, and as often happened she found some sort of escape by seeing the amusing side of it all. Her eye (and ear) for the bizarre or comic was an essential safety valve that she invariably released during the various crises in her life.

One incident involved her favourite prey, the society lady. A frequenter of Edith's Saturday tea-parties was a Lady Fitzherbert, whom Edith disliked but tolerated because her wealth made her a candidate for a portrait by Pavlik. Osbert's valet called her "Bitch-herbal," and the label stuck. At one tea she arrived with Edith's publisher Tom Balston, of Duckworth's, and Geoffrey Gorer. Balston related a story about Harriet Cohen, the pianist, who had been at Edith's house the week before, telling how she had embarrassed everyone by saying that two men were marrying others out of spite just because she wouldn't have them. "Bitch-herbal," obviously thinking of Edith's relations with Pavlik, turned to Edith after hearing the story, and remarked in an acid voice, "Women say that sort of thing when they've passed a certain age and think they ought to be married and aren't married. . . . We shall," she said to Edith, "have you doing that sort of thing next." Edith, whose relations with Pavlik were causing her great anguish, was furious, but she had her revenge. She had arranged to have tea with Lady Fitzherbert, but now she declined to go. Ethel, a sixteen-year-old maid who gave Edith no end of entertainment, was unused to the telephone, and Edith, who was teaching her how to use it, asked her to tell Lady Fitzherbert that she was unable to go to tea. Ethel duly dialled the number and then in her broad cockney voice said, "Is that you Bitch 'erbal? Is that you? This is Miss Sitwell speaking, and she won't see you." "Ethel!" Edith said. "You must not say that. You must say, 'Miss Sitwell sends her *love* to Lady Fitzherbert and to say she is sorry etc.' You must not call her Bitch-herbal." "Why not?" Ethel asked. "Because," Edith replied regretfully, "we have to remember Mr. Manners."[37]

But Ethel lasted the course as her maid, for however Edith appeared to her public, she inspired devotion in those who looked after her. And at Weston Hall, Sachie's home since his marriage, Georgia's maid Gertrude "did" Edith's clothes and was her confidante. At Renishaw, where she was untidy and threw her clothes in a heap, she charmed her maid, Barbara, into finding "nothing any trouble for Miss Edith." But Miss Edith's patience

with Ethel was tried when, returning to Pembridge Mansions
after a visit at Weston, she found a letter on her dressing-room
table from a certain Miss Sims, who had apparently invited a
boy-friend up to Edith's bedroom. Miss Sims, the fat daughter of
the local greengrocer, was a friend of Ethel's, and soon Edith was
invaded by processions of women complaining about the behaviour of their sons and daughters who they suspected had "used"
Edith's bedroom, and were demanding proof so that they could
punish their unvirtuous offspring.

The rumours spread round the district about Edith's house,
until the young man to whom Miss Sims had addressed the letter
marched in one day while Edith was having lunch and convinced
her that he had *not* been in her bedroom. He told her that the
wretched girl was the bane of his life, and that if the lies did not
stop he would have the flat watched and all the men who came
up or down traced.

Edith replied, "Some of the gentlemen come up to see *me*,"
but the "boy-friend" was not convinced, believing they all called
to "oblige" the greengrocer's daughter. Edith consequently interviewed half the young men and women in the area, but because
she thought Ethel basically a "nice and good girl" refused to
blame her for turning her house into a notorious lovers' hide-
away.[38]

It was not Edith's first contact with the neighbours, for she was
well known in the Bayswater streets, where her appearance attracted attention. Often she was seen buying fish, because it was
cheap, and on one occasion, after she left with her purchase, the
fishmonger turned to another customer and said, "That's a very
odd-looking young person." The customer replied, "You know
she is one of our most notable poets." "Oh," remarked the
fishmonger, "well, in my opinion there's too much of that sort of
thing nowadays."[39]

But it was her local herbal cosmetic shop that Edith most enjoyed, and visits always provoked conversation like the following
she recalled in a letter:

EDITH, to the assistant: "I want a message of hope for my dewlaps."
ASSISTANT: "Yis Modom". [They had a long helpful talk about dew-
laps.]
EDITH: "Do you realize that God has only relented about my hands

and my ankles and that if the joints on them enlarge it will be the river for me?"

ASSISTANT: "Yis Modom", then continued, "For craggy joints use brand X."

"Craggy joints", Edith mused as she left, "Now have I craggy joints?"[40]

But if London street humour amused her, Edith appreciated even more the humour of the music hall and especially of Nellie Wallace. In fact, Lady Ida had met the comedienne in a Scarborough hotel, and after Nellie overheard Lady Ida remark, "Isn't that Nellie Wallace?" she replied, "Yes dearie," and they became friends. Sachie had persuaded Cecil Beaton to take photographs of Nellie Wallace, and it was also at Sachie's suggestion that his sister first went to see her. She was an instant convert, and whenever Nellie was performing in London, Edith would try to be there. It was an enthusiasm she shared with the poet John Freeman, who wrote to tell her about a performance of Nellie's in the Lyceum that Edith had missed. She was genuinely disappointed:

Nellie Wallace is an extraordinary mimic, has great personality and has the most significant appearance I have seen in an English actress. Everything acts; her cheeks, which she flaps as if they were blown by a wind, when she cries, her hands, her feet, her body. She is very tragic although she is a low-comedy actress, the epitome of starvation. . . . I never go to the theatre excepting to a Mozart opera or a certain Russian opera, or the Russian Ballet, but Music Hall delights me, and circuses even more.[41]

With Nellie Wallace's delight in a bizarre and personal style of dress, her individuality appealed to Edith. She used to go often to see her with Geoffrey Gorer, who recalled:

Nellie Wallace wasn't very often in the West End. We had to go to the more suburban music halls to see her. We went one evening to the *Finsbury Empire* and enjoyed a performance of Nellie. When we were coming out, a group of girls, who were waiting at the stage door shouted in broad Cockney,—pointing to Edith—"Oh look, there's Nellie!" Edith was absolutely delighted.[42]

FIVE

Friends and Enemies

Miss Edith Sitwell and Mr. Osbert Sitwell have pleasure in calling a General Amnesty—this does not apply to habitual offenders.

Newspaper notice

NELLIE WALLACE proved a diversion, but there was always
the grind of Edith's biography of Pope to return to. While Edith
was slaving over it, she was involved in a row with Siegfried Sassoon. Her quarrel with him arose out of a misunderstanding, but
all the same she felt Sassoon deserved the "ticking off" she gave
him.

Too often her affection for others was not returned, and if
there was one fault Edith was unable to forgive it was what she
regarded as disloyal behaviour. In Sassoon's case, she was indeed
fond of him and was hurt when Sassoon kept postponing an en-
gagement to see her in Paris with excuses which she realized
were fabricated. And a row at Siena, Italy, at a Festival where
Façade was presented, had not improved their relations. Now
she complained.

A boy who collected autographs had tea with "the Aged old
Earl" (her name for Sassoon) and Sassoon showed his guest an
article about the Sitwells by another writer, where Sachie was described as a "Harlequin," Osbert not even mentioned, and Edith

was called "Morbid, hysterical . . . out of touch with life . . .
grotesque and nonsensical." As a result, Edith wrote and gave the
"Aged old Earl" "blazes." She told Georgia:

I've asked him what the hell he means by being so disloyal as to dis-
seminate abusive nonsense of that kind. I have told him Osbert, Sachie
and I perfectly realise his attitude towards us, that we have understood it since last summer [the Siena Festival].[1]

Later it transpired that Sassoon had shown the autograph-collec-
tor the paper because it contained one of his poems. Sassoon was
determined not to quarrel with Edith and told her so. He arrived
for tea and gave her a cigar box from Trumper's which he had
decorated with tinsel as a peace offering. Unfortunately for him,
Edith caught her fingers in the lock, and, almost with relief on
her part, any hope of reconciliation vanished.

The reason for Edith's annoyance was more deeply rooted than
simply the offensive article. Sassoon had formed an emotional attachment with a wealthy young artist, and with a pang of jealousy Edith felt Sassoon had neglected her and all his friends, and
that the broken meetings had been caused by his attention to his
artist friend.

She was consequently cynical about Sassoon's marriage, commenting in a letter to Georgia in 1933: "And I suppose the bridal
pair will want to adopt [Sassoon's friend]." In the next paragraph
she complained about Sassoon's picking off another target into the
bargain, by making a damning remark about the newly founded
Sexual Reform Society, which had been pestering Edith for her
name to support tolerance for homosexuality.

Her bitterness against homosexuality was partly caused by the
realization that so many of the men she fell in love with or developed a penchant for were homosexual: Guevara, Pavlik, and now
Sassoon (although there are no details, it is probable that she was
in love with him, a fact confirmed by Sachie). "I shouldn't have
thought anybody needed encouraging . . . and really we have
quite enough of it without *training* fresh ones," Edith commented
bitterly.[2]

Less justified was an attack Edith made on a snoring neighbour, but again it was clearly a device to which she often resorted, namely, shifting the blame for her own worries onto
others. Although unhappy, she regarded her work, however tedi-

ous, with a completely professional attitude. Nothing must prevent her from working, and when she went to bed early, exhausted after writing her book, she was furious to find that a retired professor who lived downstairs had developed the "intermittent habit of mooing like a cow and hooting like an owl all night. It was exactly as if I had been shut up in a combined byre and a nest." Complaints from Edith proved ineffective, and the noise continued for several months until it sounded more like "a herd of bulls." Eventually, in reply to a complaint, Edith received a letter from a stranger who told her that she was "now free to continue your foolish scribblings. The silence below you is the silence of death." Unable to accept the accusation in the letter that she was "cruel and heartless," Edith replied with a curt note that said:

(a) Go to Hell
(b) Go to the cinema stage
(c) Attend revivalist meetings[3]

Her complaints appear an over-reaction, but it must be said that her emotional state arose partly from the subject-matter of her book. As she would constantly seek a sense of identity through her imagination, lacking it through the affection of any close friend, her choice of Pope was hardly surprising.

He was then an unfashionable poet, but Edith was attracted to him because they both had similar preoccupations with language and both were interested in "texture" in poetry. Sachie, in fact, had introduced her to Pope's *Rape of the Lock* when he was at Eton in 1915, and although she used to like telling a story about having learnt it "by heart" en route to Montegufoni as a young girl, she fell in love with him as she had with Swinburne. There are, in fact, striking similarities between Pope's life and her own, and it is impossible to feel at times that she is not writing about herself, as in the following extract:

The childhood of a poet is in nearly all cases a strange weaving together of the ecstasy that the poet knows and the helpless misery that is known by a child who is lost in the unfamiliar street of a slum. He is in a foreign place, and the faces around him are dark and strange. . . . He must suffer within his heart the mad tempests of love for the beauty of the world of sight, sense, and sound, and the mad tempests of rage against the cruelty and blindness that is in the world.

But he must suffer these dumbly, for among the tall strangers there is none to understand him, and among the small strangers there is nothing but noise and buffeting. The children are terrifying to him; their eyes are on a level with his own, but they are like the blind and beautiful eyes of statues—they see nothing. . . .[4]

A list of parallels can be drawn. Pope was a dwarf; she had curvature of the spine. He liked to claim he was an aristocrat; she was an aristocrat. Above all, they both had a vitriolic hatred of unsympathetic critics. All this went into her life of Pope.

As a prose writer, Edith could hardly keep her private personality out of what she wrote. Because she had little formal education, she was unable to present her researches in a scholarly way. Her genuine enthusiasm outshone the analysis in the book, which she published as *Alexander Pope* in 1930. It began, in a small way, a Pope revival, although it did not please the critic of the *Yorkshire Post*, who had once heard her "spouting her pretentious nonsense at Oxford." The reviewer, who signed himself "G.G.," was none other than Geoffrey Grigson. He wrote:

Miss Sitwell asks for it by her annoyance, her arrogance, her self-satisfaction, her superiority to mere critics and scholars. She exasperates the writer into forgetting his rules and his politeness and retaliating with her own weapons.[5]

He attacked her for "inaccuracy and ignorance in psychology" and blamed her for not researching the book properly. If Edith "had asked for it," she got more than she expected from this first attack, for Grigson was young and had become friendly with "dear old Wyndham Lewis." Edith's reply was caustic as usual; reviewer-baiting was the only sport in which she indulged, but she was completely unable to see the damage she caused herself by her usual methods of replying to bad reviews. The newspaper announcement at the beginning of this chapter was typical of her reaction.

The paper blamed Sachie for apparently being unable to forgive, but unlike his brother and sister, he rarely replied to attacks, except for a drawn-out battle with Ernest Newman over Sachie's books on Mozart and Liszt.

As a result of a fall shortly after *Alexander Pope* was published, Edith damaged her head and was suffering from a lack of balance. This injury meant that, more than ever, she was in no

mood for the annual family ritual stay at Renishaw in August. It
was not an event looked forward to by anyone, except perhaps
Sir George, who would wander round the estate making suggestions to Osbert about wildly fantastic improvements for it. Lady
Ida was fond of social gatherings and always invited a large stock
of her friends to help avoid the rows and tensions that often arose
in the family, especially between Osbert and his father whenever
the subject of money was raised.

Lady Ida's solution was also taken up by her family, who
brought their own friends to stay at Renishaw. The young, snobbish, but acidly observant Evelyn Waugh was delighted to be
asked, and arrived on August 23, 1930. He doubtlessly exaggerated his impressions when he recorded them in his diary, but has
nevertheless perfectly caught the eccentric atmosphere that still
survived at Renishaw and had first been noted by Constance Talbot Sitwell in the first decade of the century.

After being met at the local railway station by Sachie, Georgia,
and William Walton, Waugh was taken to Renishaw Hall, where
he found amongst others Arthur Waley, and of course the "entire
family."

Ginger in white tie and tail coat very gentle. Ginger and Lady Ida
never allowed to appear together at meals. The house extremely noisy
owing to shunting around it. The lake black with coal dust. A finely
laid out terrace garden, with a prospect of undulating hills, water and
the pit-heads, slag heaps and factory chimneys. . . .[6]

A chef from the Ritz had prepared excellent food, which the family complained about. Waugh was impressed by the fact that

the household was very full of plots. Almost everything was a secret
and most of the conversations deliberately engineered in prosecution
of some private joke. Ginger, for instance, was told that Ankaret's [a
house guest] two subjects were Arctic exploration and ecclesiastical
instruments; also that Alastair [a friend of Waugh's] played the violin.
Sachie likes talking about sex. Osbert very shy. Edith wholly ignorant.
We talked of slums. She said the poor streets of Scarborough are terrible but that she did not think that the fishermen took drugs very
much. She also said that port was made with methylated spirit: she
knew this for a fact because her charwoman told her. . . .[7]

Waugh also noticed the unusual relations the family enjoyed with
the servants, and felt that they

lived on terms of feudal familiarity:— a message brought by footman
to assembled family that her ladyship wanted to see Miss Edith upstairs. "I can't go. I've been with her all day. Osbert you go." "Sachie, you go." "Georgia, you go." etc. Footman: "Well come on. One
of you's got to go" . . .[8]

Shortly before leaving London for Renishaw, Edith gave a
party at Pembridge Mansions on July 22. Amongst her guests was
Virginia Woolf, who recalled the occasion in her diary the following day and observed:

Edith Sitwell has grown very fat, powders herself thickly, gilds her
nails with silver paint, wears a turban and looks like an ivory elephant, like the Emperor Heliogabalus. I have never seen such a
change. She is mature, majestical. She is monumental. Her fingers are
crusted with white coral. She is altogether composed. A great many
people were there—and she presided. But though thus composed, her
eyes are sidelong and humorous. The old Empress remembers her
Scallywag days. We all sat at her feet—cased in slender black slippers,
the only remnants of her slipperiness and slenderness. Who was she
like? Pope, in a nightcap? No; the imperial majesty must be included.
We hardly talked together, and I felt myself gone there rather mistakenly, had she not asked me very affectionately if she might come
and see me alone. . . .[9]

Virginia Woolf and Edith shared a common enemy in Wynd-
ham Lewis, who had attacked them both in his novel *The Apes of
God,* which was published in June 1930. Rumours had reached
Edith that she was included in a chapter of the satire entitled
"Lord Osmond's Lenten Party," and she told the novelist Sydney
Schiff (who published under the name of Stephen Hudson) that
she was refusing to read the book. But of course she did read it,
and, as she wrote to Choura Tchelitchew:

A writer and painter well-known in London (I had sat for him nearly
every day for a year seven years ago), having tried to make a personal
conquest of me in vain, has revenged himself on me and my family
. . . naturally, because I am a lady, I cannot say, except to intimate
friends, the reason for this attack.[10]

It was because she was "a lady" that Edith still had principles
that made her feel it was caddish for a man to attack a woman.
She was well aware that Lewis was not a minor writer like the
gossip columnists, who would soon be forgotten, and she was

genuinely afraid of his power to damage her reputation. "Unfortunately," she went on, "the author of *The Apes of God* is also a great writer."[11]

The vehemence of Lewis's attack had surprised her, for although relations had become strained during the time he painted Edith's portrait, she had a grudging admiration for him, as he was well aware. He had been to Renishaw many times as a guest and had even stayed in Scarborough with her brothers. But his persecution mania had developed to the point where he imagined that people were looking down on him from the ceiling. Beginning to feel that his friends hated him because they were unable to tolerate his paranoia, he diverted all his bitterness into *The Apes of God*. Osbert became Lord Osmond; Sacheverell, Phoebus; and Edith, Harriet. In fact, Edith does not enter at all until quite late in the chapter, after Osbert has been shredded by Lewis:

You will see them all sit round in a great family circle of militant minors—Lady Harriet Finnan Shaw (whose last book of verse Willie Service handed you, I hope yesterday) will be here after dinner. Harriet is about forty and very bright in a stately, cantankerous fashion— she is the image of Phoebus—she will be accompanied by the friend with whom she lives, Miss Julia Dycott, who is about fifty and a perfect kitten.[12]

Helen Rootham was Julia Dycott, and Georgia was "a certain New Zealand Jewess, Babs Kenson," whom Lewis described as trying to "land Phoebus with magic of her Maori moneybags." Much of the satire is unreadable, because the humour is so esoteric that it seems to have strayed out of a school magazine. Nevertheless it is clear, for example, that a long passage is meant to attack *Façade*. Other parts designed to make Edith bristle were "A Book of Old Harriet's all about Arab Rocking-Horses, true Banbury-Cross breed"; "Still Making Mud Pies at Forty"; "Harriet Turns Forty easily on the scales with a bit to spare, she is a forty-year-older and as for that old chum of hers there, Julia, she is a fifty-tonner . . . she p'raps weighs eight or ten summers more than Harriet."

The part of the book that annoyed Edith the most was the suggestion that she enjoyed Julia, i.e., Helen, as a "woman-mate."

Edith believed that Lewis was "seized with a kind of *schwärmerei* [passion] for me":

I did not respond. It did not get very far, but was a nuisance as he *would* follow me about, staring in a most trying manner and telling our acquaintances about the *schwärmerei*. . . . He revenged himself, in *The Apes of God*, by insulting me most grossly, calling me "a womaniser" and saying I had change of life! (I was about thirty-two.)[13]

It was less likely to be a slip of memory than a deliberate lie, for Edith was in fact forty-three when the book appeared. With her touchiness over Pavlik, who appears briefly in *The Apes of God*, it is not difficult to see why she disguised her real age.

Naomi Mitchison reviewed the book in *Time and Tide*:

Those who have three guineas and quite as many free mornings to spend ought to buy *The Apes of God*. . . . As to the Sitwells, eleven years ago one of them was very kind to me. He didn't know who I was and I've scarcely seen them since, nor do I know anything about their private affairs, but because of that kindness (in the time when we were both really young) I feel impelled to say that I think Wyndham Lewis has behaved pretty badly about them, and artistically it has spoilt an important section of his book.[14]

Support for Edith also came from W. B. Yeats in a letter he wrote to Lewis, reproving him for attacking Edith. She was very proud of Yeats's letter and often used to quote his lines but, characteristically, only to suit herself. The relevant part of his letter read:

Dear Wyndham Lewis . . .
I have heard that you attack individuals, but that drove me neither to detraction nor admiration for I knew nothing of it. . . . Somebody tells me that you have satirised Edith Sitwell. If that is so, visionary excitement has in part benumbed your senses. When I read her *Gold Coast Customs* a year ago, I felt, *as on first reading "The Apes of God"* [italics added], that something absent from all literature for a generation was back again . . . passion enobled by intensity, by endurance, by wisdom. We had it in one man once. He lies in St. Patrick's now under the greatest epitaph in history.

> Yours very sincerely,
> W. B. YEATS[15]

It was the comparison of *Lewis* with herself and Swift that Edith conveniently and naturally left out. But seeing that she was compared to Swift, why not write about him in an imaginative sense, and come to that, why not sharpen her claws on Lewis in the same book? The ideas must have occurred to Edith as she considered the theme for what was to be her only novel, *I Live Under a Black Sun*. About Edith, Lewis himself also wrote, in his memoirs:

I hope that Geoffrey Grigson will stop knocking her about in public. He should remember that although as brave as a lion, she is only a woman . . .[16]

and later in his memoirs he commented on various other critics:

I'd a damn sight rather have Edith than those cowards who skulk beneath a nom de plume and peashoot you from an ambush.[17]

After *The Apes of God*, Edith had no intention of letting "that old daisy," Wyndham Lewis, step on her. "Trampled to death by geese," she used to say, quoting Kierkegaard, and writing to Choura in September 1930:

My book of *Collected Poems* has had an enormous success. It is curious, and so unexpected after years of prejudice. I suppose that it is always like that. The only success which is worthwhile in the Arts is the success which comes after some years of suffering. I know that. If one had an immediate success it would mean one had neither vision nor mystery in her art.[18]

"Only," she added sadly, "the years are so long and the persecutions are terribly hard on the nerves." She told Choura that she and Pavlik would "triumph at the end of it all" although there would be "years of battling in the future." Lewis had stung her bitterly with his innuendo that she was a lesbian, and she was now more resolved than ever to keep Pavlik's friendship, something she desperately needed anyway.

Sachie was leading his own quiet life with Georgia at Weston Hall, and now that Osbert was installed at Renishaw with his friend David Horner, Edith had few immediate friends to confide in. Helen Rootham, who had once been a prop to her, had soured towards Edith, who recalled in her memoirs, *Taken Care Of*:

But then, suddenly, life rotted. Helen, a wonderful friend to me when I was a child and young girl, seemed to become semi-poisoned by the smell of money and a silly wish to "get into society." She and her sister . . . sprouted into such high super-lineage that it became obvious to me that they were absentees from the *Almanach de Gotha*. . . .[19]

After being told by various Serbian or Croatian friends that she was a reincarnation of a certain Princess Yellena, Helen became

unusually troublesome (a) because she realised that she was really a Princess (this she had always known subconsciously), and (b) because every single human being she saw became, automatically, the advancing Turkish army [Princess Yellena had expelled the Turks], and had to be repelled. . . . Anybody who spoke to me and did not confine their entire attention to her must, necessarily, have criminal instincts, otherwise for what reason could they possibly wish to speak to me?[20]

Life in Paris was, as Edith said, often "unmitigated hell." She declared that she did not mind taking the "boîte à l'ordure" down the stairs every night, for there was no sanitation. But she did object to

the open accusations of wickedness, and the threats that I was going mad. "Have you looked at yourself in the glass?"[21]

Edith desperately needed Pavlik, but still had to endure Allen Tanner. There was no choice but to take them both; Pavlik knew Edith would overlook anything, as long as she could see him. Her devotion was not always unrewarded, and she knew that, unpredictable as he was in his behaviour towards her, he really understood her as few others did. His tenderness was also unpredictable. When he showed her some sympathy, Edith felt that their relationship was worthwhile; for example, after she received an affectionate letter from him, like the one thanking her for trying to find portrait sitters:

How are things at present, dear friend? . . . Tell me a little about your ideas and what you think about everything that torments my mind—about Art—painting. . . . I think that in London the question of selling pictures without an exhibition is probably very difficult. I thank you once again for the care and trouble that you take on my behalf. Dear friend, I shall never forget.[22]

Pavlik was now completely dependent on Edith for practical help, as he had been rejected by Gertrude Stein and Alice Toklas. With Edith, he had called on the women in the Rue de Fleurus only to find that Gertrude was "not at home" to them. Pavlik was

furious when he learned that Miss Stein had banished his work
because it bored her and placed it with the work of other artists
in a room she never sat in. He was beginning to realize Gertrude
collected artists like bric-à-brac. Speaking of one of his last visits,
Pavlik wrote to Edith:

I went with Choura to say "how-do-you-do" to old mother Stein. My
God, what a bore she is! Old, a typical Jewess, pretentious and
wicked. Alice is a monstrosity, with a moustache à la Gauloise and her
hair frizzed like the Queen of the Gipsies. They are both historical
monuments, a pair of curiosities who cease to interest anybody except
little Americans who suck up to them. It is so strange how they have
changed so suddenly. They didn't behave very graciously to us. I
really don't care, I've done my duty and that's all there is to it.[23]

Alice Toklas did not like Pavlik from the first meeting. She
disliked his haircut, but, more important, considered that he was
malicious. "Pavlik," she recalled, "was not interested in life as he
saw it, as it was. . . . He wanted to use it. . . . Pavlik was a
dreadful little arriviste. . . . As I see him beside other men of his
generation, his attitude towards life wasn't clear. If you get into
Pavlik deeply, you'd find a weakness."[24]
Gertrude Stein apparently had liked Pavlik, because, as she
told him, she didn't understand what he was doing. Long after
they quarrelled, Pavlik took his revenge painting both Stein and
Toklas in his canvas "Phenomena"; Gertrude Stein is depicted as
an Indian chief, surrounded by broken canvases, and at her side is
Alice Toklas, knitting, with an evil expression on her face.
Edith knew that she had to remain in Paris, near Pavlik, but
she had also to continue her work on her latest prose book. This
was a study of Bath, a subject in which she was scarcely interested at all. But her publishers Faber & Faber had commissioned
it for the spring of 1932, and in August 1931 she still had 90,000
words to write. Only the various eccentrics who had lived in Bath
in the eighteenth century interested her, and she refused to visit
the city. *Bath* seemed very remote from poetry, and the nearest
she got to this was her compilation of an anthology of other people's, which appeared in three volumes spanning 1930–32.
But above all it was essential, if Edith was to succeed as a
writer in Paris, that she must keep her friends and make more.
Next to London, Paris was the most important literary centre,

and many of the English and American writers Edith had met in
London would gather in Paris at the bookshop Shakespeare &
Company. A meeting place for both the established and the
aspiring literati, the shop had initially earned its reputation
through its owner, Sylvia Beach, who had made friends with
James Joyce and Gertrude Stein. Miss Beach invited Edith to
give a poetry reading, and because Gertrude Stein and Alice
Toklas were to be there, it was expected Edith would read some
of Gertrude's work. That Edith had no intention of doing, for she
was aware of Gertrude's conduct. Gertrude had been nasty to
Pavlik and therefore must be made to feel Edith's disapproval.

It was a difficult decision for her to make, as she stood to lose
by it. At Gertrude's house she had met Picasso, who had offered
to draw her because he found her face a "real collector's" piece.[25]
The drawing never materialized, very possibly owing to Gertrude's intervention. Edith undoubtedly cut off other opportunities of self-promotion by offending Gertrude Stein, but even the
presence of other influential figures, such as Joyce, at the reading
made no difference to Edith in her resolve to punish her enemy.
The occasion was remembered by Natalie Barney:

Edith sat majestically remote above her audience. Her long Elizabethan hands, bearing no papers, met in their virginal loveliness,
sufficient unto themselves. . . . She rose to read, but what were those
strange un-Steinian rhythms now scanned by this unique poetess's
lips? Were they not some of Miss Sitwell's own?[26]

As Edith's reading came to an end, Miss Stein grew angrier and
angrier. "She sat bolt upright, meditating, in spite of a twitch of
her hands, a more gentlemanly reprisal than immediate exposure."[27] Drinks followed, but Miss Stein was not there to enjoy
them. She had gone home piqued, and the following day Edith
received a curt note from her, expressing her anger at not being
included in the reading. Tanner wrote to Edith, trying to prevent
the breakup of the friendship:

Edith, I entreat you, however, not to quarrel with Gertrude—I mean,
not to "break", that is a better word, on our account. You must be quite
unconcerned and just as *false* as you can manage to be, and we will
find out many things in that way.[28]

It was too late; Miss Stein and her mischief-making had gone
out of Edith's life. One positive advantage Edith must have felt

was that Gertrude could no longer be regarded as a competitor for Pavlik. In one sense, she never had been, but any doubts Edith may have had were dispelled and she knew that whatever Pavlik wanted from women could now come only from her. But still Edith required a confidante to help her relationship with Pavlik, and now she turned to Stella Bowen, her Australian artist friend who had consoled her over the *stolen book.* Stella had been treated badly in her turn by Ford Madox Ford, whom she had been living with, and found a sympathetic listener in Edith.

At the beginning, however, Edith's aristocratic manners puzzled Stella, who scolded her for bringing across the Channel the prejudices of an Englishwoman. This was nothing new—Pavlik had also insisted on telling her that an artist "had no business to be a lady"—but Edith found the more seedy aspects of Paris and Guermantes difficult to accept, and she refused to go into cafés to see Bohemian life there. Instead she often attended parties given by Stella, sitting on a covered coal-box, on which she had once been enthroned while Stella painted a portrait of her.

Grateful as Edith was for Stella's friendship, the artist's constant complaining sometimes reminded Edith too much of her own difficulties with Pavlik, and Stella was

such a nuisance, poor dear, about her troubles. I really will take nearly every trouble in the world, but people must make up their minds what they want. I can't have poor souls weeping for six hours a day because they have to tell me then for six hours the next day because the man won't see them and that is what is happening.[29]

More reliable as a morale booster was Allanah Harper, who would often take Edith out to concerts. Although there was no piano in the shabby rooms of the Rue Saint-Dominique, Edith had never lost her early love of music. Allanah would arrive in a car and they would often drive to the Théâtre des Champs-Élysées. At that time Beethoven was Edith's favourite composer, a swiftly changing accolade, and she made Allanah attend a performance of his Ninth Symphony in an effort to convert her. Like her taste in poetry, which often changed, Edith's taste in music fluctuated so much that she could write:

Though I admire Mozart I admire him less, which is my fault, preferring infinitely Gluck because he is less sweet. Bach is my god; he seems to have created a perfect world in which there is no sin and in which sorrow is holy and not ugly.[30]

Music was a world in which she had sought refuge as a child when life was difficult, and it was to music that she returned now. Important for her, Bach seemed religious, in that he provided an excuse for and justification of her own suffering. She had always tried to convince herself that "sorrow is holy," and his music was the most powerful persuasion she knew.

With the pressure of work on the despised book on Bath, Edith's health suffered. Like her father, she was a born hypochondriac and always exaggerated her illnesses, but this time her ill health was real, and she was surprisingly stoic when it came to enduring injections in her arm. (She was probably anaemic.) Illness meant less money, for she was prevented from writing, and to fill in the time profitably she resumed her work on her anthology, *The Pleasures of Poetry*.

Edith lacked any decent secretarial help, and her untidiness and carelessness in the preparation of her manuscripts often meant misquotations. One particular mistake over Baudelaire, a favourite poet of Edith's, was noted by a lady who complained to *The Times Literary Supplement*. Mercifully for Edith, John Hayward (the editor of John Donne) intercepted the letter, which he gave to his friend T. S. Eliot, whose support of Edith (for once) stopped the editor, Bruce Richmond, from publishing it. It was a lucky escape for Edith, but it was to give her a false impression of Eliot's loyalty. Whatever Eliot had done for Edith behind the scenes, he never publicly lifted a finger to protect her or speak in her defence, despite her constant support of him.

SIX

Murdered Love

There is a terrible groping animal
Consciousness that lumbers to appal
The heart . . . this only knows the flowering dire
And urge of its hot blood and earth desire.

Prelude to a Fairy Tale

IN APRIL 1931 Edith was looking forward to going to Weston Hall "to help" with her nephew Reresby, who was born in 1927. Having no children of her own, she was very proud of Reresby and of Francis, born in 1935, and she always enjoyed her visits to the pleasant house that Sachie and Georgia had transformed into a comfortable home. Exotic needlework—bed and chairs which had been worked by her ancestress Mrs. Jennens—appealed to her own taste, and she was particularly impressed by the fact that they had been worked with wool and feathers. At Weston Hall she could relax, reading some hundreds of recipes for medicines, compiled by an even earlier ancestress, Anne Blencowe, in 1694:

If one had "rheum" she insisted that the invalid should take a worm boiled in milk and drunk when lukewarm. Imagine having a red nose, running eyes in front of her, and the worm wasn't even cut into pieces.[1]

Although Edith needed money from her journalism, she wrote only one essay in 1931, "Life's Tyrannies." In it she declared: "It is better to love than to be loved" and, echoing again her beliefs about suffering artists, continued, "And believe me, to be celebrated in one of the arts is the worst horror of art. The art without the celebrity is the ideal possession."[2]

After Edith's publicity-hankering it was a surprising statement, but at the time she believed it herself. More surprising was her conclusion: "The only possessions which are in truth worth having, if we look back through our lives, are a clear soul, a warm heart and simplicity."[3]

To the public reading this it must have seemed that a new Edith Sitwell had arrived, and they must have wondered what had caused the apparent change. The answer was Pavlik. Her own financial position and the constant barrage of letters from Pavlik and Tanner, often harping on their own state of poverty, made her hate even more the whole society she had attacked viciously enough in *Gold Coast Customs*. Whatever her difficulties with Pavlik, she could understand him when he wrote after a visit to London in August:

It was a great pleasure seeing you again in London . . . full of good humour and telling amusing stories, because when you are well you have such a charming expression of goodness and lively mockery in your eyes which is adorable. The more I know you, the more I become attached to you, I am sure you will write some wonderful poems, you who are too great even for your brothers to understand. How much I would love to see you in Paris. We could be together and read and work and laugh at things. If one doesn't die of hunger, this epoch is ideal for painting because no-one looks at what we do, but we feel sad because of the isolation of what we do vis-à-vis human society.[4]

Almost uncomplainingly, Edith sent Pavlik more money, but to her cost, as it turned out. She ran into a grave financial crisis, and after a session "in dock," as she termed it, with her bank manager, she was told her overdraft must be reduced. In desperation she appealed to Sachie for help, but he himself was poor and unable to lend anything. He managed, however, to borrow £500 for her from Siegfried Sassoon. She wrote to Sachie:

I really shall never be able to tell you how grateful I am to you. It has

made and is making the whole difference to my life and I shall feel
able to work again once this nightmare book of *Bath* is over. Actually
there is nothing that one can say that doesn't sound so dreadfully
inadequate. . . .[5]

At least Pavlik was grateful, and any doubts that arose in her
mind were dispelled by letters such as:

There is sometimes such—hell in my soul that it is frightful to touch it
and you know that there isn't a single person who can understand and
console me more than you.[6]

Her bitterness towards Sassoon changed to gratitude, and although she still had reservations, she was now able to write:

His virtues are of an entirely opposite character to those of Mr. Lewis.
He is home loving and extremely exact and tidy and his friendships
(whilst they last—he is very changeable) are almost fantastically loyal.
The bravery which made him so great a figure in the war is reflected
in his appearance, and he is the most generous minded man I have
ever known. . . .[7]

But this description of him was intended for publication, and in
fact she had charitably struck out a passage referring to his artist
friend: "Siegfried Sassoon found it hard to condone any luxury
until the last two years, in which he seems to have suffered a sex-
change."[8]

Her financial aid helped the Pavlik household besides helping
to buy their friendship, and she spent Christmas in Paris with
them. It was an intensely happy time for her and she longed to
stay on indefinitely. But she still had Pembridge Mansions to look
after and her overdue *Bath* book to complete. Reluctantly she returned to London.

One of the few reliefs of the new year of 1932 was the pleasure
of knowing that *Bath* was nearly at its end. When it was published, even Desmond MacCarthy, whom she disliked, gave her a
good review:

One of the most charming books of its kind. If I add that I have not
read a book quite like it, illogically that pre-empts the compliment.
Yet, as every reader who has been thoroughly pleased by a book
knows, it is in such contradictions that appreciation first expresses itself.

And another critic wrote in a provincial Somerset newspaper:

If and when Miss Sitwell visits Bath I shall expect the Major and other civic dignitaries to arrange a pageant at least as impressive as that with which Queen Anne and her Consort were received when one hundred young men of the city . . . came to the borders of Somersetshire to meet them. . . . I myself should be willing to design the procession and act as Master of its ceremonial.

Bath sold most of the 1,500 copies in very quick time, and Fabers at once contacted Edith to ask her to write another prose book, on English eccentricity. If *Bath* was "wretched," her *English Eccentrics* was "confounded," for by December 1932 Edith was working seven hours a day on it. Checking facts and visiting the London Library (she always had overdue books) bored her to distraction, but at least the subject of eccentricity was close to her heart. Her gallery of oddities was created with more enthusiasm than *Bath*, since Edith shared the same love of the ridiculous that her subjects enjoyed displaying. To some extent she sympathized with many of her characters in the way in which they were misunderstood, and felt an affinity with their peculiar foibles. In a letter written about the same time as her *Eccentrics*, Edith displays her sense of the ridiculous, and it shows her humour at its best; it describes a disastrous journey made in the train from Italy:

A friend . . . presented me with a bouquet of chloratic pink roses obviously just torn from some old lady's grave, surrounded by what looked like sea-jaded groundsel. This floral offering afterwards played old harry with my destiny.

Everything went peaceably enough until we were in Switzerland, and the wind which had been non-existent in Italy, had by now become a polar hurricane. It tore through my wide open window, dashed through my compartment, tried to tear my teeth from my head and finally hurtling itself at the bouquet, flung the bottle of water in which it was contained, onto my sheets, and broke it there.

I got up to shut the window. But before I could shut it, I had to unloose the blind. No sooner, my children (believe me, or believe me not), had the blind got me in its grip, than it tore madly out of the window, taking a large part of me with it. The blind and the wind rushed along at a thousand miles an hour, and tried to fling me onto the line. I resisted but the blind was becoming too strong for me, and I was racing through the window after it, when it suddenly changed its mind, flapped at me like an eagle, hit me on the nose, flung me all round the compartment, then it tore out of the window again taking me with it. . . .

Luckily *that* time, it knocked me onto the bell, and just as I was rushing out of the window, again, the sleeping car attendant arrived, seized me in a firm grasp, tore me with terrific difficulty, away from the blind which was just disappearing out of the window with me attached and flung me onto my bed. He then sat down, mopped his forehead, and said, "C'est bien étrange, ce que vous faisez là, madame". From that moment on I did not know a moment's peace.

At 7-15, a voice that obviously belonged to the young games-mistress of a girl's school, called outside my compartment: "Miss Pyke, Miss *Pyke*"

"Yes, dear" an older, rather patient voice replied.

"Oh Miss Pyke, Mr. Hoare is in the lavatory."

"Well dear, what if he is?"

"Yes Miss Pyke, *but they won't let him out!*"

"Wait till I come, dear"

But I never found out what *was* the end of that, because the sleeping car attendant after my night's adventure, wouldn't let me out of my compartment, for fear I should be lost altogether. . . .[9]

Describing the adventures of a ham actor and would-be society climber in her *English Eccentrics*, Edith relates how Robert Coates took part in a performance of *Romeo and Juliet*:

. . . in the duel scene where Romeo kills Tybalt, all was ruined, and the house was convulsed with laughter at the appearance of a bantam cock, which had strutted at the very feet of Romeo, at whom it had been thrown. Mr. Coates was in despair, but luckily, at the last and darkest moment, old Capulet seized the cause of the trouble, and bore him, crowing loudly and flapping his wings, off the stage. . . . The play continued, though, when Romeo left the stage after killing Tybalt, he stood in the wings and shook his sword at the box from which the cock had been thrown on to the stage, with the result that the occupants of the pit yelled that he must apologise for shaking his sword. Mr. Coates, very naturally, refused to do so, and the interruptions continued until the occupants of the pit turned on the interrupters and pelted them with orange peel. The play continued, then, without any further interruption until the moment came when Romeo kills Paris. Then the latter, lying dead upon the ground, was raised to life by "a terrific blow on the nose from an orange". The corpse rose to his feet and, pointing in a dignified way to the cause of his revival, made his way off the stage. Mr. Coates, we are told, was "considerably annoyed" during the Tomb Scene, by shouts of "Why don't you die?" . . .[10]

Along with her declared love of poetry, Edith possessed considerable talents as a prose writer, and it is not difficult to see why *English Eccentrics,* well written "from the inside," as it were, was one of her most popular books.

Edith was now worried about her mother's health, although she was reluctant to admit it. "Your Aunt Ida," she told her cousin Veronica Gilliat, "nearly had pleurisy and nearly had bronchial pneumonia." This sounds like a change of attitude towards Lady Ida, but as Osbert Sitwell recalled in *Laughter in the Next Room,* by 1923

> my mother, who had so cruelly ill used her [Edith], had come to love her society, her wit and perception, and it was symptomatic of Edith's fineness of character that she responded and, now that my mother was growing old and her spirits flagging, set herself at a great waste of her own energy and time, to amuse her—and there was little else one could do for her. . . .[11]

But however much Lady Ida's health worried Edith, there was little time to see her. In August 1932 the task of packing her manuscripts, books, and other scanty belongings had to be done, for Edith could no longer afford to keep on her flat in Moscow Road. She realized the importance of keeping a pied-à-terre in England after she gave up Moscow Road, and a house in Warwickshire controlled by her father had been left vacant by the death of her Aunt Florence (Sitwell). Edith had hopes of living there, but instead an old and tiresome retainer who had looked after her aunt, Sister Edith Woods, moved in under the terms of her aunt's will. Sister Edith had long ago earned the title of the "Scarlet Woman" from Osbert because of her considerable girth, and Edith remembered her as "a bursting woman like an advertisement for tomatoes in a railway station."[12] That she was to live in Long Itchington completed Edith's unhappiness. Many years later, when asked to write about Sister Edith, she commented, "She was tireless in making mischief between my brothers and my father, and deprived me of one third of my income. Let us hear no more of that sordid woman."[13]

There was little consolation back in Paris, where Edith felt imprisoned with Helen. England seemed far away, but a scene that March with Vivienne, T. S. Eliot's estranged wife, must have made her feel glad that she at least had her sanity. Vivienne Eliot came for tea with Georgia and her mother, Mrs. Doble. She had become addicted to ether, and Edith noticed the smell, "as if four bottles of methylated spirits had been upset." Edith's maid, who had been a nurse, told Edith quietly that if Vivienne started anything she was to "get her by the wrists, sit on her face and don't let her bite you. Often it has taken six of us to hold her down." "Tea," Edith reflected, "was undiluted hell."[14] The last encounter with Vivienne was to be in Oxford Street that summer. Edith greeted her with a "Hello, Vivienne," but Vivienne only looked at her in amazement and answered, "Who do you think you're addressing? I don't know you!" "Don't be silly, Vivienne," Edith replied; "you know quite well who I am!" "No, no," were Mrs. Eliot's last sad words to her, "you don't know me, you've mistaken me *again* for that *terrible* woman who is so like me . . . she's always getting me into trouble."[15]

With her memories of the previous Christmas in Guermantes, Edith felt that life in Paris could be a treat despite *English Eccentrics* hanging over her. But Guermantes was now no haven for Edith, only too aware as she was of the increasing strain in the relationship of Choura, Tanner, and Pavlik. Pavlik often had long silences between his letters to her, and it was again from Tanner that Edith received the desperate news. The matter of the stolen book was forgotten as far as Edith was concerned. She knew now that she could partly keep in touch with Pavlik via Tanner, and that Pavlik probably never knew about the letters she was receiving.

Tanner told her of the great unhappiness he had experienced as a child, having lived with unsympathetic parents, and of his misery on realizing that he was homosexual. The housework Pavlik made him do and the obstacles he placed to prevent Tanner from being a celebrated pianist had all worn him out. He told Edith he was heading for a nervous breakdown, and that the only solution was to leave Pavlik. "I want," he told Edith, "a rest from Pavlik and his all-consuming energy, his career, his painting, his personality and God knows what besides, and I am not a little angry with him for disposing of my time and strength and patience so lightly."[16]

Despite his disillusionment with his partner, Tanner was determined that Edith should not fall out with Pavlik even if he wrote her difficult letters. "Remember," he wrote, "there are never any

grounds for hurts, wounds or offences."[17] But Edith was beginning to doubt this; Pavlik made no effort to understand her
suffering or the boredom she had endured trying to write her
English Eccentrics, although he did provide the design for the
wrapper of the book. Written at one of the most unhappy times
of her life, the book might have been gloomy, but, like her malice
and wit, it had become a diversion. No one could guess from the
book, which at times is extremely amusing, what hell she was
going through.

Edith was only too aware of the complexities of her relationship with Pavlik. He often reassured her by saying that he,
too, needed her, and this made it impossible for Edith ever to
think of leaving him. Although she would never discuss sexual
matters, all her friends have indicated that she was not naïve
about Pavlik's homosexuality and could not have failed to realize
that his sexual needs were taken care of by Tanner, and others. It
was a paradox Edith probably never fully understood herself, but
she would have been horrified if—had it been possible—Pavlik
had made any sexual demands on her. As a woman she desperately needed love, but as Edith Sitwell she had to be able to handle her emotional needs so that she could continue to write
without being swamped. Pavlik's homosexuality gave her the
protection she wanted from any relationship with a man, without
the agonies of sexual involvement. There is no doubt that she
never had sexual relations with anyone at any time in her life.
Her physique was not of the kind that attracted men, and all
Edith's friends considered that as a person she was somehow outside any suggestion of sex; indeed her virginity radiated a particular spiritual quality found in few women. Sachie, in his *For
Want of the Golden City,* has described this aspect of his sister,
which impressed itself on those who knew and loved her:

Of the aphidae I call her because of her tall thinness in her youth, and
the suggestion of long waists and wimples, long thin fingers and
pointed feet. Of virginal beauty, as should be a young abbess or
palantine, not sexually, but poetically and spiritually beautiful; some
kind of throw-back from being the child of a mother who was not yet,
or scarcely eighteen years old; so that I have often wondered, never
having seen anyone at all resembling her, whether there may not have
been nuns like her. . . . More than once I have felt that little note of
affinity, which must come out of the very distant past, as though there

had been young women there much resembling her, to whom indeed one could . . . have talked of poetry. . . .[18]

Nevertheless, despite the limitations of their relationship, Edith could not fully understand or forgive Pavlik for his lack of loyalty, inevitable at times because of his own attachment to his male friends. To look at their relationship on a practical level, Pavlik could not resist the temptation to use Edith for the financial help she gave him; on a more elevated level, he required her as his artistic muse, a purely spiritual inspiration. Edith gradually realized that her money would buy her no more than that, but she still wished that Pavlik would at least appear more grateful.

Unfortunately, the dilemma affected them in different ways; the tension created in their relationship only drove Pavlik more fervently to painting, but the anguish felt by Edith, which might have found a similar outlet in poetry, had the effect of keeping her from poems and making her continue to write prose, which brought in the money they all needed. The jealousy Edith felt about Tanner would be expressed only later, and then only briefly, when Tanner was replaced by another boy-friend.

As an outlet for her misery, *English Eccentrics* was not enough. Edith also worked on developing the unpublished essay on Wyndham Lewis begun the previous year and began her memoirs, which were never to be published as such. It was a way of trying to write some of the problems out of her system. The section about Lewis is called "The Ape of God":

Mr. Lewis spent a very large part of time with my brothers and me in the years 1921, 22, 23 and this was a great delight to us for we have always considered him as the greatest prose writer of our generation and as a great draughtsman. His mind is enormous, incalculable and black, his intellect tremendous and it is a pity that he should waste this intellect in barren fancies about imaginary slights and plots against him. He paid my family a visit at our house in Scarborough, arriving with a very dark complexion and a bundle in place of a suitcase. My mother, I am afraid, did not take a fancy to him and asked Osbert: "Has your friend brought a valet?" She was promptly escorted to bed and asked to remain there. The visit I believe passed off without any other incident, but I do not know for I was not there. He visited us also at Renishaw; but the visit was not entirely happy as Mr. Lewis lost his collar on the first day, and was unable to come down to lunch until he found it.

At this time however, we were counted among his friends and Sacheverell and I were inured to the ordeal of Mr. Lewis watching us from afar with that blinking look of reproachful affection to which I have referred; a look which turned upon us, varied from the expression of the canine friend in the well-known advertisement of his master's voice, to that of a returning wanderer seeing from afar the old homestead.

Mr. Lewis had unexpectedly a fine and extraordinary power of mimicry and this was used upon friends and enemies alike. It is sad to think how many friends changed into enemies (in Mr. Lewis' imagination) for no reason. He was very angry for instance with Frank Dobson, the sculptor, for claiming that Mr. Lewis was older than himself. "I am thirty-four" he informed Sacheverell in a furious voice "and I remain 34 until further notice". We all thought at the time that Mr. Lewis was rather minimising the fact. But he liked all the facts about himself to remain shrouded in mystery, for fear that Mr. Clive Bell or other evil portents of our civilisation should find out about him. He is a great writer and a most sad and solitary man having attacked and driven away every loyal friend he possessed, and all those whose admiration for his gifts is founded in reality.[19]

The memoir of Lewis also contained a section which reads like a description of herself:

When Lewis is dead I shall write the story of his life . . . and in it I shall show how every little fault and every little mistake made by this fundamentally gentle and affectionate character is the result of the fear that engrosses him, the fear that he is not loved, the crushing impressions that those on whom he has set his affections do not return them.[20]

By the time Edith wrote this, Pavlik was no longer returning any affection to Edith or Tanner because a new star had risen. He was an American poet called Charles Henri Ford, who had published poems with an introduction by William Carlos Williams and had also collaborated with Parker Tyler (who was to be Pavlik's biographer) on a novel called *The Young and Evil*, which they hoped Gertrude Stein would help them to publish. The novel had been written in 1930–31, although it was not published until 1933; Allen Tanner apparently believed, having seen an early draft of it, that he and his sister Ruth were depicted in it:

My sister is called a fly-by-night, a café-hound, a whore, oh, I can't remember half of it, it is too horrible a creation to think about. It is sinister. The book is horribly written and one naturally doesn't look for any literary value even if it were possible for there to be any in a work that has its only analogy in obscene photography or blackmail.[21]

Tanner believed that Gertrude Stein's approval of the book, with the promise of help to publish it, was another plot against him. On top of this new upset and worrying about Pavlik, Edith had the strain of Helen, whose cancer of the spine was growing worse. Much to Edith's relief there was a chance to return to England in February 1933, as Pavlik had an exhibition at Tooth's in London that she had promised to help with. Whatever troubles Edith had with Pavlik, she still would not give him up; her constant determination to help him was remarkable in view of the way he treated her. Any difficulties about his behaviour she excused, putting it down to illness, which was in fact largely imaginary.

Earlier in January 1933 she had commiserated with Choura: "I hope that Pavlik will be better and that you and Allen will not catch anything. Poor Pavlik, it is too bad that this has happened at a time when he is working so hard."[22]

The following month he was well enough to travel to London for the exhibition, but Edith travelled ahead and had a stormy passage. She was sea-sick and arrived more dead than alive, to be met in London by Georgia. Sachie and Georgia insisted that Pavlik should join them all at Weston Hall for a period of recuperation. Listing the attractions of the house, Edith had written to Choura, asking her to use her influence to persuade Pavlik to come, and his visit was planned to begin on February 27. On the twentieth, Edith went with Lord Berners, the composer, to the exhibition; it was a great success, and Edith was "too happy for words," as she said in an excited letter to Choura a few days later. Many paintings were sold and there was the hope that Lady Cynthia Mosley, the wife of Sir Oswald, would commission a portrait. "My dear," Edith continued, "I am proud of your brother's triumph with all my heart. . . . Sam Courtauld [chairman of Courtaulds Ltd. and founder of the Courtauld Institute of Art] said that he is now established as a great artist and that the only danger will be that he may follow the fashion of modern painters. . . ."[23]

Edith must have thought that with the success of the exhibi-

Edith, aged ten, with her brothers, Osbert and Sacheverell, and their nurse, Davis. (CROMACK, SCARBOROUGH)

Sitwell family group. *From left to right:* Sacheverell, Sir George, Georgia, Reresby, Lady Ida, Edith, and Osbert. (CECIL BEATON, SOTHEBY's)

Lady Ida and Sir George Sitwell. (VICTOR HEY, SCARBOROUGH)

Renishaw Hall, Derbyshire.

The first portrait of Edith by Pavel Tchelitchew, 1927.

Pavel Tchelitchew. (CECIL BEATON, SOTHEBY'S)

The Gotham Book Mart Party. *Left, seated*, William Rose Benét; *behind him,* Stephen Spender; *behind him,* Horace Gregory and his wife; *behind the seated Edith and Osbert Sitwell*, Tennessee Williams, Richard Eberhart, Gore Vidal, José García Villa; *on steps,* W. H. Auden; *standing*, Elizabeth Bishop; *seated*, Marianne Moore; *seated at right*, Randall Jarrell; *in front of him,* Delmore Schwartz; *cross-legged in centre*, Charles Henri Ford. (LISA LARSON, LIFE, TIME INC.)

Sacheverell Sitwell in the early 1920s.

tion, which she felt Pavlik partly owed to her, their relations would improve. The visit to Weston Hall should have been happy, but in the library, which Edith had boasted to Choura about in her letter, Pavlik discovered a book on a czar's coronation which he thought Sachie had left there on purpose. He took undue offence and after only one night insisted on leaving.

Edith sympathized with Sachie, who at that moment was very high in her estimation. If her own poetry brought no pleasure at this time, she was excited by his *Canons of Giant Art* and wrote to him in June 1933:

My darling,
Once again I'm more proud than I can possibly say to have this great poetry dedicated to me. You know what I've always known your poetry to be.[24]

Insisting that Yeats should have a copy, she wrote that he would probably "lay hands on you as a result, but you'll have to put up with it," and continued:

I feel writing to you rather as Yeats felt when he said to me, "You don't mind what an ould, ould man like me says—but you mind what the biggest fool that any editor has been able to find says".[25]

"What hell Renishaw will be," Edith predicted to Sachie. "I've seen the Gingers [her parents] to whom I've given a thorough fright." She was confiding to him in her letter, complaining that she was being pestered by a man "with clanking rows of teeth, with barbed wire entanglements who thinks I stole his silver toothpick when he was brought to tea with me, and is now avenging himself."[26]

In August she went to Renishaw, as was expected of her, for the annual family reunion. It was not peaceful; battles went on, Edith wrote to Choura, "between my father against Osbert, Sachie and Georgia so that I cannot concentrate. You cannot imagine what goes on. Now there is a battle that I believe may end in a legal wrangle. My father says that Osbert owes him £2,000. This is a terrible lie."[27]

Lady Ida, who had met Edith at the station, had warned her that Sir George was going to disinherit Osbert, and to relieve the tension Lady Ida had also brought an outside visitor, the A.D.C. to the ex-King of Greece. Sachie and Osbert apparently refused to talk to him, and Edith was obliged "to make polite conversation for nine hours. . . . He never tires and never rests, like the Hebrew God, and he refuses categorically to amuse himself. . . ."[28]

Meanwhile Pavlik had told her about Ford and Tyler's novel *The Young and Evil;* because of its obscenity it was banned from being brought into England, so she asked if Choura would get Ford to send it to her so that she could judge it for herself.

Edith was persuaded to go to Bath to give a reading, and there family problems raised their ugly head: Lady Ida constantly said, "Darling, what are we going to do about your father and Osbert?" Edith had just had some teeth removed because of an abscess and she was in no mood to listen. There was, however, some welcome news in the form of a letter from the Royal Society of Literature stating that she was to be awarded the King's Medal for Poetry. They had, according to Edith, "been forced by Yeats, Siegfried, de la Mare and Blunden into giving my poetry this medal,"[29] which was to be presented the following January.

Edith was delighted, but some of the pleasure was taken away by the impact of Ford and Tyler's *The Young and Evil.* Today it reads fairly harmlessly as a stylistic forerunner of Jean Genet's *Our Lady of the Flowers,* but it is easy to imagine the astonishment Edith felt as she read through scene after scene of lesbianism, homosexuality, transvestism, and prostitution. It must have been quite clear to Edith now, if she had ever any doubt, what sort of company Pavlik was keeping. Back in Paris, she gave news of Helen, who had gone to a nursing home for a second operation for cancer in November, to her cousin Veronica:

I'm expecting the Boyar to tea . . . oh, he's been so trying lately! He has started finding young English and American poets. As he can't read a word of the language you can imagine my suffering, and though he is so happy when I say what I think, they are all quite incompetent and fearfully obscene.[30]

To Geoffrey Gorer, in a letter written at the same time, she was more explicit:

I am very worried about Pavlik. I am afraid his money affairs are *very* bad again. I hardly ever see him now, though, as he is too occupied with that creature who wrote the immortal book we know.[31]

Edith realized that it was Ford who was taking up Pavlik's

time. Pavlik had actually glibly written to her to say that it was sad they were both in the same town (Paris) and only able to see each other once a week because he had a cold. "I found out," Edith continued to Gorer, "that in spite of all the disasters I have mentioned, the genius had spent his whole time there, every day!! I am not unnaturally a little hurt. I am also cross at being supposed to be a fool."[32]

Ironically, the only poem that Edith had written in 1933 was called *Romance*, which was published in November. Even in family letters she was unable to confide her misery except to tell Sachie that "life here is hell. Poor Helen is terribly weak and ill, it is perfectly dreadful. On Saturday last we had a fearful time with her and I honestly thought it was the end." All she could admit to Charlotte Haldane (wife of J. B. S. Haldane) was that she had

seen people behaving in a perfectly ugly way just lately, and I never get used to it, I mean in my personal life it has been very bad, and outside, these terrible lynchings in America and the departure last week of the French convict ship for Devil's Island have upset me terribly—nineteen hundred and thirty-three years after Christ and the righteous are still behaving like this.[33]

It was hard for Edith, always a sympathetic person, with a sharp eye for human folly, to feel detached from the horror of certain tragic world events, and she was often as upset by various disasters as if they were part of her personal problems. Her own miserable life helped her to understand the suffering of others, and because so many of her friends were Jews, she felt outraged by the deteriorating political situation: events proved her right.

A photograph of her with Pavlik in Toulon, taken about this time, expresses a remote sadness; she looks tired and haggard beside her younger friend. Pavlik alone, in his portraits, seemed to be able to express her emotional state. He would emphasize her hooded eyes to make her appear lonely and distant. His treatment of Edith is interesting; despite their quarrels, no other artist understood her as well as he did, and this is reflected in his various sensitive representations of her.

With Christmas and New Year behind her, Edith went to London in February 1934 to receive her medal for poetry. She had the satisfaction of knowing that the Royal Society was "black with rage at having to have me." "But," as she told Sachie, "a strange wave of popularity has flowed over me, I imagine as a result of it [the medal]. Mrs. [Jacob] Epstein, having forgotten me for four years has asked me to a 'Thé Dansante.' "[84]

A woman whom Edith had not seen for years suddenly invited her to her daughter's party, and she felt hurt that a medal should be responsible for her popularity. "Why? why? is what I ask myself, and one will never find out—that is what is so sad."[35] Nevertheless, it was a moment she treasured.

Loth to being called a poetess, Miss Sitwell collected her medal in a long sweeping dress of bright yellow silk, skull cap made of cock's feathers, saucer-size brooch made of eight huge blobs of amber[36]

reported the *Daily Express*, and the accompanying photograph shows her looking smugly pleased. The award was a boost of confidence, and with it she felt fully prepared to confront her enemies. Dr. F. R. Leavis had joined the enemy ranks, having declared that she and her brothers belonged "to the history of publicity rather than of poetry."[37] A new battle had begun.

Preparations had been made in the *Morning Post*, where she tried to half murder Leavis, though not "alas . . . little Grigson because he writes for them."[38] Support had come from the poets Edmund Blunden and Lascelles Abercrombie, and Edith pleaded with Sachie to join in an attack with her, telling him that he had a duty to defend poetry. Whatever she thought about Abercrombie's and Blunden's work, which was not much, "at least they do know *what* poetry *ought* to be *like* and they *are* scholars."[39] This was not the only new attack; her knife was also sharpened for Wyndham Lewis, whose books she had savaged in reviews. Because Gertrude Stein had helped to promote *The Young and Evil*, Edith wrote a malicious description to Charlotte Haldane:

A lecture was given at the American Women's Club here the other day on the subject of G. Stein, and I am *told,* though I cannot vouch for the truth of the rumour, that G. wore a white Grecian robe, with her various chests surrounded by a gold—cestus, I think is the word— anyhow, you will know what I mean. It must have been an impressive spectacle, and I can't think how she managed about her lingerie—for she normally wears dark grey knitted plus-fours under everything.[40]

"That confounded Allen," as she often thought of him, was released from the Pavlik household and replaced by Ford.

Tanner's reward for loyalty from Pavlik upset Edith, and although she had found him tiresome in the past she sympathized and wondered if she herself would be the next to go. Tanner met her for dinner and they slandered Pavlik with all their feelings. She had told Tanner in a letter:

I realize now that the rare occasions when he attempts to behave with decency or even ordinary politeness to me it is only that he realizes that with your one exception I am the only person on whom he can rely. Well, I will *never* let him down . . . but he has murdered my love for him.[41]

Remembering the earlier scenes, Edith decided *she* would "wear the pants" and would show him in various small ways how she felt, such as not turning up for a portrait sitting. "Poor Pavlik, he's a terrible fool, a real fool." A very great artist indeed had told her that she was wasting her time on Pavlik, and also "paid me the greatest compliment that I think I have ever had." He said that "any man who is an artist could do great work if you were beside him."[42] The artist she referred to remains unidentified, but could have been T. S. Eliot, or more likely Siegfried Sassoon. In any case it gave her new ammunition.

But Pavlik could also pay Edith back. When she eventually went round with Allanah Harper, he opened his studio door, saw Edith about to step in, and slammed the door in her face.

But Edith was trapped; if she could escape from Pavlik there was no escape from Helen, and the only hope of any peace at all was to take her to a cheap hotel in Italy, where Helen would enjoy the sun and where Edith could write undisturbed. She had now begun a life of Queen Victoria, and when bored with "that bloody Victoria," she worked on her book on modern poetry, where, as she wrote to Osbert, "I'm simply going to let the devils have it." Although she told him nothing about her relations with Pavlik, she complained about Ford, who "pesters me with his poems, and I've half murdered him, but still he continues."[43]

Ford was not the only irritant; the Leavises were proving a great annoyance. In the same letter to Osbert she described a meeting between Leavis and a friend of hers:

Mr. Leavis is small and harassed-looking and does coaching. Mrs. Leavis wears an emerald green jumper and has a dyspeptic-looking nose and eyeglasses. She is, of course, bobbed, and has black hair.[44]

The most appalling feature to Edith was the drink Leavis gave her friend, namely Cydrax: "I don't know if you know what that is, but it is a *non*-alcoholic drink."[45]

At Levanto, in Italy, where Edith had taken Helen to convalesce, her malicious humour did not desert her. Rounding off the letter to Osbert, she told him, referring to a certain lady friend:

X was in grand form. She was looking more like Hannen Swaffer [the journalist] than ever and was dressed with unusual splendour, bracelets of lucky gold pigs, ramps of pearls . . . but as a homely touch amidst all this splendour, she wore large check bedroom slippers. These caused a certain amount of interest. . . . On being told that Pavlik was painting a new portrait of me she said, in a burst of uncontrollable enthusiasm, "Ah 'ow I would love to be deported to ancient Greece where burning Sappho loved and sang" [*sic*]. Then looking round the room, feeling that something had gone wrong somewhere, she added, "And where the boys were ryging beauties and all the ryge". Sensation. Curtain. Shortly afterwards she was withdrawn from circulation much to my grief.[46]

Edith had been working on her volume of criticism, which was to be called *Aspects of Modern Poetry*. For her it was an ideal way to attack the poets and critics she disliked, and to praise those she was fond of. The book included a chapter on Sachie's poems. She always adopted the role of the elder sister and, believing in his poetry, refused to be prevented from saying he was a great poet because "he happens to be my brother."[47] She had an absolute determination to encourage his work, no matter what the outcome. From Levanto she sent him a draft of her essay on his work, but he was embarrassed and tactfully told her so. "Your letter," she replied, "hurt me most terribly, indeed it upset me so much that I have been unable to answer it before." Edith told him that she could not conceive how he had misunderstood her essay, explaining that the book was being written "so as to include that essay. I gave infinitely more thought, more care and more time to it than any other in the book, and everyone who has written to me about the book says it is one of the best."[48]

Taking a break from her prose, she spent a brief holiday with Osbert in Brides-les-Bains. There she met "a very pushing Swiss woman who had been told that Osbert was a famous author, so gushed at him a lot. She talked about Virginia, Eliot, Pound, Lawrence etc., and then asked me if I wrote under my name. I replied, 'I do, but you could not have heard of me. My brother, however, does not write under his own name. He writes under the name of Clemence Dane.' The Swiss lady clasped her hands, she rolled her eyes and said, 'But she is great, your Dane, she is as great as your Galsworthy, as your Barrie, as your Walpole.' I said, 'She is. And in my brother you behold her.' The news spread like wildfire and Osbert used to sit surrounded by quite a little court of admirers of *Will Shakespeare, A Bill of Divorcement*, etc."[49] Edith had no particular dislike for the West End dramatist, but the joke amused her because Dane's work was so unlike Osbert's.

When Edith returned to Paris, "her 'ell," Lady Ida, and Sir George descended on her, but she refused to miss the Christmas season to please them. With *Aspects of Modern Poetry* to be finished, she told her parents she was unable to see them because her book was already a fortnight late and she was scribbling four thousand words a day. To complicate matters, Duckworth's had inadvertently advertised her book as including an essay on W. H. Davies, which she had not written, and that had to be rushed off at the last minute. Hasty preparation of the book was to tell against Edith, but in writing it she was only concerned to praise some poets, attack others, and, of course, rap certain critics. Since *The Apes of God*, Lewis had been on her mind and with her piece on him she set the tone of the book:

Now Mr. Lewis, in spite of all his boyish playfulness, in spite of that Boy Scout Movement for Elderly Boys called *The Enemy*, in spite of being, as you might say, a Regular Pickle, has a strong vein of sentimentality underlying all his brusqueness. Just as, in that long plaint, *The Apes of God*, in the midst of worrying about those who do, or do not issue or accept invitations to lunch, tea or dinner, live in studios, or pretend to be young, he longs for his friends to love him, he longs to be *understood*. Oh, will not *somebody* be kind?[50]

Lewis, Grigson, and Leavis formed the Unholy Trinity who were given slaps, and of course they did not take them lying down. A furious row broke out when the book was published in November 1934. Edith was accused of plagiarizing from the hated Leavis's *New Bearings in English Poetry* as well as from Herbert Read's *Form in Modern Poetry*. The battle went on for weeks, each side calling up various supporters. Amongst Edith's was a young lawyer called John Sparrow (later Warden of All Souls College, Oxford) who in fact, unknown to everyone, had previously reviewed it anonymously (as was the practice at the time) in *The Times Literary Supplement*. Sparrow's legalistic mind managed to produce many points in Edith's favour, but it was Edith who rounded off the battle in December with a final whack.

There is little doubt that Edith *did* plagiarize, and it seems puzzling that she "borrowed" from the people whom she despised so much, Leavis and Herbert Read. (Read, she said once, "twittered".) Leavis had a critical acceptance and was widely read by others, but still Edith thought no one would believe for a second that she would steal from an enemy. It is easy to see that, weighed down as she was by the misery she felt over Helen's illness and the combined malice and neglect shown her by Pavlik, she was in no mood for any original research. The impatience she felt for Helen and Pavlik was relieved by hitting the critics instead.

If one is to analyse this polemic, Grigson was the worthier target, as Leavis had made only one remark and never replied to her outbursts. Grigson had written about her *Five Variations on a Theme* in 1933:

Miss Sitwell we know. Ingredients: Peel, Early Dryden, Pope, a soupçon of Darley, Beddowes and Shelley, two fluid ounces of Rimbaud and a pint of Synaesthesis. This polychromatic syrup Miss Sitwell pours out by the tumbler, rather than the liqueur glass; and the long, formless poems in this book . . . are indigestible and slightly nauseating. Miss Sitwell's pseudo-baroque mythology can surprise or deceive one no longer. Like the tired refreshment room at the Victoria and Albert Museum, it is pretentious and tiresome.[51]

That sort of unhelpful "critical" writing was in the same bantering style as the part of Edith's *Aspects* that dealt with Grigson. Edith's critical writing was coloured by the fact that although she had a marvellous eye for quotation, she had no facility for evaluation beyond her own personal methods of looking at technique. The battle over *Aspects* had been noticed by Arthur Waley, who was a close friend of Sachie's. Waley was well aware how sensitive Edith was to any criticism, and decided the time had come for her to call a halt to her fights.

Dear Edith,

I spent a lovely day reading your poems. The only other thing I have
done was to hear a Mozart Concerto and that fitted in very well. I
have read poetry in about ten languages and know none that, for technical skill and variety, surpasses yours. You, Sachie and Eliot . . . are
the only modern English poets who seem to me to be of any importance. I can't imagine passing such a day as this has been with any
other living poet's work (except Sachie's). Eliot one would have
finished before breakfast.[52]

Having given Edith praise, he went on:

Has anyone in a printed review ever said anything that has been useful to you in your work? If not, please give up reading reviews. Get
the cuttings sent to, say Georgia, who could send anything on that was
not too irritating. Nothing is gained by trying to down critics. It only
leads to your wasting in controversy time that is precious for your
work. I wonder if Helen Rootham would agree about this. If I saw her
I should try very hard to make her take this view. Living with you,
she must have a great influence in that sort of direction.[53]

Waley's advice had no effect on Edith at all, and the fight over
Aspects of Modern Poetry continued to damage her reputation,
as Waley had foreseen. The book also showed that she had no
sympathy with the poets of the Left. Although she pretended to
admire Auden when he had become famous, she never really
liked his work, as she made clear in *Aspects*. Naturally, in later
life she wished to expunge her references to Spender and Auden,
"as they are now personal friends,"[54] but in truth she never
believed that poetry and politics mixed, and could never give
these poets her full enthusiasm.

SEVEN

The Black Sun

Helen and I left for Paris.
My life there was unmitigated hell.

Taken Care Of

AFTER the public battles died down, Edith found herself once
more enmeshed in personal vendettas. Pavlik was intent on going
to America, at the suggestion of Ford, and was hoping to profit
from the rich New York art patrons. Edith was equally determined to stop his visit, for she disliked Ford's influence. Late in
December 1934 she had heard from Allen that

precious Mr. Ford has done nothing to help, and that Pavlik knows,
but nevertheless he passes the time freely with this little horror. Allen
is evidently very sad, and he says that Pavlik treats him coldly and has
given his affection to this nauseating creature.[1]

She wrote to Osbert, who advised Pavlik that it was not a good
financial time for buying in America. This failed—Pavlik insisted
that he would go nevertheless. Choura was also annoyed with her
brother, as she had almost no money and depended on him for
support; Edith suggested to her that she could perhaps knit for a
certain shop in Paris. Edith was also feeling anxious about Allen
Tanner, who had been left behind; she believed now that he had

been a good friend to Pavlik, "and I think he would miss him a great deal. And I fear a long procession of Fords, which would be very sad. . . ."[2]

The only consolation for Edith was that Cecil Beaton was also going to America, "and he will be *very* useful to Pavlik. I've written to him about it, because he knows everyone over there. . . ."[3] The farewell was a minor disaster. Edith said good-bye to Pavlik and on the way back from the station caught a chill. Then, to make things worse, Helen's sister, Evelyn, "laid a booby trap in the shape of a turned up rug"[4] and Edith sprained her wrist.

As the year 1935 passed, things showed no signs of improving. In August, just before she was leaving Paris for England, a letter written by Pavlik from America caused a bitter row. Edith had written to him detailing information that apparently contained some evidence against him, which he refused to accept.

. . . I've been made totally ill by the letter I received . . . from Pavlik. He told me that . . . he doesn't believe in the existence of the letter about which I spoke to him, and that he wouldn't believe it even if I sent it to him. That I have shown myself to be vulgar, insensitive and hard and that he is revolted. . . . When I think of the seven years of our friendship, during which I showed him a very great and true affection, I can't understand how he *can* think me capable of this conduct. . . .[5]

Edith had accepted that Pavlik's homosexuality caused him problems:

I understand only too well the moral suffering, believe me. —What Pavlik doesn't understand is that which is more annoying, his manner of entering into passionate friendships with very inferior people . . . like Mr. [Peter] Watson [the future financier of *Horizon*, a wartime arts magazine] and Cecil Beaton then neglects me all the time for them, and when they show themselves in their true colours, he complains to me. Pavlik behaved himself very badly in England under the influence of Cecil, and it was too much when he began to complain about Cecil to me. . . .[6]

Edith's nerves were completely exhausted over Pavlik; but there was London, followed by a visit to Weston Hall to look forward to. Osbert had insisted that she return to England, and Edith had been only too happy to agree. She passed the time pleasantly, going to parties given by the Courtaulds [Samuel and his wife] and also attending a Garden Party at Buckingham Palace.

But there was soon more trouble with Pavlik. It had been rumoured that he had formed an affection for Djuna Barnes, the American novelist (probably the matter referred to in the letter Pavlik refused to believe in). Edith complained to Choura:

All Pavlik's friends here are feeling sorry for Miss Barnes because Pavlik has not married her yet. They are saying that he has treated her very badly. I have told them that it is *none* of my business, and that it has no interest whatsoever for me. That they should go and make their complaints directly to Pavlik, for I can do nothing, and in any case, I think she has found consolation elsewhere. But people tell me that she is whining and snivelling the whole time. I have also told them that in my opinion Pavlik has been very nice to her; and I don't know what she's got to complain about. . . .[7]

Despite the depressing situation between herself and Pavlik, Edith found time and the humour to tease T. S. Eliot. He had declined an invitation she had given him to a cocktail party, but had hoped Edith might see him before he left London. As she wrote to Choura:

. . . So today, I have written a letter to him:
"My dear Tom, what has happened? I stayed at home all afternoon waiting for you as was arranged. I hope that you are not ill?" And tomorrow, I will write him a letter *dated last Saturday:* "My dear Tom, would you like to come and see me on Tuesday afternoon; unless you write to the contrary, I shall be waiting for you. . . ."
I don't know what he'll be able to do, and will be highly amused to see. . . .[8]

Christmas was spent in Spain, and gloomily Edith noted that she had only two letters from Pavlik,

written on the boat and posted in New York. I don't know his address, so I wrote to him c/o his dealer, for Christmas. But I don't like writing there, since I think that my letters will be opened. I suppose all the horrors, Cecil, Soapy [Peter Watson] etc., will be there. It's a great pity.[9]

By now she was becoming obsessed with jealousy about Pavlik, tortured by her ignorance of what he was doing. This is probably behind her acid reference to Beaton, because in fact her relations with him had been perfectly friendly and would be in the future, and there was nothing to inspire this bitterness, except the present circumstances. She was liable to twist facts if she had even a small idea about someone, which no evidence to the contrary would remove. Otherwise she enjoyed Spain, apart from the noise of hammering all the time, and then "all the men from this little town come to this café every evening and yell sometimes (it is right under my bedroom) till three in the morning."[10]

Meanwhile, Pavlik was still in America, and Edith managed to persuade Beaton to introduce him to successful and wealthy friends. He had another exhibition, which did not go well, but Beaton tactfully told Edith it had been successful. She replied to Beaton in March 1935:

I am so delighted to get your letter and hear what a wonderful success Pavlik is having. He thoroughly deserves it. Poor Pavlik, he was so unhappy, and everything was so beastly. It is lovely for him your being there and it makes all the difference having a great friend there.[11]

How Edith must have choked as she wrote those words, for she felt she was now forced to endure Beaton so that he could report back Pavlik's behaviour with Ford to her.

She completed her work on the life of Queen Victoria in December 1935, and sent it to her publisher Faber & Faber. Exhausted and bored, Edith could not face starting another book. But she always found poetry an antidote to tiredness and was startled to discover what she regarded as a remarkable poem by one Dylan Thomas, in a copy of *Life and Letters*. Thomas's work was already known to Edith, and she had not liked it. Without naming the writer, she had attacked Thomas's poem *Our Eunuch Dreams* in her *Aspects of Modern Poetry*.

Thomas had not been pleased, and had complained to a friend:

So you've been reviewing Edith Sitwell's latest piece of virgin dung, have you? Isn't she a poisonous thing of a woman, lying, concealing, flipping, plagiarising, misquoting, and being as clever a crooked literary publicist as ever. . . . Yes, that was my poem, absurdly criticised. I duly sent my protest to Gerald Duckworth and he replied to the effect that so many protests of a similar sort had been received, that he could, as yet, do nothing about it. It is being hoped that he will have to withdraw the book. . . .[12]

Thomas's hopes had come to nothing, and neither had the promise from Duckworth, which was presumably conveniently forgotten. Thomas had shown some admiration for Edith's and Sachie's poetry in a school essay, but any feelings he had about Edith had probably changed by now under the influence of his friend Geoffrey Grigson. Later Thomas fell out with Grigson, who then recanted his praise for the poet and derogated his verse. In January 1936 Edith wrote to Thomas:

Dear Mr. Thomas,
Though we have never met, I am unable to resist writing to tell you however inadequately, with what deep admiration and delight I have read your very beautiful poem, which begins with the title, A Grief Ago.

Edith also wrote that she did not "remember being so moved by the work of any poet of the younger generation, or when I felt such a deep certainty that there is a poet with all the capabilities and potentialities of greatness." Edith referred to her attack on her Aspects of Modern Poetry, saying, ". . . I must confess the first poem I read of yours I did not like, technically,—and felt it my duty to say so. . . ."[13] Privately she had written to Christabel Aberconway, a friend of Osbert's, and told her that A Grief Ago was not one of Thomas's best poems, "but I do think he stands a chance of becoming a great poet, if only he gets rid of his complexes. He is only twenty-one. . . ."[14]

Thomas, however surprised he must have been at Edith's letter, was delighted and showed it to his mother. He wrote a long reply which shows just how eager he was to please Edith:

I shouldn't be able to thank you enough for your letter, so I won't try, but I loved it, and I'll owe you a lot always for your encouragement. No, of course, I don't care a damn for an audience or for "success", but it is exciting—I suppose it's the only external reward—to have things liked for the reasons one writes them, to be believed in by someone who's right outside the nasty schools and the clever things one (me) doesn't want to understand, like surrealism and Cambridge quarterlies, and communism and the Pope of Rome. . . .[15]

Thomas explained that he had no money at all, apart from what his poems and stories brought in, and mentioned his "few rowdy habits." Edith was to become familiar with his "rowdy habits," at least by repute, but she always declared that he behaved perfectly towards her whenever they met. That was all in the future; in a second letter of Thomas's a meeting was arranged for February 18, and Edith promised him dinner at her club.

Now that her flat in London was gone, Edith had joined the Sesame Imperial and Pioneer Club, in Grosvenor Street. It had been suggested by Georgia, who was already a member, and although predominantly a club for women, it was mixed. The Sesame, as it was known, was to be the meeting place for all Edith's literary protégés. Robert Herring, the editor of *Life and Letters*, was also asked to the dinner with Thomas, and Edith reaffirmed her belief in Thomas's work to him:

. . . the more I read young Thomas's poems, the more certain I am that he is the coming man. Is not the progress he has made during the last eighteen months extraordinary? . . . will it bore you if we discuss them [his poems] at dinner? I want to ask him some questions and also give some advice. . . .[16]

Not only was Edith anxious to adopt the role of Thomas's sybilline adviser, she wanted to be practical. They would go round to Duckworth's, and then meet Mr. Wilson of Bumpus, a London bookshop, in the hope of finding a job. Dylan replied gratefully in his second letter to her:

Are you sure you really don't mind taking this on, all this trouble? I'm so very grateful to you. You must have listened to a great deal of woes of young poets. And to take a regular job is the most sensible suggestion in the world.[17]

Edith had indeed listened to the woes of Tom Driberg and Brian Howard, who had come to little as poets. Thomas was young enough to be "managed," or so Edith thought. He was worried about meeting the "grande dame" of forty-nine and was too terrified of her to misbehave, so all went well. Edith was completely charmed.

In May "bloody" *Victoria of England* appeared, and it was an enormous success. It was not a book that produced any surprises, but Edith's work on the Widow of Windsor managed to convey her sympathetic understanding of Victoria's life, especially her childhood. As in all her prose books, there was nothing conventional about her approach to her subject, and what her book on Victoria lacked in scholarly method was compensated for by her original and imaginative reconstruction of the known facts.

By August she had received £356 from her publishers; the first printing of 4,000 copies had immediately sold out, and the book went into another impression of the same number. It was also taken by a book club and bought by Houghton Mifflin in America. The sudden popularity of *Victoria* had surprised Edith, but its success was perhaps due to Edith's having no personal feelings for her subject. There was no reason for any identification with Victoria, as there had been with Pope, and the book was better written as a result. The historical subject had been a refreshing change because there were no literary allusions, except to Tennyson, whom Edith liked.

There were complaints that Edith had plagiarized again—this time from Lytton Strachey's *Queen Victoria.* "Old Jane at it again," Wyndham Lewis wrote of Edith to Geoffrey Grigson. "Have you seen her Victoria?" Grigson had, and reviewed it, complaining that Edith had "devitalised . . . the Queen and everyone else into wax fruit."

Anxious to avoid charges of plagiarism, Edith had written in her preface: . . . "if a common stock of information has been drawn upon she hopes at least to plead a different treatment of necessarily similar material."

At that moment Edith did not care what Grigson and Lewis thought, because the other press reviews were almost entirely favourable. *The Spectator* considered it was "a book of great beauty," and *The Times* thought it was "a sincere and moving portrait of a great sovereign." Most pleasing of all was the notice from *The Observer,* which declared that "her canvas invites immediate comparison with Mr. Strachey's. But it is at once broader and warmer than his. . . ." So much for Grigson!

The financial rewards of *Victoria* meant that there was the chance of her staying in England in a new flat. There would be no question of plagiarizing in her next book, for Edith was considering a first novel. It would be a new technical experiment, and a means by which she would write out her private grief without fear of exposure. A letter from Yeats had pleased her, asking if he could include some of her poems in his edition of the *Oxford Book of Modern Verse.* Yeats had made broadcasts about her work and boosted her morale by saying that the critics "sometimes attack Miss Edith Sitwell who seems to me an important poet." Yeats had also told the poet Dorothy Wellesley that

THE BLACK SUN   123

"the two Sitwells have their own great qualities" (Edith had sent
Yeats Sachie's *Canons of Giant Art*), and while he was preparing
the anthology he "re-read all Edith Sitwell and found her very
hard to select from, poem is so dependant upon poem. It is like
cutting a piece out of a tapestry."[18]

So pleased was Edith by being included in the extremely eccentric choice (Wilfred Owen was left out because of Yeats's prejudice and undue prominence given to women he had been in
love with, like Margaret Ruddock and Dorothy Wellesley, whom
Edith incidentally disliked) that she declined her much needed
fee. Taking advantage of this, Yeats wrote to thank her:

I am most grateful. I had a fixed sum of £500 and the O.U.P. pointed
out to me that a previous Anthologist had expended £150 of that sum
on authors and kept the remainder. I have exceeded the sum by £200
or £250. . . . Now I am going to ask you to extend your generosity
even further. . . .[19]

He wanted to make a broadsheet out of *The King of China's
Daughter*. Edith, recalling the letter years later, said:

I gave him the poems of mine that he put into his anthology and then
he asked for "The King of China's Daughter" to be set to music and
performed at the Abbey Theatre in Dublin for the sum of one pound.
Of course I couldn't refuse, but . . .[20]

Yeats in fact offered a guinea. The anthology appeared and Edith
wrote to thank him:

It is the greatest pride and delight to me that you should have chosen
poems of mine to appear in the book *The Oxford Book of Modern
Verse,* a most inspiring book full of beautiful works which I did not
know before. . . . I am absolutely shocked and horrified at what you
tell me about the enormous sum which has had to be paid to authors
and the fact that a large part of the payment will have to devolve
from you. What can they be thinking of? They have no sense either of
reverence or of gratitude. I think it is quite disgraceful.[21]

Edith told Yeats she considered the rival anthology *The Faber
Book of Modern Verse* to be "the . . . most tone-deaf and fum-
bling collection of modern verse ever produced."[22] Obviously
Edith did not know that Yeats was tone-deaf, but if he had no ear
for music he at least had great enthusiasm for the Rosicrucians,
and on the strength of their new alliance he tried to convert

Edith. She was not convinced, for she thought it was "such a strain and so bad for the clothes as it seems to lead to sandals and blue veils."

Helen, too, had gone through various semi-religious fads during her illness. Her mind had grown more disturbed, and Edith realized that any hope of living in England had to be abandoned because there was no one to look after Helen. Her illness was first diagnosed as inoperable cancer of the bone, and it was Edith's money that would be required to pay for the doctor's fees. When she had been strong enough, Helen had managed to give piano and singing lessons, but that small income had now come to an end. In September 1936 Edith told David Horner, Osbert's companion, in a letter from Paris, that "the poor woman suffers a good deal of pain, and *never mentions it*. One just sees her going green, and a terrified look appearing in her eyes."[23]

Edith was spared the actual nursing by Helen's sister, Evelyn Wiel, who was a trained nurse, but who took it upon herself to boss Edith as well as tend Helen, which became a trial. Unlike Helen, who had influenced Edith's poetry by introducing her to French poets, Evelyn did not understand her and made little impression. Edith often inscribed her books to her: "to Evelyn who never reads anything." But she had to be endured.

Pavlik also had to be endured, and Edith was not looking forward to his return from America. His unpopularity extended throughout the family—for some reason, after he had stayed with Soapy (Peter Watson), he had quarrelled with Osbert. Edith commented:

He insisted on taking Soapy and Mr. Ford here and everywhere, and introducing them to everyone; it was just the same the year before . . . and *frankly* they are all three of them *impossible*, especially for the English.[24]

Pavlik returned from America with Charles Henri Ford still in tow, but Edith somehow managed to be "very amiable to him, and am paying no attention to him whatsoever. I must say that he brought me the most lovely bag from America. . . ."[25] Edith knew that if he had survived America with Ford he would also be keeping house with him in France. Her attitude was ambiguous; while she could not forgive his behaviour, she nevertheless invented excuses for him and went on seeing him. She would have written off anyone else, but at the very least with Pavlik there was always the attraction that he would paint her.

In October he began a new portrait. The result, completed in 1937, seems to express her sadness. She is clothed in a kind of sackcloth, holding a quill pen, and looking pale and washed out. It was the nearest he got to an actual representation of her, and Edith, flattered by his intuitive understanding of her, was "frightfully pleased."

For a time it seemed that Helen was responding to radium treatment and was a little better, although Edith herself was becoming ill. Her physician suggested that she should go with Helen to Levanto. "I have become such a sylph," Edith wrote to Georgia, "that you won't know me. My face has returned to that awful haggard, famished look like a vulture, that made me once the most hated woman in England. (I wonder why it always annoys people so much?)"[26]

Helen and Edith left for Italy early in 1937, and if Edith had left some of her problems behind they were still not far from her mind. Work began on her novel, which was to be called *I Live Under a Black Sun*. It was to be the expression of her own unhappy relationship with Pavlik disguised as fiction. Whether it was also an indirect means of letting Pavlik know just how she felt is impossible to say, but Edith would feel a certain sense of release in being able to write down her own problems under this guise. It was the only time that she ever exposed her deepest emotions and feelings in prose.

Not long after they had arrived in Levanto in March, she took up her pen on behalf of Dylan Thomas by writing to the journalist Richard Jennings. The wonder boy had been having treatment for venereal disease and was consequently in hiding. Edith did not know this and wrote angrily:

My dear Richard,
The last time we corresponded it was on the subject of Master Thomas, who is rapidly heading for having his ears boxed. I can feel the tips of my fingers tingling to come in contact with the lobes of his ears. And it would do him a lot of good, for he was evidently insufficiently corrected as a child. *What* a tiresome boy that is, although a very gifted one. Having given us all that trouble, caused me to pester you and to write dozens of letters to busy people who must

now curse the name of Sitwell—he has now disappeared again—disappeared without leaving a trace. I have had reproachful letters from this person and that, reproving *me* because *he*, after getting *me* to ask *them* to give *him* an appointment, hasn't kept it. But not a word can we get from him. This disappearance trick seems to be a habit with the younger generation. They ought to join Maskelyne and Devants, for they would make a fortune of the place and we should see a recandescence of interest in magic. I'm practically Master Thomas's secretary now, as everyone who can't find him—(and nobody can)—addresses his letters care of me, and I have to readdress them.[27]

With the success of *Victoria,* Edith was able to send Thomas a little money with her letter, and he must have heard that he had been in the doghouse, for he wrote her a long and tactful letter in August from Cornwall:

20th August 1937

Dear Miss Sitwell,
Before anything else I want to thank you with all my heart for your great generosity and graciousness. Caitlin and I thank you for the lovely present with which we bought all sorts of things we wanted from knives and towels to a Garbo picture and paid off the clamourers. And to the man who gave me the present you enclosed, all I can say is "Thank you". I shan't ever be impertinent about his name, but I shall always think of him with gratitude. He must be a kind and splendid person.

And now I want to apologize for this apparently very rude and disrespectful delay in answering and acknowledging your present and letters. I'm awfully bad with letters, I know, but I couldn't be unmannerly or unappreciative enough to let a reply like this linger on through slackness or carelessness.

For the last ten days I have been in and out on the Newlyn fishing boats, making a little money and hardly been on shore at all during the daytime. I've just been snatching a few hours of sleep when I can, too utterly tired in head and every limb to write even the shortest sentence of gratitude for all you've done and are doing for me. This sounds weak, but it honestly is true. Sometimes over twelve hours in a rough sea in a twelve foot boat. My job is over now and I can start thinking again, not moving all the time in a kind of fish-eyed daze.

It is wonderful of you to take all this trouble in trying to get me some work, I'm sure, aren't you, that something must come out of it?

Almost above all, I should like some connection with the B.B.C. I've

done one broadcast of my own poems, and of a few poems by
[Arthur] Ransome and Auden on the West Regional programme,
and I was told that it went down quite well. That was late in April
this year and no-one's got in touch with me since. I love reading
poems aloud and I do hope Mr. Main will succeed in making the
B.B.C. interested enough to let me read some more. All those little
ninny five minute readings with a death at the end of each line. I
wouldn't mind anyway.

I should enjoy very much reading some of Sacheverell Sitwell's
poems if the B.B.C. and he, sometime allowed me: it's great and
grand aloud, isn't it? Pillars and columns and great striding figures
through a microphone.

I am writing to-day to Peter Quennell [the poet, critic, and biogra-
pher], though I know him very slightly from parties, and I'll send
Miss Reynolds my three or four new poems. A friend of mine is typing
my new story and as soon as it is finished I'll send it to you along with
the poems. I do so much want you to read them; I'm not sure of them
at all; I hope you'll tell me all about them; sometimes I'm afraid they
caricature themselves.

Life here has at last become too much even for us, who don't
demand great comforts. With smells from the fish market in front of
us, and dust from the coal yard below us, and flies from the dump
behind us we might as well live in the street. Our studio is haunted
too, and last month the landscape painter next door hanged himself
from the rafters. So we are going to go to Wales for some time, to my
mother's house. Sailing around to North Devon in fishing boats and
making our way as best we can across to Swansea, it shouldn't take us
more than a week. We start about September 1st.

I do hope this change of address won't be awkward. If any of the
people you've asked to help me want to get in touch immediately my
mother's address is, Marsto, Bishopston, near Swansea, Glamorgan.

It's impossible for me to tell you how deeply I appreciate your
kindness. I value your friendship. I'll always remember it.

Caitlin thanks you very much for your message, she's looking forward to meeting you. I hope we can all meet in London soon, and I
hope sincerely that your friend in Paris will get better.

All my gratefulness and apologies,

Yours very sincerely,

DYLAN THOMAS[28]

Thomas probably thought Edith was the Lady Bountiful, but
despite *Victoria*, which at the time was selling 150 copies per day

at a cost of fifteen shillings a copy, her finances were again in a
bad way. On February 27, 1937, her banker had written:

Dear Miss Sitwell,
Thank you for your letter but I am sorry to hear that you have been a
victim of the wretched influenza. . . . I'm glad to hear that Miss
Rootham had derived some benefit from the light ray treatment . . .
what a blessing it will be if they can succeed in destroying the root of
the trouble.

It is very kind of you to suggest sending me a copy of your new
novel, and I look forward to the happy hours I shall enjoy reading it.

I am afraid my letter will not be complete unless I touch on the disagreeable subject of finance and in this connection I notice the present
overdraft is rather high (about £935) but I note with pleasure that
you expect to send funds in April and I hope that your book will
prove to be a best seller and that after July overdrafts will only be a
horrid nightmare of the past. However, I note that during your stay at
Levanto you expect to live cheaply and I trust that this will have the
effect of improving the financial outlook. . . .[29]

The novel was "getting on very well" and she told Geoffrey
Gorer's mother that it was, of her own work, "the only prose
book (excepting for criticism) that I've ever been pleased with."
Levanto was not, however, much of a holiday. Driven by financial worry, she had to begin work at 5:30 A.M., to ensure peace,
for the hotel "has changed sadly. The food is worse, the noise
awful, and it is infested with gibberingly appalling people."[30] But
lighter moments brightened up the days and Pavlik's sister was
Edith's confidante:

The hotel is full of English . . . products of the empire . . . they knew
quite well that I am not a lady. There is a little Captain who kisses me
when his wife is not looking . . . unfortunately the only people in the
hotel who want to speak to me have learnt that Willie Walton is my
adopted brother and now all the high society want to know someone
who knows a famous man! But I show my profile and not my full
face.[31]

Choura, apparently, did not receive all of Edith's letters, and
Edith was worried that she would lose her friendship with her
and thus her one hope of keeping in contact with Pavlik. She
wrote to Choura:

My dear, I would never go to Paris without seeing you. I will always
write to you, that goes without saying. There is nothing in the world

which could come between us because I like you so much. I have very
few true friends and I would never be so beastly or wicked to quarrel
with one of my closest friends.[32]

As there was no chance of Edith going to Paris before the end of
June, because her novel had to be finished, she implored Choura
to write even a little note when she had her letter because "I am
afraid that this might get lost as well."

Edith's sense of desolation was not helped by having to work
on her novel. "It makes me cry so frightfully, I am hardly fit to
be seen. It is rough stuff and no doubt about it," she wrote.[33] Because Edith was so involved in the subject matter of her novel,
the guests in the hotel seemed to grate on her nerves more than
ever. Their society conversation bored her, and Edith was not exaggerating when she declared she retreated to her bedroom every
night "nearly dead with fatigue."[34]

This was an example of how, in her creative work, Edith gave
her whole self to whatever she was working on. The anguish she
suffered writing her novel was not helped by a nasty letter she received from Pavlik. He accused her of saying something unkind
about Ford's family, and while this was quite probably true, his
latest attack only reinforced the sense of bitterness Edith felt for
him, and her resolve to write about it in her book.

Helen's illness did not help Edith's state of mind. It was not
her fault that she was lying in a room next to Edith's, suffering
great pain; but neither was it Edith's fault, and she had to share
the burden. Torn between guilt at not being sympathetic enough
towards Helen and her sense of purpose and duty as a writer,
Edith decided that they had better return to Paris, where Helen
could be looked after by her sister, Evelyn. Exhausted and anxious about her ill friend, Edith herself suffered an attack of bronchitis when she later returned to England, in June.

Unexpectedly, in July 1937, news came from Sachie that Lady
Ida was seriously ill and had gone into a nursing home. Apparently their mother had returned from Italy with Sir George
and after a few days in London had felt unwell. Pneumonia had
been diagnosed, and after ten days in the nursing home she died.
Sachie went to see his mother during her last illness and found
her mentally alert. She had always been a gifted mimic and
amused Sachie with a skilful imitation of Christabel Aberconway.
He was with his mother when she died.

The funeral was held at the parish church of Weston in Lois Weedon, near Sachie's home in Northamptonshire. Sir George declared that he was too unwell to attend, and remained at the Curzon Hotel, where he had been with his wife before her illness.

Edith was helpful in sorting out some of her mother's affairs, but she was reticent at the time over expressing any feelings about her. She undoubtedly felt a sense of release that the woman she had once hated could no longer trouble her, but she had "forgiven her long ago."[35] It was only later, especially in old age, when Edith looked back over her life, that she was unkind about her mother both publicly and privately. Neither woman had ever really made much effort to understand the other. They had rarely met in recent years, except at what had become the traditional family meeting each August at Renishaw. This potentially explosive meeting was something that Edith, Osbert, and Sachie had always dreaded because there were repeated wrangles with Sir George over money. But although a duty visit, it was bearable for both Edith and her mother at least, simply because it was virtually their only meeting; it would have been impossible had they seen more of each other.

After Lady Ida's death the question arose of Sir George's future. Problems between him and Lady Ida had also lessened as they grew older, and Sir George had lately depended more on his wife than he would ever care to admit.

A young friend of Osbert and Sachie's, Francis Bamford, was solicited to become companion and secretary to their father. Bamford had helped edit *Dear Miss Heber*, a book of family letters found at Weston Hall, and, with his antiquarian interests (he was archivist to Lord Gerald Wellesley, later Duke of Wellington), he was to prove ideal for Sir George. He had been at Renishaw when Lady Ida had died in London, and he recalled a curious story of that day.

Osbert was entertaining friends and had taken them over to nearby Bolsover Castle. Gerald Wellesley had remained behind with Francis Bamford to measure a wall for a bookcase. When the door bell rang it was left unanswered until Bamford remembered that the servants were out. He went to the door, and the figure of a woman entered the house without a word and climbed the stairs leading from the hall. Nothing was thought of the incident until Osbert returned, when he received a telegram giving the news of Lady Ida's death. Francis Bamford then described the mysterious figure he had seen and Osbert identified her as his mother. It seemed she had returned to Renishaw at the moment of her death.

Sir George visited Renishaw briefly and soon after went off to Italy with his new companion, being now well enough to travel (he was always well enough to do what he wanted). At seventy-seven, he had good health, but he always exaggerated his complaints; hypochondria was one of his worst faults, or one of his greatest hobbies.

With Sir George out of the way and Lady Ida dead, Edith felt able to relax and enjoy a "peaceful time at Renishaw." But the peace was soon to be broken, for, returning to Paris at the end of August 1937, she found Helen's illness had become much worse. In September, Edith's novel, *I Live Under a Black Sun*, was published. Most of the reviews were disappointing, although not as bad as Edith was later to claim. The novelist and critic L. P. Hartley, writing in *The Sketch*, said of the novel:

Anyone who has an understanding of the workings of the heart will find those workings faithfully illustrated here, and anyone who loves literature will realise that they are presented with an originality of outlook and a resourcefulness of craftmanship that deserve the highest praise. Miss Sitwell writes, as one would expect of a poet, with the powers of her mind and imagination always at full stretch. . . .[36]

Evelyn Waugh, in the magazine *Night and Day*, found *I Live Under a Black Sun* to be

like a magnesium flame in a cavern, immediately and abundantly beautiful at first sight, provoking further boundless investigation. It is a book that must be read patiently, more than once, and it must be read. . . .[37]

Writing to the novelist and critic Pamela Hansford Johnson in 1959, Edith thanked her for having written an appreciative review of her novel when it was first published, and revealed that she had never seen the review and had in fact seen only one review, by the poet Wilfrid Gibson, and one "by the late lamented (but not by me) goosie gander Dr. Edwin Muir, who said the book had no point and he didn't know what it was about."[38]

In fact the poet and critic Edwin Muir had given the book a good review and had consistently praised Edith's poetry over the

years. He had been amongst the few who had taken the trouble
to study her early work, which he considered in an essay in the
1920s.

As a basis for the novel Edith used the life and the character of
Swift, but transposed him, with his circle of contemporaries, to
the background of the First World War. Into this already complex tapestry Edith wove her own feelings on some of the female
characters, introduced Allen Tanner in a new fictional role, and
used Pavlik as Swift. Edith, in fact, put all her torn feelings about
Pavlik into the novel, as well as the interrelationships among her
other friends. Her complaint about the lack of appreciation of the
book probably stemmed not so much from what was said as from
the fact that no one realized that she was writing of her own experience and longing to be understood on a personal level. It is
also possible that, because her experience was directly trans-
ferred into the book, Edith thought that her novel would be
remarked upon for its strong sense of reality.

The task of identifying the characters is not easy because sev-
eral of them have dual identities. The main figures are Jonathan
Hare (Pavlik), Anna and Lucy (both Edith), Henry Deringham
(Wyndham Lewis), and Sir Henry Rotheram (Edith's father).
The role Pavlik expected Edith to play in their relationship is
clear from the opening pages of the novel, where Hare declares:

Every human being needs to be believed in, and love is belief. All my
life through all the wretched mess of my poverty . . . I have never
doubted my greatness. . . . I must have someone who believes in me,
who is ready to give up her will to me. . . .[39]

and:

Throughout his life it had been necessary to inhabit another being,
conquer the will of another . . . only thus could he refute his poverty. . . . Now he looked at the woman beside him despairingly,
hopelessly, perceiving her weakness and her fear. She would never
help either himself or him. . . .[40]

Edith had been very worried about Pavlik's prolonged absence
in America. Her fears at the time are identifiable in the novel:
"He cannot be meaning to let me go entirely, or he would not
write to me at all. . . . I must have something in life, some hope,
something in which I can bury my thoughts—something to build.

I cannot believe that now Jonathan is sure of the future he will
bring himself to cast off the woman who has stood by him for so
many years."[41] Edith was now fifty and had arrived at the unhappy realization that she would never marry. It was a revelation
that, if it had ever been seriously considered, had come into full
view too late; bitterly Edith realized that she had

". . . devoted my whole life, the whole of my existence, all my
thoughts to Jonathan for years now, oh yes, for long years." And as she
spoke, the knowledge of the truth of her words, the realization of the
nobility of that selfless sacrifice grew upon her.[42]

I Live Under a Black Sun was a therapeutic, if painful, look at
Edith's private feelings. She had managed to examine her own
thoughts and consider those of Pavlik with considerable objectivity for the first time. The book had forced her to realize the
hopelessness of the relationship; but in reality Edith ran true to
form, and her undying love for Pavlik closed her eyes to the
truths revealed in the agony of composing the novel.

Little long-term benefit derived, therefore, from this self-
analysis. Perhaps one reason Edith always felt so misunderstood
was her inability to transmit her own deeper emotions to other
people. Ready to help others out of a genuine sympathy for them,
she was able to forget some of her own anguished feelings that
way. It was not surprising that in 1948 Edith described her novel
as her "ewe lamb, and I feel about it as I do about my poetry—I
mean, a personal feeling, as if it was part of myself. . . ."[43]

The year 1937 saw more than one Sitwell book reach the shops.
Sachie sent Edith a copy of his *La Vie Parisienne*, a study of
Offenbach, and the lively Paris setting of the book presented a
strong contrast to the gloom within the Rue Saint-Dominique flat.
Writing to thank Sachie in November 1937, Edith told him that
Sir Hugh Walpole, the novelist, had not liked her novel (another
review she had in fact seen), and she commented wryly to her
brother:

I'm so glad Sir Hugh has been made a knight. It means that when he
goes to heaven he will be able to walk in and out of doors in front of
William Shakespeare and Charles Dickens. . . .[44]

This is an example of Edith's habit, almost Shakespearean, of
softening gloomy news by preceding it with humour. It occurs

with great frequency in her letters. Apart from its providing balance, she needed the diversion of amusing incidents in her life just as much as her malicious comments, to take the edge off her own unhappiness. Helen's condition fluctuated from bad to worse, and then sometimes she appeared much better. Now the cancer had spread and Edith felt certain that the end was near—"Yet strangely enough during the last two days, I have hardly dared say it, she seems a little better. They are giving her more morphia than before. . . ."[45]

Despite the lack of appreciation that Edith felt was shown towards her first novel, she was busy planning a new one. She obviously felt happier writing imaginative prose than labouring over non-fiction, and as there was no question of poetry yet, because the advances on prose were much greater, another novel seemed the obvious step. Appealing to Sachie for advice regarding style, Edith wrote: "Please write and tell me: do you think I ought to have less decoration? I'm longing to begin it. I think I am going to call it *Spring Torrents*."[46]

The new novel was never actually written, as Edith was exhausted with worry over Helen. By May of 1938 her illness had reached a new crisis and Edith was told that she was dying. "I got back from Montegufoni ten days ago, to find her delirious and well . . . the rest I won't harrow you with. She is constantly delirious and when she isn't we have death bed scenes."[47]

Edith had found the strain intolerable, and had taken some rooms in a cheap hotel, to allow Evelyn the chance to nurse her sister in the best circumstances possible with everybody else out of the way.

Three times, [Edith told Sachie] I have been sent for because the nurses and Evelyn have thought she was dying. I am obliged to tell you this but don't be too miserable and don't come darling. There is nothing on earth you can do and it is unnecessary for anyone who doesn't have to see and hear all this to see and bear it. Father, realizing that nearly six months of looking after a patient under the worst type of cancer, could not have tried me sufficiently, asked Inez to stay at Montegufoni for the month before I left. . . . I've never known her to be such an absolutely hell-borne nuisance.[48]

Inez Chandos-Pole was a cousin of Edith's whom Sir George was fond of. Her family lived in Derbyshire and had no particular appeal for Edith. Sir George, on the other hand, liked keeping up with his relations, and kept in close touch with Inez's father, Colonel Chandos-Pole. (The Chandos-Poles were later to play a dramatic part at the end of Sir George's own life.) Inez had told Edith that she thought she had cancer because she had a terrible pain. That was enough for Edith, who replied that all she had was wind in the stomach, "because cancer never begins with pain. . . ."[49]

Helen lingered on until the end of May 1938, when she finally died. Her death was a relief to Edith, but also a terrible shock. There is very little hard evidence about the influence of Helen Rootham over Edith, except a few references in Osbert's autobiography, but it was great and formative. Edith may have destroyed any letters she had, and also any photographs, for none seems to have survived.

Sir William Walton, for one, did not like Helen, finding her rather overbearing, and "rather a Yugoslav type."[50] Her interest in various faddish semi-mystical cults bored Edith; and to give her more down-to-earth interests, Edith and others introduced Helen to various undesirable men, whom she fell in love with. Amongst them, it was said, was the painter Wassily Kandinsky, but Sachie has said she was in love with Ivan Meštrović, the great Yugoslav sculptor.

It appears from mysterious notes made by Edith that while Helen was dying but still well enough to be up, she was visited by a man whom she loved but who had always ignored her while she was still a threat. Edith had been furious at his treatment of Helen and had taken him aside and told him just how shabbily he had behaved. He had used as an excuse his "mystical" nature, which Edith told him was nonsense.

Edith was loyal to Helen, and in extreme circumstances quick to speak up in her defence, despite the difficult past. In her memoirs, *Taken Care Of*, Edith's last word on her old governess was:

Poor Helen! She had been so good and kind when I was a child and very young girl, and I shall never forget that.
Her death was very terrible.[51]

EIGHT

Return to Renishaw

I am afraid we are all a dreadful disappointment to the dear
sweet-minded Germans, and have not given them quite the welcome they expected. . . . My God, I hope we continue to give
them the thrashing they deserve. . . .

Letter to Ree Gorer

WITH HELEN'S DEATH Edith felt disorientated. There was
still Evelyn, who went with her to leave flowers on Helen's grave.
Despite her faults, Edith was grateful for her company in the
months they were left alone in the Rue Saint-Dominique. She
even felt grateful for it, but the one person she desperately
wanted to see now that she was freer in her movements was
Pavlik. He did not come near her, or offer his help in any way,
and his neglect was made all the worse because his work was
now enjoying a success in England that he had not achieved before, much of which was due to Edith's help.

Pavlik was still in England in June, and Edith had also left
France for the annual family gathering at Renishaw. She hoped
to see Pavlik alone in London, but when she went to visit him he
was too preoccupied with Ford, who was also there, to bother
with Edith. Pavlik was totally unsympathetic to Edith's feelings
and, criticizing her black mourning dress, told her rudely that it
made her "look like a gigantic orphan."[1] There was no one left to

complain to except Tanner, who had now lost Pavlik's friendship. He no doubt agreed with Edith when she said to him that Ford was a

perfectly worthless parasite, with no gifts, and a thorough slum type, throwing his weight about in England, and I am powerless to do anything. . . . P. does not mind what pain he inflicts on one. . . .[2]

For some time in the early months of 1939 Edith could not work and instead helped to sort out Helen's affairs. She remained in Paris, where her agent, David Higham, suggested that she could go on a lecture tour of America. A visit to America seemed exactly right to take her out of the vacuum she was in. But once she had clinched her contract she felt she was regarded as something akin to "a trick cyclist" by her American tour agent, Colston Leigh.

"Next they'll want me to deliver my lecture cycling round and round the platform balanced on my nose with my feet in the air, and declaiming at the same time on the effect of texture on the caesural"[3] Edith declared. So the lectures in America fell through, and life in Paris continued in the same oppressive vein; "Moby Dick," as she called Evelyn Wiel, was still annoying her; they both had flu and Edith noticed that Evelyn "succeeded in producing the phenomenon of, at the same time, trumpeting like an elephant and spouting like a whale."[4]

Sir George was also ill in Montegufoni, suffering from bladder trouble, and Edith wrote to him an unusually warm note saying she would be only too glad to do anything she could to help. The sudden upsurge of interest on Edith's behalf arose because she was at a loss to know what to do, and the company of Sir George seemed better than none at all. Sir George replied:

It is delightful to think I may see you in Paris, and if all goes well that you will come for a long stay at Montegufoni in the autumn.

Best love, darling
Your loving father
GEORGE R. SITWELL[5]

Sir George would have been grateful to have seen Edith because he was, like his daughter, desperate for some inoffensive company. Not that he was bored, for in Montegufoni he occupied himself with his various schemes to improve the castle. Osbert had asked him in 1937 what he would do if there was to be a war.

Sir George replied, "I should take refuge in the mountains."[6] Neither his family nor any possible war interested him as much as his schemes; in September 1939, just before war broke out, he began to have the statues in the grotto in Montegufoni renovated. He mused over his various plans, indifferent to the world crisis, and although he would have been glad to have seen his daughter, the visit would not have meant much. The last time Osbert saw his father he recalled his saying out of the blue, "Edith made a great mistake by not going in for lawn tennis."[7]

The projected visit, which might have prevented so many subsequent problems, was never made, for as Germany prepared to invade Poland, Osbert cabled Edith in mid-August from Monte Carlo, where he was spending the summer with David Horner, telling her to return to England. Osbert and David arrived at Renishaw from Monte Carlo on September 1, two days before Britain declared war on Germany, and found Edith already there.

Edith had been obliged to leave Paris suddenly without Moby Dick, who remained in their flat in the Rue Saint-Dominique with nearly all Edith's books and other possessions. Also fleeing at the same time was Pavlik, who had been in Switzerland, had rushed back to Paris, and had then crossed the Atlantic to New York with Ford. On September 8 Pavlik told her he was already bored and finding "this horrible city New York is slowly killing me." Before going north to Renishaw, Edith spent a few days in London and managed a visit to Brighton. After Paris, even London seemed peaceful, but she was tired of towns and longing to go to rural Renishaw.

It was surprising how quickly Edith managed to throw herself back into her old routine in London and even in her first week was back seeing old friends. Before returning to Renishaw on August 24 she went to lunch with Louis Kentner (the famous pianist), his wife, and Sachie. Renishaw could now be expected to be comparatively peaceful; Sir George was in Italy (not at war with Britain until June 1940), and it seemed that Edith would find it quiet enough to work on her poetry. Ostensibly the war was to seem almost useful to Edith. With Helen dead, and Evelyn braving it out in Paris, it was a relief to be safely with Osbert, without expense, and relatively near London, where she could renew old friendships. There was always the nagging doubt about Pavlik, but it was unlikely that the war, or Edith's absence from Paris, would make any improvement in their relations. Edith could hardly be pleased that he was in America with Ford, but at least he was safe.

But on her arrival, Renishaw was not as idyllic as she had expected. Osbert and David had spent many years away, travelling the Continent, and the house had fallen into bad repair. It was always cold, even in the summer, a fact that did nothing to encourage Edith to get out of bed, where she was in the habit of doing her writing. It was also impossible to work at night, as there were only oil lamps for light.

Although Edith was fond of Osbert, she could not confide in him, nor would he discuss any of his problems with her. David Horner was to be in London and elsewhere on war service, but Osbert never discussed the true nature of their relationship. Had he done so, not only might many aspects of her own relationship with Pavlik have been illuminated, but she might also have been spared some of the anguish and strain later at Renishaw, when David was to become her most bitter enemy. But all that was in the future, and in the meantime Edith was trying to relax in her old and familiar surroundings. Somehow they seemed less attractive when actually tasted than she had anticipated because she did not have the sense of independence that, although miserably exerted, she had enjoyed in Paris.

Her nerves were strained, and not helped by a stream of war evacuees who came to her and Osbert. Amongst them was Harold Acton, who stayed for four days in October 1939.

Poor Harold, I am really very sorry for him, because I think he has been very badly treated by his parents and by fate in general. But his visit was a little depressing because his onslaught on all the people he knows is amazing. Still one must remember . . . that he has been dragged away from China which he loves.[8]

Gollancz commissioned an anthology of poems from Edith, which was called *Edith Sitwell's Anthology* and published in 1940. Edith was rather nervous with Victor Gollancz, or "Golly," as she called him, and once managed to ask him, "When will the gollies be ready?" instead of saying "galleys."[9]

Duckworth's, her earlier publisher, had brought out her *Gold Coast Customs* in 1929, but because she had not written much

poetry since then, it was convenient for Edith to have her prose
books published by Fabers, Sachie's prose publishers, at his suggestion. She had made a selection of her own poetry for Fabers,
but that publishing house would not handle new books of her
poems. Edith had, however, heard good reports about Macmillan
and was determined to have her poetry published by them. Macmillan had offered her a 10 per cent royalty rate on her first volume of poems since she returned to England, *Street Songs*. In
1941, when she had written enough poems for a new volume, she
pleaded with Ann Pearn, her agent, and David Higham's partner,
to negotiate better terms with them. Edith told Ann Pearn:

I consider it [10 per cent] a very low royalty, and must point out that
I am a poet of such established reputation and of such fame, that the
publication of a new book of poems by me, after a lapse of years,
should, if properly handled, attract the greatest attention and obtain a
most favourable sale.[10]

The war bored more than frightened Edith, but she was sympathetic to the terrible time her friends were having. Choura was
stranded in Paris and was having problems with her husband.
The Atlantic was safely between Edith and Pavlik, and this was
a relief to her, for although the passion had gone out of her love
they could correspond. Not that their letters began well, for Edith
found that his had nothing to say, which was a disappointing
blow to her because, despite all the terrible things he had done
in the past, she still often thought about him, and now she worried about his friends. Edith was slow to realize the full signifi-
cance of the war, for she was enthusiastically expecting to return
to Paris fairly soon.

Judging from her letters to Choura, the one person who understood the situation between Edith and Pavlik, she was now desperate for news of him. Every letter to Choura contained a plea
that Choura should write back to her, but Pavlik had not been receiving all his sister's letters, and the letters Edith had from him
still gave no news. Edith wrote to Choura:

In effect there is very little to say. One sees nobody, one thinks nothing. It is as if one were a rag doll in the middle of a high wind. . . .
Here having smiled so much in the past, one cannot smile any more.[11]

Although she hated to admit it, she was also worried about her
father (still in Italy). "He is becoming more and more bizarre,

poor old man, and is becoming a little crocodile in spirit at nearly eighty. Think what we will be like at that age!"[12]

There was a distraction in a visit to Weston Hall to see Sachie and Georgia. Edith felt she should be away from Renishaw for Osbert's sake, to give him a break, but she was also aware that Sachie had a very small income, so insisted on being a paying guest. She wrote to Georgia:

I'm longing to come and see you darling. It will be heavenly, war or no war . . . of course I am coming as a P.G. We shall all three of us be able to have the first talk we have had for ages.[13]

There was a new threat that Osbert might have to work for the Ministry of Information, and Edith, being homeless, feared that she might have to live at Weston Hall permanently, for she would not live at Renishaw without Osbert. While such an arrangement would have meant Osbert's being more out of touch with David Horner, whom she was beginning to dislike, she would have been bored by the country near Weston as much as she had become bored by Renishaw. Fortunately Osbert was not required at the Ministry of Information, and Edith returned to Renishaw. She hated the war, but at the same time could not understand any lack of patriotism; the artist C. R. W. Nevinson, who had painted her portrait, did not escape censure:

Richard Nevinson telephoned through on Friday evening . . . giving Osbert details of his last terrible illness (such a moment to choose), asked if he and his wife Kathleen could come down here in their caravan and camp in the stable yard. They came on Saturday but were shown, nicely but firmly, that if they were intending to stay for ages the caravan would be their home and that we were not bound to see each other every day. (I do think Richard is rather a sickening spectacle.) He is such a *monstrous* egoist, that he had no time to think of the wretched boys who have to go into that hell, but could only moan about his own purely imaginative diseases.[14]

She catalogued his imaginary complaints, ending with "None of this, I am thankful to say, prevents him from giving interviews with newspapers."

Later she was to complain about another artist, Paul Nash; at first sight it seems tactless of her to express such annoyance about two friends of Sachie's in letters to him. Who they were did not annoy her so much as the fact that they were artists. Just as all women writers to Edith were potential competitors, so all artists were potential enemies standing in the way of Pavlik, and it was her continuing devotion to him that made her take exception to Nevinson and Nash.

Edith Sitwell's Anthology, although promised by Christmas 1939, was published at the end of January 1940. Impatiently, Edith waited for reviews. Amongst them was a Valentine's Day greeting from the left-wing newspaper *Reynolds News:*

Among the literary curiosities of the 1920s will be the vogue of the Sit-wells, the sister and two brothers whose energy and self assurance push them into a position which their merits could not have done.

One brother wrote amusing political verse. The sister produced a life of Alexander Pope. Now oblivion has claimed them and they are remembered with a kindly if slightly cynical smile. . . . Miss Edith Sitwell has been occupied in collecting her favourite pieces of poetical writing and has published 812 pages of them. . . . It would be a delightful bedside book if it were not so heavy to hold. The 160 pages of "critical introduction" well might be omitted from future editions.[15]

Osbert telephoned Sachie on March 5 to tell him about the offending article. Edith followed the call by a letter:

Will you please write immediately to Mr. Frere [their solicitor] complaining that you will join with Osbert and me in the action we are taking. He has consulted counsel who says the paragraph is libellous and being sick of this sort of thing, Osbert and I think and know that you will agree that it is about time that people *paid money* for indulging in malicious lies with the intention of injuring us. They want a lesson and money is the only thing that leathers them.[16]

Although this kind of vendetta was the last sort of thing one would expect solicitors to take up, Frere, Cholmeley & Nicholson were well used to the litigious predilections of the Sitwell family, who had been their clients since the nineteenth century. Philip Frere, whose help Edith wanted, was particularly qualified and held in high esteem. Sir George's complicated legal transactions had been skilfully and tactfully dealt with by him, and he was also used to Edith's demands, for she suspected libel in nearly every derogatory remark published about her. On this occasion, Frere was forced to agree that the Sitwells had indeed been libelled. There was a long delay, but at last Edith was told the case would be heard in February 1941.

Sachie told Edith that he was unwilling to be involved, but on Christmas Eve 1940 Edith reassured him:

What a confounded nuisance it is for all three of us . . . to have this law case on. . . . But I don't see how we could have allowed this man to say we have all sunk into oblivion and "if we are remembered it is with a kindly if cynical smile". If we had allowed it the sentence would have been repeated in paper after paper in the provinces and all over the Empire.[17]

Sachie's reluctance was not shared by Edith. She was annoyed by *Reynolds News*, but from the letter she wrote to Sachie it is also clear that she was quite simply bristling for a fight, and expected to win and enjoy it. Paris and Renishaw had left Edith low-spirited, but there was something about a libel case that reminded her of the public platform she had campaigned on during the 1920s for the sake of modern poetry. Now the roles were reversed; while she had been unable to write poems that would have kept her reputation as a poet before the public, the new left-wing poets such as Auden and Spender were in danger of becoming better known than she, and were certainly regarded as being modernistic, while Edith was often seen as an Establishment figure.

Libel would be a nerve-racking experience for Edith, but she suffered her nerves almost gladly whenever her poetic reputation was at stake. At last, with the support of Osbert and the reluctant co-operation of Sachie, Frere was instructed to proceed.

Visitors arrived at Renishaw just before Christmas 1940 and Sir Edward Marsh was a guest for lunch, as he was staying with the Duke of Devonshire at Chatsworth, nearby. Marsh wrote to Christopher Hassall (the poet and dramatist) that he had had luncheon with Osbert at Renishaw. "It was delightful but my taxi cost 45/- which as the butler said was rather a lot just for luncheon."[18] He did not realize that the luncheon was far from delightful for Edith. She wrote to Sachie about it:

His [Marsh's] toothie pegs gave him and everybody else a lot of trouble, sometimes they sound like galloping horses and at other moments they hiss like boa constrictors.[19]

Nor did Marsh report an attack Osbert made on him over Winston Churchill, whose private secretary Marsh had been. Osbert had always detested Churchill and had published a satire on him in 1919, called *The Winstonburg Line*. Edith continued:

Osbert waited until he was just going and then flew at him about Mr. Churchill which nearly reduced him to tears. I think the poor old boy must have had some kind of fit.[20]

Edith had conveniently forgotten how she had once hoped for Marsh's patronage for Pavlik.

Conveniently, too, in February, she made her peace with Hugh Walpole, who she found had liked her anthology. She wrote to him that "my temper has always been a bigger source of worry to me than it could possibly be to anyone else, and that I shall now see more clearly than ever how stupid it is for me to let it carry me away."[21] Walpole was then one of those popular novelists whose work she so despised, but she saw now that he could be used to her advantage, and that by buttering him up he could be produced as a witness for the defence. Correcting proofs for the anthology had driven her mad, and Edith resolved to try to write poems again. Her first published poem since 1936 was *Lullaby*, about the invasion of Poland, for she was now adopting a new prophetic role, and feeling more assured in her work. In her leisure time, though, she was less domineering and grateful to certain carefully invited guests whose conversation she enjoyed.

In 1937 the three Sitwells had given the annual Lord Northcliffe memorial lectures over several days at London University. Edith had spoken about modern poetry, Sachie about George Cruickshank and Palladian Art, and Osbert on the novel and Charles Dickens. In the audience had been the young Alec Guinness, and now, in 1940, he sent the Sitwells tickets for a stage adaptation of *Great Expectations* that he had written and was acting in. He was not hopeful that they would accept, but was bold enough to try his luck; with the war on, any publicity he could get in a difficult time was welcome. He was delighted when Edith arrived with Osbert. He had always admired Edith's poetry and must have conveyed his enthusiasm, for they became warm friends. Not long after their first meeting, Edith invited him to stay with her at Sachie's house, and as Sir Alec recalled:

It was a pretty eccentric weekend. Edith was on her writing-angry-letters jag. When one went down, there were letters to be posted in Edith's writing to the Editor of the *New Statesman*. The family had wondered "How do we deal with this? Do we let it go or do we secrete it?" As Sachie was terrified that Edith would make a fool of herself, efforts were made to stop the letters going.[22]

When Sir Alec was on tour in Leeds in the winter of 1941, Edith invited him and his wife, Merula (who was distantly related to her), to stay at Renishaw for a weekend. Their son was only a few months old and they were to come "only on the condition that Osbert didn't know that there would be a baby in the house as he couldn't bear babies."[23] Sir Alec felt that it was as if "their life was something of a fantasy. For of course Osbert knew there was a baby in the house but there had to be this huge pretence that he didn't know." Edith met the Guinnesses:

in a hired limousine on a rather foggy afternoon and the limousine had slightly tinted glass. Edith sat in the back seat with my wife. There was a speaking tube and I sat in the front so conversation went on through the speaking tube and in spite of the fogginess she had two blinds pulled down so we went round Derbyshire as we might have been in a hearse.[24]

Sir Alec was aware of how kind Edith was, writing letters to cheer him up and giving him a letter of introduction to Pavlik when he went into the Navy. Sir Alec met Pavlik for afternoon tea and he found him "extremely Russian, very amusing . . . in a Russian camp way," but somehow he gathered that Pavlik was then devoted to Edith. Pavlik was fairly happy and still staying with Charles Henri Ford, while working spasmodically. Extraordinarily, too, Edith had reluctantly become reconciled to Ford, and for the same reason that she had accepted Allen Tanner, Pavlik's earlier boy-friend, whom she had fiercely resented at the beginning.

In 1937 Ford had published a volume of poetry called *Garden of Disorder*. Pavlik had told Ford, "You must dedicate the first copy to Edith, inscribe it and send it. . . . if it weren't for those people around her, you would have gotten to know how wonderful she really is."[25]

The book was duly inscribed and sent, and Edith now admitted that she admired one particular poem in it. Ten years later, another step of reconciliation was taken when she began a correspondence with Ford, even though it was purely in order to find out what Pavlik was doing. (She was to find herself in a difficult position when choosing poems for her *Atlantic Book of British and American Poetry*, published in 1958, when her editor, Edward Weeks, wished her to remove her choice of Ford's poems; she loyally felt obliged to keep them in.)

Meanwhile, during the summer of 1940, evacuees settled in some of the buildings next to Renishaw Hall. Their arrival was noted by Osbert with genuine sympathy, but he could not understand the habits they brought with them:

You can't imagine the dirt and helplessness of the poor refugees [*sic*]. They are fried fish-shop types, and can hardly cook for themselves, and have no windows open. If they are given bread they throw it away. Three loaves were found in the park. . . .[26]

The noisiness of the evacuees made it hard for Edith to work, and she took refuge for a few months in the Sesame. She had begun to write poems again, but when she returned to Renishaw Hall, in October, there was a new worry about her father. Although Italy had been at war with Britain from June 1940, Sir George was determined to remain at Montegufoni as long as possible. He had sent a message to Osbert early in the month, telling him that he was "completely undisturbed."[27] "That is so typical," Edith commented to a friend; "I suppose he thinks that this is just a slight international misunderstanding, which will soon blow over. . . ."[28] By the end of the month the situation had changed. A series of letters and telegrams had arrived from Sir George that worried and disturbed his family. To Geoffrey Gorer, Edith explained:

My maddening old father is in Italy; and has sent through a message to say that if we cannot send money through to him by December, he will be starving. What an end and climax to a life in which one has been a constant nuisance to one's offspring![29]

The situation about Sir George was to prove more serious than Edith had imagined. He eventually left Italy to stay in neutral Switzerland in the spring of 1942 with distant relations—the daughter of Colonel Chandos-Pole, Olga, and her husband, a Swiss banker, Bertram Woog de Rusten. A telegram subsequently arrived that puzzled Edith and Osbert. It read: "Safe in paradise of food and wine, love Daddy." Sir George was never "Daddy" to them, signing his full name in all cases, George R. Sitwell. The reference to wine was more mysterious still, for "Daddy" rarely drank any alcohol. To Sachie, Edith complained:

Oh life has been infernal just lately, re our private lives, hasn't it? I should like to hit Woog.

Personally I think it is just a vamp on his [Sir George's] part though I didn't at first. Also his telegrams are infuriating. What does he think we ought to do? Go out there? How does he think we would get there? Leaving aside the fact that we should be interned.[30]

Edith had every right to be suspicious; she learnt that Sir George, always the most careful of persons about legal affairs, had given power of attorney to Woog. The most unsettling part as far as Edith and Sachie were concerned was the thought that Woog could easily be dwindling away the inheritance unchecked.

These were not their only worries. At last the case for libel against *Reynolds News* was heard, in February 1941, before Mr. Justice Cassels, with G. D. Roberts, an elderly and famous barrister, whom Edith nicknamed "The Buffalo," appearing for the defence. She told Christabel Aberconway that she gave the court

what I consider a really beautiful performance of a sweet, sunny-natured old lady, stinking of lavender and looped with old lace, in whose mouth butter, even in the palmy days when it could be procured, would not have melted.[31]

Edith's looks were deceptive, for she answered "The Buffalo's" questions as skilfully as she had dealt with her hecklers in the days when she read poems to predominantly hostile audiences.

Roberts remarked that she had unkindly referred in the past to Alfred Noyes's poetry as "cheap linoleum" and also that her feud with Wyndham Lewis had been notorious. Why, asked Roberts, had she not sued Lewis? Edith replied that cheap linoleum was serviceable and that no one paid any attention to what Lewis said. "It is utterly untrue to say that I have passed into oblivion," Edith went on; "I know of no fact upon which such a statement could be based."[32] Her publisher, Daniel Macmillan, supported her, saying her works sold well, and although Roberts was nasty to Arthur Waley (also a witness for the Sitwells), whom he pretended he had never heard of, the publisher's evidence helped to convince the judge, and he awarded the Sitwells £350 each.

It was a victory precious now for Edith because it would have been a disaster if they had lost. But the verdict was sneered at by the press.

"The papers, with their usual low cunning and meanness, have left out, in their reports, everything inconvenient to themselves,"[33] Edith complained to Daniel Macmillan. The gallant knight Sir Hugh Walpole wrote a letter to the *Daily Telegraph* supporting the Sitwells, to stem remarks that "the action was not a petty personal one, but an action that had to be fought for everyone's sake." Walpole also wrote to Edith:

Don't let yourself be upset by the *New Statesman*. It is always trying to be clever and therefore this most heartless of papers just cuts no beautiful ice. I was delighted to see that old Shaw lent his support and I feel really proud of having given my testimony.[34]

The Times summed up the popular feeling with a cynical editorial on the Sitwells:

They will not claim to be exempt from the sentence of Holy Writ: "our names shall be forgotten in time and no man shall have our works in remembrance". But if Sainte-Beuve rightly defines a critic as the one whose watch is five minutes ahead of other people's, yesterday's judgment is a salutary warning that the habit may be expensive. Are not the five minutes now up?[35]

Despite the papers, nothing could remove the sense of victory Edith felt. She wrote to Sachie:

I must say in spite of all the worry, we did manage to have a happy time in London, didn't we, during the case? . . . Desmond MacCarthy [journalist and critic] is going about apparently telling the story of how he was asked to give evidence, and that if he was asked he should say that he had often said and intended to go on saying that oblivion *has* seized writers! I have told my informant that Mr. M. was repeating a conversation which had been confidential and that I no more understand the behavior of this gentleman than I understand the criticism of this critic. (In future I shall always refer to him as Dingy Desmond.) I also said a good deal more. . . .[36]

Not all Edith's time was taken up by teasing MacCarthy, for her poems were appearing with new profusion in *Life and Letters*, a journal edited by an old friend, Robert Herring. Feeling tired of the war, and roused to compassion by it, she wrote *Street Song* and *The Youth with the Red Gold Hair*, and by September

1941 *Still Falls the Rain* was published in *The Times Literary Supplement*. The change of style was marked with lines such as:

> Dark angel who art clear and straight
> As cannon shining in the air,
> Your blackness doth invade my mind,
> And thunderous as the armoured wind
> That rained on Europe is your hair;
>
> And so I love you till I die—
> (Unfaithful I, the cannon's mate):
> Forgive my love of such brief span,
> But fickle is the flesh of man,
> And death's cold puts the passion out.[37]

Edith was advised by Osbert that to survive personally as a poet she had to change her subject to make an impact, or she would be compared unfavourably with the poets of the Left who were politically conscious. Edith had suffered enough, in any case, with the grief of Pavlik's infidelity, and the personal distress she felt for the suffering caused by the war, not to want to relive any private agonies in her poetry. What pain she felt, Osbert advised, should be expressed impersonally.

It was not always an entirely happy role, for Edith, reassured by sudden and welcome success, overreacted and took on an exaggerated feeling of responsibility for the "sins of the world." She did not care much about the leftist poets, but Yeats's *Last Poems* and Eliot's *Four Quartets*, being published at the time, impressed her by their sagacity and calm wisdom. Her time, as she said, "for experiment was done."[38] Early in 1942 her new poems were published by Macmillan in the volume *Street Songs*, and in the *New Statesman* Stephen Spender wrote: "This volume shows an astonishing development of Miss Sitwell's talent as a technician as well as in her material . . . a fascinating book at moments tragic and always full of charm."[39] Spender's judgement was astute; Edith's great technical skill, the hallmark of her early work, was used less self-consciously in her new poems. Because her skill in poetic craft was assured, she was able to concentrate on the content of the poems, her ideas unhindered by problems of technique. This technical skill was, however, sometimes an advantage and sometimes a handicap, and much of her later work lacks verbal invention and tends to be too repetitive, with certain symbols

such as "gold" and "bone" and "Judas coloured" being over-
worked. But that is to judge with the benefit of hindsight. With
Street Songs, a fresh and, to many critics, a new Edith Sitwell
had appeared.

Edith herself was surprised at Spender's review, for he had
been an enemy in the days of *Aspects of Modern Poetry* and in
the pages of the *New Statesman,* à propos the libel case of *Reynolds News,* Spender had rather jokingly written that he wished to
reassure anyone that they could write what they liked about him,
for he had no intention of bringing a libel action against them.
The Times Literary Supplement joined in support, its review declaring that Edith's work had "majestic assurance, noble and
unassailable simplicity."[40] The tide had turned quickly for Edith,
and she was now critically accepted in a way that she had always
dearly wanted.

Edith now emulated Hugh Walpole, who was notorious for
lavishly entertaining critics in return for good reviews (he was
portrayed as Alroy Kear in Somerset Maugham's novel *Cakes and
Ale*). Edith *needed* the reassurance of the critics, for she had
dedicated much of her writing life to poetry and, having once
achieved critical acclaim, was terrified of losing it. Edith was sincerely grateful to people like Spender, who gave her good no-
tices; and apart from the praise, she adored literary gossip, which
Spender and other new friends brought to her when she entertained them at the Sesame. He became a good friend.

Ironically, Spender as a schoolboy, impressed by Edith's early
volumes *Troy Park* and *Bucolic Comedies,* had written a sonnet
addressed to her, which was published in his school magazine.
He recalled that "my whole life would have been different of
course if I had sent it to her when I was seventeen. . . . I would
have been asked to tea, but I was much too frightened to send it
to her."[41] So this new acquaintance was an initiation for Spender.
Previously he was aware only of Edith's public reputation, but
now he and his wife, Natasha, "learned to appreciate her sensitive sympathy." Spender described her appearance in his book
World within World:

Her features seemed carved as though out of alabaster, in which were
cut narrowly watchful eyes, amused, kind, cold, sad, or even at moments, incisively shrewd. She wore magnificent dresses and large jew-
ellery—an ivory cross, or jade pendant, or gold set with large and

beautiful stones as in a bishop's mitre or cross. In her appearance, as
in her poetry, she was triumphantly herself, yet endlessly reaching beyond herself into other people and other times. . . .[42]

Spender realized that Edith's "wellbeing was bound up with that
of her friends"—not always so sympathetically, though, for when
Edith met somebody in the Sesame mutual acquaintances would
be discussed and Edith, who had inherited a talent for mimicry
from her mother, could be wonderfully amusing, impersonating
friends like Arthur Waley or his mistress, Beryl de Zoete. Edith's
attitude to Beryl de Zoete, whom she called "Baby B," was one of
extreme antagonism. As early as 1925 she had found unacceptable to her code of morality Beryl's relationship with Arthur
Waley, who was living with her. But "Baby B" was the opposite
of Edith in appearance, being small and untidy; she shared a life
of austerity with Waley, living mainly off fish cakes and spa-
ghetti. Edith could not understand this Spartan existence, since
Waley and Beryl were very rich, and Beryl's being both brilliantly clever and a woman was enough to give her a seal of disapproval in Edith's eyes. Beryl was the butt of endless jokes and
brought out in Edith a kind of childlike cruelty. Once in the Sesame Club she made a whole group, including Spender and Frederick Ashton, sprawl on the floor, pretending they were Beryl
falling off a cliff, which they all found amusing in a way, but also
humiliating.

Paradoxically, in view of her cruel *jeux d'esprit* in the Sesame,
Edith was worried sick about Helen Rootham's sister, Evelyn
Wiel, whom she believed to be starving in Paris. This contrasting
behaviour of extreme concern and mild cruelty was necessary to
Edith, each to balance the other. She required a diversion from
her lonely life made complicated by old loyalties, and only by enjoying cruel jokes could she cope emotionally with her often self-
imposed worries. There was no obligation for Edith to support
Evelyn, which she could not afford to do in any case, and she
could hardly forget Evelyn's being so tiresome when they lived
with Helen in the Rue Saint-Dominique. When France fell, Evelyn had shown great courage, nursing wounded soldiers despite
her own illness, and Edith admired this. Edith was so fascinated
by her courage that she liked to repeat a story of Evelyn's bravery from the time when her husband was Norwegian consul in
Paris, which Evelyn had told her. Preparing for a reception, Ev-

elyn opened a wardrobe to get a fur coat and to her horror felt a
heart beating behind it. She realized at once that it was probably
a man who had recently escaped from prison and who was
known to be dangerous, but she kept her nerve and said, as if ab-
sent-mindedly, "Oh damn, I've forgotten my pearls," before
going calmly downstairs to call the police.[43] But courage made
Evelyn no money, and although her brother was a well-off lawyer, he was content to give her nothing. Unhesitatingly Edith
sent her a monthly allowance. Then it transpired that Evelyn had
received none of this because of the intervention of the currency
authorities, and that £200 of the accumulated allowance had
been credited to Edith's account. Just at the time when Edith
was waiting for her *Street Songs* to appear she wrote at least a
dozen letters to the Board of Trade, and also a long document,
part of which read:

I have received with the profoundest distress and horror the news . . .
of your decision that no funds are to be sent to Evelyn Wiel . . . she is
the wife of Mr. Truels Wiel . . . former (during the last war) Norwegian Vice-Consul in Paris. He deserted Madame Wiel leaving her
destitute . . . he finally got into a scandal and left Paris. Mme. Wiel is
British by birth and ancestry. Her maiden name is Rootham and she is
the daughter of the late Samuel Rootham of Clifton near Bristol . . .
born in March 1880. She is now completely penniless.[44]

Edith told the Board of Trade that Mme Wiel's health was bad,
but to the same claim the Foreign Office replied "that the Swiss
people who dealt with the funds" insisted that (a) Mme Wiel
was not British born, to which Edith replied, "This is a lie," and
(b) that she had an income sufficient for her needs, to which
Edith wrote, "This is also a lie. She has no money excepting the
money I made for her until France fell. She was my paid housekeeper and secretary."[45]

The payment of the £10 Evelyn received from Edith was
made possible only because Edith received an annuity from her
new millionairess friend Bryher. "Bryher" was the pen name for
Winifred Macpherson, the sister of the shipping millionaire Sir
John Ellerman. She wrote historical novels and met Edith and
Osbert through their mutual friend Robert Herring, who had
come to live in Eckington during the war. She came to visit Herring and was soon a frequent guest at Renishaw.

Bryher was fascinated by Edith, who responded warmly by satisfying Bryher's endless desire to hear her read her poems aloud. They sat on the terrace in Renishaw and Bryher remembered the atmosphere:

. . . all seemed golden, while the landscape beyond us hovered in the cool Derbyshire sunshine as if a giant butterfly were protecting the grass with its coral and amber wings. . . .[46]

Bryher was more than just a lover of poetry; she was intensely practical and kind. She was aware of Edith's financial plight and gave her money to buy a house in Bath. Unfortunately Edith had no enthusiasm for Bath as a city after writing about it, and had no intention of living there, but she was excited about the prospect of owning a house of her own at last. While the sale was being negotiated she wrote to Sachie:

Now look Darling . . . I want you and Georgia to go and have a holiday in my little house in Bath that I am just buying. The sale is just going through. . . . It is 8 Gay Street which belonged to Mrs. Thrale.[47]

Edith was also worried about Sachie, who had now become Captain and Adjutant in the Home Guard. She was concerned that his work would suffer; if "you can't leave the Home Guard at Weston surely any doctor would most undoubtedly say you were obliged to have a holiday."[48]

There was also wartime news of Cecil Beaton:

Have you heard about Maysie Beaton's adventure during the Blitz? He was passing a ruined house with a friend when suddenly he noticed what appeared to be a mid-Victorian bust of white marble of a man with a heavy ole-Bill moustache and bowler hat. "Oh," screamed Cecil, "isn't that just me! Oh I must have it" and they began to scrabble in the debris and disengage the bust. After he had done this for a few minutes he thought he saw one of the eyes of the bust close. However he continued and in a few minutes, "Thanks chum," said the bust. It was an elderly plumber covered with white dust who had been unable to move, as he was pinned down. Do you suppose Cecil has been taken prisoner?[49]

If Edith hoped in jest that Beaton was taken prisoner, she was seriously worried that it was exactly what was happening to her father in Switzerland. There was still a maddening lack of com-

munication. She had written to Sir George that they were
distressed to hear that "none of our letters have reached you for
some time. . . . We are dreadfully unhappy that we are sepa-
rated from you, and most unhappy knowing how ill you are. . . .
And we all beg you to believe that a lack of letters from us means
no lack of affection or thought for you."[50]

It was in Edith's interest not to lose touch with her father, for
she feared Sir George had formed a new romantic attachment
with his nurse. It was a fear shared by Osbert, but probably unfounded. Woog now had a possible reason to believe that his own
financial advantages could be limited, as he complained to Osbert in September:

I have had a lot of trouble with the nurse he [Sir George] brought
with him from Florence. As I found out that she was a German and
not as she said a Swiss subject, I was warned that she had the habit of
persuading her patients to give her money and I strongly suspect that
all the money Sir George always wanted and got by selling out capital
at 25%–30% of the value was presented to her, and not to the Red
Cross as I was told.[51]

Woog admitted that the nurse looked after Sir George "perfectly," but he told Osbert, "I have got the proof that the nurse is
out after money and lies every moment in the ear of Sir George
to make over some cash or an annuity." He made arrangements
to have the nurse removed, a move which naturally caused great
hostility. After a lifetime of economy, Sir George's actions convinced Woog that "it was not possible that he is still clear in
mind." Sir George, while refusing to pay a certain £105 required
by Philip Frere, his English lawyer, wanted Woog to make the
departing nurse a gift of 50,000 lire (£500) and an annual allowance of the same amount to be paid after his death. "Physically
however," Woog continued, "he is in a fine state for he puts on a
lot of weight, walks now and again in the garden . . . and has a
growing appetite."[52]

The news that Edith might have to help to support Sir
George's nurse infuriated her, for she had little enough money
even for herself. Money was a delicate subject with Edith; she
was always reluctant to admit what her income from the Renishaw Estate was. Osbert's secretary, Lorna Andrade, remembered Edith's constant hints of poverty, but

I always felt that things couldn't be as bad as she suggested. This was partly because she said that she received only £50 a quarter from the Renishaw Estate and the Hollingworths, the estate agents, told me that she got more, or it may be that I knew she got more by looking at Osbert's pass sheets . . . knowing the life they all lived, whether at the Sesame Club, Renishaw or Montegufoni, Edith's hinted descriptions of her poverty certainly appalled and worried me. . . .[53]

Edith was persuaded to write a book called *English Women* for the war effort, for which she was paid a pittance. Characteristically, she wrote only about women who were safely dead and were not a threat to her reputation; Virginia Woolf, whose death in 1941 had shocked Edith, was the one contemporary she chose to include.

In September 1941 Edith had declared that her financial position was "about as bad as it could be."[54] Now, one year later, the situation was, if anything, worse. It seems clear that she could not have lived at Renishaw without Osbert's kindness, and this embarrassed her. Often Edith told the servants that she was "only a lodger" and took third place there.

Macmillan, which had initially pleased Edith, was now failing to pay her as much as she felt was her due, and in desperation she increased the pressure on the publishers for even better terms. The book in question was *A Poet's Notebook*, for which Edith had been offered £50, which she considered inadequate. Gollancz had paid Edith £500 for her *Edith Sitwell's Anthology*, which had appeared in 1940, and £100 for a children's anthology of verse, *Look! the Sun!* in 1941, and these figures seemed to Edith to represent a fairer assessment of what her work was worth. She told her agent Ann Pearn, of Pearn, Pollinger and Higham:

I must have the *advance now*. I cannot go on living as I am. My poverty is really dreadful, and I am eaten alive by demands for money. If they give me £100,—then I would take £50 *now*, and £50 and the rest of the sum earned by sales up to two months after publication, *then*. . . .[55]

Despite the fact that Edith's *Street Songs* quickly ran into three editions, more money could be made from the inevitable prose book. In September 1941 Edith had been commissioned by Macmillan to write a life of Elizabeth I of England, for which she was paid £100 advance. By March 1942 Edith was enjoying work on the book and told Ree Gorer, mother of her friend Geoffrey, that the book would be "a very sinister one. . . ."[56] Her choice of subject coincided with her own new grandeur of personality and the new public style of her poems. She had put her own feelings for Pavlik into her novel, and now, thanks to her drop of Plantagenet blood, she could identify herself closely with Elizabeth—she never tired of pointing out that she was born on the same day and at the same hour as her subject.

It seems strange that in a period of growing success she had to create a new strong identity for herself and her outside public world. As usual, it seems to have enabled her to impose herself on others without bringing her true feelings out into the light. To many she seemed impenetrable in her "Elizabethan" role, and it soon earned her the title "Queen Edith."

She always enjoyed the company of young people, especially young writers, who were more successful in gaining her affection than her "club bores." One such young writer she had befriended was Denton Welch, who had written an article on Sickert that had made Osbert and Edith "laugh until we cried"; and after corresponding they met at the Sesame Club. Welch was wildly excited about meeting Edith, for she had written a foreword to his first book, *Maiden Voyage*. He was an acute observer, and his account of their meeting on April 20, 1943, gives an insight into Edith at this time:

Into the rather drab hall of the Sesame Club, basket chairs ugliness; in a fright that I might not recognise Edith Sitwell.

Sitting down, feeling embarrassed with the other old women there. So incurious on the surface; yet I felt watching.

"Miss Sitwell will be down in a moment sir." The waiting, was almost too much.

Then the tall figure dressed all in black, black trilby, Spanish witches' hat, black cloak, black satin dress to the ankles and two huge aquamarine rings. Wonderful rings on powder white hands, and face so powder pearly, nacreous white, almost not to be believed in, with the pinkened mouth, the thin delicate swordlike nose and tendril curling nostrils. No hair, I can remember no hair at first. The rings, the glistening satin, and the kid white skin.

Down the long passage, this figure sweeping in front. Everything arranged for me.

"You will have Gin and French or Bronx?" "Gin and French please". Nervousness gaining on me.

"Now about your book, when is it appearing?"

I told her that it was still held up, but that I had heard that it was oversubscribed before publication.

"Isn't that wonderful," she said.

"It's due entirely to your Foreword," I pushed out of my mouth.

More nervousness. Hot, red.

"No it isn't. I think it's due to your article on Sickert". Here a laugh.

The Sesame Club was queer. Elderly ladies, attempts at sprightliness in the decorations, basket chairs, unfinished things, drabness, brooding unenjoyment of what meets the eye.

"And Gladys, we will have beer for lunch". Edith Sitwell called the maid by name although Gladys is only a substitute for [something] I have forgotten.

We move into the dining room. . . .

A lot of talk about the Poetry Reading.* Some cold remarks, some cool, some praising.

"Eliot reading *The Waste Land* is very wonderful. You wouldn't expect it to be read with feeling and exuberance, would you? It would be altogether too overpowering. W. J. Turner [poet and critic] went on and on and on, until the chairman had to clap his hand and then we all clapped him so much that he had to stop".

I followed Edith Sitwell down the long passage. She seemed to be talking to herself as she swept along. I wondered if I should say, "What is that?" or pretend not to hear. . . .

We talked on for a little while. I heard something of their life together at Renishaw, during the war, how most of the rooms in the great house were shut up, and about the two old servants. "When they ask for me", she added, Osbert says "Yes Miss Edith's in, she isn't busy, she is only working."

There was more laughter and as it died away, I looked over my shoulder and saw that someone [Osbert Sitwell] was approaching us. Edith Sitwell saw him too—and said "Hullo darling".

I stood up to be introduced and there seemed a general shuffle and swirling. When I was back in my corner again, the atmosphere had quite changed.

Edith Sitwell began a remark, but her brother followed closely with something of his own. It was as if she left him to talk and be amusing, now that he had come.

* This had been arranged by Osbert and Edith at the Aeolian Hall. See Chapter Nine.

He turned to her to speak to her about the poetry reading. There had been trouble or disagreement of some sort, and a letter had to be answered.

"But why write to me?" Edith Sitwell complained, "why not write to the chairman? It's nothing to do with me. I won't be the villain of the piece".

"Oh darling, don't bother about that. We all know you're not". He seemed impatient to have the matter settled with as little argument as possible, but Edith Sitwell still brooded on her answer.[57]

After he returned to his home Welch's journal entry concluded:

Remember the atmosphere in that drawing room again: dark, aqueous, cold with figure passing, repassing; the glistening door opening and shutting; Edith's head turning, her white hand lying on her breast so that the huge ring sparkled like ice on fire in the gloom.[58]

Maiden Voyage was a success. Welch's acute powers of observation and his concern for small detail, which he used in this autobiographical first novel, appealed to the war-bored reading public and to the critics. It was noticed by Sir Edward Marsh. "Someone was telling me about it in London," he wrote to Christopher Hassall. "He said it was rather unfortunate as the book was reeking with homosexuality which she [Edith] was probably too innocent to perceive."[59]

NINE

Splendours and Miseries

... our Swiss social circle is a little odd, probably murderers, indubitably swindlers, and possibly blackmailers.

Letter to Georgia and Sacheverell Sitwell

THE POETRY READING Welch heard about took place in the Aeolian Hall on April 14, 1943, but the first news of it had reached Sachie in a letter Edith wrote on November 1942:

You, Osbert and I have to read poetry for about 5 minutes each at a poetry reading Osbert and I are arranging to be held sometime in April. To raise money for Lady Crewe's "French in Britain Fund". The other readers are Tom Eliot, Walter Turner, Mr. de la Mare (we *urge* Dr. Bottomley, we hope Blunden, Siegfried, old Binyon, Sturge Moore, Lady Gerald Wellesley, Mrs. Nicolson [Victoria Sackville-West]!!!) and one or two more. Now then will you be tempted? as Mrs. Adey said. Actually, it isn't a question of temptation it is a question of *force majeure. You must.*[1]

The purpose of the reading was far from Edith's mind, and her real enthusiasm for pressing Sachie to take part came from her hopes of rekindling their old ties, of recapturing the loyalty and bravado of the small group, which she remembered fondly from their younger days when they were trying to make a name for themselves by any means. It was not a coincidence that their old stamping ground, the Aeolian Hall, had been chosen.

The preliminary arrangements brought Edith trouble from Dorothy (Lady Gerald) Wellesley. The fact that they were distantly related through marriage made no difference to Edith's opinion of her work. Edith had always been jealous of the rather excessive praise Yeats lavished on Dorothy's poems, and remarked, "Honestly, the old man's mind must have been going, for him to think her any good at all as a poet."[2] The poems were bad enough, but on top of that Dorothy seems to have formed a penchant for Edith, who complained sarcastically to Georgia:

You know that I am bisexual . . . or perhaps you know that so well that you don't have to be told about it. Incidentally did you tell Sachie? . . . The poor woman is really the most dreadful pest. She is now worrying Osbert and me nearly out of our minds to go down to stay with her and read at a reading she is getting up. Harold Nicolson refuses to go down Bruton Street because that is one of three places where she sat down on the pavement banging her stick and using frightful language about (a) the Queen and (b) me (the worst being about me). Raymond Mortimer [literary editor of the *New Statesman*] at one moment it seems took a hand and tried to keep her off me. She has now I understand forgiven us![3]

But Sachie was not tempted to join in with the reading, and neither was Siegfried Sassoon. They were replaced by Arthur Waley and H.D. (Hilda Doolittle). With Queen Elizabeth, Princess Elizabeth, and Princess Margaret as the principal guests, Edith was determined all should go well. She had not bargained for W. J. Turner; he overran his time and mistook the persistent applause meant to stop him for an encouragement to continue. Dorothy Wellesley was due to follow him, but could not be found because she had been "accidentally" locked in a lavatory by Edith. Efforts were made to prevent the Queen from hearing the trouble behind the scenes, but she recalls with amusement that Dorothy Wellesley attacked Harold Nicolson with an umbrella, and that she became aware of a commotion on the balcony. The chaos grew even worse, as Edith later wrote to Sachie:

Georgia will have told you about the remarkable scenes with which the proceedings ended. The whole was really a giant canvas and people who were in the picture, in the background, or took an active part,

(I, apart from the Lady Dorothy Wellesley herself and Harold Nicolson, was actually the chief protagonist) kept on filling the picture for us with more details. Beatrice Lillie for instance, tried to enfold her [Dorothy Wellesley] in a ju-jitsu grip and hold her down to her seat. Stephen Spender, seeing her outside, tried to knock her down and sit on her face. Raymond Mortimer induced her to take his arm and go into Bond Street where she promptly sat down on the pavement (that was before she went for me) and smacked Harold Nicolson. Now we find there was a big scene at a restaurant at lunch. All we needed was Dylan Thomas.[4]

Nevertheless, Edith, despite her relish in the comedy, and her embarrassment at the readings, felt "heartily sorry for her. . . . It was like a tiresome child looking forward for ages to a party and then the whole thing ending in tears."[5]

Dylan Thomas had been out of favour with Edith since he "misbehaved" at a party in front of Georgia and Sachie, and Edith had heard nothing from him for six years. When it suited her, later, she was loyal and obligingly covered up for him when shocked friends brought her reports of his "gyrations," as she called them.

The last time I heard anything about that pair [Dylan and Caitlin] was when they left their baby in the restaurant of some big station. Arriving say at Peterborough, they found there was just time to slip out for a quick one. They therefore dashed to the bar, taking the baby with them and found there was more time than they thought and consequently quick ones followed each other. It was not until they got to London and were met by friends or relatives that they found something was missing and what could it be? Oh the baby of course! (After a good deal of thought.) But they believed they remembered leaving him in the Bar so he was wired for and presently arrived in charge of officials.[6]

Edith's malice towards Dylan Thomas was inspired by a desire for revenge; reports had reached her from friends that Dylan was going round London pubs doing an "amusing" imitation of her. Doubtless he felt he no longer required Edith's sometimes smothering help as a prop to his reputation.

Edith always needed a champion, to provide her with support for her work and to divert her. When she came to London, thankfully leaving behind Renishaw, she adopted a new supporter. Her new find was John Lehmann, a partner in the Hogarth Press and

editor of *New Writing*. Lehmann had a talent for spotting new
writers and Edith had admired the work of a young Greek writer,
Demetrios Capetanakis, in a copy of *New Writing* Lehmann sent
her. Lehmann wanted principally to encourage new writers, but
to keep his magazine as a solid financial proposition he also
required established writers such as the Sitwells. Edith was only
too glad to help and was full of ideas when invited to contribute.
Writing to "Mr. Lehmann," she took the opportunity to praise
Louis MacNeice. She had never admired his work previously,
and had said so in *Aspects of Modern Poetry*, but John Lehmann
was friendly with many of the left-wing poets such as Auden and
MacNeice. Shrewd enough to see how useful *New Writing* would
be, Edith was prepared to relax her rigid canon of disapproval,
even if it meant sailing in the same boat as them. Before long
"Mr. Lehmann" became "John."

On Georgia's birthday, July 8, 1943, Sir George died in Switzerland. The long-awaited telegrams were despatched to the children, but if Edith had hoped to benefit from his will, she was disappointed. Instead of £1,000, originally left to her, she was now
given an income of £60 a year. Sachie suffered similarly, but
Edith took it the hardest. Ginger, who had been useless to her
when he was alive, had turned out to be useless when dead. Osbert had been left no capital but, of course, he was not poor, for
apart from his income from the Renishaw Estate he had been left
£1,000 by an old friend, Mrs. Ronald Greville. The terms of Sir
George's will, Edith declared, made her "physically sick," and
she worked out her anger on Woog, whom she and the rest of the
family suspected of the worst motives. Edith gave the matter a
great deal of consideration and wrote to Georgia:

(a) If he [Sir George] was in possession of his senses, how did Woog
get rid of a nurse whom the old man had set his heart on keeping?

(b) Then was the codicil made at exactly the same time as the
nurse's dismissal?

I think Woog's wife is just *as bad as him*. They are just two cheats. I
am wondering if there were any curious circumstances at the time of
Sir George's death. (I shall never call him father again). Oh dear! I
could weep![7]

The "curious circumstances" that Edith only dared to hint at
were the possibility that Sir George had been murdered. It was

too early for her to state her feelings positively, but while she was working up a case against Woog she read a passage Sachie had written about Lady Ida in *Splendours and Miseries* in 1943, and as a result she wrote to David Horner:

I really haven't any words to say what he has done to *me* by that chapter. . . . he has succeeded in conveying it was all *my* fault. (I suppose I maltreated *her* when I was a child of 8 or 9).[8]

Edith's interpretation only made family tension worse, but there was no such intention in what Sachie wrote, and no mention of Edith at all. Part of the passage reads:

Lady Ida, tall and thin and dark and beautiful, with straight Grecian nose, small mouth and dark brown eyes and little shell-like ears set close to the head . . . there was always something tragic in her appearance which I felt deeply as a child in spite of the gaiety and power of mimicry.[9]

Edith wrote to Sachie in dismay:

I do not need to tell you that I think most of the book is on a very great scale and is full of splendours. . . . I cannot of course see the last chapter as an outside person would see it, and therefore do not know how I see the situation. My nerves were completely broken and my nervous system ruined for life before I was ten years old. This was perfectly well known to the doctor who attended me then and those who have attended me since. One doctor after an interview with the then family lawyer, told father in terms that even he could not misunderstand, exactly what he thought of him for allowing it, and told him what would be the result for them both if anything happened to me.

My health has never recovered. When Osbert was nearly twenty-two our mother nearly succeeded in ruining his life too.

Father then, with the squalid sentimentality and hypocrisy that were his distinguishing features (nothing mattered unless it touched him personally) assured her that she had saved Osbert's life in so doing. I have forgiven Mother a long time ago and it needed some forgiving. Let us please never refer to this again. I have had just as much in one way or another as I can endure.[10]

Edith's fury about the will had made her reflect on her life with her parents and, unable to see any good in her mother, she refused to see the side of Lady Ida's nature which Sachie had known best, and which she herself had even come to love and appreciate in Lady Ida's last years. To Edith, Sachie was always "a

boy" she felt obliged to defend as the elder sister, and because he
refused to fight with the critics she had consistently battled for
him and his poetry, in which she had complete faith. She was unable to understand his shy nature, yet jealous of it; it is clear that
many of her fights were utterly selfless, attacking the new poets
whose fame was helping to smother Sachie's poetry.

And she formed her own conclusion as to why Sachie had written about his childhood world with Lady Ida at Renishaw and
Scarborough. She continued:

I realise, my darling, only too well from this chapter [in Sachie's
Splendours and Miseries] that you have been suffering from great
unhappiness, many things have gone to make this up: loneliness at
school, the first war coming when you were yet so young, your young
friends being killed in the war, the dreadful 1915 incident [Lady Ida's
trial], this war and I think too, the dreadful wave of idiocy that has
swept over this country in the subject of poetry—all these incompetent
little *bungalow** boys being treated as if they were Shelley. But don't
you realise that this has always happened? I honestly think I shall
make a Calendar especially for you, with a thought for each day in the
year about what has happened to the other great artists. You are surrounded by people who are *devoted* to you. You are at the height
of your power. Don't take refuge in some dream of childhood . . . go
straight ahead and leave the dreams behind. Now is the time to write
more poetry. You owe it to us that you should.[11]

Sachie replied at once and told Edith that he had not written
about Lady Ida just to annoy her. Edith, now that her first burst
of anger had cooled, began to regret writing her first impulsive
letter.

My darling . . . I wouldn't for anything in the world spoil your wonderful reviews [of *Splendours and Miseries*] for you . . . of course I
know that you would never want to hurt me, ever . . . only always
remember this, I do love you with all my heart. I know I must seem
very tiresome sometimes but it is not for any lack of affection—my
sadness at seeing you sad goes beyond anything.[12]

Meanwhile evidence was rolling in from Switzerland that
seemed to confirm Edith's theories about the "curious circumstances." A Sister Marguerite who had looked after Sir George

* This was Edith's term for the left-wing poets, such as Spender, Auden, and
Cecil Day Lewis. She had first used it in her *Aspects of Modern Poetry*.

found a translator who wrote to Osbert on her behalf. Edith read the catalogue of charges with mixed horror and delight:

(a) Woog pretended to be your cousin and called your father "Uncle George" to your guests, otherwise he said "Sir George".

(b) Sister M. had the impression that at the beginning, Sir George, having too much confidence in Woog, signed papers without reading them. It was only afterwards when she warned him not to sign, that he read them and often refused his signature.

(c) She could not write about the situation because she was afraid Woog would give her notice and your father would have been left completely at Woog's mercy.

(d) Sir George could not receive a personal letter without it passing through the hands of Woog and he took note of the contents.[13]

The charges against Bertram Woog de Rusten did not stop there. He had been ordering, charged to Sir George's accounts, items such as a carpet, which had disappeared, and cigars, which he never smoked. Other goods had arrived in the same way and were given by Woog to his own friends. On the day Sir George died, Sister Marguerite claimed that Woog refused to send for the British Consul, saying, "I am not going to inform him," and that she had sent for him behind Woog's back.

Edith's fury was doubled because bills were still coming in from Woog on behalf of Sir George, which Woog wanted his family to settle. But she was persuaded to be reasonable when the kindly Sister Marguerite asked for copies so that she could verify Woog's claims. Another surprise revelation was that a Sister Lisa, whom Woog had dismissed earlier for certain "crimes," as he put it to Osbert, appeared to be completely innocent of them in light of evidence sent by Sister Marguerite. Edith's beliefs about Woog were shared by Osbert, who was distressed to think of his father's fate:

As you know, the old boy was the plague and worry of my life, but this is really too much. One hates to think of what he must have gone through from fright and saying to himself, "I must be imagining it".[14]

Gradually Edith, too, managed a little sympathy for her father, which she had never felt in his lifetime, and wrote to Georgia:

Really what an extraordinary life his was, poor old man. . . . Oh I hope we can get Woog. The swine! When I realise the frightful trouble that has fallen on everyone through the old man and him.

Certainly he must have ill-treated the old man. I don't think there can be any doubt about that. But actually I am convinced in my own mind that something far more than that happened. It doesn't affect me emotionally (excepting that I wouldn't have such a frightful thing happen to my worst enemy and am filled with pity) but I am overcome with horror at such completely diabolical wickedness as Woog *and his precious wife* have shown.[15]

The whole situation seemed like a plot out of one of Edith's beloved detective novels, and her imagination worked overtime. She confirmed to Georgia her fears that Sir George's heartless wickedness had ended "as I truly believe, in his own murder—brought on solely by his own wickedness."[16]

There was not a shred of evidence that Sir George actually had been murdered, although it would have been easy for Woog or a nurse to have given him too little or too much medicine, as it was known that he had been taking sulphoral for his bronchitis. Edith convinced herself that it was this, administered as a fatal dose, which brought on his death. His murder, she told herself, was the punishment for his "wickedness." The circumstances of his death became an obsession with her, and every letter to her family mentioned Woog. In July:

I also feel that there is a possibility of our getting Woog down. I can't tell you the horrors I have had over that affair. I don't myself think that there can be any doubt as to what happened. And in any case even if he didn't, the old man must have been ill-treated.
P.S. I see our Swiss social circle is a little odd, probably murderers, indubitably swindlers and possibly blackmailers.[17]

The "horrors" Edith had were partly her own fault, for as evidence was not forthcoming from Switzerland, she determined to find it herself, and believed too readily the promptings of her imagination.

Helen had been interested in séances and Edith had occasionally gone with her, so now Edith suggested that a letter of Woog's and one of Sir George's should be given to a medium to see if the vibrations would confirm what she suspected. Osbert wrote a note to Lorna Andrade, his secretary, asking her to play the part of Miss Marple and visit "Mrs. Nell St. John Montagu, the celebrated medium and psychometrist," to see what happened. Miss Andrade set off on the trail and met the lady. She was not allowed to take shorthand notes during the interview, but did so later, and informed Osbert of the results, namely, that the medium decided Woog was dishonest and that Sir George had been in danger. Edith followed up the account with a letter to the medium pressing her for more details, and when they arrived she was appalled to hear that the medium herself felt that "the whole tragedy of Sir George has been so gruesome and appalling—and honestly haunts me."[18] And much as it haunted Edith, there was no solution.

In 1965, whilst on a skiing holiday in Switzerland, Francis Sitwell retrieved Sir George's ashes and took them back to England. They were interred near the remains of his ancestors in the parish church at Eckington near Renishaw.

TEN

Rebirth

This great flowering of her genius is her reward for years of devoted and patient labours at her work and art. . . .

                     Sir Maurice Bowra, of Edith Sitwell's work

DESPITE her preoccupation over Sir George's death, Edith managed to divert some of her unhappiness into a burst of poetic energy. Little of the circumstances of her emotional state was directly conveyed into her poems, as had been the case since she had taken Osbert's advice. Amongst one of her finest poems from her second new volume, *Green Song*, published in 1944, was *Invocation*, with opening lines that are as powerfully rhythmic as some by Yeats:

> I who was once a golden woman like those who walk
> In the dark heavens—but am now grown old
> And sit by the fire, and see the fire grow cold,
> Watch the dark fields for a rebirth of faith and of wonder.[1]

John Lehmann felt that Edith took symbols

from the widest range within our common culture, from Classical and Christian legend and history, and even beyond, from the primitive pre-history and shadowy beliefs of Europe: and she marries them with the more ancient and universal symbols of animal and flower, sea and sun and stars.[2]

Kenneth Clark, in his long essay on Edith's poetry, felt that Edith, unlike Yeats, did not

use symbols with fixed meanings. She has said of her poems that "all expression is welded into an image, not removed into a symbol that is inexact or squandered into a metaphor". The result is that although her poems may sometimes be vaguer than those of a strict symbolist, they never become mere riddles, as are some of the minor poems of Mallarmé. . . .[3]

To add to the praise of Lehmann and Kenneth Clark, Maurice Bowra had written an essay on her war poems, and his academic status (he was now Warden of Wadham College, Oxford) guaranteed that the essay would be widely read. He wrote:

With the publication of *Street Songs* in 1942 Miss Sitwell . . . has brought her technique to perfection. . . . This great flowering of her genius is her reward for years of devoted and patient labours at her work and art.[4]

After the years in Paris, the neglect of critics for over three decades, and seemingly endless nagging loneliness, Edith could hardly be blamed for feeling a great sense of triumph. If she was quick to administer a slap to those who had made little effort to understand her work, she was equally quick to thank those who were kind to her. Her letter of thanks to Bowra is marked by an almost pathetic gratitude, like that of a schoolgirl who can hardly believe that she has won first prize after being bottom of the class for so many years:

It would be quite impossible for me even to begin to say what great pleasure your essay on my war poems has given, and is giving me, or how profoundly grateful I am to you.

I wish I could express what it means to me to have my poetry so understood. . . .

There is so much to say, and so much to be grateful for, that I scarcely know where to begin.[5]

She concluded:

I said before, but must repeat again, I do *not* know how to express my gratitude to you, or the happiness your essay gives me . . . the

thought of it, the encouragement it gives, makes me inflexibly determined to work as hard as I have ever worked. It wouldn't be possible
to work harder, or I should do it.[6]

Soon Kenneth Clark joined Bowra, writing of her:

With the appearance of *Street Songs* and *Green Song*, those who care
for poetry recognised a true poetic and prophetic cry which had not
been heard in English since the death of Yeats. This was not merely
exquisite poetry, it was great poetry.[7]

Green Song became a universally acclaimed volume of war poetry, and Edith's reputation now seemed secure. It might have
seemed that the feuds that had punctuated her years of struggling could at last draw to a close. Not so. As her success was so
hard won, she was terrified that it might disappear overnight,
and she was racked with nerves if she thought any woman poet,
such as Kathleen Raine, could challenge her reputation. Whatever happened, and whatever she had to do, she would keep a
strong grip on the increasing circle of influential friends she had
acquired. Any disloyalty in the camp meant instant dismissal,
and she made every effort to frighten off anyone who might
threaten her supremacy.

Her malice to Kathleen Raine, for one, was inexcusable, but
Edith could never prevent herself from overreacting and Miss
Raine seemed to her a poet whose acclaim could spoil her own
new-found success.

Kathleen Raine, born in 1908, was as dedicated a poet as Edith
and in different ways had suffered great personal unhappiness.
The first volume of her poems, which appeared during the war,
received favourable reviews, which it clearly deserved. Miss
Raine had never attacked Edith, although she had every cause to
think unkindly of her: they shared a mutual friend who was kind
and generous but who was dismissed by Edith in the most cruel
fashion in a letter Miss Raine was shown. Edith was unaware of
this, but determined to try to stop Miss Raine gaining any reputation at all. She could never forget having been completely misunderstood in her childhood, and her bristles were her only defence,
along with her temper, but Kathleen Raine could hardly be expected to understand that. Edith's attitudes are partly explained
in a letter she wrote to Sachie in 1943, complaining again that he
refused to write or publish any poems:

Naturally I shouldn't think of warning you to do anything you don't
feel like doing at this moment, but of course you are quite wrong
about the poems, and about what could happen. (And incidentally,
what on earth do you mean about the great and wonderful poems
being "old fashioned", my darling, what do you mean? Poetry isn't a
matter of fashion excepting for a few fools who do not count and to
whom nobody now pays any attention) . . . I didn't write poems for
ten years but came back to my poetry more fresh than ever.

Now is our time—the tide has turned, we have many and powerful
adherents. . . . You speak of not being able to bear being torn to
pieces. I can assure you that amongst all the others, the many powerful adherents I spoke of, you have got the most powerful ally in Dr.
Bowra who, as I told you in my letter, would insist on that book [Sa-
chie's proposed *Selected Poems*] being properly treated. And to take
one example from the past: first look at your poor sister: has anyone
ever been more torn to pieces? But I am going strong. I know what
the fools who have insulted us in the past will be like in a hundred
years' time. I *know* what we are. And I'm damned if I'm going to
watch you throwing yourself away. . . . I do love you devotedly, my
darling, and worry about you all the time and cannot bear to think
of you ever having one moment of unhappiness.[8]

The parties at the Sesame that Edith now gave for her friends
and admirers contrasted strongly with the penny buns and strong
tea of her Bayswater days. Even in wartime the Club provided
acceptable food, and the pleasure of entertaining brought its own
rewards besides kind reviews. Critics like Cyril Connolly, who at
times disliked her "new poetry," found it difficult, after having
been her guest, to write what they really felt. Of course Edith
also attracted hangers-on who took her hospitality and never
repaid her kindness, but by and large she reaped benefits from
this entertaining.

Edith was fun to be with, and when she held court she never
acted the bully but was always a ready listener. The conversation
was often malicious, but as Stephen Spender said:

When one knew Edith well, one understood her, and realized that her
kindness was a completely redeeming side of her nature. She was a
very compassionate woman. . . . One knows enough about people to
realize that these seemingly irreconcilable things, are really very rec-
oncilable.[9]

The life Edith enjoyed at the Sesame made her feel guilty

about seeming wasteful to others. Sachie, as a result of Sir George's will, was in a state of financial crisis, worsened by having to keep Reresby at Eton, and his income sank to a low figure. Edith knew that Osbert's attitude to his brother was mean, but because she lived with Osbert and was partially dependent upon him, she had to transfer the entire blame for Sachie's misfortune onto Sir George. Apologetically she wrote to Sachie:

You must not think, my darling, that because you see a large luncheon party that your troubles are out of my mind . . . at Renishaw I spent no money, until I came to London in the autumn [1944]. . . . I had not been in London for a year and everybody has to have some relaxation. Surely the Swiss business will be settled. Also that Reresby's education will be nearly accomplished. I know how it is very easy to say that, but at least it is someone speaking who has been dragged down or might have been dragged down by financial worries for years, so she knows what she is talking about. . . .[10]

The luncheon party had been given after a reading at the Churchill Club in which Sachie had taken part with his brother and sister. By an uncannily dramatic stroke of coincidence, just as Edith was reading *Still Falls the Rain*, her poem about the bombing of London, a doodle-bug (flying bomb, or V-1) passed overhead. The incident was remembered by John Lehmann in his memoirs:

I do not imagine that anyone who was present will ever forget it. . . . Edith had, I believe, never experienced a doodle-bug raid before but she seemed quite unperturbed as she finished the passage:

> "Still falls the rain,
> Still falls the blood from the starved man's wounded side
> He bears in his heart all wounds"

The rattle grew to enormous proportions and it was impossible not to think that the monstrous engine of destruction was pointed directly overhead. . . . Edith merely lifted her eyes to the ceiling for a moment and giving her voice a little more volume to counter the racket in the sky, read on. . . . She held the whole audience in the grip of her discipline, the morale of her unspoken assertation that poetry was more important than all the terror that Hitler could launch against us. Not a soul moved and at the end when the doodle-bug had exploded far away, the applause was deafening.[11]

But not everyone was applauding Edith's poetic performance: Julian Symons murmured in the columns that her poetry "was removed from life,"[12] and Edith was predictably furious. Why Edith, who had earned the praise of Bowra and Clark, should have cared what Julian Symons wrote about her can only be ascribed to her oversensitivity. Symons, a poet and critic, was a friend and admirer of Wyndham Lewis, and she feared unjustifiably that they were plotting against her.

As she worked on her biography *Fanfare for Elizabeth,* she more and more came to identify herself with Elizabeth, almost convinced that she was a reincarnation of her. Unable to face up to the reality of her personal unhappy life, and afraid that she might reveal her true shy nature, Edith developed her "queenly" manner, using it with no holds barred in numerous vendettas. She wrote to Sachie after a victory won over Kathleen Raine:

I am beside myself with triumph. . . . Osbert says he never saw anything to equal it. I have told everybody where they get off and we get on. And they are trembling with fear, and write me crawling letters to which I reply much as Queen Elizabeth (Tudor) would have done.[13]

Street Songs, Green Song, and *The Song of the Cold* had been inspired by the war and, to quote the critic Alan Ross, "her heart began to beat more in time with the world's heart; her imagery became less artificial. . . ."[14] But even when the war ended, Edith's commentary was not over. She had flourished in this period and found her truest and most successful style. Having been moulded by this new experience, she continued in the same vein, and was in no way outmoded simply because the armistice had been signed. She wrote three poems inspired by the dropping of the atomic bombs, *Dirge for the New Sunrise, The Canticle of the Rose,* and *The Shadow of Cain.* "They have a hugeness of conception, an emphasis that goes towards identification of feeling, that despite a monotony of pitch is impressive and moving,"[15] Ross concluded.

In March 1946 a surprise letter from Dylan Thomas brought him back into her life. Thomas confessed it was

nine or ten years since I last met you . . . and all this time I've very much missed being able to write to you occasionally and to send you poems and to ask you about them, for I value with all my heart what you've said about them in the past. I find it so easy to get lost in my actions and my words and I know that, deeply lost so many times I could, after writing to you and through your writing, come somehow out, and up so much less sufferingly than I did into the miraculous middle of the world again.[16]

Thomas told Edith that he realized that he had in some way offended her through some

thoughtless irresponsible written or spoken word and I can't forgive myself that I can't remember exactly what the offence was . . . whatever it was it seemed to stop, as though for ever, our writing to one another let alone our ever meeting.[17]

He continued:

May I say now, as I know I should have said many years before how sorry and inarticulately, more than that, I am that some minor (or I hope so minor) presumption, conceit, seeming ingratitude, foul manner or worse, yes indeed far worse, interrupted our friendship just beginning, and lost for so long to me, the honour of being able to send my work as it was written to you, and to write to you of the never-ending problems of craft and meaning and heart that must always besiege us.

If my apology, true as my love of your *Song of the Cold* reads to you as stiltedly as quickly writing it sounds to me, I am sorry again, and can only say how hard I find it to move naturally into the long silence between now and nine beautiful, dreadful years ago.[18]

Thomas had been glad to forget about Edith, but he had read her review of his poems and was

profoundly moved by the experience of your profound and loving understanding of the poem. . . . I hope you will write to me, forgive me for a long gone never meant boorish blunder. . . . I hope you will let me meet you again. For months and months and grey months I have basemented in London . . . we are so miserably poor blast it, blast it. . . .

And I should like to tell you how I feel about all your poems written during the war if one day I am forgiven, and I may. . . . There is always a need to say what great work means to one man, how your creation is revelation and this revealed acceptance meet in a point . . . did Yeats say it of light? But I have written enough and too much, pass over it if you can and the tongue knotted awkwardnesses, these stammers for nine years back and I must wait now hoping all the time to hear from you.

Yours sincerely,
DYLAN THOMAS[19]

It was an extraordinary letter, revealing exactly how well
Dylan Thomas understood Edith; he flattered and admired her
work, and she could hardly ignore his apologetic pleas for forgiveness. Anyone other than Edith would have looked for motives: why did Thomas really wish to renew their friendship?
Moreover, Edith knew that he had often complained that she did
not really understand his poetry, but she ignored this. Thomas
knew that she would often forgive those who slighted her if she
admired their work. When Edith was in comparative obscurity
she was of little use to him, but now, in his desperate moments of
poverty, Thomas was strongly aware of Edith's growing reputation, and he must have assumed that with her family background
she had to be rich. The kindness Edith had shown him in the past
was a strong and fairly safe indication that Edith would not ignore his present appeal for help.

Edith did forgive him and, true to form, invited influential
friends who might be of use to him to the Sesame Club for dinner. They included John Hayward, T. S. Eliot, the "greatest living poet," Sachie, and Georgia. The dinner should have been a
triumph for Edith, flanked by three of her favourite poets, but a
warning came from Georgia that a lady was in distress in the
cloakroom. She tried to help and then went to tell the others
about what she had seen. "My wife," Dylan Thomas replied, and
when she emerged they sat down. Thomas was always a little
afraid of Edith, and he and Caitlin had probably braced themselves for the dinner with "a quick one."

All went well until Dylan Thomas turned to Eliot—then the
most widely admired poet writing in English, with an unassailable reputation—and flew at him about a reading of Milton he had
given that afternoon. "He muttered across me to Tom," Edith
wrote, "'I'm surprised we were allowed *Milton* this afternoon; I
thought he was dead.' Then in a tone of scorn, '*Dislodging* Milton
with very little fuss,' [Dylan Thomas continued, quoting what
F. R. Leavis had written about Eliot's criticism of Milton]. Tom
said mildly: 'I can't be responsible for what Leavis says.' 'Well,
you ought to *stop* him,' said D."[20]

Edith sat up in horror, but worse was to come: "And look here.
Why does a poet like you publish such *awful* poetry. *You know* it
is bad."[21] Edith's stature as a hostess was impaired, and the inci-

dent preyed on her mind. When she returned to Renishaw, she
wrote to Georgia:

Oh darling, I am still thinking of that most unfortunate dinner party.
Just how much havoc do you think it caused my carefully laid plans.
Dylan has disappeared off the face of the earth. But of course I can
see it is awkward for him.[22]

Thomas had taken fright, but once again he approached Edith
with contrite heart, begging her forgiveness, and once again
Edith forgave her favourite young poet. Had it been anyone else
they would have been ejected unceremoniously from her Olym-
pian court, but Edith was "really unable to think after the two
letters he wrote to me, that he could wish to be either rude or
hurt my feelings. That young man thinks us the most wonderful
family!"[23]

Shortly after the "unfortunate dinner" Evelyn Wiel arrived
from Paris, and in the New Year, Edith took her on holiday to
Bournemouth. Her patience with Evelyn was surprising considering that she really found her rather a bore; deaf and talkative,
making every conversation a strain, Evelyn still did not exhaust
Edith's loyalty. They had only the past to talk about, for Evelyn
"has no brains in particular"[24] and was not interested in poetry.
Edith herself was suffering from a bad winter cold, but there was
something about Evelyn's courage that made her forget her own
health. She listened enthralled to Evelyn's war adventures.

You know she has a heart of gold that makes my own nature seem so
bad in comparison. Utterly uncomplaining, sweet, sympathetic with
everyone else and with a dreadful resignation. She fell down in the
street in [occupied] Paris from weakness due to hunger! She has recently been starving partly because of the black market, she lived on
bread and butter and weak tea for tea and a supper of potatoes
(when there were any) and partly because she owed £100 to the
bank . . . she had kept this from Osbert and me.[25]

The slow return to normality after the war brought Edith a
sense of peace of mind, and she was even feeling humble enough
to take advice from Stephen Spender, although her letter seems
ambiguous in tone. "You show me where you go wrong," she
wrote to him, "and where I go right. Nothing could be more valuable to me. It is constructive criticism the whole way. . . . I am
never tired of working, never tired of learning. . . ."[26] Her corre-

spondence with Spender did not, however, mean that she accepted the rest of the Macspaunday Group;* although she felt her own reputation was less vulnerable than it had been, she was still afraid for Sachie.

What I mean is that Dylan absolutely eclipses Auden and tiresome as he is behaving, *he thinks you are a wonder.* He told me you can write everyone off the world. And he is right. Don't you see darling, that a new generation has arisen since Auden (who denigrates us). Now is the time. Now is the time. We have the new generation with us. (They'll never forgive Auden.) And Maurice Bowra is now Professor of Poetry at Oxford. Everything is in our hands. We are not where we were ten or fifteen years ago, I beg, urge and implore you to . . . *produce a new book of poems.*[27]

Edith had admired Eliot for many years, and for as long they had been good friends. The ever cautious Eliot had steadfastly refused to mention in print any of the Sitwells since he had reviewed some of their early books after the First World War. But now he was forced to recognize that Edith's reputation had reached great heights, and whatever he thought of her privately, he was able to ask for the first time for her official help. Eliot's old mentor, Ezra Pound, was the problem, as Eliot wrote to Edith:

3rd April 1946

My dear Edith,
As you know, Ezra Pound is in America awaiting trial for treason, for which the sentence might be the death penalty or a long term of penal servitude. He has been pronounced insane by a board of psychiatrists, has appeared before a jury which decided that he was unfit to stand trial, and has been placed in a hospital in Washington. It is possible, however, that after some mental equilibrium has been established, he may be pronounced fit for trial.

While it would not be in Pound's interest that any appeal on his behalf should be made by British writers at the present juncture, I have thought it desirable to draft the enclosed letter, with a view to enlisting the support of a small number of poets. You will observe that certain details are left incomplete, as the letter will be made public only after the sentence has been pronounced. The letter does not concern itself with the question of guilt or innocence: it is simply a statement

---

* "Macspaunday" was a composite nickname invented by Roy Campbell, referring to MacNeice, Spender, Auden, and Day Lewis.

affirming the importance of Pound's services to literature, and a plea
for clemency. It is intended to reinforce any efforts made by American
writers on his behalf. It is quite possible that there will be no occasion
to make use of this letter. But the statute under which Pound has been
committed to the hospital provides only that a person who is unable to
stand trial because of a mental condition shall be committed to the ju-
risdiction of the court if the mental difficulties are overcome. It may
well be that if Pound is tried, the sentence will be quickly given: and
it may then be too late to collect signatures in time to be of any use. I
shall therefore hold this letter against such a contingency.

If on the other hand Pound is eventually recognised to be permanently unfit for trial this letter will be inappropriate and will not be
made public. A wholly different legal situation will then be created
which will have to be met in quite a different way. I am sending this
letter to twelve or fifteen poets only. I shall be grateful if you can return it with your signature: or if you cannot, I shall be glad to receive
any criticism you may think fit to make.

I enclose together with this letter some extracts for your information
from the statement made by Pound's attorney to the District Court in
Washington.

Yours sincerely,
T.S.E.[28]

I do especially want your name, because there is no other woman poet
whose name would carry the necessary weight. I have not asked Osbert or Sachie because I feared that three names together would make
the American readers think I was packing the jury.

Pound had not exactly been one of Edith's favourite poets, and
she used to laugh good-naturedly behind his back, but she responded to Eliot's plea:

My dear Tom . . .
I am overcome with horror at this dreadful thing, and of course have
signed the appeal at once.

I can't bear to think of the man, and I can't bear to think of the poet
—I mean of his misery. But of course I *have* thought of it continually.
I've never allowed anyone to speak against him in my presence.

Even if he is not tried, what on earth will his future be like?
The extracts from the affidavit are quite unbearable.[29]

Edith was actually more concerned about Dylan, and just as
she had invoked Robert Herring's help ten years before, she now
pleaded with Maurice Bowra to persuade an American professor
to invite him over to the United States to give lecture recitals, so

that he could earn money for himself. Aware of his unpredictable behaviour, she once more adopted a parental attitude of knowing what was best for him and took him in charge:

On *no* account must Dylan go there [U.S.A.] to *live*, without the possibility of coming back, if he doesn't like it there, and if it doesn't suit him. . . .

I suggested to him he should go and lecture and read there (so as to look round) taking Caitlin, but not the children, with him. This would mean that their fares were paid, there and back. They must be.[30]

To John Lehmann she wrote that Dylan must be the "sole beneficiary" of a fund that had been set up to provide a travelling scholarship for authors. This fund was in fact the result of Edith's pulling strings, and was meant for her own protégés. She had persuaded her friend Bryher to make the initial contribution, and then used her as a mouthpiece for her own views:

The Anonymous Donor [she wrote] does *not* wish *journalists* or people of minor talent to get it. She wants the greatest artist in poetry or prose who can be found.[31]

Edith was afraid that Thomas would think her a "fussy old lady" if he discovered the lengths she had gone to, but this was far from the truth. The old lady still had claws left for Thomas's former friend Geoffrey Grigson, who she had heard was going to give a lecture in Sheffield. It was unthinkable to her to have an enemy on her own territory, and she earnestly (and quite erroneously) believed that Grigson was going there just to insult her. Edith wrote to the society that had invited Grigson to complain, and also instructed her lawyer to tell Grigson that she believed he "was indulging in a campaign of malice and calumny against her personally."[32]

Grigson answered the charge with great tact:

9th December, 1946

Dear Miss Sitwell,
May I ask you to be courteous enough to read, ponder and acknowledge this letter? . . . You will know by now what my solicitor replied: that the only ground on which I have written at any time about your poems has been the poems themselves. You will agree that if a critic holds his view strongly enough about any kind of book etc., he

has a right, if not a duty, to express those views. I should not grudge that right to you (indeed how many times have you exercised it!) and I do not expect any writer to grudge it, in his turn to me.

But the matter isn't quite so simple: you and your brother seem to think that I am preparing or executing a campaign of criticism. No, I have had my say; and though I am reprinting one of my articles, modified somewhat, and have referred once to your work in one other book, and once in one other article, both of which have been delayed in the printing, and though I have written strongly an imo ex corde upon the views and practice of poetry of a poet you much admire, there, I repeat, my criticism ends. I am not sure I do not regret (as Arnold regretted reaffirming his views on Tennyson) reprinting any adverse criticism; because as one approaches middle age one realises the priority of affirmation beyond attacks.

You say you have held your peace for ten years. I acknowledge that. I shall hold mine, partly for the reason I have just given; partly because a decline into reviving an old public discussion would be distasteful and without dignity; partly and importantly because (as you know) you, your brother and myself happen to share certainly one close friend, to me a very close friend, for many years. Dissensions of this kind interfere with friendship. He respects your personal kindliness and accepts your hospitality. I conclude that I must believe, as a friend, in his judgment. You will not expect me to recant my criticism of the past; I cannot expect you to recant yours. But if we can agree upon that expectation we may perhaps agree upon keeping for the future our judgments relating to each other's work to ourselves.

Yours sincerely,
GEOFFREY GRIGSON[33]

It seemed that at long last a truce was going to be made, for Edith replied:

Dear Mr. Grigson,
Your honest and honourable letter reached me by this afternoon's post. I shall of course reply to it at length, but in order to catch the post that goes early to-morrow morning I am writing meanwhile, this brief note to thank you for your letter, to say that I appreciate it greatly, and that I accept it in the same spirit as that in which it was written. May I say at the same time, that I have always admired your strong championship of the works you care for.

Believe me,
Yours sincerely,
EDITH SITWELL[34]

The second letter has not survived, but despite this conciliatory note there was no end to the feud. Lehmann, possibly not
realizing that Grigson had mentioned in his letter to Edith items
which were still to appear but which had been delayed in the
printing, had seen one of them. Shortly after she wrote to Grigson, Edith wrote also to Lehmann, apologizing for not having returned the "Grigsonia" before.

The poet Grigson referred to in his letter to Edith was Dylan
Thomas, and his attack on Thomas's poetry finally confirmed
Edith in her course of confrontation with Grigson. As she wrote
to Sachie, "I am in the midst of getting dear Mr. G. down and
under. He has asked for an Armistice, though in a most curmudg-
eonly way. . . ."[35] A chance for peace was lost, but for all Edith
complained about her feuds and enemies, they were a necessary
part of her life, both diverting her and keeping her alert.

One victim of her habit of jumping to conclusions and venting
impulsive anger was Lawrence Durrell, who had remarked that
at any other time the work of the Sitwells "would have been only
printed in private presses."[36] It was a careless comment, made
worse when Durrell inadvisedly wrote to Osbert asking for his
help to publicize an exhibition of Henry Miller's paintings. Edith
wrote an angry letter to Lehmann: "I for one am sick of being attacked by persons of no talent, and of a small talent like Mr. Durrell's."[37] Durrell's insult had reminded her of Noël Coward's
revue that had upset her in the 1920s. Both incidents, to her
mind, were foul and groundless attacks, and in the case of Durrell the offence she felt was exaggerated out of proportion because she really admired his work. Many years later, when her
annoyance was forgotten, she was actually defending him:

Mr. Lawrence Durrell, who is the editor of the new P.E.N. anthology,
is in trouble with the reviewer of that book because he is a fine writer
and therefore famous. . . .[38]

It was declining poetic standards that Edith really hated,
though she always considered herself the sole arbiter of taste.
Her arguments, because she lacked the intellectual or academic
method of analysis, often fell into the trap of being only witty,
but nevertheless she could demolish arguments with a simple
phrase and was a force to be reckoned with.

Eventually, however, as he had warned, Grigson's attack on

Dylan Thomas's work appeared in *Polemic* and Edith turned to complain to Bowra: "The editor has had the temerity to ask me, of all people in the world, to answer it! I am returning his letter to him, with a few very sinister remarks."[39] Edith relied on Bowra more and more for his support and influence. Cyril Connolly was not entirely enthusiastic about her poems, and so he had been toppled out of favour: the "Chevalier," as she called him, had shocked her because he had "the impertinence to contradict you [Bowra] in matters of poetry. It springs from this idea that the dilettante is always right! . . ."[40]

Enemies were made, but so were friends. Benjamin Britten wrote to her asking if she would read the entertainment *Façade* at the Aldeburgh Festival. She had met Britten in Sheffield after a concert at which the Griller Quartet played a composition of his for strings at Renishaw. She had enjoyed the music, and friendship with Britten soon flourished; musicians were important to her, for there was always the chance that they would set her work. By September 1951 he was writing:

Thank you . . . for sending me the "Canticle of the Rose" poems. I find them, the later ones especially, profoundly moving. . . . Several of them appeal to me for music—if ever the ideas blossomed, would you allow me to set them? I'd do my best for them. . . .[41]

The following May an honorary Litt.D. was conferred on Edith by Leeds University at the instigation of Bonamy Dobree, the Professor of English Literature there. As might be expected, she was delighted; indeed so proud was she to be called Dr. Sitwell that she began the irritating habit of signing her name on the back of envelopes with her honorary doctorate, even on letters to her family. Because she had never attended any school, she regarded her doctorate as an enormous achievement. She particularly regretted not having attended university, because there she might have studied Latin and Greek, and as she had no knowledge of either, she felt she had missed out on the whole field of classical literature.

In her speech to Leeds University on the day she received her honorary degree she said:

It was my strong ambition as a girl to be sent to University. But this was not allowed, and for the oddest reason. Nobody could admire Tennyson's great poetry more passionately than do I, but my father was under the sway of Lord Tennyson's longer poems . . . regarding him, not as we should as one of the greatest lyrical poets . . . but as an infallible law giver and philosopher. Instead of seeing *The Princess* as a farrago of condescending nonsense, interspersed by some of the most wonderful lyrics in the English language—he gained from that poem the impression that for a woman to be an undergraduate at a University would result in her becoming unwomanly. He did not seize the point that Tennyson made that the segregation of women was a mistake as indeed it most certainly is. Rather he concentrated on the false assumption that learning makes women unfeminine, foreseeing I might write:

> Awful odes
> And dismal lyrics prophesying change.

Well of course that was exactly what, a few years later I was going to do.[42]

An event that pleased her as much as her doctorate was the news that Sachie was going to publish a volume of *Selected Poems*. Her kindly bullying and carefully planned meetings with Dr. Bowra, who also encouraged Sachie, had worked. Three letters in a week arrived at Weston Hall, and in one Edith wrote:

No words could ever say how proud I am to be your sister, my darling, it seems almost incredible considering how much I love poetry that I should have the supreme happiness of being your sister. Osbert's preface has just come . . . it is perfect, exactly what is needed.[43]

Although Osbert had written the preface in return for Sachie's help in a similar volume of Osbert's, Edith was having to write his letters to Sachie. Relations had become strained between the two brothers because of Osbert's continuing selfishness, and Edith was placed in the difficult position of acting as mediator. Behind Osbert's back she wrote to Sachie:

About what you say about feeling a distance from Osbert, darling, there is no distance. Osbert is absolutely and completely devoted to you, there is no change in him. . . .[44]

Blaming Sir George, she continued:

I think I can explain exactly what it is you feel . . . that old devil of a father of ours has naturally caused the most ghastly worry and unhappiness . . . you and Osbert are both sick with unhappiness and worry . . . and why? Because when you see each other it brings the unhappiness to the surface. The unhappiness is then talked of, the talk continues and nothing else is spoken of but worries. . . .[45]

Edith's solution—for she refused to be disloyal to Osbert—was that Osbert and Sachie should meet and *not* discuss the problems. Desperately she tried to convince Sachie that all was well.

Nothing has happened to spoil Osbert's love for you . . . get it absolutely out of your head this thing about Osbert . . . after all was there ever a family who had more in common? Was there ever a family that was more truly devoted?[46]

Edith took Osbert with her to the presentation of her honorary doctorate, but Sachie and Georgia felt unable to go, as they were aware of a difficult atmosphere between Georgia and Osbert.

The reason for this tension was a revival of the problems with Noël Coward. Both Osbert and he had been invited to Buckingham Palace by Queen Elizabeth, wife of King George VI, and Osbert found it difficult to avoid Coward after he had reluctantly apologized under the royal roof. Edith had never forgiven Coward, but there had been comparative peace for nearly twenty years, as it was only the principle that upset her. Osbert took pains to prevent her from knowing of the newly buried hatchet, but Georgia, whose candour Edith always admired, even if the initial impact sometimes surprised her, told Edith about the "palace affair." Her first reaction was fury, but there were enough family problems and Edith was anxious to make peace, so she adopted a soothing tone. She wrote:

My darling Georgia,
Do not let us think any more at all about the Coward affair. Let us never think of it again and never refer to it again. It is over and done with and forgotten . . . only think of happy things and nothing to make us upset or unhappy. . . .

I have got one of those wretched sore throats that isn't a cold . . . it is simply fatigue and excitement, I think. But it was very exciting being made a Doctor on Friday. I am to be called Dr. Edith Sitwell in future and have my envelopes addressed: "Miss Edith Sitwell, Litt.D."[47]

ELEVEN

Pavlik and "Queen" Edith

Dear me, how much I *do* like the Americans. Anyone who doesn't, must really be mad. . . .

Letter to John Lehmann

IN EARLY 1948 Pavlik sent a card to Edith informing her that he was going to France, accompanied by Monroe Wheeler of the Museum of Modern Art in New York, to see Somerset Maugham, and that he hoped Edith would meet Wheeler to discuss the possibility of a lecture tour in America arranged by the Museum. Arrangements were made, and this time the difficulties Edith had over her proposed tour of 1939 were not encountered.

In preparation for her visit, the publisher James Laughlin, a friend of Charles Henri Ford, organized a volume of tributes from Edith's friends and admirers. Planned for some time, it was published by New Directions as *A Celebration for Edith Sitwell*. The editor, José García Villa, wrote to Arthur Waley, amongst others, for a contribution. Waley, who had been well aware of Edith's wrath over his mistress, Beryl de Zoete, and who was eager to avoid possible repercussions over any accidental offence he might cause in his essay, was wary about writing about Edith, but as he had told her:

I at once replied to García Villa that I couldn't because although I like

reading poetry, I hate writing about it. But you . . . have this unfair
dominion over me. You give one such exquisite pleasure by your art
that one simply cannot refuse anything you ask. . . . I fear it will go
badly wrong . . . and probably we shan't be on speaking terms for
weeks. . . .[1]

Edith was more anxious to have an essay included by her new
friend Jack Lindsay. The Marxist poet had written fulsome praise
of her work, and to her his politics did not matter; he was soon
"that great critic." Acceptance by a Marxist writer pleased Edith,
even though she did not understand politics. Lindsay had placed
her as a "poet of the people" and had even derived an interpre-
tive message from Edith's *Façade*. This was flattery Edith could
not ignore, although she herself had largely rejected her earlier
work, believing that her later philosophical poems contained
what she wanted to be remembered by and praised for. Now
Lindsay had made the early work critically respectable, and no
one could accuse her of having socially bribed him, as he had not
even met her when he wrote this appraisal of her work.

His understanding of her work encouraged her to develop
what might be described as a more socially conscious style in her
poetry. Soon, too, second-hand books on mythology were arriving
at Renishaw. Edith was doing her homework, and Lindsay also
helped her to understand some of the myths. As Pavlik was so
obsessed with myth, there was another benefit in the prospect of
thus strengthening the bond between them. Jack Lindsay's essay
was a "great inspiration and excitement for my mind,"[2] and as
the visit to America drew nearer, Edith sat boldly marking the
books under the oil lamp that made her eyes ache, ready to ingra-
tiate herself with Pavlik.

She sailed in October 1948 with Osbert and David. The voyage
was exhausting. They were at sea long enough for her to feel anxious about Pavlik, whom she had not met for ten years, although
they had exchanged letters twice a week since the outbreak of
the war. Pavlik had now cast Edith in the role of "La Dame
Blanche" in his private mythology, and in his imagination she
continued in her old role as his muse. But of course Edith could
not read Pavlik's unpredictable moods, and her memories were of
their last meeting, which had ended on a sour note. This was the
occasion when, in 1938, she had worn a black mourning dress as
a tribute to Helen Rootham and he had told her it was unsuita-

ble, making her look like a "giant orphan." Now it would be
different, and Pavlik had written her a message of hope before
she left for New York, with an affectionate, almost protective
warning:

Soon you will be here, and we will be able to talk about many things—
I would be so glad—I can't believe it. You'll find New York very childish and very exhilarating, also very trying—but you have to know how
to protect yourself from some people—they devour one if one lets
them.[3]

Pavlik was undecided about whether or not to meet Edith at
the pier, and he had still not made up his mind an hour before
the ship was due in. Charles Henri Ford suggested to him that it
would be "grotesque" of him not to meet her, after all she had
suffered through the war.

Pavlik had been working on a huge canvas that was a visual
representation of his mythological ideas, and had kept Edith informed of its progress. When the work was completed it was
called "Hide and Seek" and it was bought by the Museum of
Modern Art, where it still hangs. Spurred on by the thought that
Edith would soon see his masterpiece, he dressed hurriedly and
went to the pier.

Pavlik had been afraid that the reunion might prove to be an
anticlimax, half aware that he cherished Edith too idealistically in
his imagination, like the "Great Sybil" portrait he had made of
her in 1937, and that in the flesh she would be less inspiring. Surprisingly, everything went well, and Pavlik, who enjoyed ceremonial occasions, was pleased that he had gone to meet her.

In her posthumously published autobiography, Edith wrote
that her "first impressions of New York were overwhelming. Everybody appeared to be young. It was not possible to imagine
that people so alive could be old."[4] When they arrived at the
Hotel St. Regis, where they were staying, Edith insisted on bend-
ing over the endless flowers that had arrived for her until at 2:00
A.M. an attack of lumbago drove her to bed.

During the war years Edith had been friendly with Alice Pleydell-Bouverie, the sister-in-law of Mrs. Vincent Astor. The Astors
had agreed to underwrite the expenses in the event of the tour's
being a financial loss, and because they owned the St. Regis
Hotel, it was the natural place for Edith and Osbert to stay. The

hotel was the setting for a reunion dinner given for Pavlik by Osbert and Edith. David Horner was there by Osbert's side, and they also invited the ballet critic Lincoln Kirstein, and the director of the Museum of Modern Art, Monroe Wheeler.

Pavlik had kept his good looks although showing signs of balding. He preferred to dress more casually now he was in America and, dinners apart, often wore sweaters, baggy trousers, and tennis shoes. Since he had last met Edith she had grown plumper, partly because, unlike the old days in Paris, there was no reason to take walks, which she had always hated and always avoided if she could, and partly as a result of the better food she was eating at Renishaw and in the Sesame.

To please Pavlik, Edith wore a dress made out of gold and black material which he had sent her, and with which she tried to conceal her fuller figure. In his mythology he saw her as a bee-princess, and incidentally, she had written several poems with bee imagery, inspired by the Upanishads. As with the black dress she wore when they last met, the cut did not please him, and he told Edith it was "unlike the Mediaeval style he had suggested."[5] He did not realize that many of her clothes were made by a dressmaker at Eckington, a large mining village near Renishaw, because Edith could not afford the services of a London couturier. Gradually the tension relaxed and Pavlik made arrangements for Edith to see "Hide and Seek" the next morning.

Unfortunately Edith's lumbago prevented her from going to the Museum, and Pavlik interpreted this as an excuse. He had written her lengthy letters about the work while it was being prepared and expected her to rush to see it as soon as possible. Feeling piqued, he tried to withdraw from a lunch to which he had been invited, but Osbert pressed him to attend, as it had already been ordered. He agreed to come, but could not control his disappointment over the abortive visit to the Museum. He launched yet another attack on Edith during the meal, this time over her red turban. He declared that it was "too fixed," and Edith, anxious to excuse herself again, explained that she had not made it. Pavlik interrupted, insisting that "those she made herself were better." The whole atmosphere depressed Edith beyond words, sensitive as she was to personal criticism. To try to impress on Pavlik the regard with which she was held by some friends in Britain, she left telephone messages to him from "Dr.

Sitwell." Pavlik was, understandably, only scornful of the use of the title between the two of them.

At last the moment arrived when Edith and Osbert stood before "Hide and Seek" with the artist. The intense personal feeling Pavlik had for this work, which he considered the culmination of his artistic technique and his private mythology, made him nervous in anticipation of her reaction, knowing him as well as she did. Edith said nothing. Pavlik seethed with rage, unable to believe that there could be no response from his closest friend. Did Edith see nothing in it, or everything, he wondered.

Later in the afternoon she wrote him a long letter, full of praise for it, which he received the next morning. Ford told Pavlik he was foolish to place too much value on Edith's silence in the gallery, but Pavlik refused to be placated as he considered the letter was *too* gushing and merely an attempt to placate him after the event.

The painting itself is difficult to comment on. A predominant mass of embryonic shapes is detailed with delicate blue and red veins. It is unlikely that Edith, who knew Pavlik so well, was unaware of what the painting meant to him. With the tension that had built up since they met again, she was terrified of saying the wrong thing on impulse and was being a little too cautious. Pavlik would have been satisfied only with a theatrical gesture of approval, and Edith, out of politeness at least, must have remarked that she liked it, however quietly. After Pavlik received the letter, Edith went to see him, but there was no mention of the painting.

Amongst the first to welcome the two Sitwells was the owner of the Gotham Book Mart, Miss Frances Steloff. Her bookstore had become as legendary as Shakespeare & Company in Paris, but the modest Miss Steloff was uncertain whether Edith and Osbert would accept an invitation for tea there. In late September Edith had gratefully accepted the invitation, which had been arranged by Charles Henri Ford. She wrote to Miss Steloff: "It is very charming of you to ask us. We both think a day *after* a reading better than a day before a reading because of our voices. And for the same reason intensified we never do anything on the actual day of the reading."[6]

The party was arranged for November 9, in collaboration with Edith's American publishers, Vanguard, who published her book of poems *Street Songs* on that day. It turned out to be the party of the season. *Time-Life* photographers arrived and fought their way through the huge gathering, selecting candidates to make up group photographs. Their choice was not entirely tactful: William Carlos Williams was excluded, as was William Saroyan, who was so disappointed that he never returned to the store.

Everyone had brought a friend, and the hubbub was chaotic as the press photographers knocked drinks out of guests' hands in an effort to reach Edith and Osbert. Edith pined for a cup of tea, but Miss Steloff's efforts to reach her from the tea-table were in vain. Edith had attracted, as Bennett Cerf, the American humorist and publisher, wrote, "the darndest assortment of celebrities, freaks, refugees. . . ."[7]

But Edith enjoyed it thoroughly, as it gave her a chance to make new friends and renew old friendships. Her books were displayed in the shop and attracted the attention of Vera Stravinsky, the wife of the composer, who was paying a visit to the bookshop with Robert Craft, Stravinsky's assistant. Miss Steloff told Craft that she could arrange for Edith to sign any of the books for Mrs. Stravinsky. Craft spoke to Mrs. Stravinsky for a moment and returned to say that Mrs. Stravinsky would like to meet Edith. When Edith was told she was delighted and suggested that the Stravinskys and Miss Steloff should dine at the St. Regis with Osbert and her. But the Stravinskys were in New York only for a day, so they replied with an invitation to the Sitwells to sit in their box with them and W. H. Auden during a performance that afternoon of Stravinsky's works. Edith had always had the greatest respect for Stravinsky, whom she referred to as "Mr. Stravinsky," claiming that his music had been an influence on her poetry, and was delighted to accept.

Another figure associated with Stravinsky was Jean Cocteau, an old friend of Sachie's whom Edith had never met, and Charles Henri Ford arranged for them to lunch together, with Glenway Westcott, the novelist and critic. Cocteau, in his usual electric manner, tried to hold court, while Edith, displaying great patience, listened courteously. Cocteau was full of his idea for a film based on the life of Joan of Arc, with Ingrid Bergman in the star part, and he elaborated on it at great length. Edith would have been amused if she could have known that the project was never to be accomplished. Meanwhile she was silent, saving her thunder.

"As a matter of fact," Cocteau said, "a fact that foreigners are apt not to realize, even francophile foreigners such as you, Mademoiselle, is that French people really do not like Joan of Arc."

Mademoiselle Sitwell was ready. "Oh, Monsieur Cocteau," she replied, "I am glad to know this. For as it happened it was one of my ancestors who burned her, and this has often embarrassed me when talking to my French friends." Unfortunately for Edith, although Cocteau took no offence, her humour, which was often ice-breaking, failed on this occasion.

"Quelle merveille!" Cocteau replied. "C'est la vraie morgue anglaise." ["How wonderful! True English arrogance."][8]

Although Edith was never to become a close friend of Cocteau's, because she still disliked his work, their friendship later developed sufficiently well for him to send her drawings in return for the gift of her *Collected Poems* in 1957. "Ce remerciement est venu de mon coeur qui vous aime (c'est à dire qui vous admire)" ["These thanks come from my heart, which loves you (that is, which admires you)"], and later, "Je peux rapprendre l'anglais de mes rêves et de mon enfance dans votre livre de poèmes. Les gens oublient que le génie existe. . . . Restez ce que vous êtes et ce que nous émerveille." ["I can learn again the English of my dreams and of my childhood in your book of poems. People forget that genius exists. . . . Remain that which you are and which astonishes us."][9]

Meanwhile, such meetings as Edith had with the famous were resented by Pavlik, who was jealous of the publicity they were given. Pavlik, not being a writer, was often left out of the company and had not been invited to the *Time-Life* party. It infuriated him to read the *Life* report on the Gotham Book Mart party, where the Sitwells were described as "the senior members of England's most celebrated living literary family who gave the New York literary set its biggest thrill in years."[10] He felt that Edith did not pay enough attention to his young friends and was desperately anxious that she should get on well with Charles Henri Ford and his actress sister, Ruth.

After years of neglect in Britain, and the strain of interminable battles there, it was exalting for Edith and Osbert to be greeted with the same attention usually paid to visiting royalty. Edith soaked up the praise that the press gave her. *Life* continued its report:

The Sitwells behaved more like lambs than lions. They gave a joint reading of their poetry at the Town Hall where the largely female audience bustled rudely in and out during the performance, but the Sitwells read patiently on. At big cocktail parties they surprised everyone by their polite habit of shaking hands with and saying goodbye to everybody. At appointments they were punctual to the second. While Edith had 'flu, Osbert dashed off to give lectures at Montreal and Buffalo. . . . Edith swept around New York looking like a medieval sorcerer, in flowing capes and gowns topped by a vermilion turban.[11]

Such reports made Pavlik say to friends that Edith was "loitering in the public eye." As an artist he had never received such acclaim, and because he felt the credit was his for arranging the visit, he had hoped he might share her glory. His attitude to Edith was now completely coloured by the "Hide and Seek" incident and she was at once demoted from "La Dame Blanche" and made to fit a new image. This time it was "Isis," the butcher of the body of Osiris in the Tarot pack, because he happened to be reading about the subject at the time.

It is hardly surprising that Pavlik's insistence on forcing himself and Edith into an artificial mythology put strains on their relationship. At times, however, he spoke of Edith with great insight and told Ford that "there are two people in her I can't put together."[12] Like many others, he could not reconcile her poetry with her public manner. Pavlik wanted Edith to be more feminine, which recalls his complaint once that *he* wanted to be the man, and that she was not to "wear the pants."

Apart from the strain of Pavlik's behaviour, Edith liked being in New York. "I enjoy myself most of the time very much. And we *seem* to be having a great success, if I may say so," she wrote to John Lehmann. Crowds had to be turned away from many of their halls where they were giving readings, and in Yale they read before an audience of fourteen hundred. They spent Christmas in Boston in deep snow and returned to New York in January for a recital of *Façade* at the Museum of Modern Art. During the dress rehearsal Edith was given a standing ovation. David Horner also took part, reading *Tango-Pasodoble*.

When the Sitwells were due to return to England in the middle of March, a farewell dinner was given at Voisins, a fashionable

New York restaurant, and this gave Pavlik his chance to humiliate Edith publicly. He had already confided to Ford that "she has neither intelligence nor heart. . . . I'd like to slap her face, and have her kneel at my feet and crawl like a worm."[13]

During the meal, in earshot of those at her table, he rebuked her loudly for her behaviour and told her that their "affair" was finished. It did not have the desired effect; by now Edith was used to his insults and, although bitterly hurt, managed to ignore him and showed no emotion at that moment. But when she left the restaurant, she burst into tears. When Osbert and Edith finally departed for the boat, she gave him a note:

Though you are for some reason angry with me, I do not know the cause. You must know in your heart that I have been a devoted friend to you for over twenty years. It was a most terrible blow to me, coming to New York to find that you were unhappy and then ill—really it was one of the most terrible blows of my life.

You gave me no opportunity of showing you what I felt, but I was really shattered by it, as Osbert knew.[14]

Although the trip had been a resounding success for Edith as a poet, it was with considerable relief that she and Osbert disembarked at Southampton. They were exhausted, and Renishaw in the early spring provided a complete and welcome relaxation after the past few hectic months. But the peace was soon interrupted by a letter from Pavlik. He accused Edith, amongst other things, of ingratitude to himself and Ford, who had made it possible for the Sitwells to be in America in the first place, and for turning her back on his "left-wing" artist friends. In a letter dated March 28, 1949, which Edith wrote in three drafts because she was trying to be tactful as well as firm, she removed her opening sentence: "Your heartless and callous letter reached me this afternoon." Despite her bitterness at having to write, she knew Pavlik too well to let her first impulsive anger provoke him further.

I have never since I first met you, put myself before you. I have not changed in the sense of which you accuse me of changing. . . . I knew from the evening after we arrived in New York, that you had changed towards me. You could not even pretend to want to talk to me. I quite understand that I had been looking forward to seeing you for ten years—it doesn't matter. I shall get over it, and shall never refer to it again, only I can't let you say that this is due to my alleged treatment of your artist friends. I had not even met them.[15]

She also explained that she had undergone an operation on her throat for the removal of a growth, which might have been malignant, and that she suffered great pain, but "I did not tell you this because I did not think it would be of the slightest interest to you." Edith concluded her letter with the words:

You have been turned against me by various people who are merely envious because audiences enjoy my recitals . . . you are wrong in thinking you have to make all personal relationships clear to me; it is quite unnecessary. I have neither the right nor the wish to make any claims upon your time. I have made no claims of any kind at all; I have no wish to disturb either you or your great work.

As ever, and hoping your health is already much better,

EDITH[16]

Walking later in the gardens of Renishaw, she met a gardener who was working on the hedges. He remarked that he had read something in the paper about "Hide and Seek." Turning away, she told him, "That painting will be left to me, and when I get it you can cut it up and put it on your beehives."[17]

TWELVE

A Sense of Betrayal

I have had a few years very near to despair . . . and becoming
friends with you means so much to me. . . .

Letter to Carson McCullers

IN SPRING 1949, after the trip to America, Edith was bored and
unhappy about her disastrous scene with Pavlik. Their correspondence was now hardly lukewarm and soon became so nasty
that after one letter Edith burst into tears and took down all
Pavlik's pictures from her room, even giving away a few of them.
Life seemed empty and could be brightened only by a new interest or something to boost her morale. This materialized in a setting of *Gold Coast Customs* by the musician Humphrey Searle,
who was, she told Sachie, "a really great composer . . . it is really wonderful music . . . someone . . . I can't remember who
[this phrase often meant herself] said it was the greatest work
since the *Sacre du Printemps*."[1]

That was a claim that even Searle could not make, but her excitement, combined with the flattery Searle gave her, made her
enthusiasm uncontrollable. American audiences, she knew, were
very different from the British ones, and however much she could
get away with queenly behaviour in America she knew she could
not always take it for granted that her reputation was secure in

England. Edith's style, her wit, and her aristocratic background
appealed to the Americans, who adored "characters," but while
the popularity Edith achieved in the United States helped to sell
her poetry, it also accidentally created an unhelpful critical atmosphere for her work. The rapturous enthusiasm was for Edith
herself, as a curiosity, rather than for her work; and those who
were fascinated by her personality rarely understood her poetry.
A comment by a critic sums up the feelings felt by many: "It is
not what she writes, but what she is, that exerts the real fascination."[2]

In July 1949 she went to Durham for her second honorary degree (D.Litt.), and it was a "great day" for somebody with such
a love of ceremony. The only regret she had was that she couldn't
wear her doctor's robes in "ordinary life":

They were wonderful. A pale strawberry red silk, burdened with real
cloth of gold, in consistency like almond paste, with dim gold sparkles
over it. And a cap of soft black velvet, diamond-shaped and looking as
if it was going to sprout with feathers at the corners. The ceremony
was wonderful. . . .[3]

By now Pavlik had deserted her, and she needed a new champion. Her latest find was Roy Campbell, the South African poet
who was best known for his support for Franco during the
Spanish Civil War. Edith had been unkind about him in the past,
although he was never an "official" enemy. Now she wrote to
Sachie:

I am sure I should deplore the fracas that took place at the B.B.C. tea
rooms yesterday . . . the tea room where the B.B.C. boys have their
elevenses, but as it is . . . I don't.

Grigson was sighted in the tea room and the news reached Roy
Campbell in his office. Telephoning his secretary to telephone me and
also to ask us to come and occupy ring seats (unfortunately I was
out), Roy marched in to the tea rooms and there in the presence of
many witnesses he marched up to Grigson and said "Stand up, coward", hauled him to his feet, took off Grigson's spectacles and put
them in his pocket, shook him violently and protractedly and then
gave him what he calls "a couple of good ones". All the time Grigson
was crying, yes crying and saying, "Please don't Roy, please don't hit
me".[4]

There was not a word of truth in Edith's account; it was simply another instance of her believing what she wanted in order to suit her own fantasy. Campbell had not even attacked Grigson, although they had a meeting, during which they had a slight and brief quarrel over the critic Desmond MacCarthy. Nevertheless, Campbell became her newest champion and took his place amongst the guests at the Sesame.

She harped on about the incident in a tactless manner, seemingly oblivious of the fact that her friend Spender had indeed been physically attacked by Campbell on that same day. Also, their mutual friend Cecil Day Lewis had been the subject of an article by Campbell which, had it been about her, would have occasioned a letter to her lawyer. This, too, she disregarded. She persuaded herself that Campbell was defending her, and when William Plomer, the novelist, a friend she liked, dared to suggest she should be reasonable she reacted by calling him "odious." "Well," she wrote, "I think Plomer is very right to take the side of a great poet like Day Lewis instead of a woman who is the *poet* I am. And yet I think I know whose poetry will be remembered."[5]

The attention she had received in the United States not only caused Edith a loss of confidence when back in Britain, but also helped to promote her own *folie de grandeur* as compensation. The wartime wave of her popularity in Britain was declining, something she had always feared, and she was writing very little poetry. The less attention she was given by the press, the more desperate and irrational she became, and she resolved with an absolute determination not to "sink into obscurity." *The Canticle of the Rose* appeared, really a new volume of selected poems, and many reviewers who had previously written about the same poems felt unable to give the volume long reviews. This was the last straw for Edith, and she announced that she would "never, never allow the British public to see one of my poems again. Never. They shall all be published in book form in America and I will give them to my friends here."[6]

She worked her nerves up to a pitch that fresh family problems did nothing to diminish. Osbert now scarcely maintained even polite relations with Sachie and Georgia, and the tension was always a source of regret to Edith. As Osbert was now fifty-seven and the early symptoms of Parkinson's disease had appeared in him, Edith felt she could cite his age as a reason for refusing to attach any blame to him. But she well understood Sachie's position and constantly sympathized with him. A scapegoat had to be found to resolve her divided loyalties, and it was again poor Georgia who received a few raps in a series of letters to Veronica Gilliat, her cousin:

Life here is really hell, and I don't think the breach will be made up. I love Sachie dearly and cannot bear to think of everything that has happened . . . on the one hand I have got S. thinking he had been chucked out of the family by our going to America without him. Thinking also that he was promised money by Ginger which he hasn't had, and on the other hand I have got O. thinking that a monstrous suggestion has been made to him. Between the two of them, I am devastated. . . . G. is behaving hysterically also because one of Osbert's lawyers told her that Osbert doesn't like her. . . .[7]

Georgia had tried to tell Osbert frankly that they were desperately poor, with a family to support, and that they needed his financial help. A visit to America would have helped Sachie and Georgia enormously financially, but they would not have countenanced the embarrassing grand manners of Edith and Osbert when over there. Furthermore, Georgia loyally believed that Edith's behaviour to critics and others was not helping Sachie's career. He was encountering his own friends, such as the novelist Rose Macaulay and the artist John Piper, with whom Edith had quarrelled, and was constantly being placed in difficult situations because of his sister's quarrels. It did not, of course, lessen his love for Edith, as he had long been used to her battles and admired her courage; but Georgia felt that if Sachie was going to say nothing, *she* would have to speak out and the quarrels would have to stop, if he was to continue writing.

Edith could only see the situation as an attack on her and Osbert and, into the bargain, was reminded of a subject she did not want to think of, her own overdraft. Difficult as her financial position was, she herself never dared to ask Osbert for help. The large sums she spent to encourage struggling writers by giving them lavish meals and praise, the parties she provided, and all the expenses of her busy London social life were taking a heavy toll on her income.

More than ever, Edith seemed to be echoing the life of the woman she had so despised, her mother. The martinis were grow-

ing larger; Edith found that alcohol kept her warm in the freez-
ing rooms of Renishaw and helped to stave off her worries, or so
it seemed. Going upstairs with Lorna Andrade, Osbert's secretary, whose room was next to hers at Renishaw, Edith asked, "Do
they still send people to prison for debt?" This horrifying question made Miss Andrade shudder; she realized Edith was thinking of Lady Ida. Reassuringly Miss Andrade replied, "No, and in
your case they wouldn't kill the golden goose that laid the golden
egg."[8]

The one person from whom Edith needed comfort was Pavlik,
but her hurt feelings would not allow her to approach him. Instead she had received worrying news of his health from Charles
Henri Ford: Pavlik had colitis. Guilt superseded her bitterness
towards him, and she longed to see him again. A chance came
when he went to Rome with Ford and wrote to her for the first
time since their quarrel, trying to get money out of her. "If only,"
he appealed, "some of the rich people in New York could get an
idea to give me a yearly income on which I can rely and get some
work done in peace and not in fear and misery."[9] Edith tried to
tell herself that she was no longer hurt by him, but she had been
wounded too often before and realized that a meeting in Rome
would be a mistake.

It was easier for her to see Pavlik in Montegufoni, where, as
guests, he and Ford would have to be polite, and in early May
1950 Edith set off for Italy. There were the familiar travel disasters that she always suffered en route, mainly because she carried
an innumerable number of cases which always caused delays at
the customs. (One case that always went with her contained old
newspapers and cuttings.) Amongst cuttings that arrived with
her at Montegufoni was one from an Oxford undergraduate magazine, *The Isis*, about a performance of *Façade*. Edith had gone
to considerable trouble to meet some students who wished to perform *Façade*, even letting them come to the Sesame to hear her
own recent American recordings. The item that displeased her
most read:

During the vacation John Catlin arranged an audience with Miss Sitwell, and all those readers domiciled in the metropolis wilted into the
Sesame Club to meet the *doyenne* of drawing-room letters. . . . Later
tea was served and the literati sat at Edith Sitwell's feet; I saw the

shade of Harold Acton run along the window curtains as the at-
tenuated atmosphere of the twenties pervaded the fragile afternoon.[10]

From Montegufoni one small but explosive letter was sent to
her publisher, Macmillan, who had originally arranged the meeting. She told Daniel Macmillan that although she had liked the
performers very much, "those dear young people recite it as if
they were performing an egg and spoon race. . . . I have given
permission for it to be performed, withholding my full opinion of
horror of the performance."

What I did not expect was the enclosed grossly impertinent cuttings
written by a lout who accompanied them, and uninvited by me, made
his way into my presence and enjoyed my hospitality in order that he
might write in this outrageous manner about me. It is really shocking
and will have to be punished.[11]

The "grossly impertinent offender" was Robert Robinson, then
editor of The Isis, later the writer and broadcaster, and Edith
wanted him to be sent down (expelled from the university). Instead, a reprimand was mailed to his tutor.

Robinson later remarked: "'Sent Down by Edith Sitwell'
wouldn't have been a bad epitaph. I doubt if the old besom could
have envisaged the simple pleasure she gave to a humble undergraduate by acknowledging the fact of his existence in such vi-
tuperative terms. What did make me feel shy for her was her
willingness to tell fibs: I had indeed been invited to tea with her,
along with all the others who had volunteered to read her poems
—she took us through them at the Sesame Club, and the more I
heard her read them the more they seemed to get mixed up with
the little pink cakes she gave us to eat."[12]

The Façade incident gave Edith a chance to let off steam satisfactorily and release some of the nervousness she felt about seeing Pavlik. Osbert was also dreading it in case there were going
to be fireworks. Edith had to wait nervously for a month, whilst
working on her anthology Book of the Winter, before the fateful
meeting.

When Pavlik arrived with Ford, they stayed for a few days.
The atmosphere was completely calm and quiet, too quiet for
Edith to be her usual self. Pavlik's biographer, Parker Tyler,
learned from Ford that Edith hardly opened her mouth "except
for the most commonplace exchanges." Ford, who was com-

pletely bored, commented that "never before was she really
mute!" After they left, Edith had lunch with Lincoln Kirstein and
told him that Pavlik "was so sad that it was really heart breaking.
I could hardly bear to see it." But she added, as if to reassure herself, "he is a very great genius."[13] It was all that was left. She
finally realized that their love was over.

Edith returned to England in early June since she was to read
at the Aldeburgh Festival. She was "dead bored," as she wrote to
Sachie, but her brooding over Pavlik was interrupted by a new
worry:

I am very sorry to tell you Osbert is in a very serious state of health.
He has just seen the specialist again and the report is everything but
satisfactory.[14]

Parkinson's disease was suspected, but there was an agonizing
month to wait before Osbert was to see the famous physician Sir
Henry Cohen (later Lord Cohen of Birkenhead) for a second
opinion. Narrowly avoiding staying on a chicken farm with distant relations at Aldeburgh, she returned to give Evelyn her annual treat in London. Then in early August 1950 a letter arrived
at Weston Hall about Osbert with "burn this" scrawled in red ink
at the top.

Sir Henry Cohen's diagnosis was not bad. It is the *condition* not the
disease. There is no reason why it should get any worse. Sir Henry
thinks it will go on the same for ten or fifteen years. He is to go on
with his normal life, as far as possible.[15]

Comforted as Edith was by this reprieve, it was still a terrible
shock to her. Despite Sir Henry's optimism, the disease was to become progressively worse and Edith's sympathy for Osbert increased accordingly. From now on Osbert was a "saint" who
could do no wrong.

Because of the success of the first American tour, Edith and
Osbert were asked to give further readings. A second tour was arranged, starting in November 1950. With his illness, which he
bore stoically, Osbert found the prospect of the United States
daunting, but the climate, Edith told him, would do him good,
and she herself desperately needed the flowing dollars, so they
decided to go. After they arrived there, Osbert sent a note to
Sachie telling him they had arrived safely and adding: "Edith is

to read the part of Lady Macbeth at the Museum of Modern Art on November 16th.”[16]

It was not quite the programme Edith had planned; with the success in 1948 of *Façade*, which had been performed in New York, she now wanted to take the role of a triumphant Elizabethan Queen in a ballet Frederick Ashton was to write from Britten’s music to Rimbaud’s *Les Illuminations*. Lincoln Kirstein proposed to Edith that she should sit on a throne decked out with flowers and jewels and read from a poem about the state of England to be called *The Great Seal*. The grandeur of the idea appealed to Edith, who even hoped that Stravinsky would write the music. But the plan collapsed from lack of financing, and the Lady Macbeth performance that replaced it was disastrous. Edith insisted on reading the part “because she was one of my ancestresses,” but also insisted, “I don’t wish to compete with Judith Anderson but to read as a poet.”[17]

The performance was dreaded by all involved except Edith, but because it was a benefit concert for the museum funds the authorities found it difficult to refuse her. Every rehearsal was a full-dress occasion and most of the invited audiences wriggled with embarrassment. Edith, ever the egoist, was unable to realize that the performance *was* so bad. Her dress, which was described as a *robe* in the programme, was “in Italian figured velvet donated by Scalamandre Silks Inc.” and gave her a confidence that no one else felt. Of course Edith carried the part with great dignity, but the rather bizarre photographs of the occasion show her in spectacles looking overbearing and grandiose. The press were not convinced and said so, but Edith nevertheless considered it a great performance, and it was to be repeated in future visits to America.

Her grand role was privately detested by various “friends,” although they continued to call at her court because the association was socially advantageous. They failed to find any of the warm kindness in reserve behind the grand manner, which Edith extended to friends whom she decided she could trust. At the final rehearsal for *Macbeth* and the performance, new friends were invited: Tennessee Williams, Carson McCullers, and her cousin Jordan Massee. Williams had given a party for Edith and invited Carson McCullers, Massee, and Gore Vidal. Massee recorded in his diary:

Edith and Neil Porter rehearsing for the performance of *Façade* at the Chenil Galleries, London, in 1926.

William Walton. (CECIL BEATON, SOTHEBY'S)

Georgia and Edith. (FOX PHOTOS, LONDON)

Edith. (CECIL BEATON, SOTHEBY'S)

Edith. (CECIL BEATON, SOTHEBY'S)

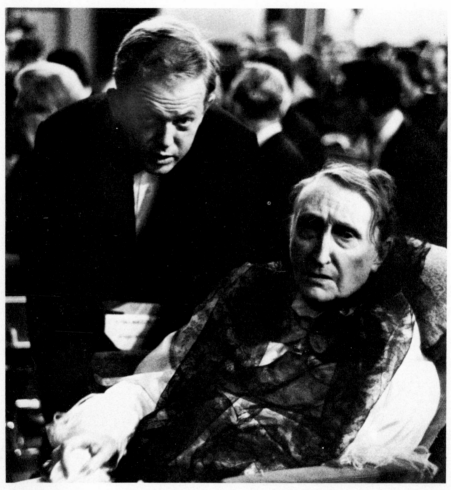

The last photograph taken of Edith, with Malcolm Williamson after a performance of the opera *The English Eccentrics*, 1963. (ERICH AUERBACH, LONDON)

One of the few parties I ever enjoyed. Before Edith arrived, Tennessee Williams remarked that he considered writers as a group together were worst, but he added "I encourage people to talk about themselves which is what interests them most".[18]

It was a foolproof recipe for Edith, and when she arrived,

she was very dignified and very grand but with natural good manners, like genuine royalty, not a pose. She had chosen to wear a huge gold bracelet . . . a long black dress and a long black cape, both to the floor, and a rather peculiar hat. She took her seat in the center of the sofa and we were presented.[19]

The whole party was rather surprised to find the private face of Edith so much nicer than the public one they had heard about, and Edith put them at their ease with "her quiet charm and amusing stories." "We had expected a kind of 'exotic épater les bourgeois' but found Edith only being herself."[20]

There were more surprises: Edith herself was completely charmed with Carson McCullers, who as a woman writer would normally have been treated with remote politeness. There was something about the shy, almost schoolgirlish figure that appealed to Edith, and as Carson told her of her unhappy childhood Edith listened with great sympathy. A friendship had begun. Carson regarded Edith as a heroine and almost at the beginning fell in love with her, hardly surprising as she had a difficult marriage with a homosexual husband, was herself bisexual, and had in the past fallen in love with another writer, Elizabeth Bowen, who, like Edith, was strictly heterosexual.

If Edith had at first listened to Carson only out of politeness, she was bowled over when she came to read her novels *A Member of the Wedding* and *The Heart Is a Lonely Hunter*, which Carson sent her. A letter of appreciation was sent: four quarto sides of admiration. Edith had read the books while resting from typhoid inoculations and found they "stabbed my heart and conscience, as nothing has done for many years. . . . What a great poet's mind and eye and senses you have . . . together with a prose writer's mind and sense of construction and character." She continued: "What would not a poet have given to have written: 'The long gold sun slanted down on them and made their skins look golden also.'"[21] The line was one Edith herself might have written, and as a reward *The Canticle of the Rose* was sent

with instructions "to read the later poems first." Amongst the im-
personal introductions of the endless lectures and talks, Edith
had found a woman in whom she could confide. Carson, of
course, said the right things, but she was so genuinely overcome
by Edith's praise that she told her that her poems were as great
as Milton's and wished that "T. S. Eliot had been capable of the
same development." Extravagant, perhaps, but Carson meant it
sincerely.

Edith and Osbert celebrated the New Year of 1951 in Mexico,
en route to San Francisco, and more letters followed to Carson.
She confided in her about Osbert's illness, knowing Carson would
sympathize because she had just learnt that her own paralysis
was incurable. Edith wrote:

Oh, I've seen so much these last five years, that your noble mind and
heart should have to endure this. People, foolish people say that pain
ennobles. It only doesn't debase a nature when it is as noble as
yours.[22]

Apart from discovering a great writer, Edith had found a fellow
sufferer whose unhappiness strangely parallelled her own:

You say you are horrified about my childhood. What do you suppose *I*
am to know what *you* have suffered in that terrible house where you
found yourself locked up[23]

Thinking of herself also, Edith added:

. . . the torture and horror of being told that nothing one does, says
and thinks is "normal". Naturally a genius does not think in the way
in which an ordinary person thinks. For two years I suffered from
being told that I was "going mad". I was told that daily.[24]

Edith was anxious to hear all about Carson's childhood when
they met again, but in the meantime she was

suddenly landed with an extremely difficult and lengthy piece of work
of the kind I have never done before.[25]

The work was a film script to be written for George Cukor, the
Hollywood director, who hoped Edith would adapt her biogra-
phy *Fanfare for Elizabeth* for the screen. It was a challenge
Edith, who needed the money, could not refuse, but privately she
doubted if she would be able to write it. Cukor hoped to cast
Laurence Olivier as Henry VIII and Vivien Leigh as Anne Bol-

eyn. The schedule was more exhausting than ever with this new project besides poetry readings and the inevitable performance of Lady Macbeth to an audience of film stars, including Harpo Marx. This time a man had a fit, and someone remarked to Edith, "You ought to be awfully pleased. It was one of the most flattering things I have ever seen."[26]

Edith decided to do most of the work on the screen-play at Renishaw, and before leaving the United States she told Carson, "I have had a few years very near to despair and feeling very far from poetry. And becoming friends with you has meant so much to me. . . . I shall be coming to America very often which is wonderful to look forward to."[27] Before she left, Edith had just time to see the Carson McCullers play *The Member of the Wedding* in New York with Tennessee Williams, on March 6, 1951, but although she enjoyed it she sat through it in acute pain. A few days previously, crossing a street in New York, she had caught her heel in a trolley track while trying to avoid a car, and as she crashed onto the street her head nearly went under another passing vehicle. "The rest of my frame," she joked bravely, "with the exception of my hands is like a Gauguin."[28]

Edith and Osbert returned to Renishaw, but life there was no easier. She felt she was being driven mad by a lady who had been pursuing Osbert ceaselessly, realized there was no chance of success there, and turned to Edith instead. Her name was Alice Hunt, and Edith appropriately nicknamed her "La Chasseur" [sic]; soon the lady developed the annoying habit of telephoning her at 8:15 in the morning.

The film had to be worked on despite "La Chasseur," and Edith took it seriously, cancelling nearly all her social engagements. She began to doubt her ability to complete the screen-play satisfactorily but persisted, knowing, as she told her cousin Veronica, that it was the only chance she had to make "really big money. Mr. Cukor said to me, 'we shall be rich and famous in our old ages,' so I daren't put the thing down again!"[29]

But she did, for Oxford had awarded her an honorary D.Litt., thanks to Maurice Bowra's influence. In a state of nerves, Edith went to receive it on June 20, 1951. A degree from Oxford was the high point of her academic success and she told everyone proudly that the only other woman who had an Oxford honorary D.Litt. was the Queen. Edith even managed to go for a walk, something she hated. The following month she enjoyed a reunion with Carson McCullers, who had arrived from America on the *Queen Elizabeth*. Her husband, Reeves, was also there, but his visit had not been planned. He had been released for a day from the hospital where he was "drying out" to help put Carson's luggage on board, and without passport or money had travelled as a stowaway. When they reached Southampton, David Gascoyne, the poet, who was Carson's host, rescued him.

They all went to a party given by Edith at the Sesame, and while they all chatted pleasantly, Reeves, who had been drinking all the afternoon, slipped quietly onto the floor, where he lay in an alcoholic stupor. Edith ignored the incident, but as Carson's visit lasted ten weeks her husband soon became a strain. Reeves threatened to commit suicide (which he did do two years later), and Edith was bombarded with telephone calls from Carson in the middle of the night to find a doctor for him. The next day Edith gave Carson lunch at the Sesame, but because it was a holiday no doctor could be found. Carson wept copiously throughout the meal, pleading to be taken to Renishaw, which Edith refused to do because of Osbert. The old club ladies, most of whom Edith disliked, were delighted with the scene and thrilled when Reeves suddenly crashed into the dining-room in a foul rage, shouted loudly, and then subsided once again, dozing off, much to Edith's relief.

It was always easier for Edith to cope with "situations" by letter, and with Carson safely back in America, Edith wrote to her in July 1951 from Renishaw about the film. "It is more or less finished although I still have some work to do on it."[30] Now Edith began to miss Carson and her conversation, for she lacked a ready sympathizer at Renishaw. She was worried about Osbert's illness, but there was no one to confide in, since David Horner had the habit of hogging the conversation at mealtimes and Edith silently suffered his bursts of malice towards her. "It seems we shall have to keep our silence,"[31] Edith said sadly to Lorna Andrade, another victim of Horner's sarcasm, after dinner one evening.

There was no escape from Horner; he was with Osbert when Edith joined him in Sicily. She then spent a week at Montegufoni, and there she learned of the death from inoperable cancer of their butler's wife, Susan, in December 1951. The news left her unable to work. She adopted the role of the protective sister to Osbert, insisting that he should not be told of Susan's cancer. Inevitably Osbert found out when he returned to Renishaw, and his unsympathetic answer was to have her rooms fumigated at once. But there was one good piece of news: Roy Campbell had finally accepted the role of knight errant and gone to Cambridge to lecture to Leavis's pupils about their "pet tutor, which apparently caused a terrific sensation."[32] It was some consolation to Edith that Leavis, the high priest of modern criticism, was being insulted on his own ground. She had never forgiven him for his unwise comment in 1932, when he declared that "the Sitwells belong to the history of publicity rather than of poetry." Now Edith was beating him in a war of publicity, at which he was no mean practitioner himself, and all in the name of art.

THIRTEEN

Hollywood

My principal entrancements here are the columns of the lady gossip-writers, which I read with avidity. . . . Unable to get at me—because I wouldn't see them—one wrote "A *little* old lady" (my italics) "has just come to Hollywood: Edith Sitwell."

Letter to T. S. Eliot

WOOD END, the house where Edith was born, had been sold to Scarborough Corporation by Osbert and, after initially falling into disrepair, was now restored and converted into a Natural History Museum. A few rooms were made into a Sitwell Wing, with bookcases of their works and display tables of their manuscripts. All three Sitwells were invited to visit the newly restored house during July 1952, but as Sachie was in Norway, only Edith and Osbert were able to accept. It was a nostalgic occasion for Edith, seeing once again the house that held for her such contrasting memories. It now gave her the curious sensation that she was a "museum piece" in more than the literal sense.

Because of Osbert's health, Edith was determined that there should be little fuss, but although it was not a particularly spectacular occasion, a large press contingent had arrived to meet them. Edith told them a little about her early life: how she wrote her first poems during an attack of measles when she was twenty-

three, and how she had left Scarborough at seventeen to be
"'finished off' as I was in every sense."

Edith was now being publicized not as a poet but as an eccentric, and moreover one who was about to penetrate the mysterious world of Hollywood. When, in the autumn, the newspapers
heard that Edith's draft script had been accepted by George
Cukor, they gave her a large press conference at Claridges before
she sailed from Southampton, with Osbert and David.

Edith realized the value of this new form of publicity and, true
to form, wore a "Tudor"-style hat, as she sipped tea and looked
slightly bemused. As a showwoman, Edith fascinated the press-
men, who gazed in astonishment as she told them, "I propose to
write the story in bed. I don't intend to get up at all when I am
working excepting for lunch and dinner. . . . I have planned the
most sinister first scene imaginable."[1]

"It is not my first film," she told a film representative. Twenty-
five years ago she had made a film reading poems with her
brothers, and the technicians had told her it was "a tremendous
laugh." But Bernard Shaw had disagreed: "They are the biggest
fools I have ever seen, you don't know what you are looking at."
"That," said Edith, laughing, "was meant as a great compliment."[2]

Only the thought of America and her return to friends made
Edith feel less miserable, but it seemed as if they would never get
there. Their liner, the *United States,* was involved in a dock
strike, and the passengers had to carry their own luggage, something particularly troublesome for Edith. The visit followed what
was becoming an established routine: a few weeks in New York,
and then to Hollywood with Cukor.

Christmas 1952 was spent in New York, and a few days later
Edith went with Osbert and W. H. Auden to visit the Stravinskys
at their hotel. Auden had warned the Stravinskys on the telephone that Edith "drank like a fish," so in preparation for this,
Vera Stravinsky placed a standing order for double martinis and
double scotches to be sent up to them at regular intervals. Stravinsky arrived late and amused Edith by demanding jam in his
tea. She let them all down and drank scarcely anything at all. As
Osbert's Parkinson's disease made it impossible for him to hold a
glass without shaking, the entire contents of the tray were
finished off by Auden and Stravinsky.

The Stravinskys were hypnotized by Edith's appearance, and Robert Craft, Stravinsky's secretary and copyist, who was also there, regretted he was unable to test Auden's assertion that she was as bald as a coot, for her head was swathed in black silk. Indeed, the whole meeting was rather formal. Edith was extremely nervous; she had always admired the composer's work and had planned her opening remark beforehand so that her entry into the room would not be embarrassing. Taking off her long black gloves, she told a story, later to become a favourite with her, that a gorilla, seeing her take her gloves off, tried to do the same with his hands and then kissed her. The conversation turned to their mutual friend, Aldous Huxley, and Stravinsky, because he knew little about the Upanishads, which Edith had mentioned, changed the subject rapidly. Edith and Osbert left, and it was then discovered that Mrs. George Orwell had been giving a party in the same hotel at the same time. Mrs. Orwell had complained about the bar service and was told in reply, "Do like those Russians on the seventh floor, lady, order doubles."[3]

Osbert and Edith left New York for Hollywood; when they arrived, Walter Reisch was put in charge of the script. Edith hoped that everything would now be more business-like. Meanwhile the gossip columnists had a treat and Edith was amused to find, as she wrote in her memoirs, that she had been described as "a little old lady in an ankle-length fur coat and black sandals," and she added, "this dwarfish ancient, whose height is five feet eleven . . . has never in her life worn black sandals. . . ."[4]

In Hollywood they stayed at the Sunset Boulevard Hotel, where she was known privately as "Aunt Edie." The staff spent their time stopping reporters from invading Edith's room, pleading with them that if they did go up "the roof would fall in and she'd check right out." The switchboard received frequent calls, this time from Edith to "send someone up to clear this place at once," for she was always swamped with letters, books, and papers on the bed and over the floor.

She worked constantly at the same routine during the day, and in the evening visited old friends. The Huxleys invited her, or at least Aldous did, for Maria was not always pleased to see Edith. A friend of Maria's noted in her diary, "Edith was around a lot, Maria would groan privately and say that Edith had always been in love with Aldous and wanted to marry him. Aldous said nothing but was obviously enjoying himself."[5]

Aldous took Edith round to see the Forest Lawn Cemetery, a place she had wanted to visit ever since she read Evelyn Waugh's *The Loved One*. There they were treated with interest because, as Edith remarked, they "were both old enough to be considered for a plot."[6] The highlight of the visit for them was the discovery that the nearby bridal chapel was warmed from heat generated by the crematorium.

In May 1953 Edith returned to England and the revised script arrived from Hollywood. It was received with the usual horror of the serious artist at being dealt with by the film industry. However, although the "Walter Reisch Treatment" annoyed her, there was nothing else to do but plod on. She had

been having a terrible time with my film-treatment. . . . The film now opens with what would seem to be a sort of pillow-fight in the "dorm" of the 6th form at St Winifred's. . . . There is a lot of "rough stuff". George Boleyn comes into Anne's room when she is in a bath-towel! Henry is always . . . rolling drunk. . . . Walter has endowed the King and Anne with napkin rings!! marked H.R. and A.B. . . . Elizabeth's governess says "Give the girl some cookies!"[7]

"Oh, heavens above!" exclaimed Edith in despair. Her temper was, as she said, "like a rhinoceros's,"[8] and for relief she invited her latest plague of lunatics to see Dr. Leavis instead.

There was the inevitable trek back to America in November 1953, and while she was on the boat with Osbert and David Horner she received a cable telling her that Dylan Thomas had died. She was shocked and saddened by the news, and the minute she arrived in New York she was met by John Malcolm Brinnin, a close writer friend of Thomas's, who was in tears.

The London *Sunday Times* offered to pay for Edith's expenses to travel to Wales for the funeral, but she had to refuse because of her film contract. She now felt "numb":

What young poet can begin to compare with him? And he was a most endearing creature, like a sweet and affectionate child.[9]

She wrote this to Maurice Bowra, who replied:

No poet that I know of owed so much to another as he owed to you. From the very start you saw his greatness, for many years you looked after him and did countless things for him . . . it could have been easy to dismiss him as an impossible genius, but you stuck to him . . . you can always remember this and be as proud of it while the rest of us who know you, what you did, will remember it with deepest gratitude. . . .[10]

Scarcely had Edith time to recover from Dylan's death when a new crisis arose. A report of a play by Peter Ustinov reached her and it was based, she decided, on her family. *No Sign of the Dove*, as it was called, was about "a famous writer who is also a baronet and his sister, a famous poetess (who wears a turban) and their eccentric father, who has a beard. They were given the name of D'Urt (so witty). We are both represented as sex maniacs and one paper (*New Statesman*) which identifies them as meant for us, says 'the half witted Lord Basingstoke and the quarter witted Niobe D'Urt (me!) are trying to get into bed somewhere'."[11]

She thought that the name D'Urt was based on an old family name of her ancestors, Hurt, which attracted jokes aimed at their twentieth-century descendants, and their paranoia, from such as Evelyn Waugh. This convinced Edith that they were the models for Ustinov's play. Edith had met him in New York, where she was puzzled at his behaving "like a black beetle that thinks it is going to be killed. He seemed to be trying to crawl into the wall. Now I know why."[12] The "Ustinov Affair" was made worse for Edith because Beatrix Lehmann, who was a sister of John's, and appeared in the play, parodied Edith's clothes. The only consolation Edith had was that the play was booed off the stage after nine performances and Ustinov had to suffer the indignity that "his disgusting old mother sat blubbering in the stalls. She did the decor."[13]

The rage over the play was not entirely self-centred, for Edith saw it more as an attack on Osbert, a "poor crippled man who had never harmed him . . . grossly insulted by the brave Mr. Ustinov."[14] But she felt she was grossly insulted by the *New Statesman*, which followed up its comments on Ustinov with a profile called "Queen Edith," illustrated by a caricature of her by Vicki. The *New Statesman* began:

It was never a case of Miss Sitwell or even Dr. Sitwell, but of Queen Edith. The mask is elaborate and no mean carnival head set on mean shoulders . . . myth has been realised in person. . . . At this very moment the author of *Green Song* and *Gold Coast Customs* is riding the elephant of publicity in Hollywood.[15]

Edith herself read these phrases in Los Angeles and complained to her solicitor, Philip Frere. She told him she had written to the *New Statesman* saying that her appearance and her personality were entirely her own affair, and anyway her appearance was not "achieved" but natural, "since I have the same appearance and personality as can be seen in the Plantagenet effigies in Westminster Abbey."[16] Having heard this, Frere must have winced, and he sent a long letter dissuading Edith from taking action. She reluctantly agreed, but then a fresh skirmish started in *The Spectator* with a review of Edith's *Gardeners and Astronomers* by Anthony Hartley. Edith imagined that the rival paper was collaborating in a plot with the *New Statesman* got up by Kenneth Tynan and Malcolm Muggeridge. "I am so sick and disgusted by these creatures that I do not want to see anyone on my return,"[17] she complained to friends.

The battle finally ended when Edith was forced to see the amusing aspect of the correspondence. A "little Mr. Tompkins" wrote a letter to *The Spectator* that she disliked, and replying, she said she found it "wearisome," taking the opportunity to lavish public praise on Kingsley Amis for his novel *Lucky Jim.* Amis himself wrote back thanking Edith for her praise, taking the opportunity to reveal that he was the "little Mr. Tompkins."[18]

In Hollywood, Edith received a note of the main faults of the script:

In general, our main consideration concerned the lack of character growth and vitality for the part of Anne Boleyn. All of us felt that too many times in this script, Anne was the puppet of contrivance, and not the victim of circumstances or herself. Too many times in the present script, Anne was presented as an anemic character, and lacking blood, she lacked not only violence, but humanity as well . . . while Anne's character was indicated in many of the stage directions, it had not been dramatized with sufficient force to make her interesting and not on one emotional level.[19]

Edith replied that she agreed and, suggesting various changes, gritted her teeth and returned to Florence to make more altera-

tions. Her efforts brought little success, but had provided inci-
dental scenes of amusement, as she told Veronica Gilliat:

Walter [Reisch, the screenwriter] as I call him behind his back but
not to his face, has taken to acting the scenes on his back on the floor
(he is a most respectable man of about 58) yelling, "Harry, Harry,
come back Harry I cannot live without you, I love you Harry". And
George [Cukor] the director was looking at him with a beaming appreciative smile, when a really revolting deep-bluebottle, awakened
by the transcendental racket, sped at us from—somewhere behind me,
narrowly missing my face. As you know I am as terrified of them as
some women are of mice. . . . I shrieked, George springing to his feet
rushed across the room in the opposite direction and was brought up
short against the wall, rushed back in my direction, driving the bluebottle (which he hadn't seen) full at me. I yelled again and coward
Walter sat up on the floor as one awakened from a trance. George,
still unaware of the cause of the disturbance, flew to my rescue, ex-
claiming as he saw the bluebottle, "why good heavens it's a fly!" He
then abolished it and removed the corpse. He really is a very nice
man.[20]

Always drawn to hearing about crime, her interest having been
fostered by her reading of crime books and her gleanings from
the tabloid newspaper *News of the World*, Edith had paid a visit
to the "Skid Row" of Los Angeles, having taken the precaution of
being escorted by a friend of her highly-thought-of black maid,
Velma LeRoy. She was appalled by what she saw. Looking into a
dark street she "saw an appalling shop with no doorway filled
with unutterable and ragged clothes like the outworn flesh of the
dead."[21] It was a haunting experience which she said brought
her back to the despair she felt when writing *Gold Coast Customs* and *Street Songs*. For a moment she glimpsed her life in a
wider perspective. From that moment she knew she was fighting
a losing battle with the film and wrote gloomily:

I have got to do the whole damned film again because Walter would
Laughtonize it. One fully expects to see King Henry mowing the lawn
in his shirt sleeves after business hours. They have been trying to get
me to go back to Hollywood in July. I never wish to see the place
again, I hate it so much.[22]

Edith's maid, Velma, helped Edith to forget her own worries,
but offered no relief when she told her of the problems of black

people. Velma asserted that they *knew* life was hopeless because
they were black, but Edith replied, "Do you really think that
God is pink or white as if he had just come from Elizabeth Ar-
den's or Madame Helena Rubenstein's salons? When you go to
heaven perhaps you may find that God is a coloured man."[23] Underneath this joking, the race problem was one she took seriously.
As a declaration of her views, she had wanted to appear publicly
with Paul Robeson, whom she admired, and refused to take the
advice of Geoffrey Gorer, who told her it would be politically
compromising because of Robeson's communist beliefs. But to
Edith's disappointment this public appearance never came off.

She returned to London exhausted, still smarting from the
wounds inflicted by the *New Statesman* and *The Spectator*, and
wanting only a quiet time to see a few friends, and to return to
her poems, which were to reflect the grimmer side of her Hollywood experiences.

Then in June 1954 Edith was awarded a D.B.E. (Dame Com-
mander of the British Empire) in Queen Elizabeth II's Birthday
Honours list. Amongst others, T. S. Eliot wrote at once to congrat-
ulate her:

I was very happy to hear yesterday that the Sovereign had recognised
the judgment of the world of letters and conferred an honour, which,
while it may seem unimportant to yourself, will not only give pleasure
to your friends and satisfaction to your admirers but redound to the
credit of the source from which it originates.[24]

But it *was* important to Edith, who celebrated with champagne
and was quick to add her accolade to the back of her envelopes.
For anyone who had troubled to remember she was a doctor and
had to be addressed as such, the next test was to remember she
was a *Dame*.

Before Edith, Osbert, and David sailed again for America, in
November, there was an exhibition of Pavlik's work in London.
He was travelling from New York via Rome to be present. The
rows had all been settled, but Edith agreed to go to the exhibition only rather grudgingly, since her love for Pavlik was over.
She wrote to Georgia, enlisting her and Sachie's aid, and explained:

In re Pavlik, the whole thing is going to be a fearful strain and most painful for me, and I don't want anything to happen which would be an added strain.

I have been asked to go and open his exhibition on the 26th [October]. What I am doing I am doing simply because he is a very great artist. For no other reason. I am afraid I do not feel the same. I shall be very amiable to him, but as I say, I do not feel the same. I am only fearfully worried because I do not think people are buying pictures. If you can think of anyone who is rich and *might* buy, do for God's sake ask them to the show.[25]

She told the audience in her opening speech that Pavlik's work was, in Browning's words, "the instant made eternity." In its review of the exhibition the *Yorkshire Post* saw Edith as a "lone gaunt figure" as she spoke from the balcony of the Hanover Gallery, London. "Here was a Portia on Juliet's balcony," it concluded. They were bitter words for Edith, and hard to swallow. Although she had no real love left for the man whom she had championed for nearly thirty years, she was loyal to the memory. Edith had decided that no opportunity was to be given for Pavlik to make mischief or spoil her time in London. He was to be given a luncheon party by Georgia and Sachie at the Sesame but was not to be told about a musical party Edith was going to in case he caused any havoc. Edith had learned too much too often in the unhappy past. In the event, her arrangements made little difference, for Pavlik was too ill to travel to London.

With Pavlik at bay, Edith expected a quiet time, but La Chasseur, tired of pursuing Osbert, had sent her records that her daughter had made of Edith's *Lullaby*, which she had set to music. They were not exactly by Edith's favourite composer, and Edith managed a polite but firm reply to the "old trout":

It is alas quite impossible for me to give permission for the publishing or performance of your daughter's setting of my *Lullaby*. I had made it perfectly clear to you I did not wish the poems to be set. . . . I have played over the record . . . the music has nothing whatsoever to do with the poems and I find it astonishing.[26]

The prospect of her flirtation with the film business coming to an end made Edith much happier. Although it was disappointing for her as an artist, she felt she could not go on making the trips to America "like a season ticket holder." She also knew the visits were a strain on Osbert, who tried to live quietly, hoping to find a cure for the disease that was slowly immobilizing him. As long as he had Horner to look after him, Edith felt the "situation wasn't too bad," but Horner had seen a painter in Wilton, Connecticut, on a previous visit, and when the boat arrived in New York he left Osbert to visit him there. Edith was enraged, and waited impatiently for the deserter to return. Gossip had reached her from the "whole of the Herbaceous Border," as she called the New York homosexuals, and she now had no illusions about her brother's relationship with Horner, or "little Lord Fauntleroy," as she called him.

"Let silence be the watchword—private and confidential—destroy," she scribbled at the head of a letter to Sachie. "Do not mention this to anyone, otherwise it will get back and precipitate a hideous family row and we do not want it talked about." She explained that Horner had not been in New York during the whole of their stay (he had returned for Christmas), nor had he gone with Osbert to Florida. Osbert had had to be looked after by strangers, and unwisely Edith had not even tried to control her feelings. She had a terrible row with Osbert, "let herself go" about Horner, and was told in return "to mind her own business." Osbert insisted that they must behave as if nothing had happened; "otherwise domestic life will be hell—because we shall have him [Horner] there just the same, but hating us. We must show nothing."[27]

Osbert accepted the situation calmly; he was used to David's wanderings, and while he would have preferred them to remain together, there was nothing he could do, just as there was nothing Edith could do either. Edith's motives for disliking David Horner are not entirely obvious. She was devoted to Osbert, but not particularly close to him. As her own relationship with Pavlik had drifted to an end, it is likely that she resented Osbert's friendship with David, because she would have liked the comfort of a close relationship herself. She may have been jealously aware that David was filling the position of Osbert's confidant, which she would naturally have regarded as her own.

It was during this visit that Edith had her first meeting with Marilyn Monroe. The press were fascinated and took the subject up with a vengeance, badgering Edith for details. They found it quite improbable that the woman they regarded as a sex symbol and, in their estimation, a dumb blonde could have anything to

say to Edith. Edith herself was surprised to find Marilyn Monroe
an intelligent woman; they talked about Rudolf Steiner, a philosopher who had been one of Helen's "pets," and Marilyn told
Edith the story of her life. Eyebrows were raised over a nude calendar for which she had posed, but Edith defended her, telling
the press that the star had known great poverty and that, looking
at the gentle-mannered Marilyn, she had been reminded of a
child of sixteen or seventeen reduced to fending for herself.

Reports of the meeting were exaggerated, providing endless
gossip, and even in Renishaw village it was rumoured that Marilyn was coming to stay at the Sitwell Arms, the inn near Renishaw Hall. Fond of Marilyn as Edith was, she was tired of being
interrogated and administered a rap to Ruth Braithwaite of the
Sunday Chronicle:

Dear Miss Braithwaite,
I believe my secretary has forwarded your letter to me and has answered it as far as she is able. I have not the faintest idea what you
and your editor are talking about. I am *not* bringing Miss Marilyn
Monroe to England. Is it supposed I am a film or publicity or press
agent? I am an extremely busy person and have been caused grave annoyance by members of the press thinking they are at liberty to disturb my work, because of this quarter-witted story *which has no foundation whatsoever.* I do not allow my work to be disturbed, and in
order to prevent any further impertinent waste of my time, I shall be
obliged if you would be as good as to publish the following facts:
Miss Monroe, like a good many other people, was brought to see me
while I was in Hollywood. I thought her a very nice girl, and said to
her, as I said to others, that I hoped, if she came to London, she
would let me know and should come to a luncheon party. There the
matter began and ended.[28]

Miss Braithwaite's persistence paled beside the attention given to
Edith by Hedda Hopper, who had misreported a meeting Edith
had with Harry Cohn, the head of Columbia Pictures. Edith had
seen her first in the distance, "a badly done-up parcel that had
been discarded after a Girl Scout encampment,"[29] and an inaccu-
rate report appeared that Miss Hopper refused to retract. Rabies
had broken out in Hollywood, an epidemic Edith said was due to
Miss Hopper's biting dogs. "It is far less dangerous to stir up a
black mamba in the mating season, than it is to irritate me,"
Edith warned.[30]

Then in March, just as Edith and Osbert were preparing for the voyage home to England, David Horner reappeared in New York ready to sail with them. Edith hardly knew what to feel: whether to be glad that he was back with Osbert, or outraged because he would again play the lord of the manor and enjoy the comforts of Renishaw. (She had learnt that Osbert had been told by David that he didn't care whether Osbert lived or died.) Once again, when Edith complained, she only succeeded in annoying Osbert. "Don't mention it to Osbert unless he does to you, I have put my foot in it again by saying what I think of the creature," she warned Sachie.

She despaired during the whole of the voyage home and declared she felt too ill to leave her cabin, although when well she rarely did so either. If Osbert would do nothing *she* would, but for the time being she could not imagine what her best move should be.

FOURTEEN

A Time of Despair

> The living blind and seeing Dead together lie
> As if in love. . . . There was no more hating then,
> And no more love: Gone is the heart of Man.
>
> Conclusion of *Dirge for the New Sunrise*

EDITH had remarked that her feelings about David Horner were "uncontrollable," and nowhere could she find any consolation or happiness. She turned to friends, confiding in them her private worries, but it did nothing to allay her misery.

The answer came from, of all people, Osbert, who suggested she should become a Roman Catholic. Edith, although surprised at Osbert's suggestion, considered it carefully. In many ways it seemed an obvious step, for her poems had insisted more and more upon the salvation of man through Christ. There was something impressive, if puzzling, about the huge figure of Roy Campbell, who could be as aggressive as Edith but was like a lamb in his reverence to the Roman Catholic Church.

This fascinated Edith, who longed for peace and was worn out physically and mentally. It had now been finally confirmed that Columbia was to shelve the film of *Fanfare for Elizabeth* because of unresolved problems over the script and casting difficulties. It brought a deflating end to her years of success. All the battles of the past with critics and Pavlik, the miserable years in Paris, the culmination of the failure of her film, must have passed endlessly through her mind. Perhaps now the time had come to find solace in the Church, for she could certainly find comfort nowhere else, tormented as she was by Osbert's illness, and the ever present problem of David at Renishaw. Privately she was afraid of her own temper, and she told many people that she would have liked to murder David. The Catholic Church would, she decided, help her to control her passions by its authority; perhaps this was something she had always sought so desperately. Nevertheless, not just any parish priest would do, and having met Father Martin D'Arcy, the doyen of Catholic intellectuals, with Roy Campbell and his wife, Mary, in London, she determined that he was to be her spiritual guide. When she wrote to him of her decision to receive instruction in the Catholic faith, he replied, "I cannot say how happy it has made me."

As Father D'Arcy was still in the United States, he asked Father Philip Caraman to give her instruction instead. For one who had always resisted advice, Edith accepted this instruction meekly and she read the books he suggested. Before long, Father Caraman became a friend. She was reading Thomas Aquinas, and wrote to him:

I believe, and trust with all my heart, that I am on the threshold of a new life. But I shall have to be born again.[1]

And later:

. . . I see that purely intellectual belief is not enough: one must not only *think* one is believing, but *know* one is believing. There has to be a sixth sense in faith.[2]

Just as she began her instruction, Edith was moved by a performance of Benjamin Britten's setting of *Still Falls the Rain*, which she heard in the Queen Elizabeth Hall. She had become good friends with Britten and Peter Pears of late since she had become a regular visitor to the annual music festival they organized at Aldeburgh in Suffolk. Although she disliked David's relationship with Osbert, she accepted the homosexual composer and his partner without question, often writing to them jointly. Britten wrote the setting of her poem in memory of his friend Noel Mewton-Wood, who had committed suicide, and he found in Edith's "very great poem from the war years . . . courage &

light seen through horror & darkness . . . something very right for the poor boy. Also playing in the programme is that most wonderful of all horn players, Dennis Brain, & I was contemplating setting it for Voice, Horn & Piano."[3] The setting was exactly right for Edith, who, in her mood of reconciliation, felt on hearing the music "each being was alone, with space and eternity and the terror of death, and then God."[4]

Edith wrote to Evelyn Waugh, asking him to be her sponsor at her baptism. In his reply he told her:

The real joy of your letter is in the last paragraph. Welcome! Welcome!

Will you be so very kind and send me a postcard when the thing is fixed so that Laura and I may make our Communions for you. I know so many people who will want to thank God for you, and many priests who will want to remember you in their Masses. But I presume you don't want the matter spoken of, so shall mention it to no-one until you give the word.

Waugh was, of course, one of the leading Catholics in the world of arts and letters, but privately he was apprehensive about Edith, knowing her fondness for ceremony, and hoping there was more to her conversion than just that. He wrote to Caraman to express his hope that her baptism would be suitably humble and quiet and, above all, his feeling that the press must be excluded. "There are so many malicious people about to make a booby of a Sitwell. It would be tragic if this greatest occasion in her life were in any way sullied. . . ."[5]

Sir Alec Guinness received a peremptory telegram from Edith saying she would like him to attend her reception. Sir Alec recalled:

I went to that, and it was when I first met Evelyn Waugh. . . . It seemed to me that most of the other people who turned up, turned up in a kind of mourning, as if some terrible event was taking place. I came in a sort of smart dark blue suit, but I wore a rather jazzy tie, which I thought was the right note to strike. Evelyn Waugh came in a bright get up, with red and blue ribbons in his straw hat.

The ceremony was a moderately hysterical thing. . . . Evelyn Waugh and I got the giggles before it started, although I had never met him, because one of her guests [Evelyn Wiel] dropped a whole lot of bangles which rolled all over the church. We found ourselves on hands and knees searching for these things. . . .[6]

Evelyn Waugh also remembered the occasion in his diary:

. . . at 11.45 to Farm Street [the headquarters of the Order of Jesuit priests in London] where I met Father D'Arcy and went with him to the church to the Ignatius Chapel to await Edith and Father Caraman. A bald shy man introduced himself as the actor Alec Guinness. Presently Edith appeared swathed in black like a sixteenth-century infanta. I was aware of other people kneeling behind but there were no newspaper men or photographers as I had half feared to find. Edith recanted her errors in fine ringing tones and received conditional baptism, then was led in to the confessional while six of us collected in the sacristy—Guinness and I and Father D'Arcy, an old lame deaf woman with dyed red hair whose name I never learned, a little swarthy man who looked like a Jew but claimed to be Portuguese, and a blond youth who looked American but claimed to be English.* We drove two streets in a large hired limousine to Edith's club, the Sesame. I had heard gruesome stories of this place but Edith had ordered a banquet—cold consommé, lobster Newburg, steak, strawberry flan and great quantities of wine. The old woman suddenly said: "Did I hear the word 'whisky'?" I said: "Do you want one?" "More than anything in the world." "I'll get you some." But the Portuguese nudged me and said: "It would be disastrous".[7]

Before she left for Montegufoni for Christmas, Edith was finally confirmed as a member of the Catholic Church on October 2, 1955. There was no splendour. A friend of Sachie's, Lady Hesketh, was another sponsor, and the ceremony was held before twenty Catholics in a private chapel at Farm Street.

Instead of going to Italy with Edith and Osbert, David Horner was off to America again. Having confidence in Father Caraman, Edith had tried during her conversion to understand David, and Caraman did his best to try to let her see the positive side of David's relationship with Osbert, namely, his kindness and loyalty in the past. She had told Caraman, "I am under daily temptation to great anger because of something terribly cruel that has been done to my dear Osbert. . . . It is a great difficulty to me. I have so far shown no anger but I do feel it. I must of course remember my own grave faults."[8] For a short time Caraman's pastoral advice helped, and Edith wrote,

I am very grateful. . . . yesterday I almost pitied the man [D.H.] of

* The old lame deaf woman was Evelyn Wiel, and the Portuguese was Alberto de Lacerda, a young poet friend of Edith's.

whom I spoke. He is a Catholic convert and had been to church. . . .
He hasn't, I think, any idea of the terrible thing that he has done. Osbert always tries to find excuses for him.[9]

Now, a few months later, she was also a Catholic convert, and
at Montegufoni, without David, she might have been expected to
have found the peace she searched for. But she was still feeling
unsettled, and it was then that in desperation she started sending
out "The Form," a leaflet devised with Sachie's help to deal with
the constant plague of postal pests:

A.   Name in full (Block letters as throughout)

     . . . .

B.   Specimen of usual signature . . . .

C.   Passport number . . . . (This must be accompanied by
     six photographs 2½ inches by 4, and these must be signed both
     by a clergyman and by a Justice of the Peace. They must, also,
     have been taken within the last six months. Old photographs
     cannot be accepted.)

D.   Finger Prints number (if any) . . . .

E.   When were you born . . . .

F.   Where were you born . . . .

G.   How were you born . . . .

H.   If not, why not . . . .

I.   For what purpose are you going there . . . .

     . . . .

J.   And if so, where . . . .

K.   Of what sex are you . . . .

L.   Age, sex and weight of your wife . . . .

     . . . .

M.   Father's name in full . . . .

N.   Mother's maiden name in full . . . .

O.   Has any relative of yours ever been confined in a mental home

     . . . .

P.   If not, why not . . . .

Q.   If so, give full details, with accompanying photograph . . . .

     . . . .

R.   Did you ever meet Burgess and Maclean, or anyone who ever
     knew them? This last must be accompanied by an attestation
     taken in the presence of a Commissioner of Oaths . . . .

     . . . .

Although its actual composition must have given her fun, and it
was, after all, supposed to be an antidote to anger and sarcasm, it

did little to restrain her from replying to those who offended. An example was the reply Edith sent to a lady who had accused her of being a fraud, suggested that she would "rot in hell" when she died, but nevertheless would be very grateful for Edith's opinion of her poetry. Pretending the letter was written by a secretary, Edith wrote:

Dame Edith Sitwell asks me to acknowledge the receipt of your letter, and to return your stamp. Dame Edith Sitwell made it abundantly clear, not only on the occasion of her last broadcast, but every time she has spoken on the subject of poetry in public that she strongly objects to unsolicited manuscripts being sent to her.

In spite of this, every time she broadcasts and makes this pronouncement, she is bombarded by hundreds of verses, invariably completely without a vestige of the slightest talent, and she is expected to put down her work and waste her time on reading, criticising and finding publishers or editors for verses that under no circumstances *could* find anyone willing to publish them. . . .[10]

She continued with a threat that the answers she hoped for on "The Form" would be part of *The Sitwell Report,* which she maintained was being compiled by her, with the aid of her brothers, and had been inspired by a talk Osbert had with Dr. Kinsey. *The Sitwell Report* was of course pure imagination on Edith's part, a joke she invented.

Many of the so-called angry letters were sent out in this tongue-in-cheek manner, for as Edith once remarked, "a terrible sense of fun comes over one, and one just does these things. . . ."[11]

"The Form" and the accompanying letter were only a new part of her familiar defence mechanism, which provided a safety valve for her feelings by scattering a handful of grape-shot broadcast instead of making a direct attack on the source of her annoyance. She was still unforgiving about David, but that was because there was always the reminder of the helpless Osbert, with his difficulty in eating and his uncertain walk, and it made her furious at David's neglect. Now that she felt cut off from Pavlik her affection seemed concentrated on Osbert instead, so much so that some cynical observers even suggested she was in love with him. Horner himself felt that Edith realized that he was too close to Osbert for her not to feel jealous, and was aware of the affection between the brother and sister, which she had never

shared with anyone. Edith could say nothing about the intolerable situation in which she found herself, but her antagonism towards Horner shows how little she understood his relationship
with Osbert. Osbert knew that however badly Horner treated
him now, it could never remove the happiness they had enjoyed
in the past, the memory of which he would enjoy for several more
years to come.

But it is also clear that Osbert tried to control some of Edith's
financial affairs. From a draft in Osbert's handwriting it appears
that he not only forced Edith to alter her will in favour of him,
but also, in the event of his death, in favour of David Horner.
There must have been manipulation by Osbert to get Edith to
agree to this, and indeed it seems from the draft that she tried to
resist, but without success. Osbert noted that the will was
"alright" [sic] apart from the omission of the clause which he
wanted added:

I leave to my brother Osbert or to David Stuart Horner (if my brother
should no longer be living) the sum of £3,000 at present put aside in
order to buy a house, or if the house has been bought, I leave the
house instead of the £3,000 in the same way.

The contents of this house should be offered at a fair valuation to
either O.S. or D.S.H. whichever is the owner, should he desire to buy
it. This not in trust, but absolutely.[12]

There were other reasons for her hatred of David: he disliked
Edith intensely and made this obvious to her. While for Osbert's
sake she was quiet about David, Osbert did nothing to stop his
friend's remarks about Edith.

None of her misery was betrayed to the outside world as she
struggled on preparing her newest anthology, *The Atlantic Book
of British and American Poetry*. After she returned to England
early in 1956, Benjamin Britten wrote again, telling her:

I have always been keen not to write just another song, but to make a
true frame to your poems. A real prologue, an epilogue. I have devised a kind of question and answer, each preceded by a fanfare for
the horn. I want to take a piece or two from your religious poems for a
question something like "what are the seats of the Universal fire to
burn the roots of death in the world's cold heart? . . ." and for an answer, either the last line from *Metamorphosis* "out of the dark see
how real our great spring begins . . ." or some of the last lines of
Invocation. I know these are not a true question and answer, but

more like opening the doors to your great religious thought and then gently closing it. . . .[13]

Britten's letter pleased her, but even his enthusiasm could not distract her from her worry about Osbert and David, which was now becoming obsessive. Osbert had gone to the United States without her and she heard he was bringing David back with him. It was more than she could bear, and having tried every means possible to control her feelings, she had now come to the end of politeness. She wrote to her doctor:

Please may I consult you about something exceedingly important that concerns Osbert very gravely. I am having also to consult Philip Frere, a friend and solicitor . . . we might all three meet. Something has to be done to protect Osbert. He is being made much worse by a situation that is horrible, grotesque and vile. He is too ill, too shocked, too despondent to do anything himself so I am going to do it for him. We cannot go on like this.

Love from
EDITH

I think Osbert had better be put into a nursing home while the situation is being put an end to. It will poison all his few remaining years if it goes on. If I were a man I wouldn't have to bother you.[14]

Edith persisted in believing that David could be forced to leave Renishaw and be got rid of forever—but of course when he returned all was forgiven as far as Osbert was concerned. But not as far as Edith was concerned. Outwardly life went on as usual; visitors came frequently to Renishaw for lunch, and Edith appeared perfectly benign to Cecil Day Lewis or L. P. Hartley. But after they left, they would be the innocent victims, quietly shredded by Edith and Osbert, who would encourage their butler, Robins, to give one of his excellent imitations of their guests.

Much of Edith's time was spent in bed working at her anthology, and in the evening she would knit pullovers for Marilyn Monroe or Sachie. The atmosphere was tense and often unbearable for visitors. When rows blew up, Miss Andrade, for one, would often have to escape to the village for peace.

The only consolation for Edith was a refuge in alcohol, as it had been her mother's, and she became particularly fond of white wine, which she drank in increasingly large quantities. Osbert had the wine watered down, but Edith noticed this and changed to red, whose colour betrayed an interference of this sort. Never an adroit mover, she now had potentially very dangerous accidents. In the Castello di Montegufoni, where Edith spent part of the summer, the flow of wine was even more plentiful. With her increased sense of loneliness she drank more until "I fell with a crash on to my face, and came to to find myself lying in a lake of blood, my dress, three towels, and all the handkerchiefs . . . swamped in blood, with Miss Andrade holding ice to my head. . . . I cannot *think* why I didn't break my nose. But I didn't. However, my face is completely black, blue, green, and yellow."[15] Visitors were disconcerted to hear loud crashes coming from her room during the night, but might have been puzzled as to the cause, since Edith's heavy drinking was never referred to.

While Edith was feeling at her worst, there arrived unexpectedly at Montegufoni a new collection of short stories sent by the then unknown author James Purdy. Edith read them with great excitement and, pushing aside her own problems, wrote at once to Purdy, thanking him for sending the collection, *Don't Call Me by My Right Name.* "I think several of the stories . . . are superb: nothing short of masterpieces. They have a terrible, heart-breaking quality."[16]

Edith told Purdy that she had already written to Victor Gollancz recommending his work for English publication. For Purdy, acclaim by Edith was to be one of the most important and helpful events in his life, giving him the encouragement he should have received earlier. For Edith, at her loneliest, his work with its great compassion, insight, and mastery of language provided all the ingredients she needed for consolation. She was able to identify with the mood of his stories, and was also overjoyed to have discovered a new writer in whom she sincerely believed.

Shortly afterwards she received a copy of his *63: Dream Palace* and again was not disappointed, for it was "a masterpiece from every point of view. There can't be the slightest doubt that you are a really great writer."[17] Gollancz was to publish both books in one volume, but first there were problems with censorship. Gollancz insisted on changing the section at the end of *63: Dream Palace* where Purdy had chosen, to convey the exact tragic feeling he intended, certain words that were bound to offend. The phrase that was objected to was "little mother-fucker," and Gollancz suggested to Edith that they might arrive at something else. Edith, however, was adamantly opposed to any change, as always refusing in artistic matters to compromise her beliefs. She saw no reason why James Purdy should do so either, when the language was deliberately chosen for a purpose.

The censorship problem annoyed her especially because J. R. Ackerley had written a book she considered "exceedingly filthy," *My Dog Tulip,* and it had been allowed a review in *The Sunday Times* by E. M. Forster in "shall we say *frank* language." "It is permissible to publish meaningless filth about a dog," she complained to James Purdy, "and when a man writes a most noble book as yours is, 'the pity and the pain' as Victor Gollancz calls it, must be 'ruinously diminished'—again to use Victor's phrase."[18]

In January 1957 Edith heard that her old friend T. S. Eliot had remarried, ten years after the death of his first wife, Vivienne. Various versions reached her ears of how he had "abandoned" his flat-mate, John Hayward, and she was beside herself with annoyance at this example of the most contemptible of vices in her eyes, disloyalty. She wrote to John Lehmann:

Oh what a beast she is . . . you wait . . . I'll take it out of that young woman! As for Tom, he will never write anything again. . . . It makes me sick to think of the pain John [Hayward] has endured that waking up at 5.30 in the morning to be told his greatest friend, on whom he depended in his unspeakable physical helplessness and humiliation had done this sly brawling lethal cruelty. I feel I never want to see Tom again.[19]

Edith was not to know then that Eliot's wife, Valerie, was to give him the happiest years of his life, but in fact "that young woman" was not the point of her annoyance. Still obsessed with Horner's treatment of Osbert, she could see Eliot's and Hayward's situation only as involving exactly the same principles, for Hayward was partially paralysed and confined to a wheel chair.

Horner returned to London from Italy to meet his painter friend, and Edith had to stomach travelling with him and Osbert on the boat for what was to be her last visit to America. She was now worried about Pavlik, who was ill with double pneumonia in Rome, but had to leave Europe to make money from the readings

in New York. Before she left she received a "sermon" from James
Purdy, and replied:

I was very grateful to you for sending me the Sermon . . . it is impossible for you to write without distinction in anything you do. This
work, though it has all your distinction, I do not cherish as I cherish
your other work . . . because of my beliefs. I am a Catholic. I don't
believe God hates even the worst of the beings He made. And on such
a question one is bound to have one's mind coloured by one's beliefs
. . . but of course I see all the . . . grief which inspired it.[20]

Edith was still trying to reconcile her faith with her feelings
about Horner when there was a new development on their arrival
in New York. It was reported back to Sachie in March 1957:

We arrived the evening before last, 36 hours late. After what the stew-
ard said was the worst crossing they had ever known. . . . As soon as
we got on to the boat Osbert came to my cabin and told me that the
animal was going off again with the same old animal as before. Osbert
said it was "a very good thing as we need a little holiday". I must not
refuse to talk to the second animal, for if I did, the other would make
a scene. The impudence! The blackmail! The sickening horrible creature! And they simply aren't housetrained, if you could have seen
them on the dock.

Edith confided in the Astors, who were virtually the ring-masters
of the New York artistic scene, and ensured that Horner and his
artist friend "would not be received." She also made Minnie
Astor speak to Osbert to try to persuade him to "prevent the
creature from returning to England. If he does we'll see to it that
there will be no queening it at the American Embassy."[21]

In the midst of the troubles she met James Purdy in the St.
Regis Hotel on St. Patrick's Day 1957. At this time he was one of
the few people who, albeit unwittingly, helped her to survive
emotionally and to face the strain of another round of exhausting
poetry readings. Edith cabled him to come to her hotel, and he
remembered the visit:

I met Edith only once, but we corresponded from 1956 until her
death. I felt I had known her always. She was the first important literary figure to recognize me, and she was unwilling to leave America
without seeing me. I was dreadfully poor in those days, and I had to
borrow both money and clothes to get to New York to see her. I felt
immediately at ease with her. She wore a dark long beautiful gown

and a kind of headdress which made her look like a great queen. A queen of mourning but of great vitality, wit, and dynamism. I found her wit much to my liking. She was greatly incensed that Victor Gollancz had had the "effrontery" to censor the text of 63: *Dream Palace* without consulting her since it was she who had sent him the privately published books from which the first commercial printing of any book of mine was done. Later Dame Edith wrote me she thought Victor Gollancz was a "Fool" for having rejected *Malcolm* [generally regarded as one of Purdy's finest books] on the grounds that it was "unintelligible". [Secker & Warburg later published the book in London.]

I admired the way Edith pursued her enemies—to the death. Like me she had received recognition only slowly and painfully, but as she pointed out, in her early days of struggle she was not fortunate as I was to have someone like her who so unstintingly championed him. I believe Edith was the kindest and most generous and big-hearted person I have ever met outside of some members of my own family. She had none of the dry constipated detachment of T. S. Eliot. She was always sure of her own tastes and never afraid to come out for a writer before he was well known and respectable. I think the fact that two writers whom she had been critical of, Noël Coward and John Cowper Powys, came to be her great admirers partly because all three of them found they liked my books so much. . . . Edith was always going to write to John Cowper Powys and thank him for his championing of my work. He continued to praise her courage and generosity in letters to me. Edith was greatly incensed by a review of 63: *Dream Palace* in *The Observer* which attacked the book. It was written by one of the little followers of the very pale conservative critic V. S. Pritchett. Later John Davenport reviewed 63: *Dream Palace* very beautifully and enthusiastically on the occasion of Secker and Warburg reissuing the book free of the censorship and bowdlerizing which Victor Gollancz had felt constrained to give it. I greatly enjoyed Edith's barbs at a very conservative would-be Marxist critic who assailed the book in *The Encounter* (we did not know at the time the C.I.A. controlled *The Encounter*). Edith began a wonderful military campaign against the critic whom we called "Goat-Beard" who styled himself a revolutionary although he drinks martinis and writes for the arch-conservative *The New Yorker*.

I believe that Edith must have written to me at least twice a month for eight years. She never faltered in her belief in me. I was always at a loss that I could give her so little return except my devotion and love. Without her, I doubt that my work might ever have been published at all, for American publishers and reviewers are among the most benighted in the world, the most indifferent to works of the imagination and style, and the most frightened of what John Cowper Powys [the novelist, poet, and essayist] called in his defense of my book against *The Observer* the world "under the skin" or as some would call it "the unconscious". Edith often sent private messages to me through [celebrated] visitors . . . and other less known persons who had attended her gatherings at the Sesame Club. It was one of her fears that I would be reduced to silence by the attacks on *63: Dream Palace* which had stemmed from the V. S. Pritchett circuit. She was therefore greatly pleased when *Malcolm* and especially *The Nephew* received such a good press in Great Britain and America. I believe one of Edith's greatest gifts was her genius in "spotting" (her word) new talent. She was both intuitively and actually very much connected with "reality" and the originality of new talent. Her death was a great personal loss to me. But her encouragement and belief in me has kept me writing in a world of coarse and short-sighted men and rank commercialism and shoddy vulgarity. She touched many lives and remains a vital force in letters.[22]

Edith too was grateful and later wrote to him, "It gave me so much happiness to meet you at last. May we meet again very soon."[23] The problem of the "offensive" word in *63: Dream Palace* was still unresolved; Gollancz proposed several "tamer" alternatives that would be acceptable in England, and after Edith heard more from Gollancz while she was in New York, she continued in the same letter to "James" (they were now on first-name terms):

Worried to death, I *now* think that the best thing to do would be to add the word "old" to "little bugger". I think if it was printed "little old bugger" the word "old" would give point though not the impression of heartbreaking love.[24]

Even Edith's modified phrase was unacceptable to Gollancz, and the book was published with the ending also cut so drastically that it removed the whole point of the story. Edith commented bitterly when she received her copy, "It is a pity that the custodians of our morals never by any chance, attack the right things. . . ."[25]

Edith left New York to make a tour of readings which included a visit to the University of Texas at Austin, where she saw the library that eventually would buy her manuscripts, the Humanities Research Center. The tour was proving successful: for a single

reading at Austin she received $1,000. In May she returned to
New York, and a reporter told her of the death of Roy Campbell,
who had been killed in a motor accident. It was a great grief to
her, but the show had to go on, and she recited in another performance of *Façade*. But soon an even greater blow to her spirit
followed. Not long after she had returned to England with David
and Osbert, a telegram arrived from Rome telling her that Pavlik
had died, on July 31, 1957. Sachie sent a letter of commiseration
and she replied:

Yes it was a dreadful shock: so much that I have been quite numb.
One can only say that he was so ill that I doubt if he could ever have
painted again and that would have made life hell for him.

I think someone might have told me he was dying. I knew he was
very ill but he had been so since January. If I had known I should
have written to him. It has been an awful year. First dear Roy's death
and now Pavlik's.[26]

Beryl de Zoete had written a kindly letter expressing her con-
dolences over Pavlik, but Edith refused to accept her sincerity:

That vulgar old woman, Beryl de Zoete has now written to me and said
"I feel the death of Pavel (which he was never called by anyone)
must have much distressed you. I am much distressed myself." She
had then said he had begged her to write to him and she wished she
had. But at least he knew she admired him. He loathed her.

I replied that yes, I was distressed and . . . it was sweet of her considering how extremely slightly they were acquainted to be distressed.[27]

Pavlik was gone and would be guarded as sacred personal
property. Edith refused to believe that his death could deeply
distress anyone but herself (although Beryl had probably written
only because she knew how unhappy Edith would be). Edith's
feelings of bitterness about Pavlik were tinged with guilt, for she
had loved him very deeply in the past and could never forget
that. Her grief was sincere, but her annoyance at Beryl was due
to other causes. The "Vampire Trout," or La Chasseur, as Edith
called Alice Hunt, had joined the ranks of the bores and lunatics
who kept Edith from her work. As compensation for losing Osbert's interest she was "trying to make mischief between me and
my confessor . . . telling lies about my private life,"[28] as Edith
wrote furiously.

To make things worse, by the middle of August Edith had secretarial trouble when her previous secretary, a Miss Fraser, left
her to go to Sweden. Edith claimed that while she was in America
the secretary had done very little work. *Fanfare for Elizabeth* had
been about the childhood of Elizabeth Tudor, and Edith had
now been commissioned by Macmillan to write a larger, full-
length book on the life of Elizabeth, to include the power struggle with Mary, Queen of Scots. It was to be a mammoth work,
and Edith was finding difficulty in completing it without a secretary. "Confounded Elizabeth" had held up her correspondence
for nearly a year, and now it was overdue. Apart from secretarial
worries, Edith was unable to put Pavlik out of her mind. She
wrote to Choura on September 22, 1957:

I must write in English, because I cannot express myself in
French. . . . Yesterday was our Pavlik's birthday. Oh what a birthday
for us who loved him. I still cannot believe he is no longer with us and
am still at moments, numb with grief. . . . And my soul bleeds for
you and Charlie [Charles Henri Ford] in your grief and loss.[29]

Already Edith was hoping to arrange an exhibition of Pavlik's
work at the Tate Gallery, and on the same day that she wrote to
Choura she also wrote to Sachie:

Remembering darling, that you angelically said that you would write
about Pavlik if his sister sent you photographs [of his paintings], I
have written to her by this post.[30]

Because Edith loved the man, she loved his work; the two were
inseparable. Had it materialized, the exhibition would have given
Edith great pride, in at least honouring his memory, but it never
happened. She was later delighted with the success and appreciation of a memorial exhibition that was held in New York in the
spring of 1964, but for now she was frustrated.

Edith's *Collected Poems* had been published in London in July
1957. *The Times Literary Supplement* reviewed the volume favourably but gave it only 655 words. *The Observer* was unkind
about it, and when Jean Cocteau sent her two drawings, one in
praise of her reciting and the other in praise of her poems, Edith
wished *The Observer* could have known. It had just published an
article by Cocteau on writing, and Edith felt if the *Observer* people had known of Cocteau's praise they would have been "driven

mad with fury." The review that pleased Edith most was by Cyril Connolly in *The Sunday Times*, who, heading his notice "England salutes a major poet," praised poems from each of her various poetic periods. From her early work he isolated her *Sleeping Beauty*—"It overwhelms me with an astonishing tour de force"— and *Gold Coast Customs*, which "reaches a pitch of despair hardly matched by any other work between the wars." He concluded his review:

When we come to compare the collected poems of Dame Edith Sitwell with those of Yeats or Mr. Eliot or Professor Auden, it will be found that hers have the purest poetical content of them all. The honey may sometimes fail, the comb never.[31]

As regards the adverse reviews, Edith was completely mistakenly convinced that Geoffrey Grigson was at the bottom of it all, and "of course, *The Observer*, *Daily Telegraph* and *Spectator* were all in league. . . ."[32] This was completely untrue, but the attacks, as often, brought back recollections of Noël Coward, as she told James Purdy, who had also suffered similar insensitive reviews:

When I was a very young woman, immediately after I wrote *Façade* Mr. Noel Coward produced an alleged parody of this in a stage revue, in which he presented me as writing unspeakably degraded and filthy poems. I endured this for six nights and two afternoons weekly, for nine months. . . .[33]

And she added: "Neither you nor I could write basely if we tried. . . . Oh I have not your patience. . . . I *hate* the stupid . . ."[34]

At the same time a certain Lady Deena Hanson was pursuing Edith in the pages of *The Spectator*, declaring only Edith's brothers admired Edith's work. Edith declared she must be Hanson's disease, and when friends called the Sesame she managed successfully to spread a rumour, which was generally believed, that *The Spectator* had been bought up by the American scandal sheet *Confidential*. Neither was she finished with the lady. "When I am long dead," she told the composer Malcolm Williamson, "and there is grass growing over my grave, a boy will run upstairs into Macmillan's office and say 'Please Mr. Macmillan, sir, I have found it', and producing a piece of paper the size of a postage stamp will say, 'I have found Lady Deena Hanson's family tree.' "[35]

FIFTEEN

Indian Summer

There are moments when I feel it would be better to retire into a lunatic asylum. I don't mind people saying they are the Emperor of China, but I *do* mind non-stop fussing.

The Last Years of a Rebel

EDITH was now becoming a familiar part of the Aldeburgh Festival, and in June 1957 she went there to read Blake with C. Day Lewis. It was also the occasion when she met her new secretary, Elizabeth Salter, for the first time, although the meeting, over luncheon, was not entirely successful. In her book *The Last Years of a Rebel*, a memoir of Edith Sitwell, Elizabeth recalled:

I should like to say . . . that Dame Edith recognised my intrinsic worth behind the façade of indifference. In fact she did nothing of the kind. She took an instant dislike to me.

Not that I was allowed to see this at the time. Her manners were far too good.[1]

But Elizabeth afterwards wrote to Edith to thank her for seeing her, and Edith, touched by courtesy, which she always appreciated, appointed Miss Salter her secretary when they next met, this time at the Sesame.

Once Elizabeth overcame her initial nervousness, she found that Edith respected the guidance of a firm but gentle hand. One reason they managed to collaborate successfully was that Eliza-

beth wrote detective novels, a genre to which Edith was affectionately devoted. More important, Elizabeth had an instinctive
understanding of what lay behind the formidable façade of the
celebrated poetess. She had arrived at a crucially desperate time
in Edith's life, when Edith was finding it harder than ever to
cope with Horner's presence. For Edith, her choice of secretary
was to prove one of the most fortunate decisions of her life.

When Edith went to Italy that autumn, she felt more relaxed
about David Horner. Now that some of her worries were being
taken care of by Elizabeth, there was less opportunity to use
David as the constant scapegoat. The problem was still there,
though, and Edith wrote to Sachie:

. . . something to which I won't go into isn't too intolerable at the moment. I mean it might be worse. But of course something may blow up
at any moment.[2]

At that time Edith's only annoyance was that David was trying to
become friendly with her friends Jeanne and Sherman Stonor,
who lived at Stonor Park, near Dorchester, although this seemed
harmless enough. Predictably, however, it was not long before
something did "blow up."

Just before Christmas Edith wrote to Georgia, sending her season's greetings and adding that there was no news excepting

that the other night, that abominable creature that infests this house,
insulted me so terribly, and with such unutterable evil that I was ill,
and had to remain in bed for three days and a half.[3]

Edith's yearly pattern of living had become fairly fixed since
the Second World War. Because she hated the cold she spent the
winter with Osbert and David at Montegufoni. She was also with
them for summers at Renishaw, and she was alone only when she
was living in her club for part of the autumn.

In 1958 Edith returned slightly earlier than usual from Italy,
because her *Collected Poems* had earned her the William Foyle
Poetry Prize. Anything Edith did was news, and the publicity the
award brought attracted a large number of fan letters. Many of
them were kindly meant, but all too often a request for an auto-
graph was accompanied by pages of the life history of the sender.
Worse were the malicious letters, such as:

You gay old cat—who do you think you are, with those so obviously
Woolworth "jewels". My Niece from Horsham buys all mine from

Cartiers, but I don't suppose they'd even serve you, even if you could afford them. You are just a stupid, vain and pretentious woman. Come to me, and I'll set my darling little Bonzo on you. Come to think of it, he's a pedigree Bulldog, and too good for you. . . . I'd rather pop a ferret through your letterbox. . . .[4]

One woman wrote to ask if Edith wore a wig. The letter began:

You fool,
In a thousand years' time—yes—in a thousand years' time, the common people will be calling you that! . . .[5]

Edith returned the letter with the terse comment "Who let you out?"

Fortunately Elizabeth Salter was settling down and dealt with the "lunatic" mail. She was also learning when not to send out Edith's "bombs"; after all, it was the writing of them, not the sending, which relieved Edith's feelings. It did not particularly matter if they were never posted; they had served their purpose.

From these letters it is clear that it was Edith's manner of dress, familiar to a large non-poetry-reading public from constant photographs in the newspapers, that contributed to the way in which she attracted cranks. As Edith grew older and was accorded more recognition, her clothes became more distinctive. Her hats, in particular, were considered by many to be ostentatious, as was her collection of large rings, a well-known feature from the early 1950s. Edith was particularly fond of aquamarines, and also coral. She frequently chose large stones because they were shown to great advantage on her elegant fingers and helped to emphasize her pale skin, of which she was very proud.

It was not just an increasing wish to be noticed that made Edith dress the way she did. As she grew older her profile became more "acrid," as she put it herself, and she refused to hide it, believing it should instead be emphasized. Her friends found hers a fascinating beauty, and she carried off their interest quite naturally. "Why not be oneself?" Edith once wrote; "that is the secret of a successful appearance. If one is a greyhound, why try to look like a pekingese? . . . I am as highly stylised as it is possible to be. . . ."

To many it was an appearance that suggested a defensive façade, and there was some truth in this. Elizabeth Salter was slowly realizing that Edith managed to give the impression of public bravado but was in truth a shy and insecure person under-neath.

The Sesame Club became more important to Edith; she used it as her base from which she could amuse and be amused by friends she invited there. She particularly liked the company of the young. Few of her friends would ever resist her invitations, which in a sense were like a summons gladly acceded to. The only excuses Edith would accept for the non-appearance of her guests were work or a virus. Like her brothers, she had a horror of catching colds, and was always suspecting someone of having carelessly given her some offensive germ.

At this time Edith began to confide in Elizabeth, telling her some details about her early life and especially the cruel manner in which Lady Ida treated her.

Although haunted by her unhappy childhood, Edith had by now found it difficult to separate fact from fiction in the tales of her suffering. Her brother Sachie does not accept many of the stories his sister circulated about her early life. She told so many of her friends the same stories that it is likely that she herself came to believe in a particular version of the truth because she had repeated it so often. What is clear is that Edith *felt* that her mother had treated her badly. She told Elizabeth that her mother's face, when she was young, had "the pomp and magnificence of a Roman mask," which in old age was "still magnificent and its pride unbowed, but it was empty." "Little things," she told Elizabeth, "water-drops or bee-wings, fretted her away and made her utterly unhappy. Much of her talk was full of these painful little cold water-drops, but there were mo-ments when it flashed with brilliance. . . ."[6]

Edith was now seventy, and it was thirty-five years since she had performed in the first concert of *Façade*. In April 1958, she received an invitation to recite the speaking part in Oxford, in a performance on May 8 that was to be conducted by Peter Stad-len, before an audience of undergraduates. It was, in fact, the last performance she took part in.

Edith accepted, and travelled to Oxford with Elizabeth, in time for the rehearsal. An incident happened that would have given anyone but Edith a bad fright. The screen, designed by John Piper, behind which the speaker read was being attached to a wooden frame when suddenly it fell forward, narrowly missing

Edith's head. It was prevented from crashing onto the instrumentalists by the conductor's wife, who lunged backwards to break its fall. Incredibly, this left Edith unmoved.

The performance passed without incident and Edith received a standing ovation from the students. When she went backstage, she was met by Colin Wilson, a writer she admired. Edith was amongst the first to recognize the quality of his *Outsider*, but it was her interest in crime that made her agree to review his *Ritual in the Dark*, a study of psychotic murderers, including Jack the Ripper. Detective novels had always held a fascination for her; she also had an almost obsessive interest in 10 Rillington Place, where the real-life Christie murders had taken place, and where the bodies had been hidden. Mr. Raper, a chauffeur whom Edith hired when she required a driver, took her past the door on several occasions and Edith declared she found it "a horrible lonely house. I felt plainly that it was haunted. . . ."[7]

It is interesting to speculate why Edith was so interested in crime. In retrospect, we can deduce it sprang from her reaction to Lady Ida's difficulties, which had made such an impact on her. Her unusual interest in crime was as strange as her obsession with diseases. When she inadvertently offended the stepmother of a leper by a thoughtless remark ("I have had every disease known to man, except leprosy") published in a tabloid newspaper after a reporter inquired about Edith's health, she was drawn into correspondence with the lady, who complained to her. The leper's stepmother took pleasure in contrasting her life with Edith's and told her how she was living in great poverty with her husband, a man who had a mania for undressing in public.

As Edith, in bed and wearing a bed jacket, opened these letters she handled them with gloves, fearing she might catch some infection. Her first reaction to her careless remark was guilt, and she had a food-hamper sent from Harrods to her correspondent and her husband. But, as often happened, Edith's kindness was capitalized on unfairly. The woman plagued her mercilessly for more food and money until Edith's patience was stretched, and the correspondence ceased.

The first half of the programme at Oxford had been taken up by a performance of Schoenberg's *Pierrot Lunaire*, a work Edith heartily disliked. It was one that Elizabeth Salter gave an amusing parody of. This Edith knew, and when Sir Alec Guinness asked if he could see her urgently, Elizabeth was asked to be there to give an impromptu parody of the Schoenberg.

It was not an easy meeting for Sir Alec, because *Time and Tide,* in an article on him, had included a paragraph saying that he "told a wonderful story about Edith's reception into the Roman Catholic Church when she was, according to the magazine, 'brought down the aisle on a white satin cushion.'" Guinness had read the article with horror, for the account was untrue and had probably arisen from Evelyn Waugh's inventive gossip. Well aware of Edith's sensitivity, he telephoned her club and told her he must see her. She at once invited him to lunch, which he felt obliged to decline in the circumstances, and when he met her, gave her the magazine. He was careful to explain that had it been truly his authorship he would hardly have come to see her. Edith nodded and read on. When she came to the offending paragraph her pale face blushed red for a second, but when she finished reading she responded, "I believe you." A moment later a friend, anxious to cause trouble, rushed in with the magazine, only to be deflated by Edith. The atmosphere was soon relieved by Miss Salter's performance of *Pierrot Lunaire,* which, although it caused the performer the greatest embarrassment, made everyone else laugh. Nevertheless, Sir Alec never quite felt he was forgiven, for on a visit to Edith and Osbert at Montegufoni, his wife was kissed warmly by Edith but he received the cold treatment of the "long distant aquamarined hand."[8]

In September 1959 Edith made her last long journey in Britain, this time as far as Edinburgh, to read at the Festival. Elizabeth Salter travelled beside Edith in "the motor" driven by Mr. Raper. They were given pleasant rooms in the Roxburghe Hotel, which overlooked the attractive Charlotte Square.

The rehearsal for the reading had been a careful one, with people positioned at various points of the theatre. Edith had not, however, taken into account the different acoustic effect prevailing when the hall was filled, and during the performance various people complained that they could not hear her voice.

Robert Muller, a journalist from the *Daily Mail,* was in the audience, and reported that Edith

wagged a heavily bejewelled finger at her audience, and told them— "Get a hearing aid. I am not going to shout with my voice. . . ."[9]

The complaints continued, and Edith, putting down her papers, told the complainers:

I have earned my living by reciting all over the world and if you can't hear me there is something wrong with you. I have no intention of ruining my voice to please you.[10]

Various other people throughout the theatre joined in the complaining chorus, and Elizabeth, panicking because she thought there would be an angry army of people demanding their money back, went to instruct the stage-hands to lower the curtains. By the time Elizabeth arrived backstage there was complete silence, the unrest had passed, and the curtain was fortunately not lowered.

During the interval the writer Sir Compton Mackenzie, who had been unable to hear, suggested another microphone. When this was done, the second half continued without interruption. Afterwards Edith was unrepentant:

I know how to hold my own, despite such interruptions. There are always people who have something to complain about. Do you think after all the reciting I have done that I don't know my onions?[11]

The fracas had drawn huge publicity and crowds waited for an hour outside the theatre to see Edith. They cheered and waved as she drove off. Pleased with the reception her fans gave her, Edith commented to Elizabeth, "The Scots always like a fighter."[12]

Earlier that day Edith had given an interview with Robert Muller for the *Daily Mail*, and what she said reveals a growing feeling of insecurity, which had no doubt been behind her rather tactless remarks in the theatre. From the very beginning Edith was overdefensive, telling Muller:

The reason that I'm thought to be an eccentric is that I won't be taught my job by a lot of little pip squeaks. . . . I will not allow people to bore me. I am an unpopular electric eel in a pond full of goldfish.[13]

Outwardly Edith sounded as if she was bursting with confidence and Muller decided Edith was "formidable, but not forbidding." But with the wit was a drastic undertone of fear:

My little trouble is that when people don't know who I am they like me. Widows used to follow me from pillar to post. In trains. Everywhere widows. Why is it that people loathe me so much?

And she ended, "You will be kind to me, won't you? Because people hate me so very much."[14]

The interview in Edinburgh was a complete contrast to one she had given to John Freeman in his television series "Face to Face" only four months earlier, in May. She had answered or avoided difficult questions with great skill and showed herself to be a brilliant performer, even in front of the camera.

Edith readily told Freeman about her ancestry, including Joseph Denison, who had founded the family fortune on her mother's side. Family history was something of an obsession with Edith as it had been with her father, and she told Freeman, with more fiction than fact, that Denison had been an errand boy and had "walked barefoot from Leeds to London and built up a large fortune. I'm extremely proud of his having walked barefoot from Leeds." When asked about her childhood, Edith remarked that she had "forgiven her mother long ago" and "didn't want to talk about it," but she did say that her parents had "resorted to everything which could possibly humiliate me."

When asked why she liked the country, Edith replied that it was because of "the quiet, and not having to be bothered by silly questions." Freeman was undeterred, realizing that Edith was enjoying talking to him, and he next suggested that those who did not know her considered her to be forbidding: what did Dame Edith think of that? Dame Edith had a very quick and sharp answer ready:

I don't think that I'm forbidding, excepting when I absolutely refuse to be taught my job by people who know nothing about it. I have devoted my whole life to writing poetry, which is to me a kind of religion, and I'm not going to be taught by people who know nothing about it. I think it's very impertinent. After all, I don't teach plumbers how to plumb. . . .

The interview revealed an Edith Sitwell who was confident but not overbearing, and many of her viewers overwhelmed her with praise. The few cranks who wrote to her then upset her only slightly, but in September, after Edinburgh, similar letters of abuse depressed her out of all proportion to what they said.

Apparently more vulnerable than ever to unkind criticism,

Edith seemed less able to take care of herself. She was gloomy and consequently relied increasingly on alcohol to boost her morale.

There is no straightforward explanation for Edith's increasing fondness for drink. At the Sesame she always drank socially, and although this included wine with the meal, a few cocktails, and perhaps a brandy afterwards, it had little noticeable effect on her. When at Renishaw, however, driven to distraction by boredom and loneliness and the ever-present David Horner, she drank larger quantities of wine to console herself.

The Sesame provided Edith with some sort of diversion that often helped to keep away her bouts of depression. But now Elizabeth noticed that Edith had

brandy taken at night to calm her *angoisse,* the strong martinis beforehand and the liberal quantities of white wine. . . . Unfortunately, these were only temporary palliatives; in the long run both sickness and despair were accentuated.[15]

Edith was becoming afraid that she had dried up as a poet, and once after a few drinks she told Alan Pryce-Jones of *The Times Literary Supplement* that she *knew* that her poetry was worthless. It was a terrible moment for everyone present; spoken with utter frankness, it was a remark quite untypical of Edith's attitude towards herself and her work.

She was still working on her long life of Elizabeth Tudor and Mary, Queen of Scots, *The Queens and the Hive,* a response to the ever-present need for money. Just how serious this was no one knew until she confided in Elizabeth:

I have been very ill indeed, though better today. For three days I couldn't keep any food down and got no sleep at all. The nights were an absolute nightmare of retching and a kind of mental horror. This was simply brought on by the Income Tax badgering me to send them money I have not got. . . .[16]

Undoubtedly the fresh financial worry had increased Edith's feeling of failure, but this was not known to her friends or guests at the Sesame, and it seems unfair to lay all the blame at the Inland Revenue's feet.

The novelist Pamela Hansford Johnson had recently become a friend of Edith's in unusual circumstances. Her husband, C. P. Snow, had written to Edith saying that a publisher's reader thought he detected what might be considered a malicious parody of Edith in one of his wife's novels. Sir Charles (as he then was) asked Edith if she would mind reading the manuscript, for:

if there were anything in the book you didn't like, my wife would wish to cut it out. . . . I know it is an infliction to put extra work on to you and we wouldn't think of asking you if we were not bewildered. . . .[17]

Edith was delighted to have the opportunity of knowing the Snows. She admired their work and wanted to meet Lady Snow because she had known the youthful Dylan Thomas. An amusing reply was sent to Lady Snow:

Dear Lady Snow,
How much I laughed when I received Sir Charles's letter!
   I am, at the same time, alarmed, for I am at the moment finishing a book called *The Queens and the Hive*, which is about Queen Elizabeth I and Mary Queen of Scots, and contains a rousing account of Catherine de Medici planning the massacre of St Bartholomew's Eve. I am now terrified that this may be supposed, by any readers I may have, to be a malicious portrait of you. After all, you are not Italian, do not persecute Protestants, and are not the mother-in-law of Mary Queen of Scots, so the likeness springs to the eyes! . . .
   Nonsense apart, it is an ill wind that blows nobody any good. I am a very great admirer of you and of Sir Charles, and have longed, for ages, to know you both. And now I shall. . . .[18]

Lady Snow wrote a short memoir of Edith that is useful because she did not know her well until 1959 and so it gives an impartial view of the elderly Edith, and also because there is no suggestion of any of the problems Edith was suffering at the time.

We met her for the first time at luncheon at the Sesame where she was supposed to hold court. I say "supposed" because I think this is a psychological misconception. She first sat in the corner, looking spectacular and courts formed round her. I have seen people whom I shall not name, bow so low before her that their buttocks shot up at an angle of 45 degrees. She was not a "room-talker" a type I detest. Like to talk she did, but she was also a good listener. She could be a savage foe, (though this was really another dressing up part, consisting largely of schoolboy japes) but, I personally, have never known her to be the first to attack. . . . She contrived for herself a unique style of dressing . . . she usually chose majestic hieratic hats . . . and robes of the richest embossed material. Round her neck were exotic ornaments of

heavy gold. On her exquisite hands were loadings of aquamarines.
One wondered how she could even lift them from her lap.

I only once saw her without a hat, and this when she dined at our
flat. Her hair was fair and sparse. But she was magnificently robed in
a gown presented to her by the Metropolitan Museum of Art (New
York) for her poetry recital there. She told me at once that she had
worn it to give me and my guests pleasure. She did, we were all
delighted. But, so robed, she did not over awe us. It was not part of
her plan. Her plan was simply to please. . . .[19]

Clearly, then, her friends saw no outward signs of distress. Social
invitations provided by the Snows and other friends all helped to
make Edith feel she was wanted.

When she was alone at the Sesame at night or at Renishaw, the
alcohol began to take its cumulative effect, and by early winter of
1959 it was a different story and Edith became the victim of a
series of accidents.

The first of these happened just before she was due to leave for
Montegufoni. Elizabeth received a telephone call at midnight
and heard the faint voice of Edith explaining that her bed at the
Sesame had collapsed and thrown her onto the floor. She had
struck her forehead against the corner of a bedside table, and as
a result had received "a lump the size of an ostrich egg over my
right eye."[20]

Bravely she refused to cancel a huge party she was giving for
over a hundred guests the following morning, and several days
later she caught the train from Victoria Station, her eye hidden
under a black veil and the lump concealed by a tall witch's hat.

Not long after she arrived in Italy, there was another accident
at Montegufoni in early 1960:

Because my electric light near my bed had not been mended, I had a
candle but no matches. I got out of bed to try to find another switch—
couldn't, and felt my way back to bed—caught hold of what I thought
was the bottom of the bed but it wasn't—it was a very flimsy chair,
which gave way, hurtling me to my spine on the floor, where I lay in
agony for about five hours till I was called, then I was picked up and
put on my bed really screaming with pain.[21]

While Edith was in Italy, Elizabeth was attempting to sort out
some of the income tax problems, a complex series of enquiries
which led her to Paris. In fact, when Edith had been preparing

for the "Face to Face" interview in May 1959, Elizabeth had gone to Paris to visit Evelyn Wiel, who still lived in the Rue Saint-Dominique. Apparently when Edith had hurriedly left Paris in 1939, she had left all the paintings she owned behind in the flat. On hearing about this, Elizabeth suggested that some of the paintings should be sold to pay off her debts at the bank. (Edith's overdraft was at this time £14,000.) In Paris a search in Edith's dusty bedroom revealed a stack of Tchelitchews, so Elizabeth selected three and brought them back to Edith. Definite plans were being made to stabilize Edith's finances. Meanwhile, Edith, who was in Italy with Osbert and David for the winter of 1959–60, retreated increasingly into herself through worry. Her income tax problem, added to the overdraft, constituted a terrible debilitating threat, and away from the interests and security of her club her physical condition worsened. Confronted with the sad presence of Osbert, whom Parkinson's disease had left unable to write and difficult to understand, there seemed little point in Edith's even getting out of bed. In the past she had desperately written to clinics all over Britain, trying to find a cure for her brother, and her lack of success only depressed her further.

Sachie wrote to Osbert for a report on his sister's health and Osbert sent a cheerless reply in early December, typed by his secretary, Lorna Andrade:

You ask me in your letter about Edith. Alas I feel very pessimistic. At the moment she seems alright in the mornings, but becomes rather exaggerated in conversation towards the evening. I have got Guido's niece to sleep in the room next to her for a few days. It is partly my fault that she is still in bed, as I was opposed to her getting up, because of her weakness and the stairs as you will remember are like ladders of stone, very steep and narrow and difficult. . . . I don't think she is having any brandy, except yesterday morning, and Luigi is beginning to water the wine again but she eats nothing and one litre of wine a day as well as glasses of Vermouth are quite enough. There is something mysterious about the whole thing. (I'm afraid this does not make for cheerful reading.) She is no better, or does not say that she is and has now been in bed for five weeks and refuses to get up for any reason at all. The details are infinitely distressing but what can I do?[22]

Apart from the alcohol problem, Edith's general health was good, and her doctor felt there was no reason why she should not get up. The result of being in bed for nearly two months was a weakening of the muscles, which made walking almost an impossibility, but Osbert had a frosty reception from Edith when he tried to suggest that she should go to the Blue Nuns' Nursing Home in Florence for massage. She continued to work in bed, writing angry letters to the newspapers, including, as Osbert wrote,

one to *Time* who had not printed the article to which she objected at all, it having appeared in *Life*; this was only discovered after the letter had been posted.[23]

A constant problem about Edith's health was her ability to confuse her doctors by making light of her condition. Her doctor in England had found her condition perplexing, and it is likely that she herself was not aware of its seriousness. It is also possible that subconsciously she was trying to use her illness to gain sympathy from Osbert, though consciously she said she did not want to worry him. David still upset her, and her financial difficulties were still kept from her brother. She adored him but, perhaps remembering her mother's troubles and the effect they had on Osbert, was afraid to ask for his help.

Once she was removed from the trying situation at Montegufoni, Edith's health would improve, but the New Year of 1960 was holding few cheerful prospects for her and little to cheer her. By the middle of January she was making an effort to come down for luncheon but would return to bed again for the rest of the day. As Osbert wrote again from Italy:

Edith seems quite well in herself. Her state of mind is the thing to worry about, I'm afraid.[24]

Despite appearing at luncheon, Edith had no appetite, though now that the prospect of returning to London was nearer she looked forward to giving huge parties at the Sesame. Her return was planned for April, and, telling Georgia this in a letter, she spoke of her financial woes:

On No account tell anyone at all about my worries. Osbert is not allowed even the slightest worry. He knows nothing about my having worries. On no account—I really beg of you—mention it to anyone at all. . . . I simply cannot stand anything more. The last two years what with his illness and the return of that low animal have turned

me into an old woman. And I cannot stand the hell upon earth rows I
should have to endure . . . the sickening way that awful Christabel
[Aberconway] sucks up to the little Lord![25]

Lady Aberconway was an old friend of Osbert and David, and
fond of them both. Edith corresponded with her and they often
met, and although Edith was not very friendly with her, she
knew Osbert enjoyed her company. She was terrified that Christabel would defend David against her, and was always watching
out for a conspiracy.

Physically, Edith had grown fatter in her body, but her arms
and legs were thin and weak. Moving was now an effort and her
back began to trouble her. This was partly a result of her childhood curvature of the spine, but also because her long days in
bed had made her legs almost powerless.

Once Edith was back in London in the security of her club, her
health improved again. Elizabeth cheered her up with the news
that her financial problems were being taken care of—a sale at
Sotheby's of paintings and manuscripts was being arranged—and
as a further tonic her friends called to see her. A party was given
to show off the "last portrait Pavlik did of me (a very fine
one),"[26] and work she had been doing on a selection of Swinburne's verse was resumed. Edith even managed to make a television appearance in which she reminisced about Gertrude Stein.

She returned to Renishaw for the summer when her club
closed down, and once she was back with Osbert and David her
health worsened again. All the old symptoms returned, and Osbert was alarmed to discover that Edith's legs and arms were
now as thin as matchsticks. She was refusing all food except soup.

After an incident at dinner, David Horner was furious and
gave Osbert a "knowing look" as Edith was helped to bed. This
had an important effect on the household, since David told Osbert that either Edith would have to leave Renishaw or he would
depart himself.

Edith's doctor was called in, and Sachie wrote to Osbert asking
for news of what the doctor said. Unable to visit Renishaw, because he was never asked, Sachie depended upon the letters of
Osbert, the same man whose influence kept him away from the
family home.

The doctor thinks she is quite well in her body, but she can't get out of bed herself and in spite of the slenderness of her arms and legs, she is too heavy for the servants to carry her up or down the stairs.[27]

The most distressing feature about Edith now was her mental state. She was constantly in tears, probably due to remarks made by David, and when questioned by Osbert as to why she was so upset she simply replied "Why do you think?" David Horner wrote Georgia a long letter about Edith's state of health, for Osbert was unable to write with any ease himself. He told Georgia:

Her condition both physically and mentally has greatly deteriorated. To begin with, she says she has cystitis which she has not got. . . . She refuses to eat anything but is drinking heavily. Yesterday for instance she finished off half a bottle of brandy and a whole bottle of white wine. Apart from anything else this form of diet is the highroad to cirrhosis of the liver. She never moves from her bed as she can't walk; her legs and arms are like sticks but she is very fat otherwise so that her legs will not support her weight. She has gone down to luncheon once when two American women came and made no sense, being absolutely plastered. It took two of the servants to take her upstairs again—so much for the physical.

Her mental state is far worse. The underlying trouble is the persecution mania with its logical corollary of paranoia. For instance, her latest fabrication to Miss Andrade and Dr. Atkin is that she wanted to marry several young men but Osbert prevented her on the grounds "that they had not sufficient quarterings". This is a perfect example of persecution mania and paranoia with frustrated sex thrown in. Her most repeated story, this time to two servants, Miss Andrade and Dr. Atkin, but never to Osbert or to me is that Lord Henry Somerset was implicated in the Wilde scandal, was given a revolver to shoot himself by his brother officers, did not use it and fled to the country. This story ends in floods of tears. It is rather bad luck on poor Lord Henry whom she had mixed up with Lord Alfred Somerset [Douglas] who anyhow had nothing to do with the Wilde scandal whatever his own little scandal is. . . .[28]

Horner then described how Edith had refused to see a specialist, in fact a psychiatrist, when Osbert was trying to make her see one. He ended:

There are two alternatives; either a nurse here which means more work for the staff and permanent friction, or, as Dr. Atkin thinks, she should be sent to a private mental hospital probably for a long time. It seems to me that this is the only solution as she certainly will not be

able to go to Montegufoni for the winter—the staff had quite enough
of it then as her behaviour was quite unrepeatable and as she is to all
intents bedridden, she could never manage the journey. . . .[29]

According to Horner, Edith was deranged. While it is true she
was at times confused and unstable, her remarks about Lord
Henry Somerset, her second cousin, show a calculating rather
than an unhinged pattern of thought, since he was involved in a
Victorian homosexual scandal, the Cleveland Street Affair. She
understood and resented the relationship between Osbert and
David, but significantly she talked openly to neither about it.

Towards the end of June 1960, at her doctor's insistence, Edith
went to the Claremont Nursing Home in Sheffield, and her slow
recovery began. True to her old form, she gave Osbert a list of
people she intended to cut when she left the home. It turned out,
despite what Horner said, that she had suffered a neglected attack of cystitis many years ago, which had now resulted in in-
fected kidneys. This condition had been largely responsible, the
doctors said, for her mental state, and had even helped to cause
many of the outbursts of malice and the familiar battles. Her
health was improving remarkably quickly; underneath everything she had remarkable recuperative powers and an indomi-
table spirit. Lorna Andrade, who went to see her at the end of
July, found her comfortable and contented and even liking the
home. Gradually, too, the doctors were reducing her alcohol in-
take and her appetite improved.

The problem of how to face the future remained, and while it
was being discussed, Edith wanted to return to Renishaw to sort
out her affairs. She wanted to live permanently in London and
considered sharing a flat with Elizabeth Salter. The prospect infuriated David Horner, especially when Edith said she would
therefore have to collect her things and spend a week at Renishaw organizing the move. For above all he wanted to be rid of
her and was afraid she would remain at Renishaw once she returned and was better. He wrote again to Georgia:

I suspect that Edith has been writing to that tiresome Miss Salter. Her
visit here must be stopped. All this is a manifestation of cunning; she
waits until you and Sachie have gone [Sachie and Georgia had seen
Edith in the nursing home] and then starts to get round O. I foresee
that extreme sternness will be needed.[30]

Georgia realized that Horner's motives were selfish and wrote a reply to him:

Dearest David,

Thank you for your letter. It seems tragic and ignoble that poor darling Edith is more of a problem because she is better. I realise, of course, that Sachie and I have been spared all but the worry of it, which at a distance is comparatively little and I know that Osbert's devotion to her and the fact that you and she don't get on has made the burdens in different ways almost insupportable but *please try not* to provoke Sachie's loyalty so that controversy is added to the other horrors of the situation.

Georgia told Horner that Edith ought to be allowed a normal life if she could find someone to share a flat with her, and that it would be much cheaper than her club. Georgia emphasized:

She must be allowed to do so. It would be too cruel and we should have it on our consciences if she were not given another chance. . . . I am sure O. in spite of all he has been through on Edith's account would never forgive himself if he felt he had been unkind to her and that would be dreadful for you as *you would eventually be blamed* as having taken the initiative.

Also don't forget you have had the benefit as well as the disadvantages of having her with you. Being the only other woman in the family and loving her as I do I have a haunting feeling of sympathy and responsibility; . . . all I can say is that if you both think it is best I will go and tell her. It would make a ghastly scene but it might help her more than a doctor's approach.

Georgia ended:

If only you had given us the chance of seeing her at Renishaw or Montegufoni in the last years we might have been able to ward off her decline.

But this sincere letter, one of the few occasions when somebody pleaded for sympathy for Edith, cut little ice with Horner. He repeated his ultimatum that Edith was to go to a home or he would leave Renishaw. Osbert, in a pitiable state of health himself, quietly agreed.

In the end the decision was made by Edith. She announced to Elizabeth Salter that she would live permanently in London, no longer being well enough to continue her frequent trips abroad, and would return to her club.

SIXTEEN

The Last Years

. . . But now I know
That even the hunters in the heart and in the heaven
At last must sleep.

Conclusion of *Dido's Song*

THE RETURN to the Sesame in November 1960 was only a
short-term answer because, apart from the question of Edith's
health, the expenses were appalling. A typical week there cost
her nearly one hundred pounds, and as she had been unable to
work during her illness it was essential that ways be found to re-
duce expenses. Despite all this, she decided to celebrate her return by giving a huge dinner party, and the guests enjoyed a
four-course meal of smoked Scotch salmon pâté, roast beef and
green peas, roast or creamed potatoes, pear Melba, and canapé
Ivanhoe.

The diagnosis of paranoia was kept from Edith as she would
have been horrified by the suggestion. Most of the time she appeared quite well and happy, only occasionally lapsing into what
the doctors described as "exaggerated conversation." She did
have something to complain about when interminable drilling in
the building next door sounded through her bedroom wall in the
Sesame. With the lingering effects of her illness and her "alarming mixture of megalomania and inferiority complex," she

believed the drilling and noise was a deliberate act to evict her from the club. She announced, "They are not going to make me move out of my room. Who do they think I am? Do they imagine I would go away to please them?"[1] And she threatened to enter the offending next-door house with the press "and to use to the workmen all the words to be found in *Lady Chatterley's Lover*, together with some others in French and Italian: (I swear like a trooper in both these languages)."[2]

Lady Chatterley's Lover had been much on Edith's mind of late, for D. H. Lawrence had been the subject of a long article in *The Times Literary Supplement* in December 1960, during the "battle of the Noise," as the wrangle over the alleged obscenity and banning of the novel came to be known. Edith had read:

Among these enemies of love whom Lawrence had encountered elsewhere were the bright little intellectuals of his day. Though a conspicuous trio of these, the Sitwells, had their headquarters not far away in the Dukeries, intellectuals were not by and large prominent in coalfield society.[3]

This was offence enough, but what really incensed Edith was the suspicion that her family were being maligned by Lawrence in only the most thinly veiled fashion. The part of Lawrence's book that confirmed for Edith that Sir Clifford Chatterley was a parody of Osbert read: "Chatterley came home crippled from the wars, his disablement being such as to deprive him of his sexual capacity. He took up writing with immediate success." And later: "The Chatterleys had a baronetcy": "thereby," Edith wrote, "pinning it onto Osbert, that poor desperately ill man."[4]

Edith had heard many years before that Lawrence had based *Lady Chatterley* on the Sitwell family, but because of Osbert's illness he resembled Chatterley more now, years later, than when Lawrence wrote his novel, when he was healthy. In fact, an earlier privately printed version of *Lady Chatterley* had more clearly identified Lawrence's cast with the Sitwells: Lady Ida, Osbert, and Sachie were in it. But even earlier, Aldous Huxley, who was a mutual friend of Lawrence and the Sitwells, persuaded Lawrence to tone down the then recognizable portraits. Lawrence agreed, for he had found Edith and Osbert curiously touching; and he rather liked them.

Edith had gone with Osbert to have tea with the Lawrences in

Italy in May 1927. Edith had met Lawrence with her old friend Alvaro de Guevara and had liked him; she admired his poetry, but not many of his novels. In return Lawrence had tried to see the Sitwells in the late 1920s, but when he called at Renishaw the house was empty. Osbert met Lawrence for the first time during a tea-party in the Tuscan villa where Lawrence lived with his wife, Frieda.

Referring to this in her memoirs, *Taken Care Of*, Edith noted that Lawrence "seemed to be trying to make us uncomfortable by references to the contrast between his childhood and ours."[5] The account of this meeting in Osbert's autobiography is quite different, for he remembered the Lawrences as being "extremely courteous." Lawrence himself wrote to a friend:

Osbert and Edith Sitwell came to tea the other day: They were really very nice, not a bit affected or bouncing: only absorbed in themselves and their parents. I never in my life saw such a strong, strange family complex: as if they were marooned on a desert island, and nobody in the world but their lost selves. Queer![6]

Stephen Spender has suggested that Lawrence would have seen Edith and Osbert as "sexual disasters," according to his own philosophy. Spender knew Frieda Lawrence well, whom he recalls as referring often to "that poor Edith Sitwell."[7]

In Frieda Lawrence's memoirs, *Not I but the Wind*, she recalled Edith and Osbert's visit in much the same terms as her husband:

They moved us strangely. They seemed so over sensitive as if something had hurt them too much, as if they had to keep up a brave front to the world, to pretend they didn't care, and yet they only cared too much. When they left, we went for a long walk, disturbed by them. . . .[8]

Osbert had always admired Lawrence's work and had announced publicly that he considered him to be a genius. Edith did not agree and now wrote two letters to the editor of *The Times Literary Supplement*, Alan Pryce-Jones. One, she explained, was private, and the other for publication. Part of the published letter read:

. . . the fact that my brothers and I are not in the least bit interested in the goings on to be witnessed (though not in print) in Monkey Hill does not mean that we are "enemies of love".[9]

In her private letter she was more threatening and protective; she mentioned Osbert's illness and said that perhaps the editor could imagine her feelings on reading the article. While she knew the identity of the author of the review, "he need fear no reprisals from Osbert, but he has me to deal with and sooner or later I shall deal with him."[10]

Meanwhile, the noise through to her bedroom at the Sesame continued. Edith tried to find help from the Noise Abatement Society, but an agreement they helped her obtain to limit the noise made by the drilling was not kept. At this point, Edith called in help from Henry Cecil, the novelist, who had become a recent friend. The construction firm responsible for the noise had as a director a man who was a warden at Henry Cecil's church. Cecil explained Edith's troubles to him, and it was agreed to regulate the noise and to complete the work that caused it by a certain date.

The plan worked for a while, but once again promises were broken. In revenge, Edith wrote nasty letters to the offenders and sent a telegram to Elizabeth:

These liars have made life impossible all day. It is against the law and unless they behave immediately, I shall contact solicitors. Please send name and address of architects, I will deal with them. . . .[11]

Edith obstinately refused to move her room "to please them," and was instead hatching plots to get rid of the workmen. "I am going," she told her secretary, "to occupy myself by buying vipers from the Pets Dept. at Harrods, nurture them in my room until they are fully grown, and then send them parcel post next door."[12]

Perhaps it was a comment upon Edith's advancing age that her threats had no effect. She simply had to endure the noise until it at last stopped in the spring of 1961.

The work that had been disturbed was the first of a series of reminiscences, published in *The Observer*, which were later to be incorporated into her autobiography. The first and second, on D. H. Lawrence and Dylan Thomas, passed unremarked, but the third victim of the series, Wyndham Lewis, whom she wrote about in "Hazards of Sitting for My Portrait," provoked a backlash from an old friend. The writing was embittered by her illness and the anxiety that the incessant noise had caused her. T. S.

Eliot, who had been friendly with Lewis until Lewis died in 1957, was annoyed and wrote to *The Observer,* where her article had appeared, on November 11, 1960:

I have only just read Dame Edith Sitwell's account of her acquaintance with the late Wyndham Lewis. . . . I presume that I came to know him better in his later years than Dame Edith did. . . . I came to feel . . . a warmth of sympathy and friendship which no-one would ever suspect from Dame Edith's account that he would ever arouse.

Edith was bitterly hurt and wisely decided not to reply. But all the same, it sealed the end of her long friendship with Eliot.

She was still pressing on with her book on Elizabeth Tudor and Mary Stuart, and Coutts, although they always remained polite, reminded Edith that her overdraft was £9,542. They wanted the manuscript and typescript of her book for security, pointing out that "we would not of course sell the typescript or the manuscript without first consulting you in the matter."[18] Elizabeth Salter decided that the nightmare problem of insolvency must be removed and went to Renishaw to recover more of Edith's manuscripts and a few paintings, which she took to London in her own car. The rest of the pictures were sent on by van, and Sotheby's was called in to arrange a sale for the end of 1961. Apart from organizing the sale, Elizabeth had also been trying to find a flat for Edith, as the Sesame always closed in August and there was now no question of Edith's staying at Renishaw. At last she was successful, and 42, Greenhill, Hampstead, was Edith's new address, in early August 1961. The flat was small and not luxurious but comfortable enough once Elizabeth and friends had repaired Edith's old furniture, left over from her Pembridge Mansions days, which Osbert sent from Renishaw. All now seemed to be well, for Elizabeth Salter had both solved Edith's financial problems and had found her a home, indeed the first home of her own that Edith had ever lived in. A carefully programmed routine was fixed:

8.30 Take in papers, open post.
8.40 Wash and change Edith. Give her papers.
11.45 Prepare lunch for Edith and staff. Lay table.
12.30 Evening staff on duty. Both staff exercise Edith.
1.15 Lunch served.

2.00   Exercise Edith.
2.15   Put back to bed and prepare for afternoon rest.
3.55   Buy afternoon paper.
4.00   Change patient, tidy room.
4.30   Talk to Edith if required or set up room if guests expected.
5.00   Prepare Edith's dinner.
5.20   Edith up in dressing gown to dine in dining room.
5.45   Edith back to bed.
7.00   Sit with Edith.
8.00   Change bed. Settle Edith for night with biscuits, water, books, cotton wool, Kleenex etc.[14]

It was an exacting duty sheet, beyond the capacity of a secretary but not that of any trained nurse; it had to be worked out so as to interfere as little as possible with Edith's daily working routine. At all costs Edith had to be kept walking, and the middle of the day was chosen, when she was not tired or particularly anxious to work. The first nurse who was appointed was however, completely unsuitable, for reasons that no one could have foreseen. Elizabeth Salter had to resume her search for a nurse all over again. Doris Farquhar was found and was to remain for the rest of Edith's life.

Writing to Georgia about the various problems, Elizabeth told her:

These months have taught me many lessons about the management of Edith and her flat which I hope will benefit the new arrangement. . . . You can be sure that I will do everything in my power to bring about a happy working arrangement, as, for Edith's sake I am so anxious there should be one.[15]

Life was not entirely easy as Dame Edith's secretary, and Elizabeth wisely remained in her nearby Hampstead flat, which would make it easier to see Edith daily, but avoided the close involvement of living with her, which might have eventually alienated her because of Edith's unpredictable moods. Some of Edith's friends might have thought Elizabeth overprotective, but she knew exactly how vulnerable Edith was, and was a real help in coping with the many problems. Edith had appreciated her efforts in moving her out of the club, which she had come to find an absolute nightmare, a mixture between a "Butlin's camp,* a

* Butlin's camps are a chain of inexpensive vacation camps sometimes accused of being overregimented.

good old-fashioned penthouse and a lunatic asylum,"[16] and as she
cheerfully remarked to Georgia:

I think you'll like the flat when you see it. It is just big enough for
ghosts.[17]

And her visitors, more necessary than ever, trekked faithfully "to
that Greenhill far away."

Ill and tired as she was, Edith always managed a good appearance for her guests, with her wit often as spiky as when it was
directed towards her enemies. Amongst new friends welcomed to
Greenhill was Marjorie Proops, the popular columnist from the
Daily Mirror. Edith always had affection for the paper that had
published her first poem, and it was partly for this reason that she
agreed to be interviewed by the famous journalist. The result was
Dame Edith Sitwell grandly giving advice: "Spend one day a
week in bed. Every woman no matter what should have a day a
week in bed. Tell the husbands." And she talked about her dress:

When I was young I was made to wear tweeds and oval hats and
fluffy pink and blue in the evening and I hated them but when I was
eighteen I was given £4, so I went along to a sale and bought
a long black velvet dress with long sleeves. Everybody was quite
shocked for in those days young girls simply didn't wear black velvet.
I realised at once the shock value of my long black velvet and I knew
I was right to look different from the other girls because I was
different and individual. I've never looked back. I often buy rich furnishing stuff for my dresses. My favourite one was earth-coloured
brocade embroidered all over with gold lions and silver unicorns.[18]

"An evening dress?" Miss Proops enquired.
"Oh, no," Edith replied, sounding slightly shocked, "a day
dress."

Before leaving the Sesame, Edith had received a visit from
Paul Hindemith, who wanted to write an opera based on Edith's
English Eccentrics. Hindemith had been searching for a li-
brettist, and Edith would not have been pleased if she had
known that he had already approached other writers, including
Peter Ustinov, before he wrote to her in May 1961:

Would you not be interested to write a sort of one act musical comedy? I am always looking for librettos of this kind, and it would be
wonderful if an opera could be created without the usual operatic

nonsense—perhaps in the spirit of your English (or any other) Eccentrics?[19]

Because Edith had a special affection for Thomas and Jane Carlyle, and had recently extended her *English Eccentrics* to include a new chapter on them, she sent Hindemith a scenario on Carlyle's domestic sufferings. Hindemith replied:

I considered and reconsidered your suggestions of a libretto derived from your splendid account of Carlyle's domestic sufferings, and I hope you will not be too cross with me if I voice some doubts as to the feasibility of this theme. The charming essence of your narrative, is of course, that we know; here is a great man, with whose achievements as a historian and philosopher we are acquainted, and that now we see him in incongruent and unexpectedly awkward situations. . . .[20]

Hindemith went on to say that he felt that Edith's theme was too large to be dealt with adequately in the short one-act opera he proposed to write. He apologized for probably appearing to Edith "as an old fastidious wise cracking bore, worse than Mr. Carlyle," and hoped that Edith might come up with more ideas; but as Edith was too ill to work, the project came to nothing. Hindemith and his wife called to see her at Greenhill, and instead of the opera he decided to set two of her poems to music, *Dirge for the New Sunrise* and *Heart and Mind*. But before he could do this he died, in 1963.

In December 1961 the sale of Pavlik's work was held at Sotheby's and Edith wrote a preface to the catalogue. To her credit, be it emotional or financial, there was no hint of the sadness she had suffered in their relationship:

His power for living was great, I cannot believe I shall never see him again. Thinking of him now I see him as I saw him shortly after our first meeting. The snow was thick on the ground and he was leaping in the air and clapping his large painter's hands together because the snow reminded him of his childhood and earliest youth before the misery and the grandeur began.[21]

The sale of her manuscripts brought in £6,000, and the paintings brought the total up to £15,000. Throughout Edith's financial difficulties she had resolutely refused to tell Osbert, although he was aware she had problems, if not of the extent of them. Osbert was the one person in the family who could have helped Edith, but even when approached by Elizabeth he said Edith's pride would not allow her to accept anything from him. In truth, Edith was so vague about money matters that an annuity could have been provided without her knowledge.

Osbert and David went to Montegufoni for the winter of 1961–62, and it turned out to be a depressing time. Osbert was unable to talk much, while David Horner sparkled with health. One night early in March, Horner finished his glass of brandy and went off to bed. The corridors were dark and, strangely for one who knew the house so well, he took the wrong turning and walked through the wrong part of the house. Thinking he knew where he was, near his bedroom, he stepped forward into space and crashed down to the bottom of a flight of stone steps. He lay there all night in a pool of blood until he was discovered the next morning. He had broken both his legs, crushed his right hand, and cracked his skull. The head injury had the effect of a stroke, leaving him for a time speechless.

As he was driven off to Florence in an ambulance it seemed that he would not even survive the journey. To Edith it seemed a kind of justice and almost as if, as with her father's "murder," Horner was being punished for what she saw as his wickedness. She wrote to Christabel Aberconway, whom she did not really like (because "she sucked up to Jackal Horner"):

He ought to be in a nursing home. He has been a confounded nuisance for nearly forty years. I am all for the Sardinian casting his evil eye over him—excepting he has not brought anything on my side to a much desired conclusion.[22]

Horner did not die, and with great determination began retraining himself to speak and to write with his left hand. He was still seriously handicapped but could now recall the events before his accident. He claimed that he had the sensation of being pushed down the stairs, and there was gossip that Osbert's Sardinian servant was responsible. The Italian obsession with superstition began to operate: the crop failure, the illness of Luigi Pestelli, the caretaker, in fact all the disasters at Montegufoni were being put down to the "evil eye" cast by the blameless Sardinian. Edith, too, speculated: "It is most sinister about David. His last memory before he fell was very creepy. Like you," she told Christabel, "I wonder."

The verdict that justice had been done was a natural one for

Edith, but she was also aware how upset Osbert was about the accident. Her one justification of her attitude was the cruel way David had treated her, but not unnaturally David only saw Edith as trying to wreck a relationship that was not her concern. It was not the homosexuality that Edith disapproved of. She always accepted people for what they were and would not cut certain people out of her social circle, as was sometimes suggested to her by well-meaning friends, because of gossip about their sexual habits. On one occasion, when a certain eminent friend was involved in a homosexual scandal, Edith saw the headline in the evening paper and asked that it should be taken away, refusing to read evidence that would be expected to make her refuse to receive her friend socially. She was asked to sign a petition demanding that the law against homosexuality be changed and wrote to Elizabeth Salter: "I suppose I ought to do something about it. . . . I think of course the law should be changed," and, perhaps thinking of Osbert and Tchelitchew, added, "but I do think it is a very nasty messy subject. I could yell when I think about it."[23] Nevertheless, when she learned of the lack of support for the Wolfenden report, which urged liberalization of the law, she wrote a sympathetic poem of support called *The Outcasts*.

In November 1962, Edith agreed to write her memoirs. When previously approached, in the 1940s, by John Lehmann to write them, she declined, because of Osbert's own autobiography, which she did not want to rival. Now her editor, Graham Nicol of Hutchinson, came to visit her weekly with a tape-recorder, and with the help of notes, essays, and autobiographical jottings begun in the 1920s, a book was eventually put together. Parts of the book show great brilliance, but too much of it is spent attacking certain critics. Her long campaign against F. R. Leavis was out of all proportion to the one sentence he had said about the Sitwells.

Dr. F. R. Leavis' pronouncements are a constant pleasure to one. For one thing, he has a transcendental gift, even when he is writing sense, of making it appear to be nonsense. . . . When [he] writes of Mr. D. H. Lawrence, he seems to combine the fervour of a dear old country clergyman preaching a sermon on the Woman Taken in Adultery, with the powers of expression of those interesting persons who are placed in charge of a Sultan's harem. . . .[24]

The book was Edith's last bid for revenge and all the bitterness of her old age was evident:

Were I not too kind to laugh at the cruel disappointment and envy suffered by certain poor little unsuccessful writers, I might be amused by the fact that although I am now seventy-seven years of age, the unsuccessful are still thrown into what is practically an epileptic fit brought on by envy and malice at the mere mention of my name.

I understand that persons of that kind think I am laughing at them.

On the contrary, I think it is very clever of them to discover each other—although when they do so it must give them the feeling we experience when coming face to face with our own image in a mirror— they are all exactly alike. Still they can admire each other, mirrored, and that must be a great comfort to them. I have nothing against them as writers excepting for three things:

  I. They have not an idea of any importance.
  II. They do not know one word from another.
  III. They can't write.[25]

Not all the book was a vehicle for invective. Edith remembered friends such as Dylan Thomas and Roy Campbell with affection and paid loyal tribute to her two brothers. Pavlik was, however, given only a few pages, but they were written with great devotion.

The year 1962 was perhaps the greatest year of triumph for Edith; three of her books were published to celebrate her seventy-fifth birthday, including her study of *The Queens and the Hive*. It had been written under great difficulties, and Edith had roped in Michael Stapleton, a young publisher, to help with the research. To produce a book of five hundred pages was an achievement at her age, and it resulted in excellent reviews. Boring as Edith's identification with Elizabeth Tudor was at times to others, the subject had nevertheless interested her enough for her to work on it every day. Her *Fanfare for Elizabeth* was reissued, and *The Outcasts*, which was to be her last book of poems, was published in August in London, and in the United States as *Music and Ceremonies*, in 1963.

The poems were particularly poignant because Edith, sensing she was nearing the end of her life, had made this last volume cyclic. Phrases from the poems of the twenties were altered and worked into the new ones, together with work of her various later periods. The heavy "gold-laden" images had gone. *A Girl's Song*

in Winter had been written during Edith's last troubled days at
the Sesame, and although it was partly derived from a poem written in the 1940s it had a simplicity and freshness that the original
did not have.

A *Girl's Song in Winter*

That lovely dying white swan, the singing sun,
Will soon be gone. But seeing the snow falling,
          who could tell one
From the other? The snow, that swan-plumaged
          circling creature, said,
"Young girl, soon the tracing of Time's bird-feet
          and the bird-feet of snow
Will be seen upon your smooth cheek. Oh, soon you will be
Colder, my sweet, than me!"[26]

Edith celebrated her seventy-fifth birthday in September, and
the New York *Times* announced that "Dame Edith Sitwell, 75
today . . . is still a candid lady of letters." She told the press that
she did not much relish the fuss, but the reporter considered
Edith "appears to be at the peak of her life." "If you asked if I
have had a happy life," she went on, "I must say no—I have had
an extremely unhappy life." She was, however, looking forward
to a celebration in the Royal Festival Hall to mark her birthday,
commenting, "Very few people have had the honour of being
present at their own memorial service."[27] The concert was organized by Francis Sitwell, her nephew, and the Park Lane Group,
the musical organization in which he was closely involved. Originally intended to be a performance only of *Façade*, Francis saw it
as an occasion for a full celebration of her life and work. It was to
be her last public appearance in a lifetime devoted to the arts.

Edith agreed to read some of her poems. The preparation was
a painful effort for her, and she knew she would be rewarded
only on the actual night. Her speech had suffered in old age, and,
knowing it to be indistinct, she practised reading her poems constantly, almost despairing that she would ever be able to recite to
her own satisfaction. Her appetite improved in the nervous
excitement of anticipation, and as an endeavour to gain
strength; and she also endured the manhandlings of a physio-
therapist. On the evening of the concert, October the ninth, she
was ready, and after a manicurist and beautician had attended to

her she was wheeled into the Royal Festival Hall by Francis Sitwell, with Elizabeth Salter at her side. Wearing a red velvet dress, which had been chosen years before by Pavlik, and the gold collar given to her by the Duke of Verdura, an admirer, she must have reflected on how far she had come from her childhood dreams. Her family were there—Osbert bravely leaning on his stick, Sachie, Georgia, Francis, and Reresby with his wife, Penelope. So different from those days in Paris and London when she kicked over the teapot going to admit Yeats and was seen hurrying through Bayswater to buy fish!

The audience that packed the Festival Hall included many friends of the family. Sir Kenneth and Lady Clark, Sir Charles and Lady Snow, Cyril Connolly, John Lehmann, L. P. Hartley, Father Caraman, Stephen Spender, David Horner, and many others were among the sixty guests who were invited to dinner afterwards. Also there was Harold Acton, who had declaimed Edith's poetry in a loud voice in the quadrangles at Oxford and had written admiringly of her in his *Memoirs of an Aesthete:*

A hieratic figure in Limoges enamel . . . the pale oval face with its almond eyes and long thin nose has often been carved in ivory by believers. Her entire figure possesses a distinction seldom to be seen outside the glass cases of certain museums.[28]

In 1978 Acton recalled the figure who still must have shone through the elderly lady in a wheelchair:

All her public image of being a fighting, quarrelsome person was part of the defence that she put up against the outside world, because she was used to leading a solitary life. . . . She saw very few people, and she felt that she was always tense. Her social dealings with people were an effort for her. She was a very virginal person. You felt it, you could see it. Her face, everything about her was virginal, I'd say Gothic virgin. When she had this deep affection for certain people like Pavlik, she possessed them.[29]

Sachie wrote a tribute to Edith in the programme and chose the music for the first half. Edith opened her concert with a reading of some of her own poems. This was followed by Britten's setting of *Still Falls the Rain,* sung by Peter Pears; then a Rossini sonata and a Mozart divertimento completed the first half of the programme. After the interval, the concert ended with a performance of *Façade,* conducted by the composer, with Sebastian

Shaw and Irene Worth. At the end of the concert the applause was deafening. The three-thousand-strong audience turned to the Royal Box, where Edith sat with her family, her nurse Doris Farquhar, and Elizabeth Salter, and cheered and clapped. It was an emotional moment; Edith tried to struggle out of her chair to acknowledge the applause but was too weak. She waved, the tears rolling down her face.

The supper party was more of a nightmare, as the strain of the concert had left Edith exhausted. Conversation with her was not easy, and guests found it difficult to talk to her. Then Carson McCullers got stuck in a lift with Cyril Connolly and panicked, for she was as frail and weak with her paralysis as the "beloved Edith" to whom she had come to pay homage.

The excitement was over and Edith suffered a relapse because of it. She was amused by one pressman's apocryphal comment:

A wonderful, exasperating, intelligent woman, before she pulled up the sheets and slipped into sleep, she said, "Be kind to me. Like the poet Yeats said, *I have spread my dreams under your feet. Tread softly because you tread on my dreams.* Don't trample on me because so many people do." And then our greatest woman poet fell asleep.[30]

"Goodness!" was Edith's retort.

On the heels of her Memorial Concert came her appearance on "This Is Your Life," the biographical television programme. Although the programme was usually sprung on the "victim" as a surprise, Edith had been warned that she was to be the subject because her doctors had just diagnosed a heart murmur, which made any shock a potential danger.

Consequently, the guest list was scrutinized by Edith beforehand, and she approved the programme only because Velma, her black maid from the Hollywood days, was to be specially flown over. The programme did not generally please Edith, who commented, "It simply did not happen like that."[31] However, as anticipated, Velma gave Edith great pleasure by telling her that she was "the world's most marvellous woman," and this alone justified the event for her.

Past difficulties with Cecil Beaton were forgotten, as she told him afterwards:

I am grateful to you dear Cecil, for what you said of me during the "Inquisition" and for all the great friendship most truly valued and

over so many years, you have always and unfailingly shown to us.
Everytime I see you I feel young again.[32]

There was also a luncheon party at Beaton's house for Queen
Elizabeth the Queen Mother in November 1962, and Edith told
Beaton that she was writing to apologize for being unable to
curtsey. "I still can't get out of my wheel chair and have to be
carted about in an ambulance. Such a bore." Edith had often
sent Queen Elizabeth the Queen Mother her books, and Her Majesty was amused and fascinated by Edith when they met, although she has admitted to being a little nervous of Edith. But
the occasion at Beaton's was a great success, and Edith felt she
had enjoyed every minute of it. "The Queen Mother has a kind
of genius for making everyone happy,"[33] she told Beaton in a letter of thanks.

After the excitements of 1962, Edith plunged into a period of
deep boredom. Everything seemed an anticlimax, and by the
New Year of 1963 she was suffering from acute depression. Her
physical condition was also deteriorating, and her conversation
was indistinct. Elizabeth Salter wrote:

Sometimes when I went to her room I felt that the Edith I knew was
not there. Her speech would be muzzy, her eyes owlish. At other
times her mental energy would reassert itself, acting as the dynamo
that consumed her scanty fuel, so that her body remained frail and
devitalised.[34]

Her nurse, Sister Farquhar, to whom Edith had become devoted and trusting, suggested that if Edith was to survive the
winter it was imperative that she should be out of Britain. Edith
herself suggested a world voyage, knowing that the change
would do her good and also give her the facilities to go on working at her memoirs undisturbed.

Early in March she set off with Sister Farquhar and Elizabeth
Salter on the S.S. *Arcadia*, bound for Australia, along with Sachie
and Georgia, who were travelling as far as Gibraltar. Such a long
voyage was a risk, but the advantages appeared to outweigh any
possible hazards. There was a full medical staff on board and life
would be governed to fit as closely as possible the usual London
routine, only now without the plague of journalists and other
hangers-on. She was given a comfortable cabin and settled down
to her memoirs.

For some time there was bad weather, which did not trouble
Edith, though it did Elizabeth Salter. They sailed to Colombo, Sri
Lanka, where Elizabeth disembarked, later returning to the ship
with several jewels for Edith, from which she was to select an
aquamarine. The buying of the jewels had been the bait to in-
duce Edith to go on the voyage in the first instance. Elizabeth
had remembered a jeweller who, on a previous visit some years
earlier, had had an interesting stock. Edith chose a large aquamarine. Elizabeth discovered too late that she had inadvertently
committed a crime by bringing unbought jewels on board, although happily it passed undetected. They sailed on to Australia,
where Edith gave various press conferences. These exhausted
her, but she was a success with the Australians, one of whom
later sent her notebooks as a gift, while another offered an oint-
ment made by a Maori doctor as a treatment for her back. She
liked Australia and "her strange beautiful room in Sydney with a
wonderful view of the sea, and a garden view at the back with
dark glittering leaves. . . ."[35]

Elizabeth noted that Edith had not looked so well for many
months, and wrote to Sachie and Georgia: "her fortnight in Sydney was just what she needed and she gave a really tremendous
press conference."[36]

No one could have foreseen the disastrous weather that was to
blight the return voyage, across the Pacific in a new ship, the
Willem Ruys. Elizabeth sent another account to Sachie and
Georgia of what followed:

Until we embarked on this ship in Sydney, the trip was a hundred per
cent successful. Edith was well and happy and working, but alas,
after Sydney the weather became bad and we had rough seas for very
nearly a fortnight. . . . She bore up well, but she was not nearly as
happy with the ship, as her cabin was small. . . . Still, all was well
and her spirits were wonderfully good, and then when we arrived in
Miami, she had a stomach upset, which culminated in a degree of
bleeding while she was vomiting.

The ship's doctor was in constant attendance and quietened her
down so that there has been no more sickness, but although he was
perfectly happy to take her on to England, both Sister and I felt we
should have a second opinion and arranged for a Doctor to come on
board here on Bermuda. Having seen her he advised that she be
brought off the ship for a day or two's rest after which she will fly

back. . . . It is particularly tragic because she lost all vestiges of the
virus she was suffering from, was in really top form, and charmed everybody she met, including the Australian Press. . . .[37]

The situation was not as bad as had been feared, as the haemorrhage was due to a burst vein in her throat. Edith was flown
to London with Sister Farquhar, while Elizabeth followed on
board the ship to look after the luggage. All was not disaster; depressing as the last part of the voyage had been, Edith was no
worse than before she left, and she had written part of her memoirs. She would often eat very little, however, and she frequently
and disconcertingly fell asleep in the middle of a conversation
after a little to drink.

She still managed to write, firing her slings and arrows at the
critics as sincerely as ever, and even took up fresh campaigns.
Now it was the defence of animals, and letters were written
about blood sports: "Sport is sport and fun is fun and I wish I
had a pack of man-eating tigers." When she wrote a letter to the
press about a "cruelty to cats" case she had read about, she received many letters from old-age pensioners who told her to continue, because she was famous while they were not, and therefore
she was able to do so much good by her influence. The editor of
the *Daily Express* told her that her letter resulted in one of the
biggest post-bags they had ever received. She had her own beloved cats, Leo and Shadow, and two strays, Belaker and Orion,
who had invited themselves to stay. Pets had always been a consolation to Edith, from the days as a child when she had befriended her peacock, Peaky, who to her sadness deserted her
when her father found him a wife. Edith had had two cats in her
flat in Paris and adored them. When she made her will in 1936,
she asked that they should be looked after, since she felt she
"could not die happy unless they were provided for. . . ."[38]

But inevitably the long hours of boredom made her bitter, and
this bitterness was poured into her memoirs. Nevertheless, new
loyalties were still forged. Lawrence Durrell, whom Edith had
complained about so fiercely in the 1950s, was now adamantly
defended in a long correspondence that, although lacking her
sharpest wit, at least diverted her.

In the autumn of 1963 she survived another crisis, an attack of
pneumonia, and when she returned to Greenhill the news that
old Evelyn Wiel was seriously ill was kept from her. When she

was finally told, Elizabeth Salter went to Paris for a last visit to
bring back the remainder of Edith's possessions from the empty
flat she once shared with Evelyn. She found a pile of Pavlik's portraits, including one of Edith, hidden behind the old bookcase. A
further search revealed that Evelyn had papered over a cupboard
to prevent the marauding Germans from ransacking Edith's
things—when it was opened, Elizabeth found a treasure trove,
fifty-six of Edith's manuscript notebooks. The manuscripts were
successfully sold, but the Pavlik portrait was restored and hung in
Edith's bedroom, valued more highly by Edith than her own
work.

In May 1964 it was decided to find a quieter home for Edith,
and so Elizabeth found a cottage in Keats Grove, Hampstead.
Before moving in, Edith went with Sister Farquhar on a last holiday to Bournemouth, where she was visited by Francis Sitwell.
Elizabeth remained behind to make the necessary arrangements
for the move from Greenhill. When Edith arrived all seemed to
be well. Those of her belongings which had previously been at
Renishaw, Paris, or Greenhill were now all brought together in
Bryher House, and there was a patio for Edith's four cats. All this
guaranteed that Edith herself would be pleased with her new
home.

Not long after she settled in, Edith began to sleep right
through the days, as Elizabeth Salter noted:

When she woke, her speech was vague. A short conversation was
enough to tire her and her visitors had the disconcerting experience of
watching her eyes close as they conversed with her. To talk work or
business, to ask her for decisions, even on simple household matters,
became impossible.[39]

Inevitably concern over Edith's health caused tension amongst
the household staff, who were all trying to do their best for her.
Few visitors were allowed, and Edith's suspicion of conspiracies
and plots against her was rampant, because various medical restrictions meant that she was out of touch with what was really
going on. Her life was governed by her own imagination, without
the restraint of reality, and the staff needed the patience of Job to
cope with her. The autumn of 1964 was a difficult time for those
who were looking after her, but Edith inspired great loyalty from
them all the same. This made the situation tolerable, but only

just, as Edith often misunderstood their kindly motives and complained about them without reason.

Many years earlier, Pavlik and she had considered doing a stage production of her book *English Eccentrics*. This had never materialized, but Malcolm Williamson had now written the music for what was to be a brilliantly successful opera. His collaborator was the librettist Geoffrey Dunn, and the work was produced by Sir Robert Helpmann. When it was first put on at Aldeburgh, Edith had shown great interest in it and had contributed many ideas. When the opera came to London in May she was determined to be present at a performance.

Confined as she was to a wheelchair, she was too ill to dress with her characteristic care, for her weakness was such that every movement was a strain. Osbert had also decided to attend, and they arrived together in ambulances and were wheeled into the performance. Edith looked old and frail in the last photograph that was taken of her, on this occasion, but there is a noble grandeur in her face that marked her great courage. As the opera drew to a close, the figure of Beau Brummel is left lonely and deranged, playing a solitary game of cards. This moved Edith and Osbert to tears, and they both had to be wheeled away. As Brummel threw down his cards in a scattered heap, Osbert's crutch fell on his wheelchair with a macabre clatter.

A few days later, the composer arrived with the cast to visit Edith. Robert Helpmann was also present, and the cast went up to Edith's room in turns to be presented to her. Edith was in bed surrounded by her cats, and Sister Farquhar remarked, "Soon your book will be out."

"So shall I," Edith replied.

Mr. Williamson saw Edith looking strangely beautiful and said, "Edith, what do you mean?"

"Dead of course," was Edith's quick retort.

"Nonsense," said Sister Farquhar, "we all start dying the moment we are born."

"Huh!" Edith exclaimed dismissively, waving her hands in the air.[40]

In November 1964 a new doctor came to see Edith, and although the changes he made were taxing for her they produced a temporary recovery. Once again Edith was practising her poetic technique and writing letters to amuse her friends. She was also reading and appeared to be her old self again. But unfortunately she was allowed to see an article that Julian Symons had written about her in the *London Magazine*.

It was published as part of a series called *Reputations*, and with it Alan Ross, the editor, had hoped to start a Sitwellian battle. Symons was a noted writer of detective novels, and not a poetry critic, and he declared in his article that

what is attempted is less literary criticism than the history of a reputation. . . .[41]

Although entitled to his opinions, it was more than a little unfair of Symons to remark on the opening lines of *Still Falls the Rain:*

> Still falls the Rain—
> Dark as the world of man, black as our loss—
> Blind as the nineteen hundred and forty nails
>   Upon the Cross . . .

Is it merely pernickety to point out that rain is itself not black, nor even dark, and even with its symbolic meaning (Rain = Bombs), black does not seem a right or powerful word?

Is it impermissible to ask why the nails on the cross are blind, and to wonder how they could possibly see?[42]

Symons's article upset Edith far beyond anyone's expectation, for she was well aware he had no reputation as a poetry critic. Weighed against the praise of Yeats in the past ("Miss Edith Sitwell seems to me to be an important poet") Symons's article ought to have been dismissed as unimportant and impertinent. But Edith's lifelong sensitivity to criticism, combined with her illness, made her more vulnerable than ever to the ill-timed outburst. She felt that she had been made the laughing-stock of literary London, but was too ill to reply quickly to the *London Magazine*. Others went to her defence instead, including John Lehmann:

I have been reading Mr. Julian Symons's article on the reputation of Dame Edith Sitwell in your November number, and have been shocked by the distortion of its criticism and the badness of its manners. . . . Mr. Symons tries to belittle the famous opening lines of 'Still Falls the Rain' by the most absurd arguments, that seem to me to show a total failure of imagination. . . . Mr. Symons seems never to have experienced a thunderstorm, nor a rain mixed with soot as so often in London, because he makes the staggering suggestion that rain can appear neither black nor dark. . . .[43]

Symons had quoted an excerpt from Yeats's *Second Coming*, which ends with the line "A gaze blank and pitiless as the sun," to show the superiority of Yeats's work to Edith's. Symons played into Lehmann's hands, however, for he continued:

More extraordinary still, he praises Yeats for calling the (inanimate) sun "pitiless" but pours scorn on Dame Edith for calling the (inanimate) nails "blind". The truth is prejudice is blind.[44]

The correspondence continued until after Edith's death, when Symons wrote in the *London Magazine*, in February 1965, in reply to John Lehmann's letter:

Death adds its sting to an accusation of "bad manners", which could otherwise be ignored and makes it necessary to answer the criticism that such a piece of mine should not be published when its subject is ill. This seems to me irrelevant. What in the view of an admirer like Mr. Lehmann, would be the right time to publish such an article? Answer: Never.[45]

After the article first appeared, friends arrived to cheer Edith up, including John Freeman. He had been to an exhibition of Pavlik's work in New York with Bette Davis, and told Edith that they had both agreed that the portrait of Edith that Elizabeth had found and Edith had loaned was the best exhibit there.

During what was to be the last week of Edith's life, she seemed to be more cheerful. She saw her agent, David Higham, and was pleased to hear from him that *The Sunday Times* had bought the serial rights of her memoirs. A carefully considered reply had been composed to answer Symons's article, and it is clear that Edith's wit was as sharp as ever:

"And did you once see Shelley plain?"

I did not. But I did once see a Mr. Julian Symons looking extremely plain.

It is obvious from Mr. Symons's writing as I have now brought myself to read, that I have got on his nerves. He wrote about me sluggishly and at great length in a book called *The Thirties;* but I paid no attention to this as I had never heard of him. Indeed, I have only now, after multitudinous attacks on me from his ever-busy pen, discovered that he is not a gossip-columnist, but is a compiler of de-

tective stories. This, of course, makes him eminently worthy to criticize my poetry.

I make every allowance for class hatred and envy, but Mr. Symons
has now overstepped the mark in a 14-page personal attack on me in
the *London Magazine* of November 1964. In this, Mr. Symons, with
becoming modesty, says, "What is attempted is less literary criticism
than the history of a reputation."

I cannot claim to be an aristocrat like Mr. Julian Symons, yet to
speak of me as *vulgar,* is part of that originality which would be admired in Mr. Symons if anybody noticed him. It is strange that one of
Mr. Benjamin Britten's noble works was a setting of *Still Falls the
Rain.* It is possible that Mr. Britten may be remembered when Mr.
Symons is remembered only for his expectations. His fellow-*nouveaux
gentile homme,* Mr. Ross, (after allowing me to be grossly insulted)
wrote me a whining letter asking me to continue my subscription to
his magazine: hoped, knowing that I have been grievously ill for two
years, to distress me.

It is a vain hope. I am perfectly used to expectations from the gutter; what the denizens of the gutter do not realise is that they cannot
harm me. The clean wind merely blows their filth back in their own
faces.

And there I will leave them. They can disgrace themselves to their
hearts' content for all I care.[46]

On December 8, 1964, Edith chose photographs for the first
edition of her memoirs, which she had completed some months
earlier. There was nothing to suggest any change in her health,
for although she seemed a little irritable when her editor, Graham Nicol, called to see her, by the time he left she was laughing and in a cheerful mood. Nicol had told Edith, "It won't be
long now before I bring you the proofs. . . . Your work on the
book is finished."

Edith replied, "Thank the Lord for that!"[47]

Elizabeth went out for dinner that evening and returned to her
flat at midnight. There she found a message asking her to telephone Sister Farquhar. She did so and was told that Edith had
suffered a bad haemorrhage. Immediately Elizabeth went to
Bryher House, but sat downstairs to avoid alarming Edith. The
doctor, whom Elizabeth had summoned because Sister Farquhar
had been unable to get through to him, arrived and sent Elizabeth back to her flat. He announced that there had been no
change in Edith's condition and that there was no reason for her

family to be told. Elizabeth sat up all night in her flat, until she received another call from Sister Farquhar, on the morning of December 9. Edith was waiting for an ambulance to take her to St. Thomas's Hospital for a blood transfusion and asked if Elizabeth would inform the family.

After making the necessary calls, Elizabeth returned to Bryher House just as Edith was being put into an ambulance on a stretcher. "Oh, Elizabeth, I have had such an awful night," Edith said as she bravely waved goodbye. Apologizing for being a nuisance, she was driven off.

Meanwhile Sachie and Georgia rushed to London, and Francis, who was working for Shell, nearby, saw her briefly, when she was still very weak. He called back several times, but when he, Sachie, and Georgia tried to see her, they were not allowed to go in. They and Reresby were waiting in a corridor outside with Sister Farquhar when a doctor came to tell Sachie that Edith had just died of heart failure. Elizabeth arrived five minutes later, held up on the way in her taxi by heavy traffic, and they were all taken to see her.

It was all over, as Edith had written on the last page of her autobiography, "bar the shouting and the worms."[48]

Some years earlier, when commiserating over the death of a friend, Edith wrote:

I am sure that when people die they do just feel they want to rest; and they know, which we don't until we come to die that it is only for a time. . . . That I am certain of as I can be of anything and I don't mean it only applies to people who are religious—the people who are round them hold them back quite uselessly and against their will. Uselessly, for it is only momentary, the holding back. If one is there, one remembers them when they die—not as they are at all—but completely different. When I am dying I shall not want that to happen.[49]

High Mass was celebrated at Farm Street and her funeral was held at the church in Lois Weedon, in the parish of Weston. It was near Sachie's house in Northamptonshire, where she had once shocked the neighbours by not having a visiting card.

It was the first ecumenical service since the time of Henry VIII, shared by the local vicar and Mgr. Valentine Ellis. The family and friends moved slowly behind the cortège and the coffin was carried by men from Weston village to a grave in a small cemetery where Lady Ida had been buried twenty-seven years earlier. Edith would have appreciated the fact that she was, against her wishes, accidentally buried near her mother. When this was realized, the family requested to have Edith moved to a new position in the cemetery and were granted an exhumation order by the Home Secretary.

Edith was placed in her grave wearing the largest of her aquamarines, at Georgia's suggestion. As her coffin was lowered, Lady Aberconway, who arrived late with L. P. Hartley, threw a flower into the grave and nearly toppled into it. It was an incident that Edith would have relished.

Henry Moore had already designed a small bronze sculpture that was chosen by the family as being suitable for incorporation into Edith's stone. It depicts the hand of a young child holding the hand of an old man, suggesting the continuity of life through each generation.

Georgia chose lines from Edith's *Wind of Early Spring*, which were lettered by Ralph Beyer:

> The past and present are as one—
> Accordant and discordant, youth and age,
> And death and birth. For out of one came all—
> From all, comes one.

Her stone rises against a background of trees and the nearby Monk's Pond. There the only noise is that of the cows, who, as Edith would have observed, hold a "mothers' meeting" at the side of her grave.

Appendix: Some Brief Biographies

Sir HAROLD ACTON. The most famous of the Oxford aesthetes of the 1920s, he was an early and constant admirer of the Sitwells. As an undergraduate, he used to declaim *Façade* in the quadrangles, with a megaphone. He has published many books, including two volumes of *Memoirs*, and was a near neighbour of the Sitwells in Italy, where he has spent much of his life in his Florence villa.

LORNA ANDRADE was for many years secretary to Osbert Sitwell, after holding a similar position to the novelist A. E. W. Mason.

Sir CECIL BEATON. British photographer, designer, and writer. He often stated that he owed the start of his career to the Sitwells, and his early photographs of them, especially of Edith, caught the public eye. He was also friendly with Pavel Tchelitchew, an association that caused Edith some anxiety. She nicknamed him "Maysie." One of the last letters he wrote, the day before he died, was to Sacheverell.

MARTIN D'ARCY, S.J. The doyen of Jesuit priests amongst the literary Catholic intellectuals, he was responsible for the reception into the Roman Catholic Church of Graham Greene and Evelyn Waugh. He arranged for his colleague Fr. Philip Caraman to give Edith instruction, and received Edith into the Roman Catholic Church in 1955.

BERYL DE ZOETE lived for many years with Arthur Waley, the translator of oriental literature, and was herself a brilliant linguist and an expert on the dance. Edith disliked her intensely—indeed, a feeling shared by most of her friends, because Beryl was often tactless and difficult in company. She was nicknamed "Baby B" by Edith, who was unjustly convinced that she never took a bath.

JULIAN FIELD. A cultured, well-educated crook and swindler, he was responsible for involving Lady Ida Sitwell in complicated and dishonest financial transactions, in order to reap the benefits of her ignorance of the law and money matters. His friendship with Swinburne, Victor Hugo, and other literary figures, in addition to the fact that he was socially well placed, helped to gain the trusting co-operation of Lady Ida. He was jailed for three years when he was brought to trial with Lady Ida for his part in her financial affairs.

GEOFFREY GORER. He first met Edith in Paris in the late 1920s and with his mother, Ree, provided Edith with hospitality in London, besides frequent advice and encouragement. He is a distinguished anthropologist and also an amateur horticulturist. He successfully produced a new rhododendron, which he named "Dame Edith Sitwell."

GEOFFREY GRIGSON. Poet, editor, and topographer, he edited the influential *New Verse*, a literary magazine which was founded in 1933 and which helped to publicize the work of the Auden group, of whom he was a friend and admirer. He took every opportunity to publish attacks on Edith's poetry and prose, dedicating a volume of verse to a friend and "on second thoughts, to Edith Sitwell, my publicity manager." He formerly championed the work of Dylan Thomas, but reversed his opinion in a volume of critical essays called *The Harp of Aeolus*, in which he attacked Edith's and Thomas's work.

CONSTANT LAMBERT. Outstanding composer, conductor, and revivalist of certain neglected music, such as that of William Boyce and Liszt, he was one of Edith's favourite narrators for *Façade*, which he recorded with her in 1929. He helped Walton with the scoring of the work and wrote part of one of the numbers, "Four in the Morning." His best-known composition is a setting of Sacheverell's poem *The Rio Grande*.

F. R. LEAVIS. Regarded as the most influential English critic of the century, he quickly achieved a reputation for his opposition to the literary establishment and for his narrow-minded insistence that he alone was the judge of what writer or work was worthy of serious academic consideration. He was obsessed with the work of T. S. Eliot and D. H. Lawrence, whose acceptance as serious writers his criticism did much to establish. He mentioned Edith Sitwell only three times in his published writings, but adversely. Leavis influenced an entire school of critical thought that by its nature automatically excluded Edith's work, and this was partly responsible for the misconception that she was not a "serious" poet.

WYNDHAM LEWIS. The leader of the Vorticist movement in England, which he founded with Ezra Pound. Lewis was a brilliant artist, novelist, and essayist. His many portraits included ones of T. S. Eliot, Ezra Pound, Ronald Firbank, and Edith Sitwell. He launched an attack on the Sitwells and Bloomsbury in his satirical novel *The Apes of God*, an assault that failed because of its lack of objectivity. He described himself as Edith's favourite enemy, and although their prolonged dispute was public knowledge, they had a mutual sneaking respect for each other.

JAMES PURDY. American novelist, dramatist, and short-story writer, who attracted Edith's attention as a remarkable talent with his book *Don't Call*

Me by My Right Name. She was the first person to encourage and promote his work and to insist that his texts, regarded as too "frank" by Victor Gollancz, should not be expurgated.

HELEN ROOTHAM. Became governess to Edith in 1903 and was decisive in shaping her poetic career. She was a talented pianist and the niece of Dr. Cyril Rootham, the Cambridge composer and teacher. She travelled to Berlin with Edith in 1908, where Edith considered taking up a musical career of her own, but later persuaded Edith to leave Renishaw with her, to be a writer instead. She became jealous of Edith's success, and although her ill health and constant nagging made her a burden, Edith loyally remained with her in Paris until her death in 1938. Her sister Evelyn shared the Paris flat with Edith and Helen, and acted as housekeeper and secretary. She remained in Paris throughout the war, when Edith returned to England, and died in 1963, having been supported by an allowance given by Edith.

ARTHUR WALEY. Was first employed in the Print Room of the British Museum and later in the Oriental Department there, under Laurence Binyon. He taught himself several oriental languages, and was soon regarded as the best translator of oriental poetry of the century. He was a quiet man, who hated social small talk, unlike his friend Beryl de Zoete, with whom he lived until her death. Sacheverell, whose work Waley admired greatly, regards Waley as the most learned and cultivated man he has known. Edith included him as the only living person in her *English Eccentrics.*

MALCOLM WILLIAMSON. Australian-born composer who settled in England, he wrote the music for the opera *The English Eccentrics,* the text of which was based on Edith's book of the same name. He dedicated his Violin Concerto to her memory, and, using some of the thematic material from the concerto, wrote *Epitaphs for Edith Sitwell,* which exists as an organ piece and also for string orchestra. Williamson has also set Edith's *Young Girl.* He was appointed Master of the Queen's Music in 1975 and is one of Britain's most important composers.

Notes

ABBREVIATIONS

AMP: Edith Sitwell, *Aspects of Modern Poetry* (1934).

AP: Edith Sitwell, *Alexander Pope* (1930).

CES: José García Villa, ed., *A Celebration for Edith Sitwell* (Norfolk, Conn.: New Directions, 1948).

DCPT: Parker Tyler, *The Divine Comedy of Pavel Tchelitchew* (New York: Fleet Publishing, 1967).

ILUBS: Edith Sitwell, *I Live Under a Black Sun* (1937).

LNR: Osbert Sitwell, *Laughter in the Next Room* (Boston: Little, Brown, 1948).

LYOAR: Elizabeth Salter, *The Last Years of a Rebel* (London: Bodley Head; Boston: Houghton Mifflin, 1967).

SL: Edith Sitwell, *Selected Letters 1919–1964*, John Lehmann and Derek Parker, eds. (London: Macmillan; New York: Vanguard Press, 1970).

TCO: Edith Sitwell, *Taken Care Of* (1965).

ES: Edith Sitwell

GS: Georgia Sitwell

OS: Sir Osbert Sitwell

SS: Sir Sacheverell Sitwell

PT: Pavel Tchelitchew

CTZ: Choura Tchelitchew Zaoussailoff

Texas: Humanities Research Center, University of Texas, Austin.

ONE. *A Member of a Family*

1. ES, *TCO.*
2. George Sitwell, *Renishaw Hall* (n.d.).
3. ES, *TCO.*
4. Quoted by OS in *LNR.*

5. ES, unpublished memoir.
6. ES, radio broadcast (1955).
7. ES, unpublished memoir.
8. OS, unpublished memoir.
9. ES, *TCO*.
10. ES, unpublished memoir (1922).
11. Ibid.
12. ES, unpublished memoir (1922).
13. ES, unpublished memoir.
14. Ibid.
15. Constance Sitwell, diaries, published as *Frolic Youth* (London: Christopher Foss, 1964).
16. This and preceding quotations: ibid.
17. ES, *Colonel Fantock*, in *Troy Park* (1925).
18. ES, *TCO*.
19. SS, letter to OS (Dec. 26, 1912).
20. Ibid.
21. ES, *TCO*.
22. *Daily Mirror* (Mar. 13, 1913).
23. ES, letter to Sir George Sitwell (n.d. [1914]).

two.   *London Calling*

1. SS, letter to OS (n.d.).
2. ES, *TCO* (to ". . . of the war."); rest of passage excised from typescript of *TCO*.
3. SS, *For Want of the Golden City* (London: Thames & Hudson, 1972).
4. *The Drunkard*, from ES, *The Mother and Other Poems* (1915).
5. *The Mother*, from ES, *The Mother and Other Poems*.
6. T. S. Eliot, in *The Tyro* (1921).
7. ES, in *Wheels* (1919).
8. Diana Holman-Hunt, *Latin Among Lions* (London: Michael Joseph, 1974).
9. Wilfred Owen, *Collected Letters* (London and New York: Oxford University Press, 1967).
10. ES, letter to Susan Owen (June 21, 1919), in *SL*.
11. Ibid.
12. ES, letter to Susan Owen (July 30, 1919), in *SL*.
13. *Journals of Arnold Bennett: 1921–1928* (London: Cassell, 1933).
14. ES, unpublished memoir.
15. Quoted in Michael Holroyd, *Lytton Strachey*, rev. ed. (London: Heinemann, 1973).
16. ES, letter to Marguerite Bennett (n.d.).
17. ES, letter to Brian Howard, quoted in Marie-Jacqueline Lancaster, ed., *Portrait of a Failure* (London: A. Blond, 1968).
18. *Portrait of a Failure*.
19. SS, in conversation with author.
20. Quoted by Alfred Noyes in *Yea and Nay* (New York: Brentano's, 1923).
21. Ibid.
22. Alfred Noyes, *Two Worlds for Memories* (London and New York: Sheed & Ward, 1953).

23. *The King of China's Daughter*, rev. from *Wheels*, No. 1; in ES, *Collected Poems* (New York: Vanguard, 1954).
24. ES, *Poetry and Criticism* (1925).
25. Ibid.
26. ES, *Aubade*, in *Façade* (1922).
27. ES, *Poetry and Criticism*.

THREE. *Façade*

1. ES, "*I do like to be beside the Seaside*," in *Façade* (1922).
2. OS, *LNR*.
3. *The Diary of Virginia Woolf: Vol. 2, 1920–24*, Anne Olivier Bell, ed. (London: Hogarth Press; New York: Harcourt Brace Jovanovich, 1978).
4. Harold Acton, *Memoirs of an Aesthete* (London: Methuen, 1948).
5. OS, *All at Sea* (London: Duckworth; Garden City, N.Y.: Doubleday, 1927).
6. Gerald Cumberland, in *Vogue* (July 1923).
7. ES, letter to Gerald Cumberland (n.d.).
8. ES, letter to John Freeman (n.d.).
9. ES, *Children's Tales from the Russian Ballet* (1920).
10. Ibid.
11. ES, *The Sleeping Beauty*, sect. 16 (1924).
12. Ibid.
13. ES, *The Sleeping Beauty*, sect. 1.
14. ES, *The Sleeping Beauty*, sect. 9.
15. ES, *The Sleeping Beauty*, sect. 16.
16. ES, letter to John Freeman (n.d. [1923]).
17. Ibid.
18. ES, unpublished memoir.
19. Ibid.
20. Ibid.
21. Ibid.
22. ES, letter to Geoffrey Singleton (July 11, 1955).
23. ES, unpublished memoir.
24. Ibid.
25. Ibid.
26. *The Diary of Virginia Woolf: Vol. 3, 1925–30*, Anne Olivier Bell, ed. (London: Hogarth Press; New York: Harcourt Brace Jovanovich, 1980).
27. Ibid.
28. Ibid.
29. Ibid.
30. ES, unpublished memoir.
31. Ibid.
32. ES, unpublished memoir (1922).
33. "Hernia Wittlebot" (pseud. Noël Coward), *Chelsea Buns* (n.d.).
34. Ibid.
35. ES, letter to Noël Coward (Dec. 6, 1926), in *SL*.
36. ES, letter in notebook (n.d.).
37. ES, *Colonel Fantock*, in *Troy Park* (1925).
38. ES, *Pandora's Box*, in *Troy Park*.
39. John Piper, in *CES*.

40. ES, letter to Sydney Schiff (Mar. 25, 1925).
41. ES, letter to SS (n.d.).
42. Ibid.
43. Ibid.
44. ES, letter to SS (n.d.).
45. Ibid.: from cutting enclosed with the letter.
46. Harold Acton, *Memoirs of an Aesthete* (London: Methuen, 1948).
47. Ibid.
48. Ibid.
49. Allanah Harper, unpublished memoir of ES.
50. Ibid.
51. Geoffrey Grigson, *Crest on the Silver* (London: Cresset Press, 1950).

FOUR.   *Years of Achievement*

1. *Journals of Arnold Bennett: 1921–1928* (London: Cassell, 1933).
2. Ernest Newman, in *Sunday Times* (London, July 1926).
3. Ibid.
4. OS, essay in *All at Sea* (1927).
5. P. G. Lear and L. O. [pseud. for C. K. Scott-Moncrieff], *The Strange and Striking Adventures of Four Authors in Search of a Character* (London: Cayne Press, 1926).
6. OS, *All at Sea.*
7. OS, quoted in *Evening Standard* (London, Sept. 2, 1926).
8. OS, "A Few Days in an Actor's Life," in *All at Sea.*
9. Cecil Beaton, *The Wandering Years* (London: Weidenfeld & Nicolson, 1963).
10. ES, letter to Cecil Beaton (n.d.).
11. ES, letter to GS (n.d.).
12. ES, *TCO.*
13. Allen Tanner, unpublished memoir.
14. Ibid.
15. Tyler, *DCPT.*
16. ES, letter to Allanah Harper (May [9], 1927), in *SL.*
17. PT, letter to ES (June 1927). (Letters from Pavel Tchelitchew to ES from Paris translated by Lorna Andrade.)
18. ES, in *The Graphic* (July 1928).
19. Allen Tanner, unpublished memoir.
20. ES, "Freak Parties," unpublished essay (1929).
21. ES, note preceding *Gold Coast Customs* (1929).
22. ES, *Gold Coast Customs.* (Stress marks added by author.)
23. ES, *Gold Coast Customs,* note in original edition.
24. This and preceding quotations from *Gold Coast Customs.*
25. ES, note to *Gold Coast Customs* in *Selected Poems* (1936).
26. Kenneth Clark, in *CES.*
27. ES, *Gold Coast Customs.*
28. W. B. Yeats, letter to Wyndham Lewis, in *The Letters of W. B. Yeats,* Allan Wade, ed. (London: Rupert Hart-Davis, 1954; New York: Macmillan, 1955).
29. W. B. Yeats, BBC broadcast (1936), in BBC archives and reprinted in W. B. Yeats, *Essays and Introductions* (London: Macmillan, 1961).
30. ES, letter to GS (n.d.).

31. Allen Tanner, letter to ES (n.d.).
32. Geoffrey Gorer, letter to ES (n.d.).
33. Helen Rootham, letter to unnamed correspondent (n.d.).
34. ES, letter to Veronica Gilliat (n.d.).
35. Ibid.
36. ES, letter to Veronica Gilliat (n.d.).
37. Ibid.
38. ES, letter to GS (n.d.).
39. SS, in conversation with author.
40. ES, letter to GS (n.d.).
41. ES, letter to John Freeman (n.d.).
42. Geoffrey Gorer, in conversation with author.

FIVE. *Friends and Enemies*

1. ES, letter to GS (n.d.).
2. ES, letter to SS (n.d.).
3. ES, letter to GS (n.d.).
4. ES, *AP.*
5. "G.G." [Geoffrey Grigson], review in *Yorkshire Post* (Mar. 27, 1930).
6. Evelyn Waugh, *The Diaries of Evelyn Waugh*, Michael Davie, ed. (London: Weidenfeld and Nicolson; Boston: Little, Brown, 1976).
7. Ibid.
8. Ibid.
9. *The Diary of Virginia Woolf: Vol. 3, 1925–30*, Anne Olivier Bell, ed. (London: Hogarth Press; New York: Harcourt Brace Jovanovich, 1980).
10. ES, letter to CTZ (Aug. 8, 1930).
11. Ibid.
12. Wyndham Lewis, *The Apes of God* (London: Arthur Press, 1930).
13. Salter, *LYOAR.*
14. Undated clipping in scrapbook owned by SS.
15. W. B. Yeats, letter to Wyndham Lewis, in *The Letters of W. B. Yeats*, Allan Wade, ed. (London: Rupert Hart-Davis, 1954; New York: Macmillan, 1955).
16. Wyndham Lewis, *Blasting and Bombardiering* (London: Eyre and Spottis-woode, 1937).
17. Ibid.
18. ES, letter to CTZ (Aug. 8, 1930).
19. ES, *TCO.*
20. Ibid.
21. Ibid.
22. PT, letter to ES (n.d.).
23. PT, letter to ES (n.d.).
24. Linda Simon, *The Biography of Alice B. Toklas* (Garden City, N.Y.: Doubleday & Co., 1977).
25. SS, in conversation with author.
26. Natalie Barney, *Adam* (1962).
27. Ibid.
28. Allen Tanner, letter to ES (n.d.).
29. ES, letter to GS (n.d.).
30. ES, letter to Charlotte Haldane (Dec. 5, 1933).

six. *Murdered Love*

1. ES, letter to CTZ (Mar. 31, 1931).
2. ES, "Life's Tyrannies," *Evening News* (London, July 16, 1931).
3. Ibid.
4. PT, letter to ES (Sat. [Aug.] 1931).
5. ES, letter to SS (Aug. 1931).
6. PT, letter to ES (Aug. 1931).
7. ES, unpublished memoir.
8. Ibid.
9. ES, letter to GS (n.d.).
10. ES, *The English Eccentrics* (1933).
11. OS, *LNR*.
12. ES, *TCO*.
13. ES, note (n.d. [1960s, from handwriting]).
14. ES, letter to David Horner (Mar. 28, 1932).
15. OS, unpublished memoir of T. S. Eliot.
16. Allen Tanner, letter to ES (n.d. [1932]).
17. Ibid.
18. SS, *For Want of the Golden City* (London: Thames and Hudson, 1972).
19. ES, unpublished memoir, "The Ape of God."
20. Ibid.
21. Allen Tanner, letter to ES (1933).
22. ES, letter to CTZ (Jan. 1, 1933).
23. ES, letter to CTZ (Feb. 25, 1933).
24. ES, letter to SS (June 1933).
25. Ibid.
26. Ibid.
27. ES, letter to CTZ (Aug. 15, 1933).
28. Ibid.
29. ES, letter to Veronica Gilliat (Nov. 9, 1933).
30. Ibid.
31. ES, letter to Geoffrey Gorer (Sun. [Nov.–Dec., 1933]), in *SL*.
32. Ibid.
33. ES, letter to Charlotte Haldane (Dec. 5, 1933).
34. ES, letter to SS (n.d. [Feb. 1934]).
35. Ibid.
36. *Daily Express* (Jan. 25, 1934).
37. F. R. Leavis, *New Bearings in English Poetry* (London: Chatto and Windus, 1932).
38. ES, letter to SS (n.d.).
39. Ibid.
40. ES, letter to Charlotte Haldane (Dec. 5, 1933).
41. ES, letter to Allen Tanner (Apr. 1933).
42. Ibid.
43. ES, letter to OS (May 8, 1934).
44. Ibid.
45. Ibid.
46. Ibid.

47. SS, in conversation with author.
48. ES, letter to SS (May 1934).
49. ES, letter to GS (Aug. 1934).
50. ES, *Aspects of Modern Poetry* (1934).
51. Clipping in scrapbook owned by SS (n.d.).
52. Arthur Waley, letter to ES (n.d. [SS believes it was written at this time]).
53. Ibid.
54. SS, in conversation with author.

SEVEN. *The Black Sun*

1. ES, letter to CTZ (Dec. 24, 1934).
2. ES, letter to CTZ (Jan. 30, 1935).
3. Ibid.
4. ES, letter to Veronica Gilliat (Feb. 1935).
5. ES, letter to CTZ (Aug. 8, 1935).
6. ES, letter to CTZ (Aug. 8, 1935). (Not the same letter as in note 5.)
7. ES, letter to CTZ (n.d. [1935]).
8. ES, letter to CTZ (n.d. [1935]).
9. ES, letter to CTZ (Dec. 22, 1935).
10. ES, letter to Veronica Gilliat (n.d.).
11. ES, letter to Cecil Beaton (Mar. 18, 1935).
12. Dylan Thomas, letter to Glyn Jones, in *Selected Letters of Dylan Thomas,* Constantine Fitzgibbon, ed. (London: New Directions, 1966).
13. ES, letter to Dylan Thomas (Jan. 1936), in *SL.*
14. ES, letter to Christabel Aberconway (Dec. 18, 1935), in *SL.*
15. Dylan Thomas, letter to ES (Jan. 17, 1936).
16. ES, letter to Robert Herring (Jan. 27, 1936).
17. Dylan Thomas, letter to ES (Jan. 24, 1936).
18. W. B. Yeats, letter to Dorothy Wellesley (July 6, 1935), in *Letters on Poetry from W. B. Yeats to Dorothy Wellesley,* Dorothy Wellesley, ed. (London: Oxford University Press, 1940; New York: Oxford University Press, 1964).
19. W. B. Yeats, letter to ES (Dec. 13, 1936).
20. Salter, *LYOAR.*
21. ES, letter to W. B. Yeats, undated draft in notebook.
22. Ibid.
23. ES, letter to David Horner (Oct. 28, 1936).
24. ES, letter to CTZ (n.d. [1936]).
25. ES, letter to GS (Sept. 1936).
26. ES, letter to GS (Dec. 1936).
27. ES, letter to Richard Jennings (Mar. 3, 1937).
28. Dylan Thomas, letter to ES (Aug. 20, 1937).
29. Messrs. Coutts, letter to ES (Feb. 27, 1937).
30. ES, letter to Ree Gorer (May 5, 1937), in *SL.*
31. ES, letter to CTZ (May 12, 1937).
32. Ibid.
33. ES, letter to GS (May 1937).
34. ES, letter to Ree Gorer (May 5, 1937), in *SL.*
35. SS, quoting ES, in conversation with author.
36. Quoted on dust jacket of 1948 reprint of *I Live Under a Black Sun.*

37. Ibid.
38. Quoted in Salter, *LYOAR*.
39. ES, *I Live Under a Black Sun*.
40. Ibid.
41. Ibid.
42. Ibid.
43. ES, letter to John Lehmann (June 15, 1948), in *SL*.
44. ES, letter to SS (Nov. 1937).
45. Ibid.
46. Ibid.
47. ES, letter to SS (May 1938).
48. ES, letter to SS (n.d. [early May 1938]).
49. Ibid.
50. William Walton, in conversation with author.
51. ES, *TCO*.

EIGHT.   *Return to Renishaw*

1.   Quoted in Tyler, *DCPT*.
2.   ES, letter to Allen Tanner (June 9, 1938).
3.   ES, letter to David Higham (Mar. 8, 1939), in *SL*.
4.   ES, letter to Ree Gorer (n.d. [Mar. 1939]), in *SL*.
5.   Sir George Sitwell, letter to ES (May 20, 1939). (Original letter in Humanities Research Center, University of Texas, Austin.)
6.   OS, *LNR*.
7.   Ibid.
8.   ES, letter to SS and GS (Oct. 8, 1939).
9.   SS, in conversation with author.
10. ES, letter to Ann Pearn (Sept. 21, 1941), in *SL*.
11. ES, letter to CTZ (Oct. 19, 1939).
12. ES, letter to CTZ (Oct. 2, 1939).
13. ES, letter to GS (n.d.).
14. ES, letter to GS (n.d.).
15. *Reynolds News* (Feb. 14, 1940).
16. ES, letter to SS (Mar. 1940).
17. ES, letter to SS (Mar. 1940).
18. Edward Marsh, letter to Christopher Hassall, in *Ambrosia and Small Beer*, John Guest, ed. (London: Longmans; New York: Harcourt, Brace and World, 1964).
19. ES, letter to SS (Dec. 24, 1940).
20. Ibid.
21. ES, letter to Sir Hugh Walpole (Feb. 1940), in *SL*.
22. Sir Alec Guinness, in conversation with author.
23. Ibid.
24. Ibid.
25. Quoted in Tyler, *DCPT*.
26. OS, letter to SS (Aug. 1940).
27. ES, letter to Ree Gorer (Oct. 2, 1940), in *SL*.
28. Ibid.
29. ES, letter to Geoffrey Gorer (Oct. 28, 1940), in *SL*.

30. ES, letter to GS and SS (Nov. 1940).
31. ES, letter to Christabel Aberconway (Apr. 2, 1941), in SL.
32. *Manchester Guardian* (Feb. 7, 1941).
33. ES, letter to Daniel Macmillan (Feb. 13, 1941), in SL.
34. Hugh Walpole, letter to ES; letter sent on to SS by ES.
35. *The Times* (London, Feb. 8, 1941).
36. ES, letter to SS (Feb. 1941).
37. ES, *Serenade: Any Man to Any Woman*, in *Collected Poems* (1957).
38. ES, introduction to *Collected Poems* (1957; UK ed.).
39. Stephen Spender, in *CES*.
40. *The Times Literary Supplement* (clipping in scrapbook owned by SS).
41. Stephen Spender, in conversation with author.
42. Stephen Spender, *World Within World* (London: Faber & Faber, 1951).
43. SS, in conversation with author.
44. Draft document, in Texas.
45. Ibid.
46. Bryher, *The Days of Mars: A Memoir, 1940–1946* (London: Calder & Boyars, 1972).
47. ES, letter to SS (n.d. [1943]).
48. Ibid.
49. ES, letter to GS (n.d.).
50. ES, letter to Sir George Sitwell (Nov. 22, 1941).
51. Bertram Woog de Rusten, letter to OS (Sept. 1942), detailed to SS.
52. Ibid.
53. Lorna Andrade, in conversation with author.
54. ES, letter to Ann Pearn (Sept. 21, 1941), in SL.
55. ES, letter to Ann Pearn (Sept. 16, 1942), in SL.
56. ES, letter to Ree Gorer (Mar. 9, 1942), in SL.
57. *The Denton Welch Journals,* Jocelyn Brooke, ed. (London: Hamish Hamilton: 1952).
58. Ibid.
59. Christopher Hassall, *Edward Marsh* (London: Longmans, 1959).

NINE. *Splendours and Miseries*

1. ES, letter to SS (Nov. 1942).
2. ES, letter to GS (n.d.).
3. ES, letter to GS (n.d.).
4. ES, letter to SS (n.d.).
5. ES, letter to SS (n.d.).
6. ES, letter to GS and SS (n.d.).
7. ES, letter to GS (n.d.).
8. ES, letter to David Horner (Dec. 2, 1943).
9. SS, *Splendours and Miseries* (London: Faber & Faber, 1943).
10. ES, letter to SS (n.d.).
11. Ibid.
12. ES, letter to SS (n.d.).
13. Memorandum sent to OS by a Sister Marguerite.
14. OS, letter to SS (July 1943).
15. ES, letter to GS (n.d.).

16. Ibid.
17. ES, letter to GS and SS (n.d. [July 1943]).
18. Quoted in John Pearson, *The Sitwells: A Family's Biography* (New York: Harcourt Brace Jovanovich, 1978).

TEN. *Rebirth*

1. ES, *Invocation,* in *Green Song* (1944).
2. John Lehmann, in *CES.*
3. Kenneth Clark, in *CES.*
4. C. M. Bowra, *Edith Sitwell* (Monaco: Lyrebird Press, 1947).
5. ES, letter to Maurice Bowra (Jan. 24, 1944), in *SL.*
6. Ibid.
7. Kenneth Clark, in *CES.*
8. ES, letter to SS (n.d. [1943]).
9. Stephen Spender, in conversation with author.
10. ES, letter to SS (n.d.).
11. John Lehmann, *Am I My Brother?* (London: Longmans, 1960).
12. ES, letter to John Lehmann (Dec. 14, 1944).
13. ES, letter to SS (n.d.).
14. Alan Ross, *Poetry 1945–50* (London: Longmans, 1951).
15. Ibid.
16. Dylan Thomas, letter to ES (Mar. 31, 1946) (ms. in Texas).
17. Ibid.
18. Ibid.
19. Ibid.
20. ES, letter to David Horner (May 29, 1946).
21. Ibid.
22. ES, letter to GS (n.d.).
23. ES, letter to GS (May 1946).
24. SS, quoting ES, in conversation with author.
25. ES, letter to GS (n.d.).
26. ES, letter to Stephen Spender (Mar. 16, 1946).
27. ES, letter to SS (n.d.).
28. T. S. Eliot, letter to ES (Apr. 3, 1946).
29. ES, letter to T. S. Eliot (Apr. 4, 1946), in *SL.*
30. ES, letter to Maurice Bowra (Nov. 18, 1946), in *SL.*
31. ES, letter to John Lehmann (Dec. 11, 1946), in *SL.*
32. Quoted by Geoffrey Grigson to author, from letter.
33. Geoffrey Grigson, letter to ES (Dec. 9, 1946).
34. ES, letter to Geoffrey Grigson (Dec. 16, 1946).
35. ES, letter to SS (n.d.).
36. ES, letter to John Lehmann (July 23, 1947), quoted in John Pearson, *The Sitwells: A Family's Biography* (New York: Harcourt Brace Jovanovich, 1978).
37. Ibid.
38. Quoted in Salter, *LYOAR.*
39. ES, letter to Maurice Bowra (Mar. 24, 1947), in *SL.*
40. Ibid.
41. Benjamin Britten, letter to ES (Sept. 15, 1951).
42. Unpublished typescript in papers of Elizabeth Salter.

43. ES, letter to SS (n.d.).
44. ES, letter to SS (n.d.).
45. Ibid.
46. Ibid.
47. ES, letter to GS (n.d.).

ELEVEN. *Pavlik and "Queen" Edith*

1. Arthur Waley, letter to ES (June 2 [1947]).
2. Jack Lindsay, *Meetings with Poets* (London: Frederick Muller, 1968).
3. PT, letter to ES (1948), in Tyler, *DCPT*.
4. ES, *TCO*.
5. Tyler, *DCPT*.
6. ES, letter to Frances Steloff (Sept. 21, 1948).
7. *Saturday Review of Literature* (Dec. 11, 1948).
8. *Book Week* (May 2, 1965).
9. Salter, *LYOAR*.
10. "The Sitwells," *Life* (Dec. 13, 1948).
11. Ibid.
12. Quoted in Tyler, *DCPT*.
13. Ibid.
14. ES, letter to PT, in Tyler, *DCPT*.
15. ES, letter to PT (Mar. 28, 1949).
16. Ibid.
17. GS, in conversation with author.

TWELVE. *A Sense of Betrayal*

1. ES, letter to SS (n.d.).
2. Quoted by John Freeman in BBC TV programme "Face to Face" (1957).
3. ES, letter to GS (n.d.).
4. ES, letter to SS (Sept. 1949).
5. ES, letter to OS (Sept. 28, 1949).
6. ES, letter to SS (n.d.).
7. ES, letter to Veronica Gilliat (Jan. 2, 1950).
8. Lorna Andrade, in conversation with author.
9. PT, letter to ES, cited in Tyler, *DCPT*.
10. *Isis* (1950).
11. ES, letter to Daniel Macmillan, in Simon Nowell-Smith, ed., *Letters to Mac-millan* (London: Macmillan, 1967).
12. Robert Robinson, letter to author.
13. ES, letter to Lincoln Kirstein (May 24, 1950).
14. ES, letter to SS (June 1950).
15. ES, letter to SS (Aug. 1950).
16. OS, letter to SS (Nov. 1950).
17. Jordan Massee, unpublished diary (Oct. 31, 1950).
18. Ibid.
19. Ibid.
20. Ibid.

21. ES, letter to Carson McCullers (Nov. 21, 1950).
22. ES, letter to Carson McCullers (Jan. 2, 1951).
23. ES, letter to Carson McCullers (n.d.).
24. Ibid.
25. Ibid.
26. ES, letter to John Lehmann (Jan. 17, 1951), in *SL*.
27. ES, letter to Carson McCullers (n.d.).
28. ES, letter to Carson McCullers (n.d. [Feb. 1951]).
29. ES, letter to Veronica Gilliat (Apr. 21, 1951).
30. ES, letter to Carson McCullers (July 11, 1951).
31. Lorna Andrade, in conversation with author.
32. ES, letter to SS (Jan. 1952).

THIRTEEN. *Hollywood*

1. *Northern Echo* (Nov. 20, 1952).
2. *Daily Telegraph and Morning Post* (Nov. 20, 1952).
3. Robert Craft, *Stravinsky: Chronicle of a Friendship, 1948–1971* (London: Gollancz, 1972).
4. ES, *TCO*.
5. Sybille Bedford, *Life of Aldous Huxley*, Vol. 2 (London: Chatton & Windus/W. H. Heinemann, 1974).
6. Ibid.
7. ES, letter to Alberto de Lacerda (May 22, 1953), in *SL*.
8. Ibid.
9. ES, letter to Maurice Bowra (Nov. 25, 1953), in *SL*.
10. Maurice Bowra, letter to ES (Nov. 30, 1953).
11. ES, letter to Veronica Gilliat (Jan. 19, 1954).
12. Ibid.
13. Ibid.
14. ES, letter to Veronica Gilliat (Jan. 19, 1954).
15. "Queen Edith," *New Statesman* (Jan. 23, 1954).
16. ES, letter to Philip Frere (Mar. 29, 1954).
17. ES, letter to SS (Feb. 1954).
18. *The Spectator* (Jan. 29, 1954; Feb. 26, 1954).
19. In private collection; formerly in ES's papers.
20. ES, letter to Veronica Gilliat (May 10, 1954).
21. ES, unpublished lecture on Hollywood.
22. ES, letter to Veronica Gilliat (May 10, 1954).
23. ES, "The Glamour Girls," *Daily Express* (Mar. 8, 1953).
24. T. S. Eliot, letter to ES (June 11, 1954).
25. ES, letter to GS (Oct. 1954).
26. ES, letter to Alice Hunt (Jan. 1955).
27. ES, letter to SS (Jan. 1955).
28. ES, letter to Ruth Braithwaite (Feb. 15, 1955).
29. ES, *TCO*.
30. ES, unpublished lecture on Hollywood.

FOURTEEN. *A Time of Despair*

1. ES, letter to Father Philip Caraman (May 7, 1955), in SL.
2. ES, letter to Father Philip Caraman (June 3, 1955), in SL.
3. Benjamin Britten, letter to ES (Sept. 27, 1954).
4. ES, letter to Benjamin Britten (Apr. 26, 1955), in SL.
5. Evelyn Waugh, letter to Father Philip Caraman (July 19, 1955).
6. Sir Alec Guinness, in conversation with author.
7. Evelyn Waugh, *The Diaries of Evelyn Waugh,* Michael Davie, ed. (London: Weidenfeld and Nicolson; Boston: Little, Brown, 1976).
8. ES, letter to Father Philip Caraman (May 7, 1955).
9. ES, letter to Father Philip Caraman (n.d.).
10. ES, letter in private collection.
11. Cited by Derek Parker in BBC radio tribute to ES (1965).
12. Copy in possession of SS.
13. Benjamin Britten, letter to ES (May 13, 1956) (in Texas).
14. ES, letter to Amando Child (May 20, 1956) (in Texas).
15. ES, letter to Alberto de Lacerda (Nov. 26, 1956), in SL.
16. ES, letter to James Purdy (Oct. 20, 1956), in SL. (All letters from ES to James Purdy in Yale University Library.)
17. ES, letter to James Purdy (Nov. 26, 1956), in SL.
18. ES, letter to James Purdy (Dec. 28, 1956).
19. ES, letter to John Lehmann (Jan. 19, 1957).
20. ES, letter to James Purdy (Mar. 4, 1957).
21. ES, letter to SS (n.d.).
22. James Purdy, letter to author (Apr. 29, 1978).
23. ES, letter to James Purdy (Mar. 25, 1957).
24. ES, letter to James Purdy (May 25, 1957).
25. ES, letter to James Purdy (Apr. 27, 1957).
26. ES, letter to SS (n.d. [Aug. 1957]).
27. ES, letter to Veronica Gilliat (n.d.).
28. Ibid.
29. ES, letter to CTZ (Sept. 22, 1957) (in English).
30. ES, letter to SS (Sept. 22, 1957).
31. Cyril Connolly, review in the London *Sunday Times* (July 28, 1957).
32. ES, letter to James Purdy (n.d.).
33. ES, letter to James Purdy (Aug. 9, 1957).
34. Ibid.
35. Malcolm Williamson, in conversation with author.

FIFTEEN. *Indian Summer*

1. Salter, *LYOAR.*
2. ES, letter to SS ([autumn 1957]).
3. ES, letter to GS (Dec. 23, 1957).
4. ES, letter in private collection.
5. In papers of ES in possession of Elizabeth Salter.
6. Salter, *LYOAR.*

7. Ibid.
8. Sir Alec Guinness, in conversation with author.
9. *Daily Mail* (Sept. 10, 1959).
10. Salter, *LYOAR*.
11. *Daily Mail* (Sept. 10, 1959).
12. Salter, *LYOAR*.
13. *Daily Mail* (Sept. 10, 1959).
14. Ibid.
15. Salter, *LYOAR*.
16. ES, letter to Elizabeth Salter, in *LYOAR*.
17. Lord Snow, letter to ES, in *LYOAR*.
18. ES, letter to Lady Snow (May 31, 1958), in *SL*.
19. Pamela Hansford Johnson, *Important to Me* (London: Macmillan, 1974).
20. ES, quoted in Salter, *LYOAR*.
21. ES, letter to GS (Jan. 12, 1960).
22. OS, letter to SS (Jan. 1960).
23. Ibid.
24. OS, letter to SS (Jan. 17, 1960).
25. ES, letter to GS (Mar. 1960).
26. ES, letter to SS (May 1960).
27. OS, letter to SS (May 1960).
28. David Horner, letter to GS, copy (n.d. [May 1960]).
29. Ibid.
30. David Horner, letter to GS, copy (n.d.).

SIXTEEN. *The Last Years*

1. ES to Elizabeth Salter, in *LYOAR*.
2. ES, letter to Lancelot Law Whyte (Dec. 14, 1960), in *SL*.
3. *The Times Literary Supplement* (Dec. 1960).
4. ES, letter to GS (Dec. 1960).
5. ES, *TCO*.
6. D. H. Lawrence, letter to S. S. Koteliansky (May 27, 1927), in *Collected Letters*, Harry T. Moore, ed. (London: Heinemann; New York: Viking, 1962).
7. Stephen Spender, in conversation with author.
8. Frieda Lawrence, *Not I but the Wind* (London: Heinemann, 1935).
9. Quoted by ES in letter to GS (Dec. 1960).
10. Ibid.
11. ES to Elizabeth Salter, in undated draft papers of Elizabeth Salter.
12. Salter, *LYOAR*.
13. Messrs. Coutts, letter to ES (Feb. 28, 1961).
14. Memo sent to GS.
15. Elizabeth Salter, letter to GS (n.d. [spring 1961]).
16. ES, letter to Georgia Sitwell (n.d.).
17. Ibid.
18. Marjorie Proops, in *Daily Mirror*, in clippings book of SS.
19. Geoffrey Skelton, *Paul Hindemith* (London: Gollancz, 1975).
20. Ibid.
21. Preface to Sotheby's sale catalogue *Collection of Works by Pavel Tchelitchew* (Dec. 13, 1951).

22. ES, letter to Christabel Aberconway (n.d.) (in British Library).
23. Salter, *LYOAR*.
24. ES, *TCO*.
25. Ibid.
26. ES, *A Girl's Song in Winter*, in *The Outcasts* (1962).
27. New York *Times* (Sept. 7, 1962).
28. Sir Harold Acton, *Memoirs of an Aesthete* (London: Methuen, 1948).
29. Sir Harold Acton to John Pearson, BBC radio broadcast (Nov. 1978).
30. Salter, *LYOAR*.
31. Ibid.
32. ES, letter to Cecil Beaton (Nov. 19, 1962).
33. ES, letter to Cecil Beaton (Nov. 30, 1962).
34. Salter, *LYOAR*.
35. ES, letter to GS (n.d.).
36. Elizabeth Salter, letter to GS and SS (Mar. 1963).
37. Elizabeth Salter, letter to GS and SS (May 11 [1963]).
38. Draft will (in Texas).
39. Salter, *LYOAR*.
40. Malcolm Williamson, in conversation with author.
41. Julian Symons, in *London Magazine* (Nov. 1964).
42. Ibid.
43. John Lehmann, in *London Magazine* (Jan. 1965).
44. Ibid.
45. Julian Symons, in *London Magazine* (Feb. 1965).
46. Unpublished typescript, owned by SS.
47. Salter, *LYOAR*.
48. ES, *TCO*.
49. ES, letter to Veronica Gilliat (n.d.).

Bibliography

ORIGINAL WORKS OF EDITH SITWELL

The Mother. Oxford: Blackwell, 1915.

Twentieth Century Harlequinade (with Osbert Sitwell). Oxford: Blackwell, 1916.

Clowns' Houses. Oxford: Blackwell, 1918.

The Wooden Pegasus. Oxford: Blackwell, 1920.

Children's Tales from the Russian Ballet. London: Leonard Parsons, 1920; London: Duckworth, 1928 (reissued).

Façade. London: The Favil Press, 1922.

Bucolic Comedies. London: Duckworth, 1923.

The Sleeping Beauty. London: Duckworth, 1924; New York: Alfred A. Knopf, 1924.

Troy Park. London: Duckworth, 1925; New York: Alfred A. Knopf, 1925.

Poor Young People (with Osbert and Sacheverell Sitwell). London: The Fleuron, 1925.

Poetry and Criticism. London: The Hogarth Press, 1925; New York: Henry Holt, 1926.

Augustan Books of Modern Poetry. London: Ernest Benn, 1926.

Elegy on Dead Fashion. London: Duckworth, 1926.

Poem for a Christmas Card. London: The Fleuron, 1926.

Rustic Elegies. London: Duckworth, 1927; New York: Alfred A. Knopf, 1927.

Popular Song. London: Faber and Gwyer, 1928.

Five Poems. London: Duckworth, 1928.

Gold Coast Customs. London: Duckworth, 1929; Boston and New York: Houghton Mifflin, 1929.

Alexander Pope. London: Faber & Faber, 1930; New York: Cosmopolitan Book Corporation, 1930.

Collected Poems. London: Duckworth, 1930.

In Spring. London: privately printed, 1931.

Jane Barston. London: Faber & Faber, 1931.

Epithalamium. London: Duckworth, 1931.

Bath. London: Faber & Faber, 1932; New York: Harrison Smith, 1932.

The English Eccentrics. London: Faber & Faber, 1933; Boston and New York: Houghton Mifflin, 1933; New York: Vanguard Press, 1957 (rev. and enl.); London: Dennis Dobson, 1958 (rev. and enl.).

Five Variations on a Theme. London: Duckworth, 1933.

Aspects of Modern Poetry. London: Duckworth, 1934.

Victoria of England. London: Faber & Faber, 1936; Boston: Houghton Mifflin, 1936.

Selected Poems. London: Duckworth, 1936; Boston: Houghton Mifflin, 1937.

I Live Under a Black Sun. London: Gollancz, 1937; Garden City, N.Y.: Doubleday, 1938.

Trio (with Osbert and Sacheverell Sitwell). London: Macmillan, 1938.

Poems New and Old. London: Faber & Faber, 1940.

Street Songs. London: Macmillan, 1942.

English Women. London: Collins, 1942.

A Poet's Notebook. London: Macmillan, 1943.

Green Song. London: Macmillan, 1944; New York: The Vanguard Press, 1946.

The Weeping Babe. London: Schott & Co., 1945.

The Song of the Cold. London: Macmillan, 1945; New York: The Vanguard Press, 1948.

Fanfare for Elizabeth. New York: Macmillan, 1946; London: Macmillan, 1946.

The Shadows of Cain. London: John Lehmann, 1947.

A Notebook on William Shakespeare. London: Macmillan, 1948.

The Canticle of the Rose. London: Macmillan, 1948; New York: The Vanguard Press, 1949.

Poor Men's Music. London: Fore Publications, 1950; Denver: Alan Swallow, 1950.

Façade and Other Poems. London: Duckworth, 1950.

A Poet's Notebook. Boston: Little, Brown, 1950.

Selected Poems. Harmondsworth: Penguin, 1952.

Gardeners and Astronomers. London: Macmillan, 1953; New York: The Vanguard Press, 1953.

Collected Poems. New York: The Vanguard Press, 1954; London: Macmillan, 1957.

The Pocket Poets. London: Vista Books, 1960.

The Outcasts. London: Macmillan, 1962.

The Queens and the Hive. London: Macmillan, 1962; Boston: Atlantic Monthly Press, 1962.

Taken Care Of. London: Macmillan, 1965; New York: Atheneum, 1965.
Selected Poems. London: Macmillan, 1965.

BOOKS EDITED BY OR WITH CONTRIBUTIONS BY EDITH SITWELL

Wheels. First Cycle. Oxford: Blackwell, 1916.
Wheels. Second Cycle. Oxford: Blackwell, 1917.
New Paths 1917–18. London: C. W. Beaumont, 1918.
Wheels. Third Cycle. Oxford: Blackwell, 1919.
Wheels. Fourth Cycle. Oxford: Blackwell, 1919.
A Miscellany of Poetry, 1919. London: Cecil Palmer and Hayward, 1919.
Wheels. Fifth Cycle. London: Leonard Parsons, 1920.
Wheels. Sixth Cycle. London: C. W. Daniel, 1921.
Job le Pauvre. London: Bodley Head, 1922.
Yea and Nay. London: Brentano's, 1923.
Meddlesome Matty. London: Bodley Head, 1925; New York: Viking Press, 1926.
Joy Street Poems. Oxford: Blackwell, 1927.
The Legion Book. London: privately printed, 1929.
Tradition and Experiment. London: Oxford University Press, 1929.
Lifar Exhibition Catalogue. London: Arthur Tooth & Sons, 1930.
The Pleasures of Poetry. London: Duckworth, 1930–32; New York: W. W. Norton, 1934.
Prose Poems from "Les Illuminations." London: Faber & Faber, 1932.
Ten Contemporaries. London: Ernest Benn, 1932.
Sacheverell Sitwell: Collected Poems. London: Duckworth, 1936.
Twelve Modern Plays. London: Duckworth, 1938.
Edith Sitwell's Anthology. London: Gollancz, 1940.
Look! the Sun. London: Gollancz, 1941.
Maiden Voyage. London: Routledge, 1943; New York: L. B. Fischer, 1945.
Planet and Glow-worm. London: Macmillan, 1944.
Ronald Bottrall: Selected Poems. London: Editions Poetry, 1946.
Demetrios Capetanakis. London: John Lehmann, 1947; New York: The Devin-Adair Co., 1949.
T. S. Eliot: A Symposium. London: Editions Poetry, 1948.
Sleep in a Nest of Flames. New York: New Directions, 1949.
A Book of the Winter. London: Macmillan, 1950; New York: The Vanguard Press, 1951.
The American Genius. London: John Lehmann, 1951.
William Walton: Façade. London: Oxford University Press, 1951.
Society for Twentieth Century Music: Programme. London: 1952.
A Book of Flowers. London: Macmillan, 1952.
Poetry and Children. Leeds: Edmund Arnold, 1952.
So Late into the Night. London: Peter Russell, 1952.
Cassell's Encyclopaedia of Literature. London: Cassell, 1953.

Cassell's Encyclopaedia of World Literature. New York: Funk & Wagnalls, 1954.

English Morning. London: Hutchinson, 1953.

The Fourteenth of October. London: Collins, 1954.

Ezra Pound at Seventy. New York: New Directions, 1956.

Dylan Thomas. London: J. M. Dent, 1956; New York: New Directions, 1956.

American Writing Today. New York: New York University Press, 1957.

Union Street. London: Rupert Hart-Davis, 1957.

Coming to London. London: Phoenix House, 1957.

Selected Poems and New. New York: McDowell, Obolensky, 1958.

The Atlantic Book of British and American Poetry. Boston: Little, Brown, 1958; London: Gollancz, 1959.

Hommage à Roy Campbell. Montpellier, France: Société Cevenole du Mercou, 1958.

Poems of Our Time. London: J. M. Dent, 1959; New York: Dutton, 1959.

Adventures of the Mind. New York: Alfred A. Knopf, 1959; London: Gollancz, 1960.

Collected Poems of Roy Campbell. Vol. 3. London: Bodley Head, 1960.

Swinburne: A Selection. London: Weidenfeld and Nicolson, 1960; New York: Harcourt, Brace, 1960.

Dylan Thomas. London: Heinemann, 1960.

Color of Darkness. Philadelphia and New York: J. B. Lippincott, 1961.

The Collected Poems of Ronald Bottrall. London: Sidgwick and Jackson, 1961.

The Unconscious Before Freud. London: Tavistock Publications, 1962.

The Seven Deadly Sins. London: Sunday Times Publications, 1962.

Images. London: Weidenfeld and Nicolson, 1963.

Mightier Than the Sword. London: Macmillan, 1964.

Portrait of a Judge. London: Michael Joseph, 1964.

Face to Face. London: Jonathan Cape, 1964.

PERIODICAL CONTRIBUTIONS BY EDITH SITWELL

"Drowned Suns." *Daily Mirror,* No. 2928 (Mar. 1913), p. 9.

"Song: Tell me, Where is Sorrow Laid." *Daily Mirror,* No. 3007 (June 13, 1913), p. 7.

"Love in Autumn." *Daily Mirror,* No. 3093 (Sept. 22, 1913), p. 9.

"In Remembrance." *Daily Mirror,* No. 3095 (Sept. 24, 1913), p. 7.

"Serenade." *Daily Mirror,* No. 3146 (Nov. 22, 1913), p. 9.

"From an Attic Window." *Daily Mirror,* No. 3184 (Jan. 7, 1914), p. 7.

"Song: When Daisies White and Celandine." *Daily Mirror,* No. 3191 (Jan. 15, 1914), p. 7.

"Lullaby." *Daily Mirror,* No. 3563 (Mar. 26, 1915), p. 7.

"Selene." *Daily Mirror,* No. 3584 (Apr. 20, 1915), p. 7.

"Beggarman Blind." *Daily Mirror,* No. 3616 (May 27, 1915), p. 7.

"Water Music." *Daily Mirror,* No. 3788 (Dec. 14, 1915), p. 7.

"The Blackamoor Goes to Hell." *Saturday Westminster Gazette*, Vol. 52, No. 7946 (Dec. 7, 1918), p. 12.

"Miss Nettybun and the Satyr's Child." *Saturday Westminster Gazette*, Vol. 52, No. 7974 (Jan. 11, 1919), p. 13.

"The Lady with the Sewing Machine." *Art and Letters*, Vol. 1, No. 1 [Feb. 1919], p. 8. [There are two states of this issue, the earlier bearing "Winter 1918–19" on front cover.]

"Solo for Ear-Trumpet." *Saturday Westminster Gazette*, Vol. 53, No. 8046 (Apr. 5, 1919), p. 5.

"Portrait of a Barmaid." *Cambridge Magazine*, Vol. 8, No. 27 (Apr. 12, 1919), p. 584.

"Hymns of Hate." *Daily Herald*, No. 1049 (June 4, 1919), p. 8. [Review of *Any Soldier to His Son* by George Willis.]

"Interlude." *The Monthly Chapbook*, No. 1 (July 1919), p. 23. [There were two printings of this issue, the earlier having advertisements printed on orange—not yellow—paper.]

"Queen Venus and the Choir-Boy." *Saturday Westminster Gazette*, Vol. 54, No. 8121 (July 5, 1919), p. 14.

"The Girl with the Lint-White Locks." *Saturday Westminster Gazette*, Vol. 54, No. 8167 (Aug. 30, 1919), p. 9.

"What the Goose-Girl Said about the Dean," "Tournez, Tournez, bons Chevaux de Bois," "By Candlelight." *Coterie*, No. 2 (Sept. 1919), pp. 38–40.

"Mandoline." *Art and Letters*, Vol. 2, No. 4 (Autumn 1919), pp. 145–46.

"At the Fair: The Ape sees the Fat Woman." *Saturday Westminster Gazette*, Vol. 54, No. 8215 (Oct. 25, 1919), p. 13.

"At the Fair; I: Springing Jack; II: The Ape watches 'Aunt Sally.'" *Coterie*, No. 3 (Dec. 1919), pp. 40–41.

"Mandoline." *The Living Age*, Vol. 303, No. 3935 (Dec. 6, 1919), p. 630.

"Among the Dark and Brilliant Leaves." *The Living Age*, Vol. 304, No. 3942 (Jan. 24, 1920), p. 247.

"Two Country Suck-a-Thumbs," "Pedagogues & Flower Shows." *Art and Letters*, Vol. 3, No. 2 (Spring 1920), pp. 3–5.

"Sir Rotherham's Ride." *Saturday Westminster Gazette*, Vol. 55, No. 8355 (Apr. 10, 1920), p. 11.

"The Higher Sensualism." *Athenaeum* (May 14, 1920).

"Bank Holiday, I & II," "Small Talk, I," "Dansons la Gigue." *Oxford and Cambridge Miscellany* (June [6], 1920), pp. 9–11.

"En Famille." *The Chapbook*, No. 13 (July 1920), pp. 18–19.

"King Cophetua and the Beggar-Maid." *Saturday Westminster Gazette*, Vol. 56, No. 8450 (July 31, 1920), p. 11.

"Aubade." *Saturday Westminster Gazette*, Vol. 56, No. 8503 (Oct. 2, 1920), p. 12.

"Fleecing Time." *Saturday Westminster Gazette*, Vol. 56, No. 8557 (Dec. 4, 1920), p. 13.

"On the Vanity of Human Aspirations." *Athenaeum*, No. 4734 (Jan. 21, 1921), pp. 63–64.

"On the Vanity of Human Aspirations." *Literary Digest*, Vol. 68, No. 8 (Feb. 19, 1921), p. 36.

"Herodiade." *Saturday Westminster Gazette*, Vol. 58, No. 6 (Aug. 20, 1921), p. 10.

"Serenade for Two Cats and a Trombone." *Saturday Westminster Gazette*, Vol. 58, No. 8 (Sept. 3, 1921), p. 11.

"The Doll." *Form*, Vol. 1 (Oct. 1921), pp. 30–31. [Issued in limited and ordinary editions.]

"Recent Poetry." *The Sackbut*, Vol. 2, No. 4 (Oct. 1921), p. 38. [Reviews of *The Farmer's Bride*, by Charlotte Mew; *The Chapbook*, No. 10; and *Cranks*.]

"Reviews." *The Sackbut*, Vol. 2, No. 6 (Dec. 1921), p. 38. [Review of *Poems*, by Marianne Moore.]

"Poems for Music, chosen by Edith Sitwell." *The Sackbut*, Vol. 2, No. 6 (Dec. 1921). [Two poems chosen by Edith Sitwell.]

"Poor Martha." *Spectator*, Vol. 128 (Apr. 22, 1922), p. 495.

"New Publications." *The Sackbut*, Vol. 2, No. 11 (June 1922), p. 35. [Review of *The Eton Candle*, ed. by Brian Howard.]

"Readers and Writers." *The New Age*, new ser., Vol. 31, No. 10 (July 6, 1922), pp. 119–20. [First of a series of 11 general literary essays.]

"Readers and Writers." *The New Age*, new ser., Vol. 31, No. 11 (July 13, 1922), pp. 133–34.

"Readers and Writers." *The New Age*, new ser., Vol. 31, No. 12 (July 20, 1922), pp. 148–49.

"Readers and Writers." *The New Age*, new ser., Vol. 31, No. 13 (July 27, 1922), p. 161.

"New Publications." *The Sackbut*, Vol. 3, No. 1 (Aug. 1922), pp. 31–32. [Review of *The Chapbook*, May 1922, and *Public School Verse*, 1920–21.]

"Readers and Writers." *The New Age*, new ser., Vol. 31, No. 14 (Aug. 3, 1922), pp. 171–72.

"Readers and Writers." *The New Age*, new ser., Vol. 31, No. 15 (Aug. 10, 1922), pp. 184–85.

"Readers and Writers." *The New Age*, new ser., Vol. 31, No. 16 (Aug. 17, 1922), p. 196.

"Readers and Writers." *The New Age*, new ser., Vol. 31, No. 17 (Aug. 24, 1922), pp. 210–11.

"Readers and Writers." *The New Age*, new ser., Vol. 31, No. 18 (Aug. 31, 1922), p. 222.

"Readers and Writers." *The New Age*, new ser., Vol. 31, No. 19 (Sept. 7, 1922), p. 236.

"Readers and Writers." *The New Age*, new ser., Vol. 31, No. 21 (Sept. 21, 1922), p. 261.

"Rain." *Weekly Westminster Gazette*, Vol. 1, No. 33 (Sept. 30, 1922), p. 20.

"Braga Serenata." *Weekly Westminster Gazette*, Vol. 1, No. 40 (Nov. 18, 1922), p. 16.

"Promenade Sentimentale." *Spectator*, Vol. 129 (Nov. 18, 1922), p. 727.

"Winter," "Spring." *English Review*, Vol. 36, No. 3 (Mar. 1923), pp. 201–204.

"Winter." *Rhythmus*, Vol. 1, No. 3 (Mar. 1923), pp. 48–51.

"Cacophony for Clarinet," "By the Lake." *The Chapbook*, No. 37 (May 1923), pp. 13–14.

"Daphne." *Spectator*, Vol. 130 (May 12, 1923), p. 799.

"Advice to Young Poets." *Weekly Westminster Gazette*, Vol. 2, No. 65 (May 12, 1923), pp. 16–17.

"Miss Stein's Stories." *The Nation and Athenaeum*, Vol. 33, No. 15 (July 14, 1923), p. 492. [Review of *Geography and Plays*.]

"Some Books of Verse." *Weekly Westminster Gazette*, Vol. 2, No. 75 (July 21, 1923), pp. 18–19. [Reviews.]

"The Gardener, from *The Princess in the Sleeping Wood*." *The Nation and Athenaeum*, Vol. 34, No. 4 (Oct. 27, 1923), p. 154.

"La Rousse, from *The Sleeping Princess*." *Oxford Outlook*, Vol. 5, No. 24 (Nov. 1923), pp. 110–11.

"March for a Toy Soldier," "Dirge for a Gollywog," "The Little Musical Box." *No. 1 Joy Street* (Nov. 9, 1923), pp. 96–100.

"Aubade." *Spectator*, Vol. 131 (Dec. 22, 1923), p. 993.

"Undergrowth." *The Golden Hind*, Vol. 2, No. 6 (Jan. 1924), pp. 5–7, 10–16. [Standard edition and Edition-de-Luxe of 75 signed copies.]

"Song from *The Sleeping Beauty*." *The Nation and Athenaeum*, Vol. 34, No. 22 (Mar. 1, 1924), p. 765.

"Mademoiselle Richarde." *Spectator*, Vol. 132 (Mar. 29, 1924), p. 504.

"Chanson Gris." *Vogue* (London), Vol. 63, No. 8 (late Apr. 1924), p. 46.

"Yesterday." *The Nation and Athenaeum*, Vol. 35 (May 10, 1924), p. 177.

"Colonel Fantock." *Spectator*, Vol. 132 (May 31, 1924), p. 880.

"Yesterday." *The Literary Digest*, Vol. 81, No. 10 (June 7, 1924), p. 40.

"The Country Cousin." *Vogue* (London), Vol. 64, No. 4 (late Aug. 1924), p. 32.

"Jane Austen and George Eliot." *Vogue* (London), Vol. 64, No. 4 (late Aug. 1924), pp. 32, 72.

"Song from *The Sleeping Beauty*." *The Literary Digest*, Vol. 82, No. 6 (Aug. 9, 1924), p. 34.

"Funny Loo." *No. 2 Joy Street*, Sept. 1, 1924, p. 134.

"Three Women Writers." *Vogue* (London), Vol. 64, No. 7 (Oct. 1924), pp. 81, 114. [Katherine Mansfield, Gertrude Stein, Dorothy Richardson.]

"On an Autumn Evening spent in reading Cowper." *The Fortnightly Review*, new ser., Vol. 116 (Oct. 1924), pp. 558–59.

"Pleasure Gardens." *The Nation and Athenaeum*, Vol. 36, No. 8 (Nov. 22, 1924), p. 297.

"Four in the Morning." *Vogue* (London), Vol. 64, No. 12 (late Dec. 1924), p. 33.

"Three Poor Witches." *Spectator*, Vol. 133 (Dec. 27, 1924), p. 1022.

"The Man with the Green Patch." *The Criterion*, Vol. 3, No. 10 (Jan. 1925), pp. 244–48.

"Some Observations on Women's Poetry." *Vogue* (London), Vol. 65, No. 5 (early Mar. 1925), pp. 59, 86.

"Cendrillon and the Cat." *Vogue* (London), Vol. 66, No. 2 (late July 1925), p. 29.

"The Criticism of Poetry." *Saturday Review of Literature*, Vol. 2, No. 7 (Sept. 12, 1925), pp. 117–18.

"The Work of Gertrude Stein." *Vogue* (London), Vol. 66, No. 7 (early Oct. 1925), pp. 73, 98.

"The Scandal." *The Nation and Athenaeum*, Vol. 38, No. 12 (Dec. 19, 1925), p. 437.

"Valse Maigre, 1843." *Vogue* (London), Vol. 66, No. 12 (late Dec. 1925), p. 42.

[Review]. *The New Criterion*, Vol. 4, No. 2 (Apr. 1926), pp. 390–92. [Review of *The Making of Americans*, by Gertrude Stein.]

"Poème: An Interview with Mars" (from *The Childhood of Cendrillon*). *Commerce*, Cahiers Trimestriels, Cahier VII (Printemps 1926), pp. 113–23. [With a French translation by M. V. Larbaud.]

"My Brother's Book." *Weekly Dispatch*, Oct. 10, 1926. [Review of *Before the Bombardment*, by Osbert Sitwell.]

"Who are the Sitwells—and why do they do it?" *Weekly Dispatch*, Nov. 14, 1926.

"A New Poet." *The Nation and Athenaeum*, Vol. 40, No. 14 (Jan. 8, 1927), pp. 514–15. [Review of *Poems*, by Peter Quennell.]

"Our Family Ghost." *Weekly Dispatch*, May 15, 1927.

"The Dog." *The Nation and Athenaeum*, Vol. 42, No. 2 (Oct. 22, 1927), p. 117.

"How Fame Looks to a Poetess." *Literary Digest*, Vol. 95, No. 5 (Oct. 29, 1927), p. 29.

"Panope." *The New Republic*, Vol. 54, No. 690 (Feb. 22, 1928), p. 16.

"The Peach Tree." *Saturday Review of Literature*, Vol. 4 (Apr. 21, 1928), p. 775.

"Must the World be so Noisy?" *Sunday Express*, June 24, 1928, p. 9.

"People I annoy." *Daily Mail*, June 25, 1928.

"A Poet of Fiery Simplicity." *T.P.'s Weekly*, Sept. 8, 1928, p. 598. [Review of *The Heart's Journey*, by Siegfried Sassoon.]

"Modern Poetry, I, II." *Time & Tide*, Vol. 9 (1928), pp. 308–9 and 332–33.

"Are there still Bohemians?" *Daily Chronicle*, Oct. 31, 1928.

"Modern Values." *Spectator*, Vol. 141, No. 5243 (Dec. 22, 1928), pp. 950–51.

"The Bat." *Time & Tide*, Vol. 10 (Jan. 4, 1929), p. 7.

"The Cherry Tree." *Time & Tide*, Vol. 10 (Jan. 11, 1929), p. 34.

"The Poems of Charlotte Mew." *Time & Tide*, Vol. 10 (June 21, 1929), p. 755.

"Men who Interest Me." *Daily Express*, Aug. 14, 1929.

"Oh, to be in Scarborough, Now That August's Here." *Daily Express*, Aug. 17, 1929.

[Review]. *The Criterion*, Vol. 9, No. 34 (Oct. 1929), pp. 130–34. [Review of Charlotte Mew's *The Farmer's Bride* and *The Rambling Sailor*.]

"Charwoman." *Time & Tide*, Oct. 18, 1929.

"The Ghost Whose Lips Were Warm," "The Peach Tree." Translated into French by Pierre d'Exidenil and Felix Crosse. *Exchanges*, No. 1 (Dec. 1929).

"Who wants Bets now?" *Evening News* (London), Apr. 25, 1930.

"Modernist Poets." *Exchanges*, No. 2 (June 1930).

"Life's Tyrannies—and my gospel of happiness." *Evening News*, July 16, 1931, p. 8.

"Stories of Beau Nash." *Evening News*, May 13, 1932, p. 11.

"Don't Become a Standard Person." *Yorkshire Weekly Post*, June 4, 1932.

"Why Worry about your Age?" *Yorkshire Weekly Post*, July 23, 1932.

"Miss Sitwell presents a Genius." *The Graphic*, Vol. 121, No. 3059 (July 28, 1933), p. 133. [On Pavel Tchelitchew.]

"Is our Civilization a Benefit?" *Time & Tide*, Vol. 14, No. 37 (Sept. 16, 1933), p. 1086.

"Poets wise—and otherwise." *Morning Post*, Mar. 6, 1934.

"The Truth about Blood Sports." *Sunday Referee*, No. 2999 (Feb. 24, 1935), p. 10.

"Some Notes on my Own Poetry." *London Mercury*, Vol. 31, No. 185 (Mar. 1935), pp. 448–54.

"Twentieth Century Justice through a Camera Lens." *Sunday Referee*, No. 3001 (Mar. 10, 1935), p. 13.

"Here is a Dickens of our Time." *Sunday Referee*, No. 3003 (Mar. 24, 1935), p. 12. [On the novels of Walter Greenwood.]

"It is fear that breeds War." *Sunday Referee*, No. 3005 (Apr. 7, 1935), p. 12.

"People I Meet in the Train." *Sunday Referee*, No. 3007 (Apr. 21, 1935), p. 10.

"What do we Mean by Liberty?" *Sunday Referee*, No. 3009 (May 5, 1935), p. 12.

"What is Slavery?" *Sunday Referee*, No. 3011 (May 19, 1935), p. 12.

"Prelude." *London Mercury*, Vol. 32, No. 188 (June 1935), pp. 108–10.

"Let's scrap Parliament." *Sunday Referee*, No. 3013 (June 2, 1935), p. 12.

"Testament of a Young Man." *Time & Tide*, Vol. 16 (Oct. 26, 1935), pp. 1548–49. [Review of *World Without Faith*, by John Beevers.]

"A Correspondence on the Young English Poets, between Edith Sitwell and Robert Herring." *Life and Letters To-day*, Vol. 13, No. 2 (Dec. 1935), pp. 16–24.

"Gangsters, Fraudulent Financiers, War-Mongers, Sneak Motorists. . . ." *Sunday Referee*, Jan. 26, 1936, p. 12.

"Of Calamancoes, Shalloons, Garlets, Tabbeys & a hundred others." *Harper's Bazaar* (London), Vol. 13, No. 5 (Feb. 1936), pp. 60, 90.

"Four New Poets." *London Mercury*, Vol. 33, No. 196 (Feb. 1936), pp. 383–90. [Reviews of William Empson, Ronald Bottrall, Dylan Thomas, and Archibald MacLeish.]

"Making Faces at the World." *Sunday Referee,* Feb. 23, 1936, p. 12.

"Two Songs: Come, my Arabia . . . ; My desert has a noble sun for heart." *Caravel* (Majorca), No. 5 (Mar. 1936), p. [8].

"Mustard and Cress." *Sunday Referee,* Apr. 19, 1936, p. 2.

"(Dis)pleasures of Bickering." *Good Housekeeping,* Vol. 29, No. 3 (May 1936), pp. 24–25, 131.

"The Late Miss Sitwell (Auto-obituary III)." *The Listener,* July 29, 1936.

"A Head of Feather and a Heart of Lead." *Harper's Bazaar* (London), Vol. 14, No. 5 (Aug. 1936), pp. 56, 70.

"Quintessence." *Harper's Bazaar* (London), Vol. 15, No. 3 (Dec. 1936), pp. 52–53, 112–13.

"A New Poet: achievement of Mr. Dylan Thomas." *Sunday Times,* No. 5927 (Nov. 15, 1936), p. 9. [Review of *Twenty-five Poems.*]

"H. G. Wells." *Sunday Referee,* Dec. 27, 1936, p. 12.

"That English Eccentric, Edith Sitwell." *Sunday Referee,* Jan. 3, 1937, p. 14.

"On Dramatic Clothes." *Daily Express,* Nov. 8, 1937.

"Precious Stones and Metals." *Harper's Bazaar* (London), Vol. 19, No. 5 (Feb. 1939), pp. 68–69, 82.

[Review]. *Life and Letters To-day,* Vol. 23, No. 27 (Nov. 1939), pp. 239–41. [Review of *The Turning Path,* by Ronald Bottrall.]

"On a Night of Full Moon." *Harper's Bazaar* (New York), No. 2734 (Mar. 1, 1940), pp. 84, 139.

"Lullaby." *Times Literary Supplement,* Spring books supplement, Mar. 16, 1940, p. i.

"Any Man to Any Woman." *Life and Letters To-day,* Vol. 25, No. 32 (Apr. 1940), pp. 35–36.

[Review]. *Life and Letters To-day,* Vol. 27, No. 38 (Oct. 1940), pp. 57–59. [Review of *A.B.C.'s* by Charles Henri Ford.]

"Song: We are the rootless flowers in the air." *Life and Letters To-day,* Vol. 27, No. 39 (Nov. 1940), p. 128.

"Street Song," "The Youth with the Red-Gold Hair," "Ragged Serenade: Beggar to Shadow." *Life and Letters To-day,* Vol. 28 (Jan. 1941), pp. 48–51.

"Poor Young Simpleton," "Song: Once my heart was a summer rose." *Life and Letters To-day,* Vol. 30, No. 49 (Sept. 1941), pp. 198–202.

"Still Falls the Rain." *Times Literary Supplement,* Sept. 6, 1941, p. 427.

"Any Man to Any Woman." *Vice Versa,* Vol. 1, Nos. 3–5 (Jan. 1942), p. 41.

"Bread of Angels." *Times Literary Supplement,* Apr. 4, 1942, p. 177.

"The Poet's Sister." *Spectator,* Vol. 168 (May 8, 1942), p. 455. [Review of *Journals* of Dorothy Wordsworth.]

"Some Notes on Poetry." *Tribune,* No. 303 (Oct. 16, 1942), p. 18.

"A Mother to her Dead Child." *Times Literary Supplement,* Oct. 24, 1942, p. 526.

"Green Song." *Life and Letters To-day,* Vol. 35, No. 64 (Dec. 1942), pp. 132–35.

"Notes on Shakespeare." *View,* 3rd ser., No. 1 (Apr. 1943), pp. 16–18, 36.

"Anne Boleyn's Song." *Times Literary Supplement*, Apr. 24, 1943, p. 200.

"A Sleepy Tune." *Adam*, year XVI, No. 182 (May 1943), pp. 1–2.

"Heart and Mind." *Times Literary Supplement*, June 19, 1943, p. 298.

"Lecture on Poetry since 1920." *Life and Letters To-day*, Vol. 39, No. 75 (Nov. 1943), pp. 70–97.

"Invocation." *New Writing and Daylight*, Winter 1943–44, pp. 7–9.

"O Bitter Love, O Death." *Times Literary Supplement*, Jan. 15, 1944, p. 32.

"Lo, this is she that was the world's desire." *Life and Letters To-day*, Vol. 40, No. 79 (Mar. 1944), pp. 133–35.

"Holiday." *Times Literary Supplement*, Apr. 8, 1944, p. 176.

"Why not Like Poetry?" *Woman's Journal*, Vol. 34, No. 200 (June 1944), pp. 10–11, 56.

"Heart and Mind." *Atlantic Monthly*, Vol. 174, No. 1 (July 1944), p. 61.

"The Poetry of Demetrios Capetanakis." *New Writing and Daylight*, Autumn 1944, pp. 44–50.

"Girl and Butterfly." *Penguin New Writing*, 20 (1944), pp. 93–96.

"A Song at Morning." *Horizon*, Vol. 10, No. 60 (Dec. 1944), p. 372.

[Review]. *Horizon*, Vol. 11, No. 61 (Jan. 1945), pp. 70–73. [Review of *Noblesse Oblige*, by James Agate.]

"Fanfare for Elizabeth." *Harper's Bazaar* (New York), No. 2803 (July 1945), p. 30.

From *"Fanfare for Elizabeth."* *Life and Letters To-day*, Vol. 46 (July 1945), pp. 13–27; (Aug. 1945), pp. 98–107; (Sept. 1945), pp. 152–66; Vol. 47 (Oct. 1945), pp. 6–17.

"Eurydice." *Horizon*, Vol. 12, No. 68 (Aug. 1945), pp. 77–80.

"The Two Loves." *New Writing and Daylight*, 1945, pp. 15–17.

"Some Notes on *King Lear.*" *New Writing and Daylight*, 1945, pp. 77–89.

"The Poet Laments the Coming of Old Age." *Orion* [1], 1945, pp. 28–29.

"A Song of the Cold." *Penguin New Writing*, 23 (1945), pp. 52–56.

"A Sleepy Tune." *View*, Ser. V, No. 6 (Jan. 1946), pp. 4–5.

"Some Notes on Shakespeare." *View*, Ser. V, No. 6 (Jan. 1946), pp. 8–9.

"Some Notes on Shakespeare." *View*, Vol. 6, No. 3 (May 1946), pp. 15, 25.

"Mary Stuart to James Bothwell: casket letter no. 2." *Penguin New Writing*, 27 (Spring 1946), pp. 22–23.

"A Note on *Measure for Measure.*" *The Nineteenth Century*, Vol. 140, No. 835 (Sept. 1946), pp. 131–35.

"Notes from a Poet's Notebook." *View* [Vol. 6, No. 6] (Fall/October 1946), pp. 24–26.

" 'Iago.' " *New Writing and Daylight*, 1946, pp. 141–51.

"Early Spring." *Orion*, III (1946), pp. 59–61.

"A Simpleton." *Horizon*, Vol. 16, No. 90 (July 1947), p. 6.

"Hymn to Venus (from *A Canticle of the Rose*)." *Poetry London*, Vol. 3, No. 11 (Sept.–Oct. 1947), pp. 31–34.

"Comment on Dylan Thomas." *The Critic*, Vol. 1, No. 2 (Autumn 1947), pp. 17–18.

"William Blake." *Spectator*, Oct. 10, 1947, p. 466. [Review of *Fearful Symmetry*, by Northrop Frye, and *Selected Poems*, edited by Denis Saurat.]

"Dirge for the New Sunrise." *Orion*, IV (1947), pp. 26–27.

"The Bee-Keeper." *Penguin New Writing*, 32 (1947), pp. 25, 27.

"The Coat of Fire." *Horizon*, Vol. 17, No. 100 (Apr. 1948), pp. 236–38.

"Of the Clowns and Fools of Shakespeare." *Life and Letters To-day*, Vol. 57, No. 129 (May 1948), pp. 102–9.

"Chain-Gang: penal settlement." *Sunday Times*, July 4, 1948.

"A Note on Hamlet." *Tribune*, Sept. 24, 1948, pp. 23–34.

"A Simpleton." *Harper's Bazaar* (New York), No. 2842 (Oct. 1948), p. 200.

"Poetry of Miss Bowes-Lyon." *New Statesman and Nation*, Vol. 36 (Oct. 9, 1948), p. 306.

"Song: Now that fate is dead and gone." *Orpheus*, I (1948), pp. 27–28.

"Some Notes on the Making of a Poem." *Orpheus*, I (1948), pp. 69–75.

"The Canticle of the Rose." *Wake*, No. 7 (1948), pp. 23–25.

"Dirge for the New Sunrise," "The Bee-Keeper," "Early Spring." *Quarterly Review of Literature*, Vol. 4, No. 3 (1948), pp. 231–37.

"The Song of Dido." *Botteghe Oscure*, quaderno II (1948), p. 268.

"Villa's Poetry." *The Literary Apprentice* (Manila), 1948–49, pp. 64–66.

"Out of School." *Atlantic Monthly*, Vol. 183, No. 6 (June 1949), pp. 37–38.

"Out of School." *Horizon*, Vol. 20, No. 116 (Aug. 1949), pp. 77–80.

"On My Poetry." *Orpheus*, II (1949), pp. 103–19.

"Medusa's Love Song." *Penguin New Writing*, 38 (1949), pp. 9–11.

"A Vindication of Pope." *Sunday Times* (London), Oct. 2, 1949. [Review of *New Light on Pope*, by Norman Ault.]

"Street Acrobat." *Arena*, No. 1 [Autumn 1949], pp. 4–6.

"Macbeth." *Atlantic Monthly*, Vol. 185, No. 4 (Apr. 1950), pp. 43–48.

"King Lear." *Atlantic Monthly*, Vol. 185, No. 5 (May 1950), pp. 57–62.

"A Song of the Dust." *Penguin New Writing*, 40 (1950), pp. 9–12.

"Whitman and Blake." *Proceedings of the American Academy of Arts and Letters and the National Institute of Arts and Letters*, 2nd Ser., No. 1 (1951), pp. 52–58.

"Gardeners and Astronomers." *Times Literary Supplement*, special supplement: "The mind of 1951" Aug. 24, 1951, p. iii.

"Prometheus' Love Song." *The Listener*, Vol. 47, No. 1216 (June 19, 1952).

"Bagatelle." *The Listener*, Vol. 48, No. 1232 (Oct. 9, 1952), p. 586.

"Two Songs." *Atlantic Monthly*, Vol. 191, No. 2 (Feb. 1953), p. 46.

"The April Rain." *Atlantic Monthly*, Vol. 191, No. 4 (Apr. 1953), p. 53.

"Sailor, What of the Isles?" *The Listener*, Vol. 49, No. 1258 (Apr. 9, 1953), p. 607.

"The April Rain." *Times Literary Supplement*, No. 2672 (Apr. 17, 1953), p. 246.

"From *The Road to Thebes*: II: Interlude; III: The Night Wind." *New World Writing*, 3 (May 1953), pp. 170–73.

"The Love of Man, the Praise of God." *New York Herald Tribune Book Review*, Sect. 6 (May 10, 1953), pp. 1, 14. [Review of *Collected Poems of Dylan Thomas*.]

"Sailor, What of the Isles?" *Atlantic Monthly*, Vol. 191, No. 6 (June 1953), p. 53.

"The Queen of Scotland's Reply to a Reproof from John Knox." *New States-man and Nation*, Vol. 45, No. 1163 (June 20, 1953), p. 738.

"The Road to Thebes [1]." *Atlantic Monthly*, Vol. 192, No. 1 (July 1953), pp. 48–50.

"Two Songs: A Mi-Voix; An Old Song Re-sung." *Encounter*, Vol. 1, No. 1 (Oct. 1953), pp. 34–35.

[A Telegram]. *Adam*, year XXI, No. 238 (1953), p. ii.

"Dylan Thomas." *Atlantic Monthly*, Vol. 193, No. 2 (Feb. 1954), pp. 42–45.

"Down among the Glamour Girls." *Sunday Graphic*, No. 2037 (Apr. 25, 1954), p. 4.

"A Young Girl's Song." *London Magazine*, Vol. 1, No. 4 (May 1954), pp. 13–14.

"The Rising Generation." *Times Literary Supplement*, special supplement: "American Writing To-Day," Sept. 17, 1954, p. i.

"Fruits and Flowers on a Poet's Vine." *The Saturday Review*, Vol. 38, No. 25 (June 18, 1955), p. 19. [Review of *Selected Poems* of Roy Campbell.]

"A Tidy, Natural Taste." *The Saturday Review*, Vol. 38, No. 28 (July 9, 1955), p. 14. [Review of *Birthdays from the Ocean*, by Isabella Gardner.]

"Of what Use is Poetry?" *The Reader's Digest* (New York), Aug. 1955, pp. 101–4. [Republished in the following editions of the journal: English-Canadian (Aug. 1955), Australian, British (both Sept. 1955), German, Portuguese (both Oct. 1955), Spanish (Nov. 1955), Finnish, French-Canadian (both Mar. 1956).]

"Elegy for Dylan Thomas." *Poetry*, Vol. 87, No. 2 (Nov. 1955), pp. 63–67.

"Why I Look the Way I Do." *Sunday Graphic*, No. 2117 (Dec. 4, 1955), p. 6.

"The Last Days of Queen Mary the First." *Vogue* (London), Vol. 112, No. 2, (Feb. 1956), pp. 82–83, 145.

"In Praise of Jean Cocteau." *London Magazine*, Vol. 3, No. 2 (Feb. 1956), pp. 13–15.

"Dylan Thomas: tragic American visits." *Sunday Times* (London), Apr. 22, 1956. [Review of *Dylan Thomas in America*, by John Malcolm Brinnin.]

"Sweet-Brier Leaves." *Sunday Times* (London), Feb. 3, 1957. [Review of *The Player's Boy*, by Bryher.]

"What is Genius?" *Everybody's*, Mar. 2, 1957, p. 31.

"Coming to London." *London Magazine*, Vol. 4, No. 4 (Apr. 1957), pp. 39–44. [No. 14 of a series by various writers.]

"Poets of Delight: Gordon Bottomley and Ralph Hodgson." *Sunday Times* (London), May 5, 1957, pp. 4–5. [Great Writers Rediscovered Series, 5.]

"The Priest and the Plague." *Sunday Times* (London), No. 6996 (June 16, 1957), p. 6. [Review.]

"The Progress of a Poet." *Sunday Times* (London), Sept. 8, 1957, p. 8. [A recorded interview.]

"The War Orphans." *Atlantic Monthly*, Vol. 200, No. 5 (Nov. 1957), p. 78.

"Roy Campbell." *Poetry*, Vol. 92, No. 1 (Apr. 1958), pp. 42–48.

"His Blood colours my cheek." *The Month*, new ser., Vol. 19, No. 5 (May 1958), pp. 261–62.

"Better Bye and Bye." *Sunday Times* (London), No. 7050 (June 29, 1958), p. 7. [Review of *The Shaping Spirit*, by A. Alvarez.]

"The Death of a Giant." *London Magazine*, Vol. 5, No. 11 (Nov. 1958), pp. 11–12.

"Preface to Ezra Pound." *The Yale Literary Magazine*, Vol. 126, No. 5 (Dec. 1958), pp. 42–44. [Partly from *The Atlantic Book of British and American Poetry*, 1958.]

"La Bella Bona Roba." *The Listener*, Vol. 61, No. 1553 (Jan. 1, 1959), p. 14. [Reprinted in *The Guinness Book of Poetry*, 1958–59 (Putnam, 1960), and in *New Poems 1960* (Hutchinson, 1960).]

"The Yellow Girl." *The Listener*, Vol. 61, No. 1557 (Jan. 29, 1959), p. 207. [Reprinted in *New Poems 1960*.]

"At the Cross-Roads." *London Magazine*, Vol. 6, No. 3 (Mar. 1959), pp. 11–12.

"Praise We Great Men." *The Listener*, Vol. 61, No. 1577 (June 18, 1959), p. 1058.

"Of Wrath and Writers." *Lilliput*, Vol. 45, No. 5 (Nov. 1959), pp. 41–42.

"Praise We Great Men." *Atlantic Monthly*, Vol. 204, No. 5 (Nov. 1959), p. 97.

"Choric Song." *The Listener*, Vol. 63, No. 1618 (Mar. 31, 1960), p. 576.

"A Visit to Lawrence (Personal Encounters, 1)." *The Observer*, Nov. 13, 1960, p. 25.

"Dylan the Impeccable (Personal Encounters, 2)." *The Observer*, Nov. 20, 1960, p. 24.

"Hazards of Sitting for My Portrait (Personal Encounters, 3)." *The Observer*, Nov. 27, 1960, p. 24.

"Pride (The Seven Deadly Sins, no. 2)." *Sunday Times* (London), No. 7231 (Dec. 17, 1961), p. 19. [Reprinted in "The Seven Deadly Sins," *Sunday Times*, 1962.]

"A Girl's Song in Winter." *Encounter*, Vol. 18, No. 1 (Jan. 1962), p. 41.

"The Two Cultures." *Spectator*, No. 6977 (Mar. 16, 1962), p. 331. [A note.]

"Young William Walton comes to Town." *Sunday Times* (London), No. 7244 (Mar. 18, 1962), p. 40.

"The Young Ones?" *Daily Express*, No. 19352 (Aug. 17, 1962), p. 5.

"The Yellow Girl." *Atlantic Monthly*, Vol. 210, No. 5 (Nov. 1962), p. 64.

"When I was Young and Uneasy." *Atlantic Monthly*, Vol. 215 (Mar. 1965), pp. 159–65.

"Our Childhood was Hell." *Sunday Times* (London), No. 7401 (Mar. 21, 1965), pp. 21–22.

"A Man with Red Hair." *Sunday Times* (London), No. 7403 (Apr. 4, 1965), p. 22.

"A Cast of Characters: a Bloomsbury memoir." *The Reporter*, Vol. 32, No. 7 (Apr. 8, 1965), pp. 43–45.

8888888

888

BOOKS ANNOUNCED BUT NOT PUBLISHED

"Sitwells' Omnibus." Announced: ". . . begins running early in October" in *At the House of Mrs. Kinfoot*, Sept. 1921, and as appearing "shortly" in *Dr. Donne and Gargantua, Canto the First*, Oct. 1921.

"Le Canard à Chaud." Announced as "in preparation" in *Troy Park*, 1925.

"William Blake: a selection, edited by Edith Sitwell." Announced as a forthcoming volume in the series, on wrappers of The Chiltern Library, published by Messrs. John Lehmann, ca. 1950.

TRANSLATIONS

Poème: An Interview with Mars. With a translation by Valéry Larbaud. Paris: *Commerce*, cahier VII (Printemps 1926), pp. 113–123.

Victoria, Drottning av England, Kejarinna av India. Translated by Hans Langlet. Stockholm: Hökerberg, 1936.

Victoria von England. Translated by C. F. W. Behl. Berlin: Wolfg. Krüger, 1937.

La Reine Victoria. Translated by Jean Talva. Paris: Gallinard, 1938.

Le Coeur et L'Esprit; Chanson; Toujours Tombe la Pluie (Anonymous translations.) Paris (Algiers): Fontaine, Nos. 37–40 (1944), pp. 417–20 (561–64).

Chanson Verte. Translated by Marie Laure. Paris: Confluences, 1946.

Las Mujeres Inglesas. (Anonymous translation.) Buenos Aires: Espassa-Calpe, [1946].

Fanfare für Elizabeth. Translated by Margaret Rauchenberger. Köln: Schaffrath, 1947.

Corazón y Pensamiento. [Heart and Mind.] Translated by Charles David Ley. *Acanto*, Vol. 3 (Marzo 1947), pp. [10–11].

El Coronel Fantock. Translated by Sílvina Ocampo. *Sur*, Año XV (Julio–Octubre 1947), pp. 401–9.

Canción Callejera. [Street Song.] Translated by Ricardo Baeza. *Sur*, Año XV (Julio–Octubre 1947), pp. 411–13.

Il Canto di Didone. [Dido's Song.] Translated by A. G. Roma. *Botteghe Oscure*, quaderno II, supplement. "Poeti Inglesi e Americani," p. 28, 1948.

Fanfare for Elisabeth. Translated by Per Lange. København: Gyldendal, 1949.

La Regina Vittoria. Translated by Margherita Santi Farina. Milano: Longanesi, 1949.

Ich Lebe unter einer Schwarze Sonne. Translated by Hilda Mentzel and Paulheinz Quack. Düsseldorf: Schwann, 1950.

Fanfare pour Elizabeth. Translated by Denise Van Moppès. Paris: Albin Michel, 1953.

Sotto il Sole Nero. Translated by Ferdinanda Invrea. Milano, Roma: Bom-
piani, 1954.

Genshi Jidai no Sambusaku. [*Three Poems of the Atomic Age.*] Translated
by Yōnosuke Suzuki. Tokyo: Kokobun-sha, 1955.

Fanfare za Elizabeta. Translated by Dr. Josip Ritig. Zagreb: Kultura, 1955.

Cae la Lluvia Aún. [*Still Falls the Rain.*] Translated by Esteban Pujals.
Nuestro Tiempo, 3rd year, No. 20 (Feb. 1956).

Mzroczny Spiew. [*Dark Song.*] (Polish translation.) In *Antologia Liryki
Angielekiej 1300–1950.* London: Veritas Foundation Publication Centre,
1958.

MUSICAL SETTINGS

Façade, by William Walton (1922).

Daphne, Through Gilded Trellises, Old Sir Faulk, by William Walton (being his "Three Songs" [1932]).

The Sleeping Beauty: A Masque, by Leighton Lucas (1936).

The King of China's Daughter, by Arthur Duff, in "A Broadside," new ser.,
No. 4 (1937).

The King of China's Daughter, by Michael Head, in his "Five Songs" (1938).

The Weeping Babe, for soprano and unaccompanied chorus, by Michael
Tippett (1944).

O Yet Forgive, a song, by Elisabeth Lutyens (n.d.).

Gold Coast Customs, for speakers, men's chorus, and orchestra, by Humphrey Searle (1949).

The Shadow of Cain, for speakers, men's chorus, and orchestra, by Humphrey Searle (1952).

Still Falls the Rain, by Benjamin Britten (being his "Canticle III" [1956]).

A Young Girl, a song, by Malcolm Williamson.

The English Eccentrics, opera, by Malcolm Williamson, libretto by Geoffrey
Dunn, based on ES's book (1964).

Index

Hanson, Lady Deena, 235

Hare, Augustus, 1

Harper, Allanah, 26, 60, 66; concert-go-
ing with Edith, 94; meets Edith,
57–58

Hartley, Anthony, 213

Hartley, L. P., 227, 265, 276; on
Edith's novel, 131

Hassall, Christopher, 143, 158

Hayward, John, 95, 175, 229

"Hazards of Sitting for My Portrait"
(reminiscence), 256

H.D. (Hilda Doolittle), 160

Heart Is a Lonely Hunter, The
(McCullers), 203

Helpmann, Sir Robert, 271

Herring, Robert, 121, 148, 152

Hesketh, Lady, 223

"Hide and Seek" (Tchelitchew), 187,
188, 189, 192, 194

Higham, David, 137, 140, 273

Hindemith, Paul, 259–60

Hogarth Press, 47–48, 161

Holloway Prison, Lady Ida sentenced
to, 22

Hollywood, Edith visits, 210–11,
213–15

Holman-Hunt, Diana, 26

Homosexuality: Britten, 221; Edith's
bitterness against, 83; Horner,
216–17, 230; Lewis calls Edith lesbian, 88, 90; Osbert, 90, 217; *The
Outcasts* on, 262, 263; Pavlik, 66,
103, 117; Tanner, 102

Honors: degree from Durham, 196; degree from Leeds, 182–83; degree
from Oxford, 205; Foyle Poetry
Prize, 237; King's Medal for Poetry,
108, 110; named D.B.E., 215

Hopper, Hedda, 218

Horner, David, 90, 124, 138, 139, 206;
accident at Montegufoni, 261; comes
to America with Osbert, 186–88;
Edith has run-in with, 237; and
Edith's drinking at Renishaw, 244;
and Edith's health, 247–52; relations
with Osbert deteriorate, 216–19

Hornpipe (poem), 37

Houghton Mifflin Co., 122

Howard, Brian (Charles Orange),
30–31, 121

Hunt, Alice, 205, 216, 233

Hutchinson & Co., 262

Hutchison, St. John, 40

Huxley, Aldous, 24, 210–11, 254

Huxley, Maria, 210

"I do like to be beside the Seaside"
(poem), 37–38

I Live Under a Black Sun (novel), 90,
125, 128, 129, 131–33

Les Illuminations (Rimbaud), 202

Income tax problems, 244, 246–47

Invocation (poem), 168, 227

Isis, The, 199

Jennings, Richard, letter from Edith on
Dylan Thomas, 125–26

John, Augustus, 39

John Inglesant (Shorthouse), 11

Johnson, Pamela Hansford (Lady
Snow), 131, 265; on Edith, 244–46

Joyce, James, 93

Kandinsky, Wassily, 135

Kentner, Louis, 138

Keppel, Mrs., 56

King of China's Daughter, The
(poem), 34, 123

King's Medal for Poetry, 108, 110

Kipling, Rudyard, 32–33

Kirstein, Lincoln, 188, 200–1, 202

Lady Chatterley's Lover (Lawrence),
254

Lambert, Constant, 38–39

Last Poems (Yeats), 149

Laughlin, James, 185

Laughter in the Next Room (O. Sitwell), 101

Lawrence, D. H.: reminiscence, 256;
and Sitwells in *Lady Chatterley's
Lover*, 254–55

Lawrence, Frieda, 255

Leavis, F. R., 110, 111–12, 113, 114,
175, 207; Edith on, 262

Leeds University, honorary degree to
Edith, 182–83

Legros, Pierre, 29

Lehmann, Beatrix, 212

Lehmann, John, 161–62, 229, 262, 265;
on doodle-bug and poetry reading,

Museum of Modern Art, New York, 185, 187, 192, 201

Music: Edith's lessons, 12, 15; Edith's love of, 94–95

Music and Ceremonies (poetry volume), 263

My Dog Tulip (Ackerley), 229

Nash, Paul, 141, 142

National Association of Spiritualists, 2

Nephew, The (Purdy), 232

Nevinson, C. R. W., Edith on, 141

New Bearings in English Poetry (Leavis), 113

Newman, Ernest, 85; on *Façade* performance, 61

News of the World, 214

New Statesman, 149, 150, 212–13

Newton-Wood, Noel, 221

New Writing, 161–62

New York, Edith visits, 186–93, 201–3, 205, 209–10, 216, 230, 232

New York *Times*, 264

Nicholson, Nancy (Mrs. Robert Graves), 44–46

Nicol, Graham, 262, 274

Nicolson, Harold, 160, 161

Night and Day, 131

Noise Abatement Society, 256

No Sign of the Dove (Ustinov), 212

Not I but the Wind (F. Lawrence), 255

Noyes, Alfred, 147; debate with Edith, 32

Observer, The, 122, 234, 235

Olivier, Laurence, 204

Orion (cat), 269

Orwell, Mrs. George, 210

Our Eunuch Dreams (Thomas), 119

Our Lady of the Flowers (Genet), 108

Outcasts, The (poetry volume), 262, 263

Outsider, The (Wilson), 240

Overdraft, bank, 55, 97, 128, 198, 247, 257

Owen, Susan, 27

Owen, Wilfred, 26–28, 61, 123

Oxford Book of Modern Verse, 122–23

Oxford University: honorary degree to

Edith, 205; poetry readings at, 58, 239–40

Pachmann, Vladimir de, 12

Pandora's Box (poem), 53

Paranoia, 250, 253–54

Park Lane Group, 264

Peaky (peacock), 5, 269

Pearn, Ann, 140, 155

Pearn, Pollinger and Higham, 155

Pears, Peter, 221, 265

Penny Plain and Twopence Coloured, 64

Pestelli, Luigi, 261

Petrouchka (ballet), Edith on, 42

"Phenomena" (Tchelitchew), 92

Pierrot Lunaire (Schoenberg), 240–41

Piper, John, 198, 240; on Edith's poetry, 53–54

Pleasures of Poetry, The (anthology), 95

Pleydell-Bouverie, Alice, 187

Plomer, William, 197

Poetry readings: at Aeolian Hall, 157, 159–61; at Aldeburgh Festival, 201, 236; in America, 229, 230, 232–33; at Churchill Club, 172; at Edinburgh Festival, 241; in London, 57; at Oxford and Cambridge, 58, 239–40; at Paris bookshop, 93; *see also Façade*

Poet's Notebook, A, 155

Polemic, 182

Polka (poem), 37

Poor Young People (Sitwells), 52

Pope, Alexander, biography of, 82, 84–85

Porter, Neil, 60

Pound, Ezra, 177–78

Powys, John Cowper, 231–32

Proops, Marjorie, 259

Pryce-Jones, Alan, 244

Purdy, James, 228–30; on meeting Edith, 230–32

Queen Elizabeth (liner), 206

Queen Elizabeth Hall, London, 221

Queens and the Hive, The (biography), 244, 263

Queen Victoria (Strachey), 122

Quennell, Peter, 127